ASSERTIVENESS

INNOVATIONS, APPLICATIONS, ISSUES

Robert E. Alberti, Ph.D., Editor

Impact Publishers, Inc.
POST OFFICE BOX 1094
SAN LUIS OBISPO, CALIFORNIA 93406

First Edition, May, 1977
Second Printing, January, 1978

Copyright © 1977
by Impact Publishers, Inc.

For Chapters 1, 2, 3, 4, 5, 7, 8, 9, 10, 12, 13, 14, 17, 18, 19, 20, 21, 23, 24, 25, 26, 27, 28, 29, 31, 32, 34, 35.
Chapter 6: Copyright © 1972, Pergamon Press. Used by permission.
Chapter 11: Copyright © 1976, Donald K. Cheek.
Chapter 15: Copyright © 1975, Stanlee Phelps and Nancy Austin.
Chapter 16: Copyright © 1976, Charles C. Thomas, Publisher. Used by permission.
Chapter 22: Copyright © 1976, American Association of Marriage and Family Counselors. Used by permission.
Chapter 30: Copyright © 1977, Human Sciences Press. Used by permission.
Chapter 33: Copyright © 1976, Newsweek, Inc. Used by permission.
Chapter 35: May be reproduced in its entirety without further permission.

All rights reserved under International and Pan-American Copyright Conventions. No part of this book may be reproduced, stored in a retrieval system, or transmitted in any form or by any means, electronic, mechanical, photocopying, recording or otherwise, without express written permission of the publisher, except for brief quotations in critical reviews or for quotations from other sources copyrighted elsewhere. The editor and publisher gratefully acknowledge permission of those noted in the text for use herein of materials from other publications.

Library of Congress Cataloging in Publication Data
Main entry under title:

Assertiveness: innovations, applications, issues.

Bibliography: p.
1. Assertiveness (Psychology) I. Alberti, Robert E.
BF575.A85A76   158'.1   77-5774
ISBN 0-915166-38-0

Published by   IMPACT PUBLISHERS, INC.
               Post Office Box 1094
               San Luis Obispo, California 93406

Cover Design by Sharon Wood

Printed in the United States of America

ACKNOWLEDGEMENTS

Mike Emmons got this whole thing started, when he called me one beautiful summer morning in 1970 and proposed the idea for what was to become *Your Perfect Right*. We had no idea we were contributing to what has become a virtual "movement" in the field of human behavior, or that we would start a publishing business, or write more books, or even run around the country doing workshops. But all of that and more *has* happened, mostly because Mike has the foresight to sense what's significant, and the courage to say so. Thanks, Michael.

And thanks to Drs. Joseph Wolpe, Cyril Franks, and the late Dr. Michael Serber, for their early support when most everyone was saying, "What is assertive training?"

And thanks to the contributors to this book. Most of them are as yet relatively unrecognized. They deserve to be noticed.

And thanks to my family, and to the staff at Impact Publishers, Inc., and to Connie Dexter, for providing the "facilitative conditions" which made it possible for me to edit this book.

R. E. A.
March, 1977

DEDICATION

To Deborah, Lawrence, and Melissa,
who taught me what the word really means.

CONTENTS

ACKNOWLEDGEMENTS 3
DEDICATION..................................... 4
ABOUT THE AUTHORS 11

PART ONE: BACKGROUND

1. ASSERTIVE BEHAVIOR TRAINING:
   DEFINITIONS, OVERVIEW, CONTRIBUTIONS 19
   Robert E. Alberti
   What is "Assertiveness?" ... An Overview of This Book ... Additional Significant Contributions to Assertive Behavior Training
2. ON ASSERTION 33
   Andrew Salter
   Definitions ... "Fraudulent Assertion" ... Clinical Cautions
3. THE FOUR ASSERTIVE MYTHS: A FABLE 37
   Julio J. Guerra, Patricia A. Taylor
   The Myth of Anxiety ... The Myth of Obligation ... The Myth of Modesty ... The Myth of the Good Friend

4. ASSERTION TRAINING: AN IDENTITY CRISIS
   THAT'S COMING ON STRONG 49
   Martin E. Shoemaker, Donna Olsen Satterfield
   *AT: In Search of Identity ... A Three Level Model of
   AT ... Techniques and Procedures ... AT as a Belief-
   Response System ... An Assertive Life Style ...
   Target Problems and Processes ... Summary*
5. ASSERTIVE BEHAVIOR TRAINING AND THE
   ENHANCEMENT OF SELF-ESTEEM 59
   Lawrence P. Percell

PART TWO: INNOVATIONS IN TECHNIQUE

6. TEACHING THE NONVERBAL COMPONENTS
   OF ASSERTIVE TRAINING 67
   Michael Serber
   *The Selection of Nonverbal Behaviors to be Taught ...
   The Shaping of a Nonverbal Variable ... A Case
   Example*
7. A STRATEGY FOR TEACHING VERBAL
   CONTENT OF ASSERTIVE RESPONSES 75
   Myles L. Cooley, James G. Hollandsworth, Jr.
   *Current Teaching Strategies: "Examples" and
   "Models" ... The "Components" Strategy ... Ver-
   bal Assertive Skills ... Working With The Compon-
   ents Strategy*
8. ASSERTIVE TRAINING AND THE
   EXPRESSION OF ANGER 83
   David C. Rimm
   *The Relationship Between Anger and Aggression ...
   Anger, Anxiety and Assertion ... A Clinical Model
   ... Group Assertive Training for Anger Expression ...
   Clinical Illustrations*
9. HOMEWORK IN AT: PROMOTING THE
   TRANSFER OF ASSERTIVE SKILLS TO
   THE NATURAL ENVIRONMENT 93
   John L. Shelton
   *The Concept of Homework ... Laying the Ground-
   work for AT Homework Assignments ... Using
   Homework in AT ... Homework Content ... Home-
   work Format ... Additional Suggestions for Using
   Homework ... Using Paraprofessionals*

10. COPE: A WILDERNESS WORKSHOP IN AT 101
    Paula Landau, Terry Paulson
    From Fear to Confidence ... Survival: Wilderness and Interpersonal ... Assertion Training in the Wilderness

PART THREE: ASSERTIVENESS ACROSS CULTURES
11. ASSERTIVE BEHAVIOR AND BLACK LIFESTYLES 111
    Donald K. Cheek
    The Black Experience ... New Requirements for Old Problems ... Changing to Assertiveness—The First Five Steps ... Why a White Approach Can Fail
12. GROUP ASSERTION TRAINING FOR SPANISH SPEAKING MEXICAN-AMERICAN MOTHERS 119
    Paula Landau, Terry Paulson
    An Action-Oriented Intervention Program ... Techniques of Measurement ... Results of the AT Program ... Obstacles, Husbands, and Goals ... A Note on Token Feedback ... Conclusion
13. ASSERTION TRAINING FOR ASIAN-AMERICANS 129
    Philip O. Hwang
    Self-Assertion ... Oriental Myth ... Skill Acquisition
14. ASSERTIVENESS AND ANXIETY:
    A CROSS-CULTURAL AND SOCIO-ECONOMIC
    PERSPECTIVE 135
    Brian S. Grodner
    Chicano Culture ... Socio-Economic Considerations ... Assertiveness and Anxiety ... A Comparative Study ... Conclusions ... Implications for Theory and Practice of AT

**PART FOUR: APPLICATIONS OF
ASSERTIVE BEHAVIOR TRAINING**
15. THE ASSERTIVE WOMAN: DEVELOPING
    AN ASSERTIVE ATTITUDE 151
    Stanlee Phelps, Nancy Austin
    Using Consciousness Razors ... Getting Out of the Compassion Trap ... The Compassion Trap Quiz ... Choosing Your Own Labels

16. ASSERTIVE BEHAVIOR AND CLINICAL
    PROBLEMS OF WOMEN 163
    Patricia A. Jakubowski
    *Clinical Problems: Depression; Couple Counseling;
    Psychosomatic Problems; Drug or Alcohol Depen-
    dence; Agoraphobic and Irrational Fears; Aggressive
    Problems ... Conclusion*
17. ASSERTIVENESS TRAINING FOR MOTHERS
    AND DAUGHTERS............................... 177
    Iris G. Fodor, Janet L. Wolfe
    *Assertiveness Training for Mothers and Daughters ...
    Mothers' Complaints ... Daughters' Complaints
    About Mothers ... Summary*
18. DEVELOPING ASSERTIVENESS IN CHILDREN 195
    Judith S. Thoft
    *A Format for Assertiveness Training with Children ...
    Some Observations and Suggestions*
19. CASE STUDIES IN ASSERTIVE
    TRAINING WITH ADOLESCENTS.................... 205
    William D'Amico, Jr.
    *Counter-Covert Conditioning Strategy ... Cognitive-
    Behavioral Strategy ... Summary*
20. DEVELOPING ADOLESCENT ASSERTIVENESS......... 215
    Gail W. McPhail
    *Adolescent Powerlessness ... Developing a High
    School AT Program ... Elements of the Adolescent
    AT Program ... Adolescent Assertiveness Problems
    ... Evaluation and Feedback*
21. ASSERTION TRAINING WITH
    JUVENILE DELINQUENTS......................... 223
    Lynne Garnett
    *Starting the Program ... AT Techniques with the
    Juvenile Group ... Process of the AT Group ... Stu-
    dent/Staff Relationships and AT ... Summary*
22. ASSERTION TRAINING IN
    MARITAL COUNSELING........................... 231
    Robert E. Alberti, Michael L. Emmons
    *Components of Behavior ... Facilitating Assertion ...
    Other Considerations ... Applications in Counseling*

23. **DIVORCE RECOVERY: ASSERTION
     TRAINING FOR THE DIVORCED** 239
     Terry L. Paulson, Paula Landau
     AT With Problems of the Divorced . . Summary
24. **ASSERTIVENESS AS AN
     AID TO WEIGHT CONTROL** 249
     Merna McMillan
     Social and Behavioral Implications of Obesity ... Sabotage ... Assertiveness Training as a Treatment Strategy ... AT Procedures in a Weight Control Program ... Other Behavioral Techniques in Weight Control ... Covert Assertive Methods . . Side Effects of Assertive Training
25. **ASSERTIVENESS AND THE JOB HUNT** 261
     Kathleen Wheeler
     Stages in the Job Hunt ... Self-Assessment ... Research ... Communicating Potential ... Summary
26. **FOUR MYTHS OF NONASSERTIVENESS
     IN THE WORK ENVIRONMENT** 271
     Sherwin B. Cotler, Susan Morgan Cotler
     The Myth of Anxiety ... The Myth of Modesty ... The Myth of the Good Friend ... The Myth of Obligation ... Guidelines for Assertion Trainers ... Debunking Mythology
27. **ASSERTIVENESS: ONE ANSWER TO JOB
     DISSATISFACTION FOR NURSES** 281
     Sonya J. Herman
     The Nature of Nursing ... Nursing Education ... The Value and Belief System of Nurses ... The Socialization of Women ... The Mythical Evaluation of People in Hierarchies ... The Assertive Response ... Assertiveness in Nursing Practice
28. **ASSERTIVE TRAINING IN THE
     TREATMENT OF PHOBIAS** 291
     Arthur B. Hardy
29. **ASSERTIVENESS TRAINING WITH ALCOHOLICS** 295
     Steven M. Hirsch
     The Relationship of Assertiveness to Alcoholism ... A Controlled Study of AT With Alcoholics ... Assertive Techniques With an Alcoholic Population

PART FIVE: ISSUES AND ETHICS IN THE PRACTICE OF ASSERTIVE BEHAVIOR TRAINING

30. ASSESSMENT PROCEDURES FOR
    ASSERTIVE BEHAVIOR 307
    John P. Galassi, Merna Dee Galassi
    Nature of Assertive Behavior ... Assessment Prior to Training ... Assessment Instruments ... Individualized Assessment ... Assessment During Training ... Assessment After Training

31. DEVELOPING ASSERTIVENESS:
    TRAINING OR THERAPY? 327
    Martin E. Shoemaker
    Issues in Defining Training vs. Therapy ... The Content-Process Model of AT ... Differentiating Training and Therapy ... A First Step

32. ASSERTION TRAINING WITHIN AN
    HOLISTIC-ECLECTIC FRAMEWORK 337
    Michael L. Emmons

33. SQUEAK UP! 349
    Gerald Nachman
    Crackpot Ravings ... Swaggering Defeats ... The Power of Punitive Thinking

34. ISSUES IN ASSERTIVE BEHAVIOR TRAINING 354
    Robert E. Alberti
    Theoretical Issues ... Research Issues ... Issues of AT Practice and Ethics ... A Final Note

35. A STATEMENT OF "PRINCIPLES FOR
    ETHICAL PRACTICE OF ASSERTIVE
    BEHAVIOR TRAINING" 365

REFERENCES   375

ABOUT THE AUTHORS

Robert E. Alberti, Ph.D., is Counseling Psychologist and Professor, California Polytechnic State University, San Luis Obispo. He is coauthor of *Your Perfect Right: A Guide to Assertive Behavior*, and of *Stand Up, Speak Out, Talk Back!*, and is editor of *ASSERT: The Newsletter of Assertive Behavior*. He is also Publisher and Executive Editor at Impact Publishers, and is interested in developing tools for the advancement of personal growth and human rights.

• • •

Nancy Austin, M.B.A., has recently completed work at the Graduate School of Business, University of California, Los Angeles. Formerly Evaluation Coordinator for the Behavioral Analysis and Modification project at the Ventura County (California) Mental Health Service, she has lectured and conducted assertiveness training for a variety of populations. She is coauthor of the first book on assertiveness for women, *The Assertive Woman*.

• • •

Donald K. Cheek, Ph.D., is a Counselor and Professor at California Polytechnic State University, San Luis Obispo. He also serves as consultant to a variety of colleges, universities, school districts, and governmental agencies. An outspoken advocate for affirmative action and against individual and institutional racism, Dr. Cheek is author of *Assertive Black... Puzzled White*.

• • •

Myles L. Cooley, Ph.D., is a staff psychologist and Coordinator of the Psychology Internship Program at the Palm Beach County Community Mental Health Center, West Palm Beach, Florida. He received his Ph.D. in clinical psychology from the State University of New York at Albany. In addition to conducting assertiveness training groups, Doctor Cooley has published other works on assertiveness training.

• • •

Sherwin B. Cotler, Ph.D., is a clinical psychologist in private practice and is affiliated with the Family Guidance Centers, Buena Park, California. He has consulted and published widely in the behavior therapy field, and is coauthor of *Assertion Training: A Humanistic-Behavioral Guide to Self Dignity*.

• • •

Susan Morgan Cotler, M.A., is Director of the Campus Child Care Center, Long Beach City College, Long Beach, California, and conducts assertion training workshops throughout Southern California.

• • •

William J. D'Amico, Jr., M.A., is the School Psychologist for the Falmouth Public Schools, Falmouth, Mass. He is an advanced doctoral candidate in Counselor Education at Boston University, Boston, Mass. where he is conducting research in the role of cognitive processes in assertive training and self-control. Mr. D'Amico is also engaged in a private practice that offers counseling and consultation services to school systems in the development, implementation, and evaluation of Pupil Personnel Services.

• • •

Michael L. Emmons, Ph.D., is Counseling Psychologist and Professor, California Polytechnic State University, San Luis Obispo. He is coauthor of *Your Perfect Right: A Guide to Assertive Behavior*, and of *Stand Up, Speak Out, Talk Back!* His professional interests are in holistic treatment methods, meditative therapy, and the spiritual dimensions of therapy. He lectures and conducts workshops throughout the United States.

• • •

Iris G. Fodor, Ph.D., is Associate Professor of School Psychology in the Department of Educational Psychology at New York University, Washington Square. She is among the most active assertiveness trainers in the Northeast, and is coordinator for that region for the International Conference on Assertive Behavior Training.

• • •

John P. Galassi, Ph.D., is Associate Professor and Counseling Psychologist at the University of North Carolina at Chapel Hill. He has conducted extensive research and published numerous articles on the measurement of assertive behavior and the effectiveness of assertion training. He is coauthor of *Assert Yourself! How to Be Your Own Person*.

• • •

Merna Dee Galassi, Ed.D., is Coordinator of Special Programs, Student Activities, and Developmental Counseling at Meredith College, Raleigh, North Carolina. Her research on assertive behavior and assertion training has appeared in the professional journals and has been presented at a variety of national, state, and regional meetings. She is coauthor of *Assert Yourself! How to Be Your Own Person*.

• • •

Lynne Garnett, Ph.D., is a Counseling Psychologist in the Behavioral Division of the Psychological & Counseling Services, UCLA. Her interests include assertion training with special groups, including women and men in unique environments, and cross-cultural assertion training.

• • •

Brian Grodner, Ph.D., is Psychologist and Director of Training, Peanut Butter and Jelly Therapeutic Pre-School, Infant, and Family Center, Albuquerque, New Mexico. He is currently involved with children and families in high risk situations, especially those of child abuse and neglect. Brian is also interested in gestalt and assertive therapy, especially with low income clients, and consulting and training for community and educational programs.

• • •

Julio J. Guerra, Ph.D., is a clinical psychologist in private practice in Huntington Beach, California, and is affiliated with the Los Angeles County Department of Mental Health. His professional interests have included work in the areas of stuttering, child psychotherapy, and obesity. He is coauthor of *Assertion Training: A Humanistic-Behavioral Guide to Self Dignity.*

• • •

Arthur B. Hardy, M.D., is a physician in private practice in Menlo Park, California, who specializes in treatment of phobics. He is Director of TERRAP, an organization of agoraphobics, and conducts group and individual therapy programs which utilize assertive training and other methods.

• • •

Sonya Herman, R.N., D.N.Sc., is Assistant Professor of Nursing Education, at the School of Health Services, The Johns Hopkins University, Baltimore, Maryland. She teaches assertiveness to nurses and nursing students at Johns Hopkins, Georgetown University, the University of West Virginia, and the University of Maryland.

• • •

Steven M. Hirsch, Ph.D., is Executive Director of the Behavioral Health Agency of Central Arizona, Casa Grande. He has worked extensively with alcoholic populations, and directed a major study of assertiveness training with alcoholics for the State of Texas.

• • •

James G. Hollandsworth, Jr., Ph.D., has authored several articles on assertiveness training. In addition, he is a coauthor of the Adult Self-Expression Scale, a widely used measure of assertiveness. He received his Ph.D. in Counselor Education from the University of North Carolina. After completing a one-year internship at the Palm Beach County Community Mental Health Center, he returned to academe where he is presently an Assistant Professor in the Department of Counseling Psychology at the University of Southern Mississippi.

• • •

Philip O. Hwang, Ph.D., is Associate Professor, Counselor

Education, at the University of San Diego, California. He has consulted and written widely in the areas of multicultural education and assertion training.

• • •

Patricia A. Jakubowski, Ed.D., is Associate Professor in the Department of Behavioral Studies at the University of Missouri, St. Louis. She is a pioneer in application of assertiveness training for women, and is coauthor of *Responsible Assertive Behavior* and of the American Personnel and Guidance Association film *Assertive Training for Women*. Dr. Jakubowski is co-editor of *Counselor Education and Supervision* and travels extensively as a consultant and workshop leader.

• • •

Paula Landau, M.A., is a program consultant, assertion trainer, and professional writer. Formerly affiliated with the Assertion Training Institute of North Hollywood, California, she is co-developer of the COPE Wilderness Workshops and the Divorce Recovery program. She is now with Associates for Behavior Change in North Hollywood.

• • •

Merna McMillan, Ph.D., is Director of the Community Mental Health Center, San Luis Obispo County, California, until recently holding a similar position in Southern Texas. She has worked in mental health in Arizona, Texas, and California, specializing in assertiveness training, multicultural programs, weight control, and consultation with school and community agencies.

• • •

Gail W. McPhail, M.A., is Counselor at Morro Bay Junior-Senior High School, Morro Bay, California. Her work with adolescents has included individual and group counseling, workshops, and consultation. She has developed a systematic program for adolescent assertiveness, including individual, classroom, and workshop materials.

• • •

Gerald Nachman is a free-lance writer and humorist. He is a regular contributor to *Newsweek* magazine and other major national publications. He characterizes himself as "a longtime observer of the timidity scene."

• • •

Terry L. Paulson, Ph.D., is a psychologist and co-founder of the Assertion Training Institute, North Hollywood, California. He is also affiliated with the Los Angeles Department of Health Services and the Orange County Department of Mental Health. He has conducted assertion training with administrators, teachers, businesses, and is co-developer of the COPE Wilderness Workshop and Divorce Recovery programs.

Lawrence P. Percell, Ph.D., is a Clinical Psychologist for San Mateo County Mental Health and Adult Probation and a lecturer in Psychology, St. Patrick's College, Mountain View, California. He is the author of several articles on Assertive Behavior Training and is currently training probation officers to use the technique with their clients. He is particularly interested in the application of AT to the aggressive client.

• • •

Stanlee Phelps, M.S.W., is a psychiatric social worker, formerly with the Ventura County Mental Health Department (California). She has lectured extensively and conducted assertiveness training workshops throughout the country. Currently a private consultant, she is coauthor of *The Assertive Woman*, the first book on assertiveness specifically for women.

• • •

David C. Rimm, Ph.D., a Clinical Psychologist, is Professor and Director of Clinical Training, Department of Psychology, Old Dominion University, Norfolk, Virginia. He is co-author of *Behavior Therapy: Techniques and Empirical Findings* and *Abnormal Psychology*. His primary research interests are in assertive training and cognitive behavior therapy approaches.

• • •

Andrew Salter is a psychotherapist in private practice in New York City. A founder of the Association for Advancement of Behavior Therapy, he has been called "the father of behavior therapy." His classic book *Conditioned Reflex Therapy* presented the concepts of assertiveness two decades before the current popular "movement." He has written and lectured widely, and is featured on an audio tape program *Conversations with Andrew Salter: Aspects of Assertiveness*.

• • •

Donna Olsen Satterfield, Ph.D., is a Psychologist with the East San Fernando Valley Regional Center of the Los Angeles County Mental Health Services, California. She was a co-founder and Director of the Assertion Training Institute, North Hollywood, California, prior to her present position. She is interested in holistic treatment methods, including massage.

• • •

Michael Serber, M.D., was Clinical Director of Atascadero State Hospital, Atascadero, California, at the time of his untimely death in 1973. He had done extensive research and writing on assertive training, including work with Arnold Lazarus, Joseph Wolpe, Robert Liberman, and others. He served as a consultant to the Counseling Center, California Polytechnic State University, and was very influential in the work of Robert Alberti and Michael Emmons. With Richard Laws, he produced a film, *Assertive Training*, and was coauthor with Peter Houts of the book, *After the Turn On, What?*

• • •

John L. Shelton, Ph.D., is Coordinator, Behavior Therapy Services, at the University Counseling Center, Colorado State University, Fort Collins. He has done considerable writing on behavior therapy, and his work with assertiveness includes concern for ethical implications, contraindications, and facilitator training. He is coauthor of *Homework in Counseling and Psychotherapy*.

• • •

Martin E. Shoemaker, Ph.D., is a Psychologist and co-founder of the Assertion Training Institute, North Hollywood, California. He is also affiliated with the Foothill Community Psychiatric Clinic in Glendora, California, and a part-time faculty member in the Guidance Department, California State University, Los Angeles. He is particularly interested in application of assertion training to teenagers, and in the "assertive lifestyle" level of assertiveness.

• • •

Patricia A. Taylor, R.N., is a Registered Nurse in Long Beach, California, who conducts assertion training workshops.

• • •

Judith Stone Thoft, Ed.D., is School Psychologist, Brookline, Massachusetts, and associate in Educational Counseling and Consulting Services. She is particularly interested in studying children's social development and in devising and implementing planned interventions which can help children cope with interpersonal problems and master social skills.

• • •

Kathleen Wheeler, M.A., is co-owner and director of a career development consulting firm in Sacramento, California. She has been consulting for three and a half years with colleges, government and private industry in the area of career planning, job seeking skills, and assertive training. Her current interest is in job satisfaction, particularly in large organizations.

• • •

Janet L. Wolfe, Ph.D., is Associate Executive Director of the Institute for Advanced Study in Rational Psychotherapy in New York City. She is recognized as the major proponent of the integration of Rational-Emotive Therapy and Assertiveness Training. In addition to her clinical work, she is an international lecturer and consultant, and coauthor (with Albert Ellis) of *How to Prevent Your Child from Becoming a Neurotic Adult*.

Part One:
BACKGROUND

1

ASSERTIVE BEHAVIOR TRAINING: DEFINITIONS, OVERVIEW, CONTRIBUTIONS

Robert E. Alberti

A popular cartoon depicts a young woman standing with one foot on the chest of a man lying flat on his back. As the man looks up at her in disbelief, she says "Ask me how I'm doing in my Assertiveness Training course!"

On several occasions, while displaying books at professional and trade gatherings, we have observed this scene: a couple approach our booth; the man spots *The Assertive Woman*; he takes his wife's arm firmly and pulls away, saying "Oh, no! You don't need to be any more *assertive!*"

A recent item in the publishing trade magazine *Publishers Weekly* referred to the recent popularity of books on "aggressiveness training."

Reader's Digest, in its "Increase Your Word Power" column a few years ago used the term *aggressive* to define the word *assertive*.

There are at least nineteen books available on assertiveness training (AT) as this is written (not counting this volume!). Two or three have been recognized national bestsellers. AT programs are everywhere: schools, colleges, industry, government, hospitals, clinics, women's centers, service clubs, television programs.

Can anything so "faddish" actually be a legitimate technique for therapy or personal growth? Is there a body of knowledge which sorts out the confusion and misinterpretation and presents defensible evidence of efficacy?

Faddishness, of course, is a problem which besets any new therapeutic technique which catches the public eye. AT has "caught on" in the media, and the risks of misunderstanding, oversimplification, and inappropriate application are very present. AT is a process which readily lends itself to self-help and wide application. Nevertheless, those who practice in any professional setting are obligated to concern themselves with client welfare in the broadest sense, and scrupulously avoid the "pop psychology" approach that would claim a cure-all, insist it's good for *everybody*, and declare "*you must* try it!" Careful determination of appropriateness to the needs of *each* individual client is critically important to ethical application of the process. More on this in Chapters 34 and 35.

This book represents the efforts of thirty-six professionals who have worked extensively with assertiveness training, to present the results of research and practice in a form which will advance knowledge of the value, the potential, and the limitations of the process.

All of the papers in this book are not of equal weight. Some are of greater importance than others, depending upon the needs of the reader. Some papers are quite brief, others are very extensive in scope. Nevertheless, each makes a unique contribution toward a comprehensive presentation of the state of the art. And each has been prepared with the *practitioner* in mind. Thus, this book is not a scholarly volume in the traditional sense. It is at once a useful handbook and a progress report on an evolving therapeutic/training procedure.

It has been exciting and humbling for me to observe the breadth and depth of work done by many "colleagues"—known and unknown—in assertive behavior training in the six-plus years since *Your Perfect Right* was first published. Particularly in application of the process to a remarkable range of populations and problems, practitioners have produced a virtual "movement," with little form, only a partial theoretical base, a great deal of substance, and an almost limitless potential. It is my hope that this book will present a more adequate framework than heretofore available for the development of form, theory, substance, potential, and limitations of assertiveness training.

It should be noted here that the process of assertive behavior training involves at least three elements, however it may be structured, whatever specific techniques are utilized, and whoever the trainees and trainer may be. These key elements include:

Skills training, in which specific behaviors are taught, practiced, and integrated into the trainee's behavioral repertoire;
Anxiety reduction, which may be achieved directly (e.g., through desensitization or other counter-conditioning procedures), or indirectly, as a by-product of skills training;
Cognitive restructuring, in which values, beliefs, cognitions, and/or attitudes may be changed by insight, exhortation, or behavioral achievements.

The balance of this chapter offers a schema for differentiating assertiveness, presents an overview of the book, and identifies some additional AT work and resources not otherwise included in this volume.

WHAT IS "ASSERTIVENESS?"

The term *assertive* has provided a field day for would-be semanticists. As Andrew Salter notes in Chapter 2, it is only recently that the word has come to mean anything different than "aggressive." Indeed, it may still be a relatively small proportion of the population which differentiates the two concepts.

Are we then simply engaged in a semantic argument? Is the much-talked-about difference a *real* one? Psychiatrist Edward Stainbrook has observed that "A difference which makes no difference is no damn difference!" Does *assertiveness* meet that test?

As the term is used by the professionals who have contributed to this volume, it does indeed make a difference where that difference counts most—in the lives of people. You will find, in chapter after chapter, accounts of the positive results of overcoming anxiety and developing skills in social expression.

The semantic difficulty, it seems to me, has come from our everpresent "need" to over-simplify concepts; to reduce ideas to their lowest common denominators. To *precisely* label behavior is plain hard work, and requires a good deal more sophisticated approach than most practitioners, much less lay persons, are willing to undertake. The fact is that there are no absolutes, and each act must be evaluated from several perspectives in any effort to define or categorize it.

To further complicate the matter, no less a scholar in the field of assertive behavior than Richard McFall of the University of Wisconsin has urged "careful avoidance of the term 'assertive*ness*' " because "assertion is not a trait" (McFall, in press).

Fully cognizant of the warnings of McFall and others, we may proceed, in my opinion, to characterize *particular behaviors* according to a level of "assertiveness." Serber (1972; See Chapter 6) has clearly demonstrated that specific components of behavior may be developed which contribute to the social effectiveness of the client (i.e., his or her ability to gain respect from others, accomplish goals in social interaction, express feelings, while not abusing others). Thus it appears possible to deal with a concept of "assertiveness" as a relative characteristic: *one may exhibit assertiveness by behaving, within the parameters of a given social situation, in an effective fashion, honestly expressive of one's feelings, while respecting the rights and feelings of others involved.*

In *Your Perfect Right*, Michael Emmons and I proposed the following definition:

> Behavior which enables a person to act in his (her) own best interests, to stand up for himself (herself) without undue anxiety, to express his (her) honest feelings comfortably, or to exercise his (her) own rights without denying the rights of others we call *assertive behavior.*

Others have suggested the need for a more precise definition of the concept of assertiveness. Several authors in this book offer alternatives (See Chapters 2, 3, 8, 11).

We have suggested that assertive and aggressive behavior differ principally in that the latter involves hurting or stepping on others in the course of expressing oneself. Albert Bandura notes that aggression is defined by both the *behavior* and the *social labels* applied to it. Others of a more psychodynamic orientation have proposed that *intent* must be considered. That is, did you intend to *hurt* (aggressive), or to *express* (assertive)?

In his extensive research on assertive behavior, Richard McFall has followed the assumption that behavior must be measurable according to its *effects*. Thus, if the other person gets the assertive message and responds accordingly (i.e., by reinforcing you), your behavior may be classified as assertive. If he/she pouts in a corner, or shouts "Who do you think you are?" your statement may have been aggressive, as described by this criterion.

Donald Cheek (See Chapter 11) and others have pointed out that the *social-cultural context* must be taken into account in classifying behavior as assertive or aggressive (or non-assertive for that matter). A culture, for example, which regards honoring one's elders as one of its ultimate values may regard an otherwise assertive request to a grandparent as clearly out of line and aggressive.

It is clear that there are no absolutes in this area, and that some criteria may be in conflict. A particular act may be at once assertive in behavior and intent (you wanted to and did express your feelings), aggressive in effect (the other person could not handle your assertion), and non-assertive in the social context (your subculture expects a powerful, "put-down" style). It may not be possible to reconcile such mutually exclusive classifications.

In an attempt to synthesize the many perspectives which have been suggested as relevant to an adequate definition, I have developed a schema which I call the "CRIB." The term is an acronym which represents Context, Response, Intent, and Behavior. The CRIB may help to clarify the classification of non-assertive, assertive, and aggressive behavior. Entries in the chart, of course, are representative only, particularly in the area of the response of others. A *specific* situation may vary considerably from the examples shown here. In any event, the question "Was that assertive or aggressive?" is not one which may be answered simply. The issues are complex, and each situation must be evaluated individually. Indeed, the labels *non-assertive*, *assertive*, and *aggressive* themselves carry no magic, but within the framework described here they may be useful in assessing the *appropriateness* of a particular action.

AN OVERVIEW OF THIS BOOK

This section is offered to aid the reader in viewing this text in terms of three broad areas of assertive behavior training: its *theoretical foundation*, its *form and substance*, and its *current issues*. Although roughly paralleling the organization of the book, this perspective points out a pattern which does not emerge from a review of the table of Contents.

A review of the theoretical foundation of assertive behavior training is offered throughout the volume, as many of the authors have commented upon the theoretical underpinnings of their work. However, it should be noted that the contributors are principally *practitioners*, and they have written—by design—for practitioners. Theory has not been a major criterion in preparing these papers.

Assertive behavior training is indeed a process which exists with an underdeveloped theoretical base. Although founded within the general framework of behavior therapy, and characterized initially (Salter, 1949; Wolpe, 1958; Wolpe and Lazarus, 1966) as a counterconditioning procedure for anxiety, it has integrated substantially from social learning theory (Bandura, 1969), "Gestalt" theory (Perls, 1969), humanistic-existential theory (Rogers, 1961), and the

"THE CRIB": A MODEL FOR DIFFERENTIATING ASSERTIVE BEHAVIOR

YOUR ACTIONS MAY BE LABELED AS...

	NON ASSERTIVE	ASSERTIVE	AGGRESSIVE
WHEN THE SOCIETY OR CULTURE OR CONTEXT CALLS FOR...	Strength; "Cool;" Ambition; "Macho;" Drive; Self-Serving; Hardness; Toughness; Lack of regard for others.	Honesty; Forthrightness; Firmness; Courage; Directness; Caring; Respect for others; Equality in relationships.	Self-denial; Sacrifice; Quiet; Softness; Submission to others; "Not making waves;" "Staying in your place."
WHEN YOU FEEL THIS INTERNAL RESPONSE...	Emotional pain; failure to gain your goals; loneliness; Physical ailments (headaches, etc.); Low self-confidence; Low self-respect.	Good feeling; Accomplishment of your goals; Closeness (in long run — sometimes distance at first); Confidence; Self-respect; Affection; "I did all I could."	Guilt; Loneliness; Accomplishment of your goals; Distance from others; Power; Confidence; Low self-respect.
AND THE RESPONSE OF OTHERS IS...	Scorn; Derision; Lack of respect; Pity; "Winning;" Ignoring you; "Turning off."	Good feeling; Friendliness; Affection; Cooperation; Respect; Closeness; Openness. Or sometimes: Fear; Withdrawal Or sometimes: Anger; Dislike	Fear; Withdrawal; Submission; Avoidance OR Anger; Disrespect; Dislike; Hostility OR Firmness; Assertion; Resistance.
WHEN YOUR INTENT IS PRIMARILY TO...	Deny yourself; Avoid risks; Stay out of trouble; Put yourself down; Avoid hurting others; Avoid hurting yourself; Be liked; Hide your anger.	Express yourself; Reach out; Gain your goals; Show respect for others; Be honest and direct; Stand up for your rights; Express friendship or affection; Show your anger.	Express yourself; Dominate; "Set others straight;" Win; Do it your way; Gain your goals; Disregard others.

AND OTHERS INTERPRET THAT...	You are afraid you are a pushover; You don't believe in your ideas; You don't know what you're talking about.	You are confident; You are friendly; You are honest; You know your feelings; You respect yourself and others; You care.	You want to hurt others; You are thoughtless and rude; You are mean; You have no feelings; You are pompous.
WHEN YOU BEHAVE WITH...	Downcast eyes; Soft voice; Hesitation; Helpless gestures; Denying importance of the situation; Slumped posture; Words like "anything you want is okay with me;" OR avoiding the situation altogether.	Direct eye contact; conversational voice level; Fluent speech; Firm gestures; Erect posture; "I" messages; Honesty; Positive statements; Direct response to the situation.	Glaring; Loud voice; Fluent/fast speech: Confrontation; Threatening gestures; Intimidating posture; Dishonesty; Impersonal messages.
AND OTHERS BEHAVE BY...	No eye contact; Not listening; Being pushy; Making unreasonable requests; Taking advantage of you; Disagreeing; Denying your requests; Head shaking; Manipulation.	Making eye contact; Interested conversation; Open posture & gestures; Listening; Forthright comments. OR SOMETIMES: Agreeing or disagreeing. OR SOMETIMES: giving in; OR SOMETIMES: aggression.	Backing away; Hesitating; Agreeing; Closed posture; Accepting; Giving in; Looking away or down; Head nodding OR counter aggression; glaring; hostile remarks; loud voice; threats; violence OR direct eye contact; firm posture and gestures; forthright comments.

concepts of universal human rights—the latter largely as a result of the social movements in the U.S.A. during the last decade.

In Chapter 2, Andrew Salter comments upon the evolving concept of assertion, and why he believes the procedure will grow and remain a major force in psychotherapy. Guerra and Taylor offer a fable in Chapter 3, pointing out some of the myths which have created a social environment discouraging to assertiveness. Chapter 4 is a comprehensive overview of AT's development, presented by Shoemaker and Satterfield. Percell offers evidence for AT's contribution to the improvement of self-concept—an essentially humanistic referent—in Chapter 5.

In later chapters, although the authors have looked primarily at the *practice* of AT, there are a number of contributions to its evolving eclectic theory. Rimm (Chapter 8) lends support for the counter-conditioning theory in his discussion of assertive anger expression. Cheek, Hwang, and Grodner (Chapters 11, 13, and 14) caution that *any* model of theory or practice must consider cultural differences and avoid the false assumptions that everyone is the same and treatments need not take into account the individual. D'Amico (Chapter 19) has integrated covert conditioning procedures into his approach, adding still another theoretical construct to the AT foundation. Hardy (Chapter 28), dealing with phobics, is another supporter of the anxiety-inhibition school. Shoemaker and Emmons (Chapters 31 and 32) seek to integrate the extant theoretical views and offer synthesized models which view AT in a broad, eclectic perspective. With the editor's prerogative to have the "last word," Alberti offers a discussion and some synthesis of theoretical considerations in Chapter 34.

The form and substance of AT are presented in considerable detail throughout Chapters 6 through 29 of the book. Chapter 6 is a reprint of the late Michael Serber's classic discussion of the non-verbal characteristics of an assertive action.

In Chapter 7, Cooley and Hollandsworth present an innovative approach to the problem of appropriate verbal assertiveness. Rimm's work with assertive anger, Chapter 8, has provided important evidence in support of the notion that anger is a healthy, not-to-be-feared human emotion which need not be expressed aggressively. Shelton's homework assignments offer an all-important link between clinical AT and the day-by-day experience of clients, as described in Chapter 9. In one of the more unusual AT formats, Landau and Paulson report in Chapter 10 a wilderness experience as a highly successful approach to developing both social and physical coping skills.

Chapters 11, 12, 13, and 14 present a clear and unified message—the form and substance of AT are inadequate unless adapted for cultural and socio-economic differences. Cheek, Landau and Paulson, Hwang, and Grodner all provide evidence to support the concept of assertiveness as person-and-situation-specific, and offer recommendations for modifying AT to meet the needs of ethnic and socio-economic minorities.

The use of AT with a particular population of clients is the focus of Chapters 15 through 29. Although the approaches vary widely to meet the needs of specific groups, each contribution offers useful material which may be adapted to other settings. For example, although Phelps and Austin, Jakubowski, and Fodor and Wolfe write about women's assertiveness, many of the insights, observations, and techniques reported in Chapters 15, 16 and 17 are applicable to men as well.

Chapters 18, 19, 20, and 21 describe AT programs for young people from elementary through high school. Thoft, D'Amico, McPhail, and Garnett have developed strategies which extend the benefits of AT to the life stages where it may be most important. Indeed, if their work can be widely replicated, the rest of us may not be needed at all!

Attention to the shaky or broken marriage relationship is found in Chapters 22 and 23. Alberti and Emmons describe their AT approach in some detail in the context of marital counseling. Landau and Paulson are concerned with the "recovery" of those now-single ex-spouses whose marriages have ended.

Forms of AT applied to specific problem areas are the focus of the balance of the chapters in this part. McMillan integrates AT into a weight control program in Chapter 24; Wheeler, Cotler and Cotler, and Herman address assertiveness on the job in Chapters 25, 26, and 27. Finally, Hardy in Chapter 28 and Hirsch in Chapter 29 deal with more severe clinical problems in phobic and alcoholic clients respectively.

Current issues in theory, research, and practice is the theme of the last six chapters, in an effort to synthesize and to consider "Where do we go from here?" In Chapter 30, the Galassis present an in-depth analysis of assessment in AT. Shoemaker's Chapter 31 differentiates training and therapy according to a content-process model. Emmons cautions us that AT is but one tool in an adequate therapeutic approach to the wholeness of the client, in Chapter 32. As a reminder that assertiveness is not always seen as a value, we have Nachman's humorous but pointed commentary on "teaching mice to roar" in Chapter 33. The editor's goal in Chapter 34 is to clarify issues of theory, research, and practice, as a springboard for future work in each of these areas of assertive behavior training. The statement of ethics in Chapter 35, although formally endorsed only by its eight authors, suggests a standard for AT practice which has application to the work of practitioners in all settings.

ADDITIONAL SIGNIFICANT CONTRIBUTIONS TO ASSERTIVE BEHAVIOR TRAINING

One of the truths of writing and publishing books is that a book is never really finished. Authors find the practical demands of personal time schedules, publishing deadlines, availability of information, and space limitations all contribute to a frustration about "including everything I wanted to say." This volume is no exception. Many important contributions and contributors do not appear here, in part as a result of each of those factors. In order to partially compensate for those omissions, this section will present brief reference to a number of contributions and resources in AT which will be of interest to the reader.

1) Perhaps most obvious is the omission of papers by some of the most well known *names* in assertive behavior training. The reader is urged to review the *References* at the end of the book for additional material which has appeared in the literature. The work of such names as Wolpe, Lazarus, Fensterheim, McFall, and others are critical to a thorough understanding of the development and current state of the art in AT.

2) A number of *topics* were excluded from the text, again for the combination of reasons noted above. Important work has been done with assertive behavior training for handicapped and retarded populations, senior citizens, homosexuals, inmates of correctional institutions, clients treated for sexual dysfunction, and for a host of other populations. It was simply not possible to include them all, however one may keep abreast of current developments through the references noted in item 4 below. A few items are briefly mentioned here for the reader's information.

AT in corrections work is being done in many institutions around the country, both for staff training and inmate rehabilitation. Key people in this field are Henry Novotny, California Correctional Institute, P. O. Box 1031, Tehachapi, California 93561, and James Granade, School of Education, Georgia State University, Atlanta, Georgia 30303.

AT for the handicapped and retarded was the subject of a special report in *ASSERT: The Newsletter of Assertive*

Behavior (Number 13, April 1977). Several sources are included in the report (See item 4 below).

AT as a treatment for sexual dysfunction has been a specialty in the work of Rod and Marcella Hoeltzel, San Pedro, California 90731.

AT with young children is becoming a subject of increasing interest. A knowledgeable source on this subject is Pat Palmer at the Assertiveness Training Institute, 1011 Adams Boulevard, Denver, Colorado 80206.

AT and the consumer, including an "endorsement" from Ralph Nader, was the featured topic in *ASSERT* #12, February 1977. Among other sources cited was the Assertive Consumer Program, National Consumer League, 1785 Massachusetts Avenue N.W., Washington, D.C. 20036.

A verbal response model of assertiveness, a three-step process involving *empathy*, *conflict*, and *action*, has been developed by Jan Kelley, Department of Counseling and Psychological Services, Georgia State University, Atlanta 30303, and Barbara Winship of Georgia Institute of Technology. Kelley and Winship have an AT book to be published by Nelson-Hall.

The method of contrasted role-plays, an insight-oriented model for role playing in AT groups is the work of Linda MacNeilage (Counseling-Psychological Services Center) and Kathleen Adams (Psychology Department) of the University of Texas, Austin, Texas 78712. The model incorporates a Gestalt notion of "reconciliation of opposites" by having the trainee enact three contrasting responses to a situation (unassertive, aggressive, assertive), thus experiencing the full range of emotional and behavioral alternatives.

3) No fewer than twenty books on aspects of assertive behavior have been published at this writing. Some are referenced elsewhere in this book, but for the convenience of the reader, here is a "nearly comprehensive" list which includes the present volume:

Adler, R. B., *Confidence in Communication: A Guide to Assertive and Social Skills*. New York: Holt, Rinehart, and Winston, 1977.

Alberti, R. E. (Editor), *Assertiveness: Innovations, Applications, Issues*. San Luis Obispo, California: Impact Publishers, Inc., 1977.

Alberti, R. E. and Emmons, M. L., *Stand Up, Speak Out, Talk Back!* New York: Pocket Books (Simon and Schuster), 1975.

Alberti, R. E. and Emmons, M. L., *Your Perfect Right: A Guide to Assertive Behavior.* San Luis Obispo, Calif.: Impact Publishers, Inc., 1970, 2nd edition 1974.

Baer, J., *How to Be an Assertive (Not Aggressive) Woman in Life, in Love, and on the Job.* New York: Signet (New American Library), 1976.

Bloom, L. Z., Coburn, K., and Pearlman, J., *The New Assertive Woman.* New York: Delacorte Press, 1975.

Bower, S. A. and Bower, G. H., *Asserting Yourself.* Reading, Mass.: Addison-Wesley, 1976.

Cheek, D. K., *Assertive Black . . . Puzzled White.* San Luis Obispo, Calif.: Impact Publishers, Inc., 1976.

Cotler, S. B. and Guerra, J. J., *Assertion Training.* Champaign, Ill.: Research Press, 1976.

Fensterheim, H. and Baer, J., *Don't Say Yes When You Want To Say No.* New York: David McKay, 1975.

Galassi, M. D. and Galassi, J. P., *Assert Yourself! How to Be Your Own Person.* New York: Human Sciences Press, 1977.

Gambrill, E. D. and Richey, C. A., *It's Up to You: The Development of Assertive Social Skills.* Millbrae, Calif.: Les Femmes, 1976.

Lange, A. J. and Jakubowski, P., *Responsible Assertive Behavior.* Champaign, Ill.: Research Press, 1976.

Lazarus, A. A. and Fay, A., *I Can If I Want To.* New York: William Morrow, 1975.

Liberman, R. P., King, L. W., DeRisi, W. J., and McCann, M., *Personal Effectiveness.* Champaign, Ill.: Research Press, 1976.

Osborn, S. M. and Harris, G. G., *Assertive Training for Women.* Springfield, Ill.: Charles C. Thomas, 1975.

Phelps, S. and Austin, N., *The Assertive Woman.* San Luis Obispo, Calif.: Impact Publishers, Inc., 1975.

Salter, A., *Conditioned Reflex Therapy.* New York: Farrar, Straus, and Giroux, 1949 (Capricorn Books edition, 1961).

*Smith, M. J., *When I Say No, I Feel Guilty.* New York: Dial Press, 1975.

Taubman, B., *How To Become An Assertive Woman.*

New York: Pocket Books, (Simon and Schuster), 1976.

*Dr. Smith has indicated, and I agree, that his "Systematic Assertive Therapy" is not AT. I list his book here because it is popularly identified with AT.
4) Publications and professional journals in many fields are reporting AT developments. There are a few sources, however, which are more directly concerned with assertiveness training:
AABT Newsletter, Eileen Gambrill, Ph.D., Editor. Published bi-monthly by the Association for Advancement of Behavior Therapy, 420 Lexington Avenue, New York, New York 10021.
ASSERT: The Newsletter of Assertive Behavior, Robert E. Alberti, Ph.D., Editor. Published bi-monthly by Impact Publishers, Inc., P. O. Box 1094, San Luis Obispo, California 93406.
Behavior Therapy, Cyril Franks, Ph.D., Editor. Published quarterly by the Association for Advancement of Behavior Therapy, 420 Lexington Avenue, New York, New York 10021.
International Directory of Assertive Behavior Training lists 571 professional facilitators (no certification or endorsement) alphabetically, geographically, and identifies areas of interest in AT. Impact Publishers, Inc., P. O. Box 1094, San Luis Obispo, California 93406.
Journal of Behavior Therapy and Experimental Psychiatry, Joseph Wolpe, M. D., Editor. Published by Pergamon Press, Fairview Park, Elmsford, New York 10523.
5) An annual conference devoted to AT was begun in September 1976 (in conjunction with the American Psychological Association convention). For information contact International Conference on Assertive Behavior Training, c/o Post Office Box 1094, San Luis Obispo, California 93406.

2

ON ASSERTION

Andrew Salter

DEFINITIONS

The word "assertive," in its present sense, was first used by Wolpe in his 1958 book on reciprocal inhibition. At that time the word did not catch on at all. In the words of the writer Don Marquis, in another connection, Wolpe's redefinition of assertion was "like dropping a rose petal down the Grand Canyon and waiting for the echo." That was the impact of the word "assertive" when it was first used.

But as time went on, the word "assertive" became more fashionable. But before I explain why "assertion" has caught on, and why it is the number one tendency in psychotherapy today, I will quote Wolpe's original redefinition of "assertion."

Wolpe said in 1958: "The word *assertive* has rather a wide meaning here. It refers not only to more or less aggressive behavior, but also to the outward expression of friendly, affectionate, and other non-anxious feelings. It covers *exactly the same ground* as Salter's (1949) word *expressive*." (Italics added) Wolpe goes on to say that he prefers "assertion" because it is "somewhat more specific" than "expressive." No dictionary I have consulted takes this position.

Wolpe's definition might be called a "lexicographical breakthrough." To define assertion as including warm, friendly feelings is linguistically incorrect. It's like defining "fat" to include its antonym—i.e., *fat* is everybody who is thin, as well as everybody who is overweight. If we were to interview at random a hundred adults who are not psychologists, and if we were to ask them "What does 'assertion' mean?'', they would give us a correct dictionary definition. "Assertion means when you speak up forcefully. It means that you *assert*." So, to broaden "assertion" to include friendly, affectionate, and nonanxious feelings strikes me as marrying a word to its opposite. Yet this illogical usage *has* caught on.

Why has the word "assertion," in its new, inaccurate sense, caught on? Essentially the things "wrong" with the word "assertion" are the very reasons it has caught on. The word "assertion" is an impertinent kind of word. It's an anti-hero kind of word. It's a "will-you-please-jump-in-the-lake-Mister" kind of word. This is just the reason the new "assertion" has caught on. It is a "today" kind of word. It allows the individual to reject society, to reject her environment, to reject his surroundings. It gives everybody an excuse to be "naughty." It gives people an excuse to be themselves. And, of course, there's the tremendous self-reinforcement of how much better you feel when you behave assertively.

I think that for good mental health we have to get out our friendly, affectionate feelings. Yet one of the biggest mistakes made in the field of assertion training is an excessive emphasis on nasty feelings—on aggression—on dictionary "assertion."

"FRAUDULENT ASSERTION"

The biggest anathema to assertion today is the word "aggression." Aggression is certainly unhealthy, but there are several variants of assertion that I think are equally wicked.

On the one hand, we have assertion, which is a healthy behavior. On the other hand, we have aggression, which is sick. But recently I have noticed a new and fascinating development. I call it *fraudulent assertion*, that is, people who seem so nice and friendly and warm and open, but are really being non-assertive. When you talk to them later they say, "I thought it was none of his business to know thus and so, or this and that." This fake assertion is thoroughly manipulative. It's very charming, but it's a fraud.

I have differentiated four forms of "fraudulent assertion." First, there is *lifesmanship* in which you just split hairs. They say "A," and you say "That's true, but not on alternate leap years." They then say, "Well, it is non-A," at which you say, "Yes, Jones has pointed out that there are exceptions to this." All this is hair splitting. There is no search for the truth. There is no search for accommodation. It's just a disguised steamroller. It is a sick, evil thing. Lifesmanship is one form of fraudulent assertion.

The second form of fraudulent expressiveness I call *actor's assertion*. Say, "Hello, how are you, good to see you!" (slightly breathless). Though it's nicer than being nasty, let's not confuse it with real assertion.

A third form of fraudulent assertion I call *manipulative assertion*. They're just working you over, and subtly pushing. A lot of sociopathic behavior is manipulative assertion. Of course, it's dishonest. It's not even assertion in the first place.

The last type of fraudulent assertion may be called *Pollyanna assertion*. Everything is just great, everything is just dandy. "Isn't it marvelous," "What a great day," "What a great night," "What a great moment," "What a great second," "You look fine," etc.

You can remember these four styles of fraudulent assertion with the word "LAMP." L is for the lifesmanship she taught me. A is for actor's assertion. M is for manipulative assertion, and P is for Pollyanna assertion. None of them is really assertion. Assertion is the real thing. Of course, you often can't tell if it's the real thing unless the person lets you look inside his or her head. You may think, "Oh, I have a sneaky feeling that it is really, etc. . . ." and you could be right, or you could be wrong.

Those types of fraudulent assertion are what assertion is *not*. True assertion, of course, is pure and real and honest, but that sounds like something up in the heavens beyond the grasp of mortal people. Nevertheless, the basic test of assertion is that it's *truthful*. The second test is that it's what I would call *interactive*. As I was developing my ideas, people would say to me, "Oh, yes, Talullah Bankhead, isn't she a perfect illustration of what you want us to be?" I would say, "No such thing. She's just dumping personal feeling into a bottomless pit." There's no wait for what someone else has to say. The tennis ball isn't bouncing back and forth. It's just volleys being shot at you. You may call such behavior many things, but it is not assertion.

Please notice that all the therapies around have one thing in common. They all talk about "let it all hang out;" they have primal screams; they have Freudian abreaction. They're all talking about expressing and opening up—and so do we.

CLINICAL CAUTIONS

Assertion trainers should be extremely cautious with depressed clients. In a way, treating depressed clients is an "orange sorting" problem. We have a conveyor belt with holes, and certain sizes of oranges can fall through the holes and larger sizes move on. We can handle certain kinds of clients. Certain other oranges have to go to people who can give medication and who can use biochemical approaches in treatment. As you talk to a client, and you see, quite correctly, the things that are making the person so depressed ("If she only realized thus and so about her husband," or "That situation with her mother isn't really thus and so"), you may be absolutely correct in your explanation. Nevertheless, your skills will not necessarily keep this person from going into an even deeper depression which really needs institutionalization. *The fact that you can correctly see the psychogenesis of the situation does not mean that it can be treated by anybody's assertive, psychotherapeutic, or behavioral techniques.*

I think that all assertion trainers should get a two-hour course in "How to smell out schizophrenics." It's easy to spot a schizophrenic who says, "The Pope is poisoning my coffee." But diagnosis is rarely that simple.

Assertion is applicable to an amazing number of conditions, and it should be tried in many situations. But it's not going to solve every problem. (It would be good to build up a literature of case histories that would help to determine which problems respond best to assertion.) But if you exert some elementary precaution, if you comb out the schizophrenics, if you watch out for the severely and obviously depressed, and the secretly depressed, you will find that assertion training can help some of the most remarkable conditions—remarkable in the sense that they don't seem amenable to usual treatment methods. If you do a literature search, you will find indeed that various aspects of assertiveness have helped some of the most extraordinary, recalcitrant conditions.

So, if you just watch your step in picking clients, you will find that assertion training can do utterly incredible things. Remember, it wasn't that long ago that when people had pneumonia we would say, "Well, I hope he pulls through." Now we say, "Pneumonia, what's today? Friday? Well, give him a week and he'll be back to work."

3

THE FOUR ASSERTIVE MYTHS: A FABLE

Julio J. Guerra, Patricia A. Taylor

Welcome visitor, allow me to introduce myself. I am the Prophet of the Good Friend. Do not be frightened, I shall not harm you. I am here to guide you through a journey of the mind. We shall return in time to Promisium, a long forgotten land, at one time the greatest, most powerful land on the planet. The people who inhabited the villages of this great nation were filled with pride, energy and love. Nature had been generous, providing all the crops and game needed in order to satisfy the physical needs of each individual. Thus the inhabitants had sufficient time away from the chores of survival to learn to play, love, think, and generally fulfill their needs for closer, more satisfying relationships. But alas! My friend, these people's demise came from a curse put on them by Zolo, an angry, fallen beast that had been imprisoned for untold ages by the ancient Greek goddess Psyche. This hideous creature had escaped its bondage and returned to the land of the living to inflict a pestilence on the descendants of the people of Promisium.

The evil Zolo visited the four great villages of Promisium and hypnotized the inhabitants, making them believe that they were in great danger of losing their greatest possession—the gift of love and companionship with friends and intimates. Zolo tricked the people into believing that they were unworthy of love and self-respect.

Because of this curse, the worst possible fear, the fear of rejection, fell upon the people of Promisium. What's more, Zolo visited each of the four great villages of Promisium and to each gave one myth. Each myth was a rule by which the inhabitants were to conduct their relationships, in order to avoid the pain of rejection and loneliness. The inhabitants of the land believed Zolo's fiendish tale and began living their lives by the dictates of their own village's myth. Zolo then retired to his lair in Iniquity, amused by the results of his revenge on the descendants of his imprisoner, Psyche, the wife of Cupid.

THE MYTH OF ANXIETY

The first village of the land we shall visit on our mind journey, my friend, shall be the village of Macho. Largest and most powerful of all the four villages of Promisium, Macho surrounds a great lake high upon a huge mountain. Centuries ago, the great lake had been devoid of inhabitants, and only the strongest of the Planet had gradually been able to navigate the treacherously narrow, steep paths in order to reach it. Those that were successful lived in a land of plenty. The great mountain lake had so many fish in it that it seemed that all one had to do was to dip a net into the water to be blessed with enough fish to feed one's family.

Before Zolo came, these happy villagers had used their time well, and had developed open, honest relationships with each other. Both men and women in Macho openly expressed their feelings of joy as well as sorrow. Any individual who felt afraid would simply announce to those around that he/she was feeling anxious.

Thus, in the village of Macho, no one gave it a second thought to hear two lovers, for instance, discussing how they at times were afraid and threatened by the actions of one another. For, you see, each individual was well aware that it was normal and human to experience anxiety. Everyone felt that they had a right to feel every emotion that was natural to human beings, and anxiety was one such emotion.

Then, sadly, Zolo came. He told the inhabitants that they were in danger of losing the love and affection of all their acquaintances and friends because they were not truly worthy of love in the first place. Upon receiving Zolo's curse, the people were frightened and resorted to huddling around each other in small groups. None could any longer trust that they were cared for by any of their closest friends and intimates.

Zolo then spun his Myth of Anxiety to the people, first by gathering all of the males of the village together and warning them that they were in danger of losing their homes and families. That they were in a "dog eat dog" world where only the strongest could survive, and each male must prove to all that he was tough and powerful, for only in that way would he be able to save himself from certain ruin. Zolo warned that if any male showed his anxiety, others would see immediately that he was truly weak and not worthy of respect or love. Zolo instructed the men that any male showing this base weakness must be ostracized from the village. The other males were not to talk to him, let him fish on the lake, or own any land. His family was instructed to leave him since he would not be able to protect his wife and he would be a bad influence on his children.

After his meeting with the men, the evil Zolo turned his hypnotic powers onto the women. He gathered them together and spun the female version of the Myth of Anxiety. He told the women that they were born as inferior and weak humans, since they were unable to control their emotions. He pointed out their willingness to show their anxiety and vulnerabilities as proof of their inherent weakness. He explained that it would do no good to try to control these emotions since they were biologically incapable of doing so. He insisted that their only escape from the ravages of the world would be to seduce a strong male to protect them.

Now, my friend, so that you can more easily see and understand how evil and destructive Zolo's myth was on this village, I shall allow you to experience a conversation between two lovers living in Macho approximately 4,000 years after the Myth of Anxiety was told to the inhabitants...

Be very still, for your mind is arriving at the home of Juannano, a very powerful and prominent Machonian. He is the strongest in the village, lives in the biggest grass hutch, and uses the largest fishing rod of all the men. Juannano is married to Juannana, a very beautiful and delicate creature. Juannana is known throughout the land for her charm, grace, and physical beauty. Since the coming of Zolo, all of the men of the village have secretly lusted for her companionship but have only resisted their urges for they feared the wrath of the powerful Juannano.

Look now, Juannano and Juannana are engaged in a very serious debate. This is unusual, as women do not argue with their husbands in this land, and yet Juannana appears to be standing up, speaking out, and talking back to Juannano as if she thought of herself as an equal. Let us listen:

Juannana: Juannano, I want to tell you that I have been going to a new kind of meeting lately. The leaders of the meeting call it "assertion training." I have learned and come to believe that I am not an inferior being as our legends tell us, and that I also have the intelligence and physical prowess to do the same kind of tasks as you do. Therefore, I have decided that I too want to start fishing in the great lake. Our family could always use more fish, and I would also be able to feel that I was doing something for myself. I, like you, want to earn my self-respect by being true to my values, instead of merely being a seductive showpiece.

Juannano: (feeling threatened) You what!! (becomes aggressive) Don't even joke like that, woman. Your place is not fishing in the great lake, but here in the hutch cleaning the fish that I bring you and the children. You should be grateful and thankful that I have made it possible for you not to have to go out and try to survive by fishing in the lake. That is no place for someone as you, or are you so blinded and corrupted by this "assertion training" that you would bring such a scandal to our home?

Juannana: No, Juannano, I am not corrupted, I merely want to fish in the lake so that we can have more fish. And, most importantly, I desire to go and further my knowledge of the things of the world. I do not mean to upset you or threaten you by doing this.

Juannano: (He is now really anxious and threatened by her assertions. He fears that if his wife is seen fishing on the lake, the others will think that he is unable to catch enough fish for his family, and they will think of him as weak. In addition, because of the effects of the Myth of Anxiety, he believes he must not allow anyone, including his wife, to see his fear, lest she also lose respect for him. So instead of telling Juannana that he is anxious, Juannano attempts to hide his nervousness by becoming more aggressive). I am not threatened. The great Juannano never is afraid. I simply forbid you to go fishing on the great lake! I don't understand you, woman! You have the very best I can provide for you. All I expect for this is to be able to come home and see that you have cared for my home and family. This is a small price to pay for my love and protection!

Juannana: Juannano, I fear that we are not communicating and I am also feeling annoyed that you are speaking to me in such a downgrading manner. I am simply trying to discuss with you some changes that I feel I must make in my own life.

Juannano: How can you even speak of going out onto that lake, when

	you are sitting here and telling me that you are feeling fearful and annoyed! Don't you understand that you are admitting that you are weak! How can you expect to go out into the world and compete against strong people?
Juannana:	No, my husband, I am not admitting that I am weak when I express my anxiety and other emotions. I am only expressing to you my reactions to the conversation that we are having. You act as if you never felt the natural emotion of anxiety. Juannano, surely you are human like us all, and you also feel anxious and threatened at times in your life. That is normal, but if you try to hide it, you shall feel even more anxious. You will then not only fear the thought of be me going to fish in the lake, but you will also fear that others and I shall see that you are afraid. Please, Juannano, don't torture yourself that way.
Juannano:	I will not tolerate this type of talk, woman! Cease instantly! I command you! Do not continue in this vein or I shall be forced to cast you from my home!
Juannana:	My husband, I too cannot tolerate what is occurring between the two of us at this moment, and would prefer to continue this conversation at a later time. I am now far too uncomfortable and it appears to me that you also are quite aroused. I only hope that somehow we can work out our difficulties.

We must leave now, my fellow mind-traveler. Let us continue our journey on to another village and see yet another example of how Zolo imprisoned the minds of mankind.

THE MYTH OF OBLIGATION

We are now going to visit the ancient village of Obligatus. This village was built in a vast, fertile valley surrounded by magnificent snowcapped mountains. The valley and its people were fed by the Spring of Eternal Love and Self-Respect.

Indeed, the goddess Psyche had looked favorably upon these villagers, for she had made it possible for the men and women of Obligatus to enjoy, eternally, the fruits of satisfying relationships. Each individual understood that every person had many different kinds of personal needs which could not possibly be satisfied by one individual alone. Therefore, whenever one of these villagers would discover that he or she wanted or needed something from another, he/she would simply ask for the need to be met. In the event that the other individual would not want or be able to fill that need, he/she would simply refuse the request. If, after discussing it, a mutually satisfying compromise could not be reached, the petitioner would either mourn the need or attempt to have it filled by another. Consequently, each villager had many different types of friends. Each person typically had acquaintances, friends, and lover(s) who were able to fill every legitimate need that he or she could expect to be filled by another individual. It was a glorious sight, my friend, to see friendships carried out in such a manner.

But alas, do not think that this happy situation existed for long in Obligatus. For here too, Zolo left his curse upon the villagers. He poisoned the great Spring of Eternal Love and Self-Respect, with the evil juices of Insecurity and Loneliness. The ambrosia that once had flowed from the Spring was defiled by Zolo's powers and now, instead of giving emotional strength, the spring's waters gave each individual the feeling that he/she was truly unworthy of love and self-respect. Zolo waited until all the villagers were terribly frightened and untrusting of their closest friends and intimates, then he gave the villagers their own unique myth—the Myth of Obligation! Zolo told all the villagers that the only way that they ever could hope to keep the companionship of their friends was to never refuse a friend's request. Zolo added that the only time a person could say "no" to another was if it were impossible to grant the request. For example, if someone asked a friend to spend a day of rest helping the other move to another residence, the friend had to give up his/her leisure time. The only safe way to refuse that request would be to have been previously committed, or to have had a physical disability, preventing the person from lifting furniture. According to Zolo, if any villager dared to ignore the Myth of Obligation by saying, "No friend, I do not want to help you move today," the friend would leave forever, since the only reason the friendship existed was because every request had previously been granted. This lie was easily believed by the villagers, for you see, my friend, these poor smitten people did not believe that their friends cared for them enough for the relationship to last beyond the first refusal of a favor. Consequently, the people of the village of Obligatus would continuously grant every request made of them by others. They, of course, would always appear to be pleased to grant the request(s), but deep inside their hearts they felt anger and resentment towards their friends for repeatedly asking them for favors. The pain of their unexpressable resentment was thought of by these people as the price they must pay for friendship and love.

Now, my friend and fellow traveler, so that you can better appreciate the evil of the myth, we shall visit the village of Obligatus and the home of Constantine Givings. Constantine is considered throughout Obligatus to be one of the friendliest women in the land. She is reported to have a perfect record in that she has never refused a friend's request.

Shh, quiet now, concentrate, my friend; your mind is in her presence. Listen, Constantine is speaking to Everett Mayold, her current suitor . . .

Everett: Constantine, my dearest. I must ask you for the greatest request that I have ever asked of anyone in my life. My darling, will you come to the altar of Venus with me and swear your bondage to our marriage?

Constantine: (Not wanting to marry Everett, she is caught on the horns of a dilemma! How can she say "no" to Everett and still keep the friendship that she desired to have with him?) Oh, my dear Everett, it is only a dream that I could do such a desirable thing; however I cannot, for my father would not permit it.

Everett: Ah, but my dearest, I have it from strong authority that our parents have negotiated a satisfactory agreement to join the two families together by our marriage. Now, with that obstacle out of the way, will you not sit with me and plan our marriage ceremony?

Constantine: It is not because I would not want to, but I also cannot marry you for you would not be happy living with me. For you see, my desirability is falsely portrayed to you. I have never told anyone this, but the Oracles of Healing have told me that I am unable to bear children.

Everett: My dearest, it would appear that you truly do not want to marry me. I can sense that the reasons that you are giving me are not founded in truth. I have been going to this new type of group lately, called "assertion training," and we are learning that in situations such as this, it is far better to say what one feels in one's heart. We all have the right, Constantine, to refuse our friend's requests.

Constantine: What is this talk, I have never heard of such a thing! You know as well as I, the price one pays for refusing a friend! Besides, You are confusing me and I get such a headache when I am confused.

Quickly stop visualizing that scene, my good friend.

THE MYTH OF MODESTY

Take a long, slow, deep breath of air, and as you exhale I shall transport your mind to Narcissus, the next village of our mind journey. In the beginning of time, the gods of the Sun and Earth worked together and constructed this village in homage to the beauty of the goddess Psyche. Narcissus was located in a vast plain, full of fields of yellow grain, that would gracefully flow and weave in the wind, much like Psyche's golden hair. By far this village was the most beautiful of Promisium.

The inhabitants of this village were a people of blessed qualities. The gods and goddesses had given to these people the inborn ability to respect and appreciate all forms of beauty in themselves and others. This outstanding ability was the hallmark that made the villagers of Narcissus indeed among the most kind and giving people of all the citizens of Promisium. Each readily recognized the positive qualities in oneself and others, and expressed this recognition through the frequent and easy giving and receiving of compliments. The villagers would love to "catch" each other doing something well. It was common for people to stop friends or strangers that were performing a worthy act and praise the appreciated behavior with the gleeful exclaim, "Got ya, I really like what you are doing!" Typically, the complimented person would respond by welling with pleasant, warm feelings at the fact that someone had seen and appreciated some of his/her positive attributes.

But sadly, this gratifying existence did not last. For the villagers of Narcissus were stricken with the effects of Zolo's wicked curse causing them to feel that they were basically unlovable and in danger of losing all their closest friends. He accomplished this evil deed by sending the Harpies to contaminate the crops of the village with the stench of Self-Doubt. Zolo then lied to the people of Narcissus, telling them that the curse was put upon them by Psyche, who was angered and revengeful for they had been complimenting their own beauties and not hers. He warned that if they ever accepted a compliment, they would be committing blasphemy and Psyche herself would see to it that no one would ever care for them again. According to Zolo, Psyche wanted the villagers to recognize "how ugly and frail they were compared to her divine beauties." They were instructed to emulate and try to become as physically and emotionally beautiful as a god or goddess, but to never think that they could achieve such perfection. So, you see my friend, as he had done in the previous villages, Zolo first panicked his victims then he gave them their own unique myth, this time the Myth of Modesty. Dutifully following their myth, these poor villagers of Narcissus began rejecting all forms of positive feedback by devaluating any compliments they might have received, always responding with all the reasons why the compliment they received was not true. These people would automatically tell you how bad they truly were, and nondeserving of any rewards. Consequently, these people of this once beautiful village became so self-critical that they were unable to enjoy any beauty in themselves. They felt inadequate in any friendships they tried to establish. They could not imagine how another person could see any good in them or want to spend time with them. They were always suspicious of anyone trying to be nice to them. On the other hand, because of their pervasive self-doubt, any criticism they received was automatically believed to be true.

Now, my friend, in order for you to experience the turmoil in these people's lives, I will allow you to visit the home of Prudence Disolthin, a villager of Narcissus.

Prudence has neither given nor accepted a compliment in her life. She is typically so depressed that she can literally see nothing good about herself. For instance, she has been working in the same job all her life, a job that she does not like very much. She is afraid to ask for a promotion, because she would have to go seek out her boss and compliment herself by saying she could do a good job doing something else that was more rewarding for her.

Relax and concentrate, my friend, so that you can experience Prudence at home speaking with her lover, Damien . . .

Damien: My dear Prudence, I love you so! You have been very good to me today. You have spent the entire day helping me study for the examination I have at school tomorrow. I want you to know that I really appreciate your support. Thank you.

Prudence: Oh, it was nothing!

Damien: No, really, I must insist that you hear me when I tell you, I really appreciate what you did, and I feel good about you now.

Prudence: Forget it. I'm not all that good, you are just seeing me in a rare mood. Let's talk about something else. What are you going to do tomorrow after you take your test?

Damien: Prudence, my love, I am becoming upset, because I hear you saying to me that I have bad taste, for liking you and for complimenting you for something you have done. I am saying that I see something in you that pleases me.

Prudence: (Jokingly) I cannot stand this, I am getting embarrassed. If I listened to you, I would become conceited and swell-headed. You wouldn't want someone around you with a large head would you?

Damien: Do not joke around like that Prudence. Accepting a compliment would not make you conceited. I feel that you are simply uncomfortable because I am giving you a compliment. I am tired of listening to you put yourself down. You are still believing in the Myth of Modesty. My

	dear, that legend simply is not true. I have been learning in my new assertion training group that it is not healthy or good to throw away compliments. I have learned that we all need positive stroking in order to feel good about ourselves. Why don't you simply say "thank you" when you hear a compliment? If you would say that, I would feel as if you acknowledged my good feelings about you and I think you would also feel better about yourself.
Prudence:	I am sorry, my friend, for not pleasing you. I have hurt your feelings. I seem to always say the wrong things. Perhaps the best thing for you to do would be to find someone who could make you happier.
Damien:	Wait a minute! You are not hearing me. I am not criticizing you. I am trying to tell you something that I like about you. You have been pleasing me by being so supportive. Prudence, you are afraid of compliments. You could reduce your fear by coming with me to the assertion training group that I have been attending. There you may learn to appreciate your own strengths and to publicly acknowledge them.
Prudence:	No. I would be too afraid to do that. I just could not imagine myself ever going to one of those head shrinker groups. Everyone would see how unloveable I am.
Damien:	My love, the things that are frightening you are the very fears that assertion training would help you overcome. The group leaders would teach you to relax in these situations that now make you so nervous. They would also help you practice ways in which you could better respond when you are being complimented.

Stop visualizing that scene my friend and fellow mind-traveler, and listen to my words. In each of the villages you have traveled you have seen that a force known as assertion training has entered into the lives of some of the people of Promisium. I have not allowed your mind to be exposed to it for very long for I wished to speak to you first.

The leaders of this movement state that we have the right to believe in our own legitimate values and feelings. They also say that it is healthy and normal for us to try to get our needs and wants met by our acquaintances and friends. They tell us that we have a perfect right to these things as long as we fulfill the responsibility of "keeping our mouth in gear," telling others openly and honestly what we feel or want.

Do not listen to them, my good friend. They are mis-guided villagers of Promisium that have suffered so long from Zolo's curses that their minds are deranged. To act in the way they say is not being normal or responsible to others. It is being selfish. If you assert yourself, you are putting yourself before another. I tell you my friend, if you act in this way you will lose all your friends, for people will feel you do not care for them.

THE MYTH OF THE GOOD FRIEND

You must now be told the truth. Take another deep breath of air, and as you exhale, prepare yourself to go on the grimmest of all our journeys. The fourth and final village that your mind must visit is your own village, and the villager you must experience is yourself. You see, I must now tell you that you are also a citizen of Promisium, and one of the descendants of the people cursed by Zolo. You, like all the other villagers of this land, also feel unlovable and unworthy of love and self-respect.

Do not become frightened my friend. Relax. I am here to help you and keep you from experiencing the pains of Loneliness and Insecurity. I, the Prophet of the Good Friend give you this Platinum Rule, "You will only find good friends among those who share your values and always know what you want." These "perfect friends" can only be found by setting up a relationship test. The test determines if a potential good friend is perceptive enough to "instinctively" know what and how you feel. The idea is to wait until you are with someone whom you want as a friend, and then test him/her by acting in a way different from how you really feel. For example, if a friend hurts your feelings, you can test him/her by acting angry. Good friends will be able to tell that you are hurting, and they will know that what you really want is for them to ignore your angry statements and comfort you. If you ever have to reveal your hurt feelings, then you will know that person has failed the relationship test and does not really care for you.

Assertive people would require you to tell them when you are vulnerable and hurting. They will tell you that they cannot know what you are feeling because they cannot read your mind. They will seduce you into telling them your vulnerabilities by promising that they would be willing to comfort you. However, you know as well as I that comfort you must ask for is a hollow gift because a good friend "would have known. . . ."

Again I warn you, citizen of Promisium, you are in danger of losing friends. Anticipating the needs of others is the only means of maintaining friendships. So be diligently aware of others' needs, for you too may fail someone else's relationship test. But relax, my friend, do not fear, for if you follow my Platinum Rule then you will not suffer the pains of insecurity but you shall glory in the joys of intimacy.

Now, my good friend, in a moment I will count to five and at that time you will awaken. You will feel somewhat confused and restless. You will remember this mind journey that you have taken, and you shall live your life following the Myth of the Good Friend, but you shall not remember me, your host on this mind journey, Zolo.

1, 2, 3, 4, 5, ...

4

ASSERTION TRAINING: AN IDENTITY CRISIS THAT'S COMING ON STRONG

Martin E. Shoemaker, Donna Olsen Satterfield

Morrow (1971), in a bibliographic survey of behavior therapy literature between 1950 and 1969, includes over fifty examples of the clinical application of assertion training (AT). A cursory survey of studies on AT since 1969 shows a snow-balling of interest among mental health professionals in this treatment strategy, particularly its use in a group context.

For those not interested in or familiar with these professional writings, there is now a plethora of how-to-assert-yourself type books on the market for the "living-room" trainee. Since AT was popularly presented by Robert Alberti and Michael Emmons in the first edition of their book *Your Perfect Right*, published in 1970, the titles have grown to include such notables as *Stand Up, Speak Out, Talk Back!*; *I Can If I Want To*; *Don't Say Yes When You Want To Say No*; and over a dozen more!

Similarly, the growth of self-help groups led by lay people, paraprofessionals and educators of varying backgrounds and interest has paralleled the expansion of its clinical application by the professional psychotherapist. Spurred on by various social liberation doctrines, in particular the women's movement, AT has supplied a useful technology for behavior change and a natural sequel to consciousness-raising rhetoric and group meetings. The authors' own experience supports this phenomenon as women have outnumbered men in our groups almost two to one.

The growth of AT both popularly and professionally in the seventies is somewhat reminiscent of the "sensitivity movement" or T-group phenomenon of the sixties. However, those close to this recent rapid expansion of AT are also aware of a few growing pains that often mark the development of an organism from childhood to adolescence. Central to this development has been a growing "identity crisis" which manifests itself in the diversity of answers given to the question, What is AT? This is not a new question or problem for any new burgeoning psychotherapy or, for that matter, for some of the therapies that have been around a while. However, to this most complex question this paper is *assertively* addressed!

AT: IN SEARCH OF IDENTITY

Basic to AT's identity crisis are the somewhat fluid or, at times, differing definitions given to the treatment or training procedures. Fundamental to the confusion over definition is the fact that the practice of AT has, at this date, completely outdistanced its theoretical underpinning and research base. Since its inception as a clinical application of Pavlovian conditioning theory to neurotic disorders (Salter, 1949; Wolpe, 1958), its rationale, procedures and techniques have greatly broadened. To illustrate, AT can be conceptualized at one extreme as a set of verbal techniques (Smith, 1975),[1] and on the other, a broad-based self-actualized approach to living (Lazarus & Fay, 1975; Shoemaker, 1977).

Similarly, the list of processes now used by trainers or therapists has become extremely long and involved and would include the following: role-playing, psychodrama, behavioral rehearsal, guided practice, role-reversal, mirroring, modeling, audio-video or verbal feedback, token feedback, flooding, desensitization, covert practice, coaching, self-management, homework, contracting, non-verbal exercises, value clarification exercises, self-disclosure, small group discussion, group assignments, field trips, films and selected readings.

Although the above includes a large number of processes taken from action-oriented approaches (London, 1964), most professionals doing

---

1. EDITOR'S NOTE: Dr. Manuel Smith, author of *When I Say No, I Feel Guilty*, has indicated that his "systematic assertive therapy" is *not* AT. I agree. However, this approach is often taught as AT by others.

AT also have neatly integrated a number of specific concepts and insights into their definition of AT so that the client's view of both his world and himself is substantially restructured. Just a simple idea like, "you have certain inalienable rights as a human being which should not be violated," has tremendous impact upon some individuals who need permission from an "expert" to exercise their self-assertiveness.

Compounded with this long list of intervention strategies, we have seen or heard reports of a broad range of selected target problems and personality deficits and/or excesses being treated by AT. These targets range from small objective non-verbal changes (eye contact, gestures, facial expressions, gait, posture), to large life changes, such as decreasing aggressions, passivity or anxiety, leaving a marriage, starting to date, going back to school, job acquisition skills and many, many others (Hersen, Eisler and Miller, 1973).

To add to this confusion or, if you will, expansion, AT has been used as the primary training or treatment mode for quite varying population groups. This would include college students (Hedquist and Weinhold, 1970; Rathus, 1972), neuropsychiatric inpatients (Booraem and Flowers, 1972), Spanish-speaking mothers (Landau and Paulson, 1975), delinquents (Shoemaker, 1974), prisoners (Novotny, 1975), geriatric groups (Levine, 1975), and others, some of which are described in accompanying chapters of this book. Actually the list includes almost every major diagnostic classification in a wide variety of settings. The trainers or therapists represent all of the major mental health disciplines and a number of paraprofessionals. There was a time when the authors of this paper had a file on all of the pertinent research and clinical applications of AT, but we have since given up that effort as our clinical responsibilities would have to be curtailed by such a time-consuming task.

In summary, we can say that AT is a long list of highly complex and specialized intervention strategies and techniques which are used to change the thoughts, emotions and overt behavior of just about anyone who will be treated by this highly popular and successful treatment experience. To us, this exemplifies an identity crisis of great proportions, but one that certainly "comes on strong." If this sounds somewhat familiar to you and similar to an inhouse joke about most therapies living or dead, the only difference seems to be that most treatments are *not* "coming on" as strong.

A THREE-LEVEL MODEL OF AT

Here at the Assertion Training Institute we have been struggling to define for ourselves and our professional trainees what AT is for us. In such a complex situation we would not presume to speak for all professionals engaged in this burgeoning field by attempting any final definition, however, we would like to share some of our thoughts on the subject and a broad-spectrum model of AT that includes most of what assertion trainers are doing currently.

Graphically, we have chosen to depict the whole spectrum of AT as a tri-level, inverted pyramid (see Fig. 4-1).

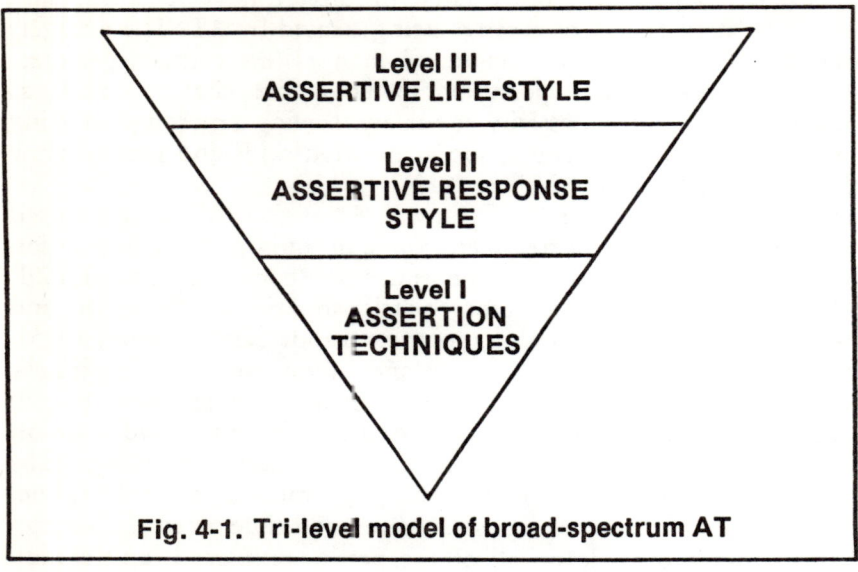

Fig. 4-1. Tri-level model of broad-spectrum AT

The very bottom of the pyramid represents all of the techniques and other non-spontaneous forms of communication skill training that various assertion trainers have originated and have perpetuated through their workshops or writings. Examples of these techniques include "broken record," "Content-Process Shift," "Decision-Delay," "Fogging," "Negative Inquiry," "Taking Distance," to name only a few. The above list includes several techniques which apparently originated in Southern California, some have a very "foggy" history and the originators are hard to determine, even for those to whom "being first" is important. Most of us who have been doing AT from its early beginnings in the late sixties learned from each other at a very rapid pace and supplemented as we went along. The senior author's early development in AT, for example, was a direct result of working with Julio Guerra and Sherwin Cotler at the L. A. Free Clinic and reading Bob Alberti and Mike Emmons' book, *Your Perfect Right*.

TECHNIQUES AND PROCEDURES

Many of the currently popular techniques had very little to do with the original formulation of AT in the writings of Salter (1949), Wolpe (1954, 1958) and Wolpe and Lazarus (1966), although Salter did describe a series of "excitatory exercises" which were later expanded by Rathus (1972). However, everywhere we go AT is more often than not associated with a series of selected and predictable techniques such as "fogging," "broken record," and "Decision-Delay," etc. To this extent then, and particularly since the publishing of a few popular books and magazine articles which advocate verbal dexterity and "getting what you want," AT will probably be associated in the minds of many with some very clever and, at times, beneficial response "tricks" prepared for those troublesome interpersonal conflict situations that occur with great regularity.

However, it is our very strong concern that AT not be reduced to or associated with these non-spontaneous verbal skills. It has been our experience that AT is seriously limited and occasionally unbeneficial to clients if only a set of specific techniques are taught and practiced. Like all pre-set ways of talking or acting, whether it be in raising children (Ginot, 1965), or in dealing with highly critical and manipulating people, the specific responses of the "other" person(s) are never as predictable as one might practice or be led to believe. While rote memorization of responses dictated by a technique can eliminate much of the anxiety associated with a troublesome situation, overworking these techniques often leads to personal inauthenticity and interpersonal callousness.

Thus, the bottom level of the model, viewed as only one dimension of AT, is filled with assorted techniques and strategies. We are sure this level is a basis for much of AT's popular appeal and the plethora of one-day workshop experiences that have been evidenced throughout the country. Such techniques have their place in AT but must be viewed in a more comprehensive perspective. They are most effective when appropriately demonstrated and taught for situationally specific deficits (e.g., handling an obtrusive salesman by using "Broken Record") and should not be looked upon as generalizable responses to most demand situations.

AT AS A BELIEF-RESPONSE SYSTEM

The middle level of our model contains what we feel to be the core and substance of AT for our groups and for those we have trained to be trainers. This level of training is best represented by the tripartite discrimination of assertive, aggressive, and non-assertive (withdrawing) response styles first clarified by Bob Alberti and Mike Emmons (1970, 1974, 1975). In this discrimination, AT is seen as a constant interpersonal response style that is characterized by open verbal expression of one's rights, needs, thoughts and feelings. The target behavior is often verbal (e.g., talking to your employer about a raise) but has grown to include specific non-verbal components that give a more self-confident and congruent message. These non-verbal behaviors have been more carefully delineated by the works of Eisler, Hersen and Agras (1973), and Serber (1972 [see chapter 6]).

Of extreme importance in the development of the assertive interpersonal response style is the comparison of assertive expression to that which is aggressive (violates another's rights) and withdrawing or passive (backing away from one's own rights). Unfortunately, and this helpful criticism has been made many times to us, the tripartite categories are not clearly defined or entirely objective (Alberti, 1976). This lends itself to healthy group discussion but can be confusing on occasion. Similarly there are often overlaps in response styles, e.g., passive-aggressive, which was extended into a fourth separate category by Stanlee Phelps and Nancy Austin in their book *The Assertive Woman* (1975), and which they label "indirectly aggressive" (see Chapter 15).

However, taken as a whole, we feel that an important aspect of AT is this response differentiation, at times oversimplified, which allows the client a simple model for viewing his or her own verbal behavior and the general social and interpersonal consequences of that behavior. The particular didactic strategies used to teach the difference between these styles vary from group leader to group leader. We have found written material, behavioral rehearsal and systematic token feedback to be quite effective (Shoemaker and Paulson, 1975).

AN ASSERTIVE LIFE STYLE

The top level, and what we are just beginning to see as an extremely exciting dimension of AT, is the development of an assertive lifestyle. Before looking at this further, let us clarify that traditional psychotherapy, and particularly proponents of the "Human Potential Movement" in psychology, have long advocated dealing with the more general or existential areas in therapy. To that extent AT is not developing some unique philosophy or treatment goals. The real difference seems to be in the language and methodology used to achieve the ends.

Fundamental to being assertive is awareness, both personal and social. Personal awareness is getting practice at "looking inside" for what I want before I look around for what other people want and expect from me in a given situation. Complementary to this, is the ability to know the probable consequences of a particular behavior in a particular setting and to take responsibility for that consequence if we choose to act. Self-desire and social consciousness are often seen as opposing forces in the causation of behavior, but we feel that both are necessary to make a judgment between alternatives. The difference is only one of primacy and timing. In other words, my own self-interest is the first question to ask and explore before I worry about the social consequence. Having delineated what I want, I then must see if the perceived consequence of my assertive action is too painful or risky, outside of my realistic control, transgresses upon the rights of other persons, or violates some other principle I hold in high esteem. The two processes form the type of awareness that we believe leads to a "benevolently self-interested" and socially responsible, assertive individual. We operate on the assumption, generally proved valid by our clients' experiences, that increased awareness and assertiveness leads to greater need satisfaction and personal fulfillment, which provides an overflow for the individual to give more positively and without resentment to others.

It is not the purpose of this paper to explore the differences in the psychotherapy "means" of behavioral vs. humanistic psychology. The point that we are making is that one of the material outgrowths of learning and struggling with the assertive verbal response style (Level II) is the desire to become more self-directed, self-interested and achieve one's potential in all areas. These concepts in themselves have often been criticized by "behavior modification purists," who find them not conducive to operational definitions and evaluation. Be that as it may, in our groups we have seen people, often those who entered timid and anxious over certain situation-specific problems, learn far more than non-spontaneous responses (Level I), or even a steady interpersonal assertive response style (Level II). They have begun to question more of their basic assumptions and goals for living. The constant practice of "looking inside" and discovering what I *really* want begins to lay bare dreams, ambitions, and values that were all covered up by the expectancies of significant others, fears of rejection and personal failure, and a host of other "intrapsychic dynamics."

So far, the best attempts at developing the "self-actualized," or what we translate as the *assertive*, life-style among the learning theory based strategies are found in the self-management literature. There is strong reason to believe that the technology of self-management and

Assertion Training now offers a link between behavior therapies and the more "free will" based psychotherapies. Self-control is such a natural corollary of self-assertion that the terms can almost be used interchangeably in the third level of development and in groups whose primary design is the assertive lifestyle. Other strategies and processes that we have used in assertive lifestyle groups are values clarification exercises and time-management (along with much support and encouragement!).

The concept of an assertive lifestyle through AT has been a very recent development. It is an advanced goal for individuals who seek out AT, and ought not to be viewed by facilitators as the only criterion of success. Broad sweeping personality or value changes as a result of a time-limited AT group is unsupported by current research. Nevertheless, broad spectrum (to use a phrase quite popular now among behavior therapists) AT *is* dealing with some of the most crucial issues in the lives of its participants and need not be confined to only the bottom and middle levels in our model.

TARGET PROBLEMS AND PROCESSES

We have presented a model of AT that we feel encompasses most of the major content areas and a few of the behavioral focuses that appear fundamental. The processes by which these are achieved are many and present the serious researcher a set of confusing independent variables. There is some uncertainty about whether AT is best defined by its *target problems* (e.g., social timidity, reliance on others for decision making) or by a set of *processes* (e.g., modeling, behavioral rehearsal) that are directed towards increasing social-interpersonal skills or reducing anxiety.

It seems to us that both target problems and the type of processes used belong in the definition of AT. The *problem* focus of AT is designed to increase assertive behaviors, some of which are non-verbal but part of a communication or message, e.g., facial gestures. Training attention is directed to honest verbalization with a specific look at content, or other non-verbal operant behaviors which develop, secure, or attain a personal desire or right. Most of these behaviors may already be in the person's repertoire, but through self-exploration and group encouragement, the whole series are brought together to achieve the desired end.

The acquisition of assertive behaviors also leads to a decrease in behaviors incompatible with assertion: social anxiety, aggressiveness, and passivity or withdrawing. Active, intentional assertiveness either inhibits or replaces these undesirable response styles.

The somewhat confusing combination of *process* strategies included under the AT umbrella is clarified considerably if broken down into four procedural categories: 1) Instruction 2) Modeling 3) Practice 4) Feedback. *Instructional* variables include a vast array of ideas and concepts that surround the philosophy, theory or rationale behind AT. For example, in this category one might include a differentiation between self-interest and selfishness, or a statement of the values that the trainer feels underlie AT. Many AT leaders pass out readings explaining various concepts, such as, basic human rights, ways to self-evaluate one's progress, or other educative resources which will reinforce the client's own personal attitude for seeking out AT in the first place.

The next major procedural class is observable *behavioral modeling*. A commonly used definition among assertion trainers for modeling is the process of role-playing by which a group member or therapist performs a specific verbal or non-verbal behavior (message related) for another member to observe and later imitate or approximate. The model does not have to be "live," but can be a videotaped sequence showing a desirable response in a specific situation (Eisler, Hersen and Miller, 1973). The objective of modeling assertive responses in AT is to enable response acquisition by teaching specific content and pointing out important *paraverbal*, (e.g., tone, loudness) and *non-verbal* (e.g., gestures, posture) components that form a message unit.

Practice appears to be the core procedure of AT and certainly one that is receiving more attention as behavior therapy literature expands. Practice or behavioral rehearsal may be personal or non-personal. Personal practice allows an individual to use the group or therapist to act out a current personal life situation, rehearsing what he or she would like to say or do. This opportunity to work on a problem area, such as giving negative feedback to an employer, may help to 1) increase assertive skill and response probability through group encouragement, and 2) act as an *in vivo* desensitization process, reducing anticipated anxiety. The improved skill and lessened anxiety generally result in an increased feeling of courage and competency in that particular problem or conflict area.

Non-personal practice accomplishes much of the above except that the rehearsal areas and roles are often prearranged by the facilitator and the practice may or may not be in an area of immediate personal concern. This usually is the case when AT is taught more as a course or in a workshop format with a large number of people present. Very personal or emotionally-laden areas are usually explored more cautiously, if at all, in these settings. An interesting application of the practice concept is the assigning of extra-group homework to be done in between sessions and reported on in the next group meeting (See Chapter 9).

The final procedural category is *feedback* and generally can be used systematically (e.g., tokens discriminating certain response styles, videotaping of rehearsal situation) or (more often) informal coaching. Typically the leader is the primary source of feedback, but one study concluded that peers or other group members are an extremely helpful source (Flowers and Guerra, 1974).

SUMMARY

Our approach to the complex and confusing issue of the "identity" of assertion training has been to develop a tri-level model, broad enough to include most aspects, advances and approaches to AT. Our definition includes the target problems and behavior, the basic processes used by AT facilitators for correcting these problems, and the broader concept of developing an assertive lifestyle. The task of definition is a difficult one and hopefully the model presented here is inclusive enough to provide a framework for the rapid development of technology and the varied procedures now used by assertion trainers.

ASSERTIVE BEHAVIOR TRAINING AND THE ENHANCEMENT OF SELF-ESTEEM

Lawrence P. Percell

Behavior therapies in general and Assertive Behavior Training in particular rest on three basic assumptions about human nature: (1) that a person's feelings and attitudes relate closely to his or her behavior; (2) that behavior is learned; and (3) that behavior can be changed. The practicing therapist, even if behaviorally oriented, is particularly concerned with the first assumption because he or she deals on a day-to-day basis with clients' feelings and attitudes as well as with their concrete, observable behavior.

The behavioral treatment of depression provides a good illustration of the inter-relationship between feelings and behavior. Often times the person who is experiencing the negative feelings labeled as clinical depression significantly decreases daily activities. He or she may cease making routine decisions or may withdraw from the social environment and live as an isolate. The behavior therapist would focus on assisting this person to increase his or her activity level with the expectation that this would result in a new emotional experience such as elation. Figure 5-1 graphically illustrates this process.

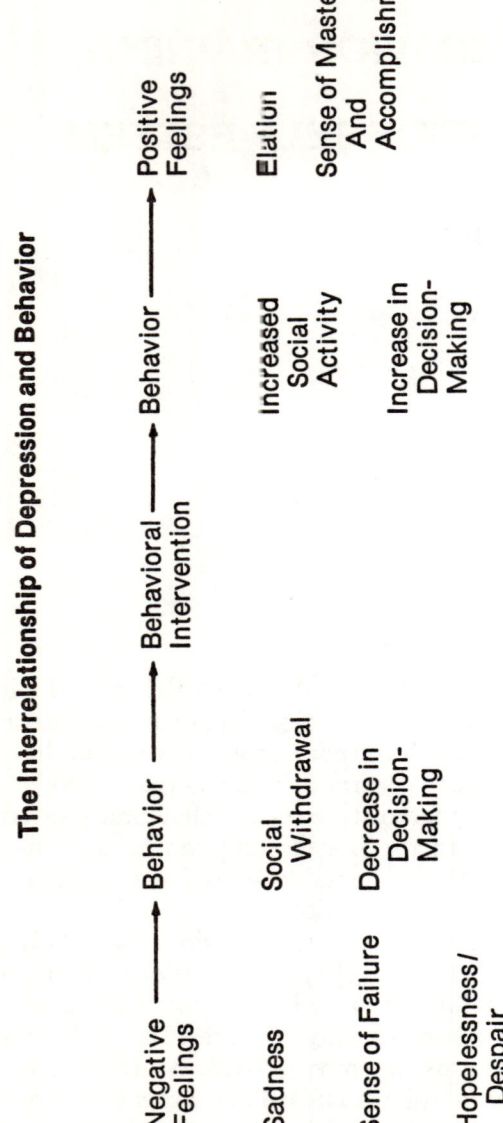

The potential for feedback between feelings and behavior is readily apparent. The depressed person who feels hopeless about life getting better but who does nothing to improve his or her circumstances, has just had those hopeless beliefs reaffirmed. If, on the other hand, the therapist can help that person take small steps toward making these decisions, the client may discover that things can change and even improve. The positive feelings which come from this discovery can prompt further action, which in turn will enhance these positive feelings and allay some or all of the depression.

A corollary to the assumption under discussion is that it is relatively easier to help someone *act* him or herself into a new way of thinking or feeling than it is to *think* or *feel* him or herself into a new way of acting. Hence, the behavior therapist focuses on changing behavior, expecting the change in attitudes, beliefs, and affect to follow.

Applying this principle to the assertive domain, it has been assumed that an assertive person is generally happier and more self-accepting because he or she is assertive. Alberti and Emmons (1970) were two of the first to explicate the relationship between assertiveness and self-acceptance. They hypothesize that the assertive individual is more likely to achieve desired goals since he or she is more expressive and able to make choices; consequently, the assertive person feels good about him or herself. The nonassertive person is more inhibited and less able to make choices, so often does not achieve his or her goals and hence does not have good feelings about him or herself.

Detailed definitions of assertive persons and behavior are treated elsewhere in the book and so will not be attempted here. There are two points, however, that I would like to raise before proceeding further. First of all, assertiveness, as I conceptualize it, is broader than just standing up for one's rights. It also encompasses acting in one's own best interest and expressing honest feelings (positive and negative) comfortably, of course without denying the rights of others. Consequently, the complex behaviors required to establish a new relationship, disagree openly with another, and change or end a relationship that is unsatisfactory can be subsumed under the assertive label. And, secondly, although I will use the term "assertive person," I do not believe there are many, if at all any, assertive *people*; nor are there passive and aggressive *people*. There is passive, aggressive and assertive *behavior*, with most people possessing some of each. Of course, many of us have developed an abundance of one particular class of behaviors and hence may be referred to as passive, aggressive, or assertive people.

The notion that "assertive people" are happier and more self-accepting is an intriguing one because most therapists hope their clients leave treatment with an enhanced sense of self-esteem. Carl Rogers (1961) is perhaps the most vocal proponent of the notion that a devalued sense of self-worth is often at the heart of client problems. Rogers advocates a psychotherapy which provides a means of establishing feelings of self-acceptance, defined as the client's perception of self as worthy, independent, able to cope with life's problems, and the subjective experience of liking him or herself.

To test the Alberti and Emmons hypothesis, Percell, Berwick, and Beigel (1974) administered both an assertiveness inventory and a self-acceptance questionnaire to 100 clients (50 men and 50 women) who were either in treatment or seeking treatment at a community mental health center. The results indicated a significant positive correlation between the assertiveness and self-acceptance measures, supporting the prediction that persons judged to be assertive would have high measured self-esteem while those judged nonassertive would have low measured self-esteem.

It would seem, then, that the cognitive-affective phenomenon of feeling good about oneself does relate closely to one's behavior, in this case the ability to be assertive. *But can it be demonstrated empirically that clients leave Assertive Behavior Training with an enhanced sense of self-esteem, as our first assumption would suggest?* Percell et al. (1974) addressed a second study to this issue. Twelve clients were given eight sessions of group Assertive Behavior Training which included the usual techniques of hierarchical presentation of problem situations, behavior rehearsal, modeling, postural and vocal analysis, constructive criticism, homework assignments and praise and social reinforcement for accomplishments. A control group of twelve clients were given eight sessions of an assertive discussion group. Such topics as the advantages of being assertive, the situational determinants of each client's nonassertive behavior, and suggestions on how to behave more effectively were discussed and explored; however, no behavior rehearsal was done. Subjects in both groups completed an assertive inventory and a self-acceptance measure before and after treatment. The Taylor Manifest Anxiety Scale (Taylor, 1953) was also administered to both groups before and after treatment in order to test the hypothesis that assertive responses can act as a reciprocal inhibitor of anxiety (Wolpe and Lazarus, 1966).

The experimenters found that the Assertive Training group showed significant increases in their self-esteem and a significant decrease in anxiety, as measured by the inventories, while controls showed no significant changes on any of these measures. Besides modifying the clients' social and interpersonal behavior, group Assertive Training was also able to improve the self-concepts of members and reduce their general level of distress as well. A more recent study reported by Henderson (1976) adds further support to this conclusion by demonstrating that Assertive Training affected changes in a number of cognitive-affective dimensions such as self-acceptance, self-regard, and self-actualizing value.

There is a three-fold process which may explain why assertive persons usually feel good about themselves. I have labeled the three components of this process (1) expectancy, (2) reinforcement, and (3) self-perception. I consider it important for the working clinician to be familiar with these components since they can be used by the therapist to enhance the phenomenon of increased self-acceptance.

First of all, it is common to give the client or trainee the expectation to feel better about him or herself as a result of behaving more assertively. It could be that this expectancy causes the individual to be more attentive to the changes which increased assertiveness brings about, changes he or she might otherwise be less aware of and, consequently, less responsive to. Of course, expectancy alone cannot bring about the therapeutic affect. In the study by Percell *et al*. (1974), both groups were given the expectation that behaving more assertively would result in feeling better about themselves; and yet only the Assertive Training group produced significant increases in either assertiveness or self-acceptance. It seems to be generally accepted in the literature that expectancy can enhance an already powerful therapeutic intervention while having little, if any, effect with a weak technique. In the research discussed, the powerful technique present in the Assertive Behavior Training group and absent in the control group was most likely behavior rehearsal, generally considered the most effective component of Assertive Training.

Secondly, the assertive person's self-esteem is enhanced by reinforcement. As Alberti and Emmons (1970) point out, the assertive person is often more likely to achieve life goals, since he or she is more expressive and able to make desires known and, consequently, feels good about him or herself. When clients do achieve their desired goals through being assertive, the therapist should be certain they attend to the accomplishment because of the effect this can have on their self-perception, the third part of the self-esteem enhancement process. Clients' hopes should not, however, be raised to expect that their assertiveness will always be met with success. I tell my clients that there are two basic goals for behaving assertively: (a) feeling better that they have communicated what they want to; and (b) bringing about some desired change. I warn them that they are likely to accomplish the former more often than the latter since there is no guarantee that others will respond positively to their assertive behavior.

Finally, the increases in self-acceptance can be explained by change in the person's perception of self. Daryl Bem, the originator of Self-Perception Theory (Bem, 1970), bases his model on the observation that when we want to know how a person feels, we look to see how he or she acts. For instance, using the depression example discussed earlier, the therapist bases a conclusion that a client is depressed on the client's verbal statements of despair and hopelessness and on his or her behavior of social withdrawal and failure to take care of daily responsibilities. Bem's theory would suggest that one also infers his or her own internal state by observing one's own overt behavior. Accordingly, the assertive client's self-appraisal changes in a positive direction probably because of the self-perception of more assertive and effective behavior. The therapist, consequently, has an opportunity to enhance this process by pointing out the client's accomplishments. Besides providing reinforcements for the desired behavior, the therapist's attention may assist a self-deprecating client, who is likely to overlook or devalue his or her success, in focusing on the positive achievement.

The self-perception hypothesis also underscores the necessity to rank order the client's problematic situations and work on them systematically and progressively, starting with the one which is easiest and most likely to be met with success. Many clients and therapists want to rush to the most important and salient situations which are usually the most difficult. Again using Bem's theory, the client who sees him or herself repeatedly failing to behave assertively and effectively in the role-play situations and homework assignments may use this information to support an already negative sense of self-worth and possibly have reduced motivation for staying in treatment.

It has been empirically validated that Assertive Behavior Training brings about both internal and external changes in trainees. Ordinarily, the internal changes early in training are not pleasant; people are anxious and uneasy about trying out any new way of behaving or relating. However, clinical and empirical data suggest that with continued practice the assertive person will come to an enhanced sense of self worth.

Part Two:
INNOVATIONS IN TECHNIQUE

TEACHING THE NONVERBAL COMPONENTS OF ASSERTIVE TRAINING

Michael Serber

Most published and verbal reports dealing with assertive training concentrate primarily on the explicit verbal message. This is also true of a recently published book on assertive training (Alberti and Emmons, 1970).

Unfortunately, a most important aspect of assertive training, the paralinguistic component—how the message is delivered—has not had its fair share of attention and has been left mostly to chance, apart from some pilot studies of limited scope (Ivey, 1968). A number of independent researchers evaluating the importance of nonverbal communication have found that in many situations the nonverbal messages are perceived as more important than the verbal by the subject (Mehrabian, 1968; Mehrabian and Ferris, 1967). In reality, it is much simpler to instruct a client to "tell off her husband" than to work out the details of an appropriate, effective message. Any experienced clinician is well aware of the fact that what ineffective persons often lack is not knowledge or courage but a command of style. Lack of style can be behaviorally defined as the inability to master appropriate nonverbal, as well as verbal, components of behavior.

To define functionally what is or is not appropriate, I am guided by

---

From the *Journal of Behavior Therapy and Experimental Psychiatry.* Vol. 3, pp. 179-183. Pergamon Press, 1972. Reprinted by permission.

what is accepted in general social usage—people don't shout during moments of tenderness, don't smile when angry, don't stand 8 feet away from friends when carrying on an intimate conversation, and speak fluently when they desire something. The number of individuals who say the right thing the wrong way is legion. This figures prominently in the folk humor of our culture. Some neo-freudian therapists, such as the gestalt therapists and transactional analysts have regarded the style of a person's communication as the object of insight and the source of therapeutic change (Berne, 1964; Perls, Hefferline and Goodman, 1951).

Wilhelm Reich in his book, *Character Analysis* (1949), vividly describes the paralinguistic behaviors or styles of communication exhibited by some of his patients. Fritz Perls, a patient of Reich's, who developed gestalt therapy (very much in vogue during the 60's) extensively employed Reichian character analysis to give his patients, individually or in groups, direct feedback about "the way" in which they said or did things. More recently, Marshall McLuhan (1964) has made much of the idea that the way people do things is what they do, or in his words "the medium is the message."

All of the so-called humanistic schools of psychology, even when they address themselves to identifying and describing a behavior, do little to teach alternative behaviors. The assumption among "non-directive" psychotherapists is that once a patient understands or feels his "character" or the "game" he plays, he will be free to adopt more appropriate behavior. My departure from this position is that understanding, whether defined in cognitive or emotional terms, is in itself not adequate for achieving longstanding or significant behavioral change. To define the behavior in need of change is only a preliminary step which has to be followed by specific instruction, modeling, role-playing and the behavioral rehearsal of alternative behavior. It is also necessary to separate out the significant nonverbal components of a total pattern and shape each one separately. In sharp contrast to traditional psychotherapeutic strategies, the behavioral approach avoids the emotional confrontation of a patient regarding behavior for which he has not developed any alternatives (Laws and Serber, 1971). Emotional confrontation may only result in raising the anxiety level of the patient, even to the point that it markedly diminishes his learning capacity.

Behavior therapy has available to it the technology necessary to shape nonverbal behavior. Information giving, modeling, role-playing, and behavior rehearsal coupled with audio-visual feedback comprise an adequate armementarium.

THE SELECTION OF NONVERBAL BEHAVIORS TO BE TAUGHT

As in the teaching of verbal behavior, the elements that are considered most important for communication are selected, giving priority to those whose shaping is likely to contribute most significantly to the end product which I call "a total socially meaningful behavior." The selection of elements depends on the requirements of the training situation. For example, telephoning an employer is simpler than telling him face to face that he has been unfair. In the phone conversation eye contact, facial expression, body expression and distance from person with whom one is interacting are unimportant—in contrast to face-to-face confrontation.

I have found it useful to break down nonverbal behavior into the following specifics:
1. loudness of voice,
2. fluency of spoken words,
3. eye contact,
4. facial expression,
5. body expression,
6. distance from person with whom one is interacting.

Loudness and fluency are vocal features that are not dependent upon the content of the verbal message. Fluency in fact may be completely at odds with the explicit message, yet if fluency is lacking from a message the overall impact of what is said is greatly diminished.

Some of the six variables listed are easily measurable—loudness of voice, fluency, distance from the other person, eye contact—but bodily and facial expression defy simple measurement. They can, in fact, be measured, but by complex techniques that are time-consuming and unnecessary for clinical work (Ekman, Friesen and Taussig, 1969). In fact, all of the variables mentioned can be satisfactorily assessed by a clinician or behavioral rater with adequate experience in working with this kind of behavior. In a study evaluating the effects of assertive training, behavioral raters were employed to rate the "softer" variables such as body expression and facial expression (Laws and Serber, 1971). The raters were trained by the use of prepared videotaped models of body and facial expression appropriate to the social settings concerned.

It may not be necessary for the clinician to rate every training session, but the fact that the variables to be shaped can be objectified makes the trainer sensitive to the fact that objective behavioral assessment could become a regular part of the overall assessment.

THE SHAPING OF A NONVERBAL VARIABLE

The conditions most favorable for the training of nonverbal behaviors are:
1. A clearly defined situation,
2. concentration upon a limited number of nonverbal variables,
3. audio-visual feedback.

I have been employing a 1/2 inch video-tape recorder and camera with a 5:1 zoom lens, and a 12 inch television monitor. The entire outfit is kept on a small cart which can easily be rolled from room to room. No auxiliary lights are necessary if room lighting is bright enough for reading and without excessive contrast.

To begin working with a nonverbal behavior it is necessary to choose a situation which can be repeated *in toto* or in part for several trials without any significant alteration. An example of such a situation would be the following: A trainee is told, "You have just met a prospective employer who is sitting behind his desk. He will act sympathetically toward you—smile, ask supporting questions, etc. It is your task in 3 minutes to begin a conversation with him and try to impress him with your qualifications for a (specific) job." The role of the employer is played by the therapist or an assistant. The patient's effort is videotaped and the most deficient element in his behavior usually selected first for modification. I have found it a good general rule to work with only one nonverbal variable at a time. For example, in the audio-visual replay of the situation it may be impossible to hear the voice of the trainee. Then our first purpose will be to shape the loudness factor.

The patient is shown a replay of his role-playing and informed which verbal variable is in need of modification. The appropriate behavior is then modeled for him. The modeling usually has to be repeated many times, and each time the trainee approximates it to the best of his ability. After several trials, each followed by videotape feedback, the patient shows progress for which he is positively reinforced by praise and given further instruction through modeling and role playing. The attention to a particular nonverbal variable continues until significant improvement has been achieved. One may then move on to another variable.

It is common when observing patients carrying out sample behaviors, to find that some non-verbal variables are already satisfactory, while others are grossly deficient. The patient who has an overall deficiency is the one who needs the most careful and concentrated work, with smaller improvements expected of him and with much positive reinforcement for each advance that he makes.

The "softer" nonverbal behaviors, such as body and facial expression, require more role-playing skill on the part of the trainer, with clear explanations and explicit modeling. Specially trained models are highly desirable. They should have been through a systematic course based on the Stanislavsky system so as to be able to give training in a wide range of expressive behaviors (Stanislavsky, 1936).

If one is not in a position to measure kinesics it is especially important to have a well-defined picture of the behavior required. A number of nonverbal techniques can be employed to develop body and facial expression. One helpful technique I have labeled the "silent movie." The trainee is told to use only his face and body to express his feelings and thoughts. He is requested to perform a timed sample exercise (2-3 minutes) in a stated situation, without any vocalization. This "silent movie" is then modeled for the trainee, and usually, after several trials, both facial and body expression may become more mobile and appropriate.

A frequent problem, distinct from lack of facial or body expression (immobility), is inappropriateness of facial or body expression. We frequently see a person delivering verbal invective with a smile on his face, or a rigid or cold individual speaking words of affection and endearment. Usually both verbal and nonverbal behaviors are in need of modification in these people, and a major goal of nonverbal training is establishing a unity of verbal and nonverbal behavior which will lead to increased effectiveness of communication. I am not suggesting that the explicit verbal repertoire be sacrificed in favor of "paralinguistic" training. The explicit message must continue to receive its necessary attention and modification.

I have made no mention of generalization of training from one behavioral variable to another. It is certainly present and obvious in sequential videotaped training sessions; but assessment of generalization has not yet been undertaken.

A Case Example

The patient, a 21-year-old male, had marked difficulty carrying on a conversation and communicating his desires to other patients and staff. He affected a silly grimace whenever he spoke to anyone. He had particular difficulty in standing up for himself, as the grin belied whatever annoyance he was trying to express verbally.

A 3-minute role-playing situation was constructed requiring the patient to deny some unjust charges. He had formulated what he was going to say and was told that the other role-player in the situation would disagree with him but he was to insist that he was unjustly accused. The entire sequence was videotaped and an assessment of the tape was made immediately after the role playing.

The assessment was as follows:

1. *Loudness of voice.* The patient could easily be heard 12 feet away from where he was standing, though he was not shouting. Loudness was satisfactory.

2. *Facial expression* was inappropriate. When the patient was telling how wronged he had been he persistently grinned and the expression on his face never changed.

3. *Body expression.* The patient's body was not rigid, and he used his arms and trunk appropriately.

4. *Eye contact.* Fifteen-second spot rating on the videotape revealed the patient to be staring at the floor in over 80 percent of the spot checks.

5. *Fluency.* The patient repeated many words and syllables within each sentence. There were many pauses of over 4 seconds between words and the speech was not rhythmic.

The behavior first singled out for modification was the chronic grin. The grin was described for him, a video replay was shown demonstrating its omnipresence, and the modeling of an alternative expression was demonstrated to him. He was requested to concentrate only on modifying this one aspect of his behavior (the grin) during the first working session. Modeling was frequently repeated, followed by his own attempt and then videotape feedback. The silent movie technique was especially helpful, the patient being required to convey his message mainly through facial expression. He began to display scowling, frowning and looking serious which were quite new to his repertoire. After a 45-minute session devoted to his facial expression he carried out a 3-minute total interaction with almost no sign of a grin. The patient was advised to practice his newly acquired nonverbal behavior in his interactions with other patients and staff, and told to return for another training session in 4 days.

During the second training session the new facial expressions he had learned were reinforced and his lack of eye contact was tackled. The appropriate behavior was modeled and the patient role-played it in several situations. He approximated the model perfectly after 15 minutes of training. The rest of the session (30 minutes) involved work on verbal fluency. The patient was made aware of his pauses between words, lack of rhythm, and repetition of syllables and words. Each fluency problem was worked on individually until the patient's behavior approximated the model to a high degree. A metronome proved of great value in training rhythmicity, as well as giving ongoing feedback as to pauses within sentences. The patient also used a tape-recorder to practice alone between training sessions. In 2 weeks the overall fluency increased markedly.

One session was then devoted to integrating all the nonverbal behaviors which the patient had recently learned. Training had taken 3 weeks and a total of five 45-minute sessions with diligent practice between sessions. His interpersonal communication improved so much that staff and other patients were taking him seriously when he voiced his desires and displeasures.

7

A STRATEGY FOR TEACHING VERBAL CONTENT OF ASSERTIVE RESPONSES

Myles L. Cooley, James G. Hollandsworth, Jr.

The goal of assertive training groups requires that trainers possess at least two general skills: expertise in *how* to teach and *what* to teach. The first skill encompasses the ability to implement effective teaching methods (i.e. modeling, role playing, feedback). The second skill assumes an ability to communicate the content of effective assertive statements. Most of the existing literature emphasizes the former skill, the "how" or process of training. Popular books in the area also focus primarily on guidelines or procedures for learning assertiveness. Relatively little attention has been paid to the actual content of assertive statements. One might assume, therefore, that trainers would have less expertise in *what* to teach than in *how* to teach. Since it is our belief that effective assertiveness training depends upon trainers possessing both skills, we have developed a strategy for teaching the verbal content of assertive statements. We have found this strategy more useful than those currently available.

CURRENT TEACHING STRATEGIES: "EXAMPLES" & "MODELS"

The original and probably most widely used strategy is what we call the "Examples" strategy. This approach involves the trainer providing examples of assertive responses in the context of role playing and modeling scenes. Many popular books (e.g. Alberti & Emmons, 1975; Fensterheim & Baer, 1975) attempt to teach the content of assertive responses primarily by examples. By avoiding instruction of specific phrases or statements, this approach has the advantage of allowing trainees to be quite flexible in forming assertive statements. We have found this flexibility to hinder the training process for many individuals, however. By relying on descriptive characteristics and lack of systematic guidelines for statements, this approach puts many trainees in the position of modeling content that is so general and vague that they question what it is they're supposed to model. To say that assertive responses are characterized by openness, directness, honesty, and appropriateness (Fensterheim & Baer, 1975) or by the open expression of personal feelings and opinions (Alberti & Emmons, 1975) may be to appropriately describe these statements. To assume that non-assertive individuals can learn to form their own statements based on these general characteristics and examples, though, is frequently unrealistic for many trainees. Also, as trainers, using this approach, we have often felt as unsure of what we were teaching as we were unsure of what our trainees were learning. In general, we have found this strategy's lack of structure to be its major weakness.

A second strategy for teaching assertive content employs the use of models. A "Models" strategy, characterized by a high degree of structure, identifies and teaches specific combinations of verbal components of assertive statements. We use the term "Models" here to describe certain structured systems for building assertive responses. This is not to be confused with the concept of "modeling" appropriate behaviors as discussed by Bandura (1969) and others. For example, Gordon's (1970) "I-Message" model has been used in assertiveness training (Cooley, 1976; Hewes, 1975). This model consists of three specific components: 1) a non-blameful description of another's behavior, 2) the tangible effect(s) of this behavior on me, and 3) my feeling about this behavior. Winship and Kelly (1976) offer another three-component model: 1) an empathy statement—the ability to see the situation through another person's eyes, 2) a conflict statement—one's rationale for an action, and 3) an action statement— what it is an individual wants to happen.

We have observed trainees forming assertive statements much more easily when they can rely on a model as opposed to relying on examples. A "Models" strategy involves teaching trainees the relatively simple task of learning the combination of components and plugging in appropriate content. We have also experienced some problems with this approach, however. Trainees frequently comment that the approach is too inflexible, that they feel like automatons unable to deviate from a model's "formula." This problem is especially apparent when a trainee tries to use the model to formulate a series of assertive responses. Obviously, relying on the model would result in a very similar response pattern that would become less appropriate the longer the discussion continued. Even when used for one-line responses, however, the available models are not effective or appropriate in many situations calling for assertive responses.

THE "COMPONENTS" STRATEGY

The development of our strategy for teaching the content of assertive statements stems from the limitations we experienced with the existing "Examples" and "Models" strategies. We desired a strategy that offered specific behavioral guidelines for assertive responses. The lack of such guidelines in the assertive training literature has contributed to the problems trainees encounter in distinguishing between assertive and aggressive statements (Hollandsworth, in press) and in forming appropriate assertive statements in different situations (Smaby & Tamminen, 1976). As trainers trying to teach these distinctions, we, also, have been frustrated by this problem. We therefore wanted our guidelines to be structured enough to help trainers teach and trainees learn while still allowing more flexibility than a "Model" strategy. A further objective was that our strategy be comprehensive enough to teach the different types of assertive statements required in different situations.

The approach we have developed to teach verbal content appropriate to these situations is called the "Components" strategy. This strategy attempts to teach seven, behaviorally defined verbal components of assertive statements. (See Table 7-1 for a list of components.) In our groups, we distinguish and concentrate on three assertive skill areas: 1) saying "no" or taking a stand, 2) asking favors or asserting rights, and 3) expressing feelings.

VERBAL ASSERTIVE SKILLS

Saying "No": The first assertive skill area we teach, saying "no" or taking a stand, is required when individuals need to respond to others' requests or demands. The verbal components of assertive statements most relevant in this type of situation are *position*, *reason*, and *understanding*. One's position is his stand on an issue. For example, "No, you can't borrow my car this afternoon" is one's position in response to a request. A *reason* helps explain one's position. Frequently, this component is preceded by "because." For example, "because I never lend my car to anyone" is one's reason for not loaning his or her car. One uses an *understanding* component to acknowledge another's position, request or feeling. "I know you really need the car to go downtown" is an example of this component.

We introduce the components in our groups by naming, defining, and providing examples of each one. The use of the components, the most important feature we want trainees to learn, is discussed in the context of modeling and role playing scenes. Modeling scenes are discussed in terms of the types and frequencies of components used. Following exposure to these scenes, trainees attempt to form their own statements in role playing situations. Throughout this process, we discuss certain features of the components in order to help trainees shape their statements more effectively. For example, when a trainee states a *position* in a hesitant fashion, we emphasize the importance of stating one's *position* clearly and confidently. We point out the appropriate use of *reasons*. Credible reasons may increase the probability that others will accept one's position. On the other hand, too many reasons given to justify one's position may be perceived as defensive rather than assertive behavior. An *understanding* component is discussed as an effective means of communicating that one is considering another's needs, feelings, etc., even though one's *position* may remain firm.

Asking favors/asserting rights: The second assertive skill area is involved with asking favors or asserting rights. We introduce three additional components, *problem*, *request*, *clarification* which are most relevant to situations calling for these types of assertive statements. A *problem* component describes a state of affairs an individual wants changed. "Your dog is loose in my yard again" states the *problem*. A *request* asks for help in solving the problem. "Would you please keep him tied up in your yard?" is an example of this component. A *clarification* component serves to obtain more information. If the dog's owner replied, "I don't understand, why is the dog a problem?" he would be asking to clarify the problem.

When teaching the appropriate use of these components in modeling and role playing scenes, we point out the importance of stating the *problem* clearly, making a specific *request*, and persisting with the request as long as necessary. The first three components are also integrated into these modeling and role playing scenes as trainees build their repertoire of statements and learn to modify them appropriately. For example, if the dog's owner should refuse to comply (*position*) with the neighbor's *request*, saying that the dog needs exercise (*reason*), the neighbor might find an *understanding* component helpful to "soften" his or her *request*.

Expressing feelings: The final set of assertive skills we teach are those concerned with expressing feelings. A final component, *personal expression*, is introduced here. Personal expression is the expression of positive or negative feelings, such as affection or anger. Examples of this component are, "I'm really disappointed," "that blouse is really nice," "that makes me angry," or "I appreciate your saying that."

Table 7-1

Verbal Components of Assertive Statements

- Saying "no" or taking a stand
  1. **Position:** Statement, usually pro or con, of one's stand on an issue or one's response to a request or demand.
  2. **Reason:** Statement offered in explanation or justification of one's position, request, or feelings.
  3. **Understanding:** Statement recognizing and accepting another's position, request, or feelings.

- Asking favors or asserting rights
  4. **Problem:** Statement describing an unsatisfactory situation that needs to be changed.
  5. **Request:** Statement asking for something necessary to resolve the problem.
  6. **Clarification:** Statement designed to elicit additional, specific information concerning the problem.

- Expressing feelings
  7. **Personal expression:** Statement communicating one's emotions, feelings, or other appropriate expressions such as gratitude, affection, or admiration.

WORKING WITH THE COMPONENTS STRATEGY

An example of a short modeling scene including all seven components follows.

Person A: Hi, I need to pick up my car by 5 o'clock and I can't find a
                              PROBLEM
ride. Would you run me down there?
                    REQUEST

Person B: Where's your car?
          CLARIFICATION
A: At Tony's Garage.
B: I can see you're in a jam, but I can't drive you down
          UNDERSTANDING   REASON
because I'm running late already, and I'm having people
    REASON   REASON
over for dinner tonight.
A: Boy, I'm really frustrated because I've tried three other
      FEELING   REASON
people already.
B: Well, how long will it take?
        CLARIFICATION
A: Ten minutes at the most.
B: Alright, I can run you down if we leave right now.
                POSITION
A: Thanks a lot. You're really a good friend.
   FEELING   FEELING

    Based on our clinical experience with the "Components" strategy thus far, we are excited about its potential for helping trainers teach the verbal content of assertive statements. In fact, the use of these components has been rated very favorably by trainees in our post-group evaluation. The approach appears to be systematic, comprehensive, and flexible. We find the latter characteristic especially helpful. The strategy allows trainers to provide choices to trainees regarding the content of assertive statements. For example, if a trainee has difficulty finding reasons for his behavior or has trouble expressing feelings, he can still respond assertively using other components. With a "Models" strategy, trainees do not have this flexibility as they are taught to use components in specific combinations. This may require some individuals to change a large portion of their verbal repertoire, a requirement we have found to be quite difficult and frequently unnecessary for many individuals.
    Another advantage of the "Components" strategy is that it enables a labeling of parts of assertive statements. After watching two trainees role play a scene, for example, the trainer may recognize that one trainee uses too many *reason* and not enough *understanding* components. Another group member might recognize that when one trainee says "no," he doesn't state his *position* confidently enough.

Feedback from the trainer and other trainees during role playing sequences helps trainees begin to shape their responses to include more or less of certain components. This shaping procedure appears to depend, in large part, on the recognition of certain components in trainee's responses. The recognition process is made much easier because the strategy provides labels for these components. The problem with an "Examples" strategy, on the other hand, is that both trainer and trainee might recognize that a trainee's statement lacks something, but identifying what is missing or needs improvement is much more difficult when this "something" cannot be isolated and labeled.

It must be reemphasized that claims for the effectiveness of this strategy are based on our clinical impressions and trainee feedback. As such, the claims are tentative, awaiting empirical investigation (which we are pursuing at this writing). We strongly believe in basing clinical interventions on available empirical data. We are aware of assertive trainers who operate on the basis of significantly less objective data. Furthermore, we share the concern that exploiters and unqualified trainers could take assertiveness training the route of faddish encounter groups (Franzini, 1976) unless we continue to build an empirical base for group procedures. Only through such a commitment can we prevent assertiveness training from becoming another psychotherapeutic commodity developed and sold on the basis of theory alone.

8

ASSERTIVE TRAINING AND THE EXPRESSION OF ANGER

David C. Rimm

In the main, assertive training in a clinical setting has focused on problems associated with timorous patterns of responding. Wolpe (1958, 1969) early on at any rate, was certainly the most influential clinician and writer in the area. For Wolpe, the primary candidates for assertion training were persons who by virtue of intense anxiety did not stand up for their rights in critical social interactions. Wolpe assumed, probably correctly, that there is something in the nature of the assertive response which inhibits anxiety. In addition to making clients feel better in the target situations, the social skills acquired during assertive training enhanced interpersonal effectiveness. Clearly both elements contribute to a more satisfying, productive life.

The research literature on assertive training, almost all of which has been published since 1970, has dealt almost exclusively with problems associated with timidity; for example, refusing unreasonable requests (McFall & Marston, 1971; McFall & Twentyman, 1973) or engaging in more complex behaviors involving standing up for one's rights (e.g., Hersen, Eisler & Miller, 1974; Rimm, Snyder, Depue, Haanstad & Armstrong, 1976).

Thus, both from a clinical and a research perspective, timidity has virtually been a synonym for lack of assertiveness. On the other hand, to an increasing degree practitioners and writers have pointed out that another class of behaviors, marked by anger and aggression, may be amenable to change through assertive training (e.g., Alberti & Emmons, 1974; Rimm & Masters, 1974; Lange & Jakubowski, 1976). Unfortunately research pertinent to the use of assertion in dealing with this class of problems is sorely limited (Sarason, 1968; Rimm, Keyson & Hunziker, 1971; Rimm, Hill, Brown & Stuart, 1974). While the present paper is intended to have an applied or clinical as opposed to a research emphasis, it is important that the reader know that what is said is based on very limited data base, which includes a few controlled investigations and the clinical experience of the author and certain of his colleagues. Given the immense popular interest in assertion training, and the profound social implications of unrestrained anger and aggression I'm quite confident the data base will grow; perhaps this paper will serve as an additional impetus for such growth.

THE RELATIONSHIP BETWEEN ANGER AND AGGRESSION

Experts do not widely agree on the definition of aggression, because, as Johnson (1972) notes, aggression is anything but a unitary thing. This is well illustrated by a few of Johnson's examples, any one of which *might* be labeled as aggression:
1. A doctor gives a flu shot to a screaming child.
2. A boxer gives his opponent a bloody nose.
3. A woman nags and criticizes her husband, and he ignores her in return.
4. Two friends get into a heated quarrel after drinking too much.

Usually, writers in the field (e.g., Feshbach, 1970, 1971) make a useful distinction between *instrumental* aggression and *drive-mediated* aggression. In the former, the aggression is a means to an end, e.g., the money and glory resulting from boxing one's way to the championship. While it would be incorrect to infer that anger is always present, it is not the primary motivator. Indeed, as any winning prizefighter knows, intense anger is usually self-defeating in the ring. Drive-mediated aggression usually involves discernable affect, and the most plausible drive or motive is anger (or hostility, which some define as an anger-like state having a gradual onset). In the case of anger induced aggression, physical or psychological injury is more or less an end in itself rather than a means to an end.

The above distinction may seem a bit academic, but in fact it is of considerable practical importance. This paper is mainly concerned with the use of assertive procedures with persons who are aggressive because they are angry. For the present, it would be rather silly to attempt to reform a hired killer, who receives ten thousand dollars for a hit, using assertive procedures, and I seriously doubt that a millionaire heavyweight champion would retire from the ring as a result of assertive training. On the other hand, a great many people engage in aggression because they are angry, and if they perceive, or can be persuaded to perceive, that such behavior is self-defeating, assertive training might be a very valuable clinical tool.

ANGER, ANXIETY AND ASSERTION

If we think of anger as a drive, then it is possible that the expression of anger (including aggressive expression) is drive or tension reducing and is therefore rewarding, *per se*. The work of Hokanson (1970) indicates that sometimes at least, this may be the case. But Hokanson also notes that a nonaggressive response may have the same effect. If this is so, then assertion may be as rewarding (i.e., tension reducing) as aggression, without the obvious negative consequences of being hurtful to others.

Another possibility is that the expression of anger is rewarding because anger inhibits fear or anxiety (the terms are used here synonymously). This assumes that psychophysiologically, anger and fear are antithetical; that is, that it is difficult or impossible to be angry and fearful at the same time. Many clinicians, including Wolpe, make this assumption. Further, let us suppose that certain people, perhaps most, would prefer to be angry than fearful, and that in an anxiety provoking situation, say things to themselves *a la* Albert Ellis, in order to generate anger (certainly there is now ample evidence that what people say to themselves affects the way they feel, see Mahoney, 1974). Finally, let us suppose that anger and assertion are on the same psychophysiological continuim. It follows that a person who usually responds to anxiety with anger and perhaps aggression, could be taught to behave assertively instead.

The above formulation may seem to blur the distinction between instrumental and drive-mediated aggression, since the anger (and consequent aggression) is drive-mediated, but it also functions to reduce anxiety. However, if we restrict instrumental aggression to those cases where an obvious external reward is involved (e.g., money, praise), the distinction is still useful.

A CLINICAL MODEL

As Lange and Jakubowski (1976) note, there is no agreed upon set of procedures defining assertive training. Nevertheless, it is possible to specify guidelines, as we did in Rimm & Masters (1974) and others have done in greater detail elsewhere (both Alberti & Emmons, 1974, and Lange & Jakubowski, 1976, are good examples). What follows is a summary of our guidelines.

a. **Assessment**: Find out how the client behaves in the target situation, by setting up a roleplay. The therapist often assumes the role of the "other person."

b. **Feedback**: The therapist tactfully provides feedback regarding both positive and negative aspects of the client's response.

c. **Modeling** (behavior reversal): The therapist models an appropriate response; it is important that both therapist and client agree on the appropriateness of the response.

d. **Behavior rehearsal**: The client then practices the new response, with feedback and repetition, until both parties are satisfied with the adequacy of the response and the client reports little if any negative affect. Experience suggests that it is important that the client receive a good deal of praise for any sign of improvement. It is also recommended that any prolonged response or interaction be broken up into small segments; they are easier to work with. It is probably best if the reader view the treatment package as a kind of shaping procedure, in the Skinnerian sense, with a good deal of guidance and prompting.

Of the many behavior therapies, assertive training may be the most stimulating to the therapist, but it is probably also the most difficult. In part this is because it is often difficult to define a socially appropriate response for a given situation. There are other factors which contribute to the challenging nature of assertive training, including those unique features in the client's learning history which have contributed to a lack of assertion. It is recommended that the serious reader refer to several "clinical models" of assertive training, including others presented in this book, as well as other detailed accounts (e.g., Lange & Jakubowski, 1976; Alberti & Emmons, 1974).

GROUP ASSERTIVE TRAINING FOR ANGER EXPRESSION

In our own studies examining the effects of assertive training on antisocial aggression (Rimm, *et al.*, 1971; Rimm, *et al.*, 1974) subjects were treated in groups. In the first, the subjects were hospitalized in a mental institution, primarily as a result of acts of aggression; in the second, they were less seriously disturbed volunteers responding to a newspaper advertisement. There are obvious advantages to group, as opposed to individual, assertive training (see Lazarus, 1971; Rimm & Masters, 1974; Lange &

Jakubowski, 1976). Group treatment is more economical; the group provides a forum for deciding on the appropriateness of a response; the group can provide massive social reinforcement for improvement and a feeling of camaraderie, which may be therapeutic.

On the other hand, experience indicates that people who express anger in an inappropriate or anti-social manner can be treated quite effectively on a one-to-one basis. Indeed, under certain circumstances, a group format is not recommended. Persons exhibiting inappropriate anger-induced aggression by no means constitute a homogenous population. As has been noted (Megargee & Mendelsohn, 1962; Megargee, 1966), some show a more or less characteristic pattern of *over-control*. They have been taught not to express anger, and keep their anger to themselves until it reaches volcanic proportions, at which point they might "blow," possibly engaging in violent behavior. Others may show a pattern of *under-control*, wherein only minimal instigation to anger results in virtually instant aggression.

While it has not been investigated, it is likely that over-controlled and under-controlled clients would constitute an unfortunate mix in group treatment, in part because the latter would intimidate or even terrorize the former. After all, the over-controlled client is probably frightened, not only of his or her own anger, but of expressions of anger on the part of others. Whether a group setting constitutes the treatment of choice for under-controlled clients, may also be debated. The camaraderie which may develop may be based on a communality of aggressive acting out which may be reinforced by the group. One or two middle class therapists may not be able to handle such a group. Perhaps the most natural clientele for group treatment are over-controlled persons; they are not likely to threaten each other or the therapist. However, as we shall now see, such clients may be treated one-to-one as well.

CLINICAL ILLUSTRATIONS

An over-controlled client. The client, a 22 year old caucasian male, had completed six months of a three year enlistment in the military. On two occasions he had been involved in fights in the barracks, the second time cutting the arm of another male with a trenching tool. The wound was not serious and the incident was never reported. He was very disturbed by his own behavior, but did not seek military psychiatric assistance because he feared, with some justification, that admitting such incidents might result in a psychiatric or disciplinary discharge. Finally, he sought help from a private practitioner. During the first session the following information was uncovered. The client, John, was an only child. His parents had been divorced when he was seven, and he had been reared by his mother. Although he was never physically punished, he recalled numerous instances wherein he was severely chastised by his mother for virtually any display of anger, which was "unchristian." He reported that his mother's favorite saying was "if you can't say anything good about somebody, don't say anything," and felt guilty if he engaged in the most trivial gossip with peers. He stated that while growing up he never engaged in fighting, in part because no one had ever taught him how.

Therapist. The second time, you know, when you went after the guy with your shovel. Tell me about that.

Client. My God, I think I could have killed him. I really went bananas.

Therapist. What made you so mad?

Client. He asked me whether I stole a shirt from his locker. I've never stolen anything in my life, except maybe a piece of fruit from a stand.

Therapist. Well, that *is* a heavy accusation, but there are other ways of handling situations like that. Has he ever bugged you before?

Client. Yeah, he sort of made comments like that before. I just clam up, but I'm really angry inside. Once I went to the latrine and threw up.

Therapist. Sounds like you let your feelings build up, until you couldn't control them. Maybe if you would say how you feel in situations like this, your feelings wouldn't build up.

Client. The things I want to say are crazy. Like "you rotten dog." It is wrong to say things like that. Or to cuss. Everybody else does, but I can't.

Therapist. So in other words, you don't say anything but get sick inside and finally you take a whack at someone with a shovel.

Client. Well, that was the first time I did that. But what if I do it again? I really feel messed up.

Therapist. Look, I think that a lot of your problem is that you just don't know what to say. Let's do a little play acting. I'll be Dick, the guy you hit . . . and you be yourself . . . but just don't swing at me, that's against the rules. Ready?

Therapist (as Dick). Man, did you take a shirt from my locker?

Client. Silent, but discernably upset.

Therapist. Well, you didn't say anything. How did you feel?

Client. Even though we were play-acting . . . first I got uptight, and then mad.

Therapist. It's good that you are aware of your feelings, but it

would be better if you had said something. Let me play you and show you what I mean. You be Dick. Just say what Dick said.
Client. OK . . . (as Dick) . . . Hey, did you take my shirt from my locker (said somewhat tremulously)?
Therapist (as client). No, I damn sure did not. And it makes me madder than hell when you accuse me.
Client. It makes me uncomfortable to swear.
Therapist. I'm glad you told me, and I guess I can see why. What about this: *Therapist* (as client). I certainly did not. And I resent your saying that.
Client. I guess I could say that.
Therapist. OK, then I'll be Dick . . . (as Dick) . . . Hey, did you take my shirt from my locker?
Client (as self). I did not (tremor in voice). That makes me angry.
Therapist. How did you feel?
Client. Kind of tense.
Therapist. Well, this is new for you, and I'm not surprised. Let's try it again.
The rehearsal continued until the client reported feeling comfortable.
Client. I see what you are getting at. But the thing is, by the time he accused me of stealing his shirt, I was already so angry at him I'm not sure . . . well, that I could pull it off . . . maybe, but I don't know.
Therapist. OK, then let's go back to the very first time he made you angry, and let's practice what we just did, so that your feelings don't build up. Let's just work on each incident . . . .

In using the term "over-controlled" we do not wish to imply that our client is possessed by some pervasive, overpowering trait which makes it impossible to assert himself in all situations. After all, he did tell the therapist that he did not wish to swear. As the reader may know, the empirical evidence supporting trait psychology in general (Mischel, 1968) and more specifically a trait of assertiveness or timidity (e.g., Rimm and Masters, 1974) is rather weak.

The above client had a history of relatively few incidents wherein he initiated physical aggression. Certainly his reinforcement history did not favor such a style of responding, and he was clearly motivated to change. This is in rather sharp contrast to the following case illustration.

An under-controlled client. The client, a 20 year old college freshman had been reared in the southside Chicago ghetto. While in high school he had been a member of a gang. Rumbles with other gangs were common place. He indicated with some pride that his gang was the terror of his high school and was quick to point out that because of his physical strength, and his prowess with his fists, chains, and knives, he was held in high esteem by his comrades. Upon leaving the ghetto and enrolling in an essentially middle class university the contingencies of reinforcement changed drastically. Early on he was involved in one or two fist fights, but quickly learned that while he might frighten others with such behavior, rather than receiving admiration he was shunned. His combative behavior *vis-a-vis* males extinguished in short order, and he reported having made some friends. His present difficulty was with females. More specifically his girl friend had broken off with him because he had beaten her up.

Therapist. Well, what exactly happened?

Client. Two weeks ago . . . it was Saturday night . . . we were talking and Loretta told me she had been seeing this other dude. Dumb bitch! I slapped the shit out of her. I'd go after the dude, but that's against the honkey rules (said with sarcasm).

Therapist. I'm not sure it is as simple as black and white. But you are right if you mean middle class rules are different from the rules of your ghetto, which is pretty frustrating for you, I guess. I know that if I had to go and live in your ghetto I'd be frustrated and scared.

Client. Scared, shit! You'd be *dead*. But I'm not scared. I can take care of myself.

Therapist. Fair enough. But why are you here seeing me?

Client. OK, man. You got me. I don't *always* do the right thing. I quit frightening dudes . . . but this shit with Loretta has got me down. She had it coming but now she won't even talk to me.

Therapist. I'm not going to say what you did was right or wrong. But I know one thing, it was self-defeating. Whether she had it coming or not, you ended up hurting yourself.

Client. No argument. But what am I supposed to do when she tells me she's been screwing around with another dude? Kiss her behind?

Therapist. Well, I certainly wouldn't. But tell me something. Did you have an understanding or agreement that she was only going to date you?

Client. The night I beat her up . . . it all started with me telling her I didn't want her seeing anybody else. She told me she didn't like being ordered around, and she *was* seeing this guy. That's when I hit her.

Therapist. Well, you asked me a moment ago what you were supposed to do with Loretta. First let me find out exactly what you did say. Pretend it is that Saturday night and Loretta is sitting next to you. Like you are actually in the situation. Say what you said, the way you said it.

Client (as client). Baby, I don't want you seeing any other guys, you understand?!!
Therapist. Sounds like you really cared about her, and didn't want to risk losing her. I can understand that, but what you said was pretty heavy. Like, if I were Loretta it would have made me defiant. Let me show you a different way you might have handled it. Pretend I'm you and I'm talking to Loretta.
Therapist (as client). You know, honey, I really care for you. It's your choice, but I'd feel better if you didn't see anybody else.
Client. That doesn't sound much like me talking. But the bitch would lap it up (laughs).
Therapist. Well, put it in your own words. Pretend you are talking to Loretta. Go ahead.
Client (as client). Baby, I really dig you. Don't go messing around with other dudes, OK?
Therapist. How did you feel saying that? Comfortable? Uptight?
Client. OK, I guess.
Therapist. To me, it sounded a lot better. You told her you cared, and you didn't sound so aggressive. But don't you think you still *told* her not to see other guys, instead of asking her? Remember, she really and truly does have a choice, and telling her she doesn't is only going to drive her away.
Client (with resignation). You're right.
Therapist. Why don't you try it again. Pretend Loretta is really sitting next to you.
Client (as client). Baby, I *really* dig you. I know it's up to you, but I'd prefer that you didn't see other guys.
Therapist. I thought that was really good. Did it feel OK?
Client. Yeah. I guess I feel less mad when I say it like that. But I keep thinking, what if she says, "screw you, I'll see who I want?"
Therapist. If you said to her what you just said in here, in the way that you said it, she might go along with you. But if she said "no" she wouldn't say it in such a bitchy way, and you wouldn't get so mad.
Client. Maybe not so mad, but I'd still be plenty pissed off. What do I do then?
Therapist. OK. Let's practice what you would do then. Suppose Loretta says "I dig you too, but to tell you the truth, I don't want to get that tied down right now."

Therapy continued until the client could deal with being told that a girl friend was not interested in an exclusive relationship.

Given this client's learning history it isn't surprising that he didn't think it was wrong to beat up his girl friend (obviously, within limits).

He could be persuaded, however, that such behavior was self-defeating, certainly in his present sub-culture. Early in this paper I suggested that often people become angry and aggressive in response to feelings of anxiety. I have found that suggesting this to certain clients (for example, client number two) is counterproductive. For some males, even the slightest intimation that they are frightened is taken as an attack on their manhood, and will probably result in defensiveness, and possibly verbally abusive behavior directed towards the therapist and even the termination of therapy by the client.[1]

Client number two was self-referred, but frequently undercontrolled individuals are referred by others, often the courts. Such referrals usually present a therapeutic challenge, to say the least. As with client number two, it is essential to persuade them that their aggression is self-defeating. Patience, and a high tolerance for frustration are minimum requisites.

---

1. EDITOR'S NOTE: The psycho-social history of the client may be a critical variable in determining his or her response to the therapist and the suggested treatment. See Donald Cheek's discussion of AT with black clients, Chapter 11.

9

HOMEWORK IN AT: PROMOTING THE TRANSFER OF ASSERTIVE SKILLS TO THE NATURAL ENVIRONMENT

John L. Shelton

Perhaps the biggest problem facing assertive trainers is aiding clients in transferring what they learn in assertive training (AT) to the outside world. After all, it is the natural environment where assertive behavior really counts. For this reason, AT is not complete when the client is able to behave assertively during relatively safe and secure training sessions. Assertive trainers must develop skills to help clients behave assertively in the "real world" as well.

Improving the transfer of assertive skills is no easy matter since the natural environment often punishes those who emit assertive behavior. Because many clients have learned their assertive behavior solely in the therapy context, the real world presents challenges which they often cannot overcome. As a result, many clients, fresh with high expectations, new insights, strong group support and a recently acquired behavioral repertoire encounter situations which are more powerful than their newly developed skills.

Clearly an approach is needed which will promote transfer during AT while at the same time adding to the efficiency of this important procedure. In my opinion, the most effective method for reaching these goals is a combination of verbal interaction and response rehearsal during office hours followed by homework assignments involving spaced practice in varied situations.

THE CONCEPT OF HOMEWORK

The purpose of this paper is to discuss the ways and means of effectively utilizing homework assignments in AT. Put another way, this paper focuses on the use of systematic homework assignments to promote transfer of skills learned during AT to the outside world.

Based on the foundation laid by Shelton and Ackerman (1974), systematic homework in AT involves the therapist and client in jointly planning and practicing cognitive, affective, and behavioral change strategies outside the therapy setting. While under the assertive trainer's direction, the client takes responsibility for carrying out various assignments, thereby greatly facilitating transfer of skills learned during AT to the actual environment in which the client lives and works. In addition, such an approach is extremely efficient since it makes effective use of the other 167 non-therapy hours of the week; time that most clients waste waiting for the next therapy session. In short, homework can make AT a 24 hour-a-day experience.

LAYING THE GROUNDWORK FOR AT HOMEWORK ASSIGNMENTS

Prior to actually engaging in outside practice of assertive skills, the assertive trainer must thoroughly understand the client's problem within the nonassertive-assertive-aggressive schema expanded by Alberti and Emmons (1970). Usually done during a screening interview, the client's assertive difficulties can usually be placed in a graded hierarchy (in order of increasing threat) composed of (1) "targets" for assertive responses, (2) the target's behavior the client hopes to change, and (3) the assertive strategy the client will employ to promote change. The following example shows conceptualization of a client's assertive problems understood within the three-part framework just outlined:

Threat Level	**Target**	**Target's Behavior**	**Assertive Behavior**
least threatening	Fred (a member of the client's carpool)	(1) Is late (2) Flips the car radio looking for sports reports	(1) Reward being on time (2) Reward not skipping plus disclosure of distress

Threat Level	Target	Target's Behavior	Assertive Behavior
		(3) Picks his nose	(3) Disclosure of distress plus mild confrontation
most threatening	Pat (client's husband)	(1) Doesn't listen	(1) Reward listening
		(2) Verbally abuses her	(2) Reward not abusing plus disclosure of distress at a later time
		(3) Excessive punishment for kids	(3) Confrontation plus leaving house with children

USING HOMEWORK IN AT

After having done the important diagnostic work described in the previous section, the professional facilitator is now ready to incorporate homework into the fabric of treatment. To effectively incorporate homework fully into the treatment format, each session should begin with a brief time in which the client or clients (in a group context) discuss their homework successes during the week. Reinforcement for success and support for "failure" is given for those having problems. After that, each AT session has as its major focus the preparation of the client for next week's homework.

Using the diagnostic schema discussed earlier each session focuses on dealing with a specific target behavior. During the session the assertive trainer involves the client in behavior rehearsal and through coaching brings the client to the point where he or she is ready for the next assignment. The use of systematic homework assignments in group AT takes the same format with general all purpose assignments being given all clients at first with more individualized assignments being given as individual client needs become apparent.

Each session then ends with the client writing down the homework assignment that he or she will engage in during the ensuing week. In all cases, the homework is jointly planned among the client, the assertive trainer(s), and (in group AT) the members of the group. However, the client, as the best judge of his or her own capacities, should have absolute veto power over all homework suggested.

HOMEWORK CONTENT

The content that each homework assignment takes will, of course, vary enormously from client to client. However, common homework examples include: initiating a conversation with a stranger on a bus, in class, etc.; entering or telephoning an office to request information; asking a favor of an acquaintance. The interested reader should read Shelton and Ackerman (1974), and Lange and Jakubowski (1976) for numerous homework examples. Regardless of what the homework assignment is, it should be interwoven into AT in the following manner:

Tasks Accomplished During Training Sessions

1. Based on earlier diagnostic work, the client chooses a target behavior and an assertive response

2. Jointly with the assertive trainer and/or members of the group, the client decides on the frequency, intensity, duration and the situation in which the assertive behavior will occur

3. The client rehearses the assertive behavior and receives feedback

4. The client masters the assertive behavior

Homework Tasks

1. Before engaging in assertive behavior, the client covertly rehearses the homework and imagines a successful outcome at least three times a day

2. Immediately prior to the assertive response, the client
   —relaxes deeply
   —visualizes a successful outcome
   —engages in homework task
   —self rewards for effort either overtly or covertly
   —calls therapist or group member for support and verbal reinforcement

HOMEWORK FORMAT

The preceding section outlined the skeleton of how homework is integrated into assertive training. Regardless of the content of the homework decided upon by the assertive trainer and the client, the format of practice assignments usually contains one or more of the following elements:

1. A *do* statement. "Read ... practice ... count ... observe ... say ... some kind of thought, action, or emotion."
2. A *quantity* statement. "Talk three times about ... spend thirty minutes ... on three occasions ask 'why' ... write a list of at least ten."
3. A *record* statement. "Count and record the number of times you say 'yes' ... each time he yells, mark your chart ... whenever the thought comes to you, click your golf counter."
4. A *bring* statement. "Bring your list ... the chart ... your spouse ... to the next appointment."
5. A *contingency* statement. "Call for your next appointment after you have done ... for each time you say 'no' a dollar bill will be deducted ... each minute you spend thinking about your rights will earn you ..."

Combining the content and format of homework yields the following illustration of a homework assignment as written on NCR (no carbon required) paper:

Homework: Betty

1. Read **Your Perfect Right**
2. Buy or borrow Salter's book and read chapters 6 and 10
3. Bring a list of ideas from reading which are especially meaningful
4. Call for next appointment when finished with No's. 1, 2, 3.

Homework: Dr. John

1. Reread Mahoney's article on use of rubber band as thought punisher.

The interested reader will observe that the preceding homework assignment involved many of the format variables discussed earlier. In each case, homework can be written on NCR paper, which can be purchased at any quality stationery store and allows the trainer the advantage of writing on one side of the paper and immediately having a copy produced on the adjoining paper. Thus, homework assignments can be written and automatically provide both the client and the trainer with a copy of the next week's outside work, largely eliminating the problems that arise from misunderstood and forgotten homework.

Of further note is the fact that the preceding homework involved the assertive trainer ("Dr. John") in a homework assignment as well. The assignment of work to the therapist as well as to the client on a weekly basis keeps the professional accountable to the client as well as vice versa, and allows the client to realize that assertive training is a joint endeavor in which the professional is hard at work fulfilling commitments toward the final goals of therapy.

ADDITIONAL SUGGESTIONS FOR USING HOMEWORK

Using phone calls: Despite extreme caution, attempts to behave assertively may be disastrous. Such is the nature of assertive training. Simply stated, assertive behavior is rarely reinforced by members of the natural environment. More often, instances of assertive behavior are punished or, at the very least, extinguished by our social peers. As a result, it is wise to ask clients to call the trainer soon after episodes of assertive behavior.

Such phone calls have several advantages. To begin with, they urge the client to complete the assignment while at the same time providing immediate reward for successful assertive attempts. In some cases, phone calls provide the support so badly needed after assertive assignments have gone awry. Many times, the assertive trainer's encouragement can overcome the punishing aspects of the environment that the client must face.

During group assertive training, the trainer would obviously be deluged if every assertive training client called immediately after every assertive attempt. As a result, one approach is to pair all group members up and request that they call each other after each assertive attempt.

USING PARAPROFESSIONALS

In some university settings, where the assertive trainers have available a number of skilled undergraduate professionals, these individuals can be an invaluable asset during homework. Some researchers such as

Pendleton, Shelton and Wilson (1976) have used specially trained paraprofessionals as targets for which nonassertive clients could practice assertive behaviors. If such persons are available, they can overcome many of the dangers associated with AT. Paraprofessionals provide a safe target whose response can be carefully controlled. Thus, before each homework assignment, the paraprofessional can be instructed as to how he or she is to behave in response to the client. Over a time, the parapro's responses can be made gradually more and more difficult. If several paraprofessionals are available, they can be rotated from client to client, thus increasing the variety of targets and therefore improving transfer effects as well. As time goes on and clients gain mastery, the paraprofessionals can be faded out in favor of "real" targets.

Trainers are urged to use these systematic procedures which require the AT client to initiate assertiveness outside of the formal training environment. They are extremely useful in enhancing the client's capacity to bring about change in his or her own life situation and behavior patterns.

10

COPE: A WILDERNESS WORKSHOP IN AT

Paula Landau, Terry Paulson

The passes get easier and finally you're just laughing over them. Every step and every strain and hard breath and heart pump is an investment in tomorrow morning's strength.

You're watching the change with your own eyes and feeling it under your own skin and through your own veins.

Fibers multiply and valves enlarge and walls thicken.
A miracle.

At least if the species has lost its animal strength its individual members can have the fun of finding it again.

Jerry and Benny Russell

The cliff stretched 80 feet above them. There was a lot of joking and laughter, but the shrill, tense note of fear rose as the last pitons were placed and the ropes readied. Each person took about a half hour to climb up, laboriously hooking in the ropes and aiders, often clumsily mixing them up. The group would fall silent, members straining their necks to look up anxiously as the next one started up. A bird flew over, breaking the silence, and everyone jumped. Then soft conversations started as they shared their nervous anticipation. The climber rappelled back down to arrive safely at the base, grinning and shaking at the same time.

That cliff became the symbol of what this small group of people had come looking for on the four-day COPE Wilderness Workshop in the High Sierras—a slightly different symbol for each one. The unique combination of wilderness survival training and assertion training was developed by the Assertion Training Institute, North Hollywood, California, because of the many parallels between the two.

Traditionally, assertion training teaches people how to deal constructively with others and to build more satisfying relationships. It also teaches them to take care of themselves—to be able to say no, to ask for what they want, to protect themselves from depleting demands and criticism and, at the same time, to be able to reach out and open themselves to others.

The depersonalization of relationships and complexity of our times have contributed to what many mental health professionals term the depression of the 70's—"learned helplessness." There are many things in the way we live today that combine to make us feel that we don't have much control over what happens to us. Jobs teeter precariously, income has long since lost the race with inflation, when something goes wrong with our marvelous machinery we don't know what to do, and even the formerly conventionalized relationships between groups and individuals have become fluid and uncertain.

Many people live their lives fearfully, often doing things they don't want to do and not getting enough of what they want. Some just give up and say to themselves "why try—there's nothing I can do about it." A growing tendency towards narrowness—sticking to the safety of the known, rather than venturing out to risk at something new—often leads people to stop themselves from doing things, to mentally accept limitations that are nowhere near their real potential.

The focus of the COPE Workshop was on building and expanding the potential strengths of each individual. The wilderness and assertion training blended together in the exhilaration that comes with extending ourselves beyond the physical and emotional limits we thought were there—slogging doggedly through that one more mile, stretching our interpersonal muscles to reach out that one bit more, and becoming increasingly aware that we can have much more of an effect on the world around us if we try.

The primitive backwoods provided a challenge which contributed to a growing sense of mastery as each person discovered the capacity to "make it" in the wilderness. Each developed renewed confidence that he or she could also regain control over his or her life and goals.

The wilderness setting and physical closeness also created a sense of community—intimate feelings were shared as easily as food and the physical tasks of bringing water and building fires. Everyone felt that this was a unique group, that they could never find this community of feeling back in the city. Gradually, they realized that it takes breaking away from the rote motions of life to really see others, and being willing to risk and experiment with new ways of interaction.

FROM FEAR TO CONFIDENCE

Throughout, the physical and emotional experiences were inextricably entwined. The group found itself thinking and talking in physical terms and vividly feeling the parallels between the wilderness experience and situations back in the "real" world. The trembling fear as you start up that sheer "unclimbable" cliff isn't very different from what you feel just before a difficult confrontation; the feeling of elation when you've reached the top is similar to your feelings when you've handled an interpersonal situation well and are proud of yourself.

They found that the anticipation was worse than the climb and realized how often anticipation had stopped them from doing things. Some laughed ruefully over how much food they'd brought, how religiously they'd tried to buy everything they could possibly need—and how much it all added to the weight they carried—and realized the back-home parallel: how often they overprepared and carried more weight than they needed to, anticipating greater difficulties than actually materialized.

Perhaps most important in this group of highly competent people, used to covering up any signs of weakness in the outside world, was finding out that it was ok to be afraid and to make mistakes—everyone does. Paradoxically, when they could drop their facades and share their fears they got more respect from each other.

A composed professional at the top of her field broke down and cried on the hike in: "I kept feeling I'd come far enough and resented not being helped more." Later, she expressed the elation she'd felt at conquering the mountain, although she'd been trembling at every move up. Another independent type found herself panicking everytime she fell behind and couldn't see the others: "I felt as if I'd lost contact and wouldn't find my way."

A young bandleader started out wary and defensive, but gradually began to loosen up and feel good about being able to both give and ask for help. He found he was liked and accepted without having to be on top.

An extremely competitive woman found herself able to let go of having to be better and of always trying to catch up or get ahead. She experienced the satisfaction of her own small achievements such as finally being able to make a fire, without having to compare herself to others. She was surprised and pleased at the respect she got from the others for the way she just kept plodding along, even if she was at the tail end.

Two of the men decided "I don't have to climb every mountain." Passing up this one meant "I don't always have to prove myself to be ok."

SURVIVAL: WILDERNESS AND INTERPERSONAL

Many of the attitudes that make an individual capable of survival in the wilderness are the same that are needed for a full and productive life in our society. We are all familiar with the stories of people who just lay down in the snow and died, and with those of the ones who made it out on sheer will to live. There are two alternatives when something goes wrong: Give up, or start trying to cope. This is as true in dealing with the problems of our daily lives and relationships as it would be in an unexpected catastrophe that left us stranded in the wilderness. Those who survive have an active will to live and a set towards tackling or going around obstacles rather than seeing them as insurmountable.

The building of a "survival" attitude is inherent to the philosophy of assertion training. "What are some of the ways you could deal with that?" "What do you want to do about it" are two of the most frequent questions asked in assertion training groups. The primary thrust of most AT groups is action—looking at alternate options, making choices, and acting on them.

A bulldozer may be able to conquer the wilderness, but a man or woman alone has to respect and learn to use its resources. Similarly, in relationships one has to respect and learn to live with others rather than try to win against them. Assertion training isn't a guarantee against failure in any given situation; the emphasis is on moving ahead, and being willing to risk again rather than wallowing in it. Failure is seen as feedback, not a final door slamming. The same creativity that is needed in the wilderness to see the potential for food and shelter in the scenery around you is needed to find new avenues to take in your life whenever one is blocked.

Along with positive attitudes, we need to acquire some basic skills to be self-reliant. In the wilderness this means learning which plants are edible, how to find water, how to keep warm—knowing enough to insulate your body with pine needles could make the difference between life and death—and how to find your way with or without a compass. Other useful skills are building fires, making pine beds and basic first aid. In relating to others, it means learning how to reach out, to communicate well and clearly, and to be both direct and open in expressing your thoughts, feelings and desires. Other skills include being able to set limits, expanding your capacity to give more freely to others, and dealing with professional and personal conflicts.

The ability to change the physical environment to meet our needs has cost the human species much of its ability to adapt. The luxury with which we surround ourselves cuts us off from even the simplest skills of survival in the natural environment. Similarly, people are often reduced to a sense of helplessness about their relationships, with little sense of control or impact on the world around them.

Anyone can buy a lot of expensive, shiny equipment, but it won't insure survival without both the drive to do so and the basic skills and ability to improvise. Correspondingly, one can rely on all the intellectual gambits and cover-ups, hide behind a role or authority, or be a scintillating conversationalist and still not know what it means to work and relate harmoniously with others on an equal footing. In a sudden crisis, stripped of equipment or role, there may be little or nothing to fall back on.

Watching one of the survival trainers start a fire with a primitive firebow, a tense, impatient lawyer commented wryly: "I can see the first requirement is patience." Before you can even begin to make a fire you have to find the wood and carve the wood block and fire bow. The teacher points out that it not only takes patience and skills, but knowing what your priorities are. "You can live for three weeks without food, but you couldn't survive for three days without water or being able to protect yourself from the cold." The students are always allowed to make some mistakes. The trainers will answer any questions, but if the students are too nonassertive to ask they may spend an uncomfortable first night. The next day they'll be told how they can make themselves more comfortable. The students are urged to tune in with all their senses. "Your eyes aren't always enough. The wild onion and a very poisonous plant look almost exactly alike; you need your nose to tell them apart."

Their careful instructions for climbing the mountain could have been taken from an assertive training lecture: "One step at a time. Look up." They spent time reassuring the group about the safety of the venture, demonstrating the strength of the ropes and harnesses. "It's ok to be afraid, everyone is sometimes, but panic kills."

ASSERTION TRAINING IN THE WILDERNESS

Much of assertion training is directed towards similar cognitive restructuring and helping people acquire the skills and confidence they need so they won't panic in difficult situations.

In the COPE experience, assertion training parallels the survival training. You build relationships with others and confidence in yourself one step at a time, just as you go up a mountain. The wilderness provides a myriad of tangible examples of how what you do affects you. Sleeping warmly and comfortably depends on where you put your sleeping bag and how you prepare the spot; how tired you get depends on the way you walk and how you time your rests; acquiring necessary information and skills depends upon your initiative in asking.

Each person in the workshop had his or her own particular frustrations to work with. A hard-driving administrator who was antagonizing his staff with his aggressive, belligerent approach knew morale was low but didn't know what to do about it. "I just always blow my stack." A young boy was so shy and timid with others that he preferred to go hungry when he ran out of food rather than ask.

Most professionals believe that assertion training is best accomplished over an extended time span, usually eight to 12 weeks, to allow for practice, supportive feedback and the slow building of skills and self-confidence. The COPE Workshop provided 15 hours of assertion training over only a two-week period—a pretrip meeting, daily sessions on the four-day trip, and a post-trip meeting. But the sense of community and cohesiveness created by the physical closeness and sharing facilitated rapid, dramatic changes. The interaction on the trail and around cooking fires carried over into the group sessions and increased their effectiveness.

Many of the Institute's usual training techniques were used: Small group interaction and dyad practice; token feedback to train the discrimination; such assertion games as "I Want," "Shoulds," and "I see, I hear, I think, I feel," canned roleplays on such areas as dealing with criticism and giving and receiving compliments, and roleplays of concrete problems. The administrator roleplayed and discussed enough work situations to feel confident that there were many different ways he could work things through without having to push around his staff "to get things done."

Homework assignments were limited to the interactions of the group on the trip; work and ongoing personal situations had been left behind. The shy, young boy was encouraged to take small steps toward participating and, with a lot of work and group support, began to trust the others and feel he had something to offer them too.

But there was no limit to the mental ranging of the participants between sessions as they began to get in touch with some of their real wants and to grapple with the contradictions between those goals and the ways they were living in their lives. Even the leaders were surprised at how rapidly the group moved past concrete problems to intense and radical lifestyle reevaluation. Two of the basic questions raised in the "Assertive Lifestyle" groups conducted at the Institute are "Do I want to continue living this way?" and "What do I really want to do with my life?" The COPE group moved past those questions rapidly to answer with a resounding "NO—I don't want to continue this way."

The lawyer said, "I've been working all my life to make money without enjoying what I do." A writer said, "I want to make some time for fun and not just plug along from deadline to deadline." The competitive woman realized that having to win all the time was a trap that kept her from enjoying her achievements.

COPE offered just a brief break in the flow of busy lives, but the intensity of the experience and some special chemistry created between the mountains and the people made it more than that. There was the feeling that the flow would never resume in quite the same way, that it had been diverted and changed. Experiencing the triumph of pushing beyond what they'd tought were their limits made them look sharply at similar self-imposed limits back in the urban world. The reevaluation and questioning of lifestyles was coupled with a new awareness of choice—they could choose to change.

A member of the group expressed the essence of the feeling: "On the trail, when the going got terribly rough, I found myself hunched over, breathing hard, and focusing all my attention on the three feet of dirty trail in front of me. I was so intent on my effort to keep going that I never took time to look around at some of the most spectacular country I might ever see. It occurred to me later that this is the way a lot of people travel through life . . . so burdened with problems and troubles that all they see is three feet of dirt in front of them, never stopping to rest, never straightening up and enjoying the beauty around them. And, the tragedy is that they may never pass that way again."

Many had hiked *in* head down and teeth gritted, but on the hike *out* everyone was stopping to savor the scenery. No one wanted to leave, even for the lures of a shower and steak. "We'll come back on your next one," they'd say, looking regretfully behind them. Some of them probably will, but whether they do or not, they face back home with a renewed assurance of their own abilities to COPE.

Part Three:
ASSERTIVENESS ACROSS CULTURES

ASSERTIVE BEHAVIOR AND BLACK LIFESTYLES

Donald K. Cheek

For his own survival, then, (a black man in America) . . . must develop a cultural paranoia in which every white man is a potential enemy unless proved otherwise and every social system is set against him unless he personally finds out differently.

William H. Grier, Price M. Cobbs
Black Rage

THE BLACK EXPERIENCE

Imagine a scene in which a black young man in his early twenties is cruising along on a late summer evening. He is kicking back, digging the sounds of Beethoven on his tape deck. Deciding to see what his partners are doing, he goes by a friend's house. Three of his friends are home, ask if they can cruise with him and jump into the car. As they drive off, one of the group loudly asks the driver, "What's that shit you playin' man, why don't you turn on some sounds?"

---

1. From *Assertive Black . . . Puzzled White*, Donald K. Cheek, pp. 43-50. Copyright © 1976. Impact Publishers, Inc., San Luis Obispo, California. Reproduced by permission.

His friend in the back seat picks up the theme and adds, "Yeah, baby, we don't need no fucked up white music bendin' our minds up." Everybody laughs and there is good natured palm slappin' among those who just "ran it down" to the driver.

How could that young man, who wanted to listen to Beethoven on his tape deck, have been helped by assertive training? What kind of assertive training did he need that could enable him to be assertive in contrast to aggressive or non-assertive? Conversely, what type of assertive training would be useless or even harmful to him in dealing with his environment? These questions are asked because traditional white-oriented therapies have had a lot of good-sounding suggestions that don't work for blacks. Following in their path, assertive training also has some great ideas, such as: "Express feelings honestly and openly," "Act in your own best interest and stand up for yourself without undue anxiety," and "Exercise your own rights without putting people down." But for blacks the issue has always been, how do you translate those high sounding objectives into the everyday activities of black folks? As some of my patients at Atascadero State Hospital's Black Project would ask, "Hey, Dr. Cheek, how can you break that shit down to something I can use—you know, like get my thang across to people without them gettin' bent out of shape?" Thus, the challenge is, how does one make those ideas and objectives of assertive training attainable (not just desirable or meaningful) to those who must live the Black Experience? Many of the lofty ideals and suggested behaviors offered by traditional practitioners are greeted with raised eyebrows and questioning glances. Many blacks with non-white clients wonder how all "that shit" would work with the folk that *they* have to deal with.

NEW REQUIREMENTS FOR OLD PROBLEMS

If assertive training is to realize its full potential of being of value to people regardless of ethnic or cultural background, then it must deal with problems that have up to now been ignored. From a black perspective this means that at least three conditions must be met:
1) A willingness to modify the traditional white middle class focus and assumptions;
2) A willingness to accept the reality and legitimacy of the Black Experience (Jim Crow Halo Effect) in reformulating the approach for black clients;
3) An openness to exploring ways of self-expression that may differ from conventional communication.

In fact, these three requirements are really a true test for *any* therapeutic approach that is to be translated to meet the needs of black people.

In mentioning the traditional white middle class focus of assertive behavior training (along with all the other therapies and techniques of the helping professions) I am asking a fundamental question. Do those who provide a psychological or mental health service *really* want to include everyone? Do we really want to help the black, the poor, the lower class, the working class, the poorly educated, the delinquent and imprisoned? Which of our psychological theories, therapies and techniques are really meant for them? Or are we assuming that all our methods or theories can really benefit only the white middle-class-oriented patient who has been the traditional client?

My assumption is that there are many professionals and laymen who would like to know ways of aiding *all* people regardless of race or social position. This is where I feel assertive training can meet the need. Since a critique of psychological theories is not the purpose of this book, I will just say that some theories have more built-in cultural biases than others. In like manner, some approaches are tested or standardized upon white populations or discussed in terms of reported results in treating only white clients. My contention is that assertive training provides an approach which is relatively free of cultural biases and therefore can be of maximum benefit to the black community.

Despite AT's potential, the way it is practiced by many whites can stamp it as useless to many blacks. As my man in the Black Project would say, "How can you break that shit down to somethin' I can use?" Thus, although there may be a willingness to modify the traditional white middle class focus there is an obstacle in the fact that most practitioners of today don't know how to "break it down" for use by a black population.[2] This is where sensitivity to the feelings of the average black person seeking treatment is necessary—sensitivity and understanding of the black client who will reflect varying degrees of suspicion, resistance, doubt, hostility and lack of confidence in the

---

2. Many black counselors have warned that real communication between the white counselor and black client depends upon the counselor becoming sufficiently acquainted with the client's cultural background to permit an in depth understanding of black verbal and nonverbal patterns of communication (body posturing, hand gestures, and facial expressions). The work of practitioners like Edward Barnes has cautioned us that a counselor who has primarily a middle class orientation may over-emphasize verbal ability and self-disclosure, and thereby fail to understand the client's non-verbal communication. This could result in the counselor perceiving the person as "nonverbal" or "unable to relate." See Edward J. Barnes, "Counseling and the black student: The need for a new view" in *Black Psychology*, Reginald L. Jones, Ed., N.Y.: Harper & Row, 1972, p. 218.

therapeutic process. To truly break assertive training down for relevance and use by black clients, these feelings and attitudes must be considered.

CHANGING TO ASSERTIVENESS—THE FIRST FIVE STEPS

With these thoughts in mind, the basic approach of assertive training from a black perspective can be considered in terms of 10 steps—the first five steps are for purposes of preparation and the last five steps are for purposes of action . . . . These initial steps can modify the conventional assertive training approach so that it begins to address the needs of the black client. The five basic preparation steps are:

1) Introduce and explain assertive training as something that can benefit most people; assess anxiety level of client (Use Assertive Inventory, Chapter VI).[3]
2) Obtain racial description of the "somebody" or "target person" with whom the client wants to be assertive. (Use Survival Ladder, Chapter VI).[4]
3) Determine tendency to use black, white or both language styles (Use Black-White Language Questionnaire, Chapter VI).[5]
4) Discuss the meaning of being assertive, aggressive or passive as related to the Black Experience. Interpret the 10 black characteristics, the Jim Crow Halo effect and the Psycho-Historical roots of black-white relationships (see "Before You Work With Blacks" questionnaire, Chapter VI).[6]
5) Discuss the social reality of black-black and black-white assertiveness (use Group Awareness Profile, Chapter VI).[7]

As the reader can see, each step, except for the introductory statement, deals directly with the interracial realities that consistently confront the black client. This is an area that has been given no attention by the popular proponents of assertive training, although it is crucial to success in helping black clients. Also, each step is accompanied by a suggested inventory or questionnaire as a guideline for increased effectiveness and sensitivity. Most important, of course, is the question of whether or not the practitioner, black or white, is basically prepared to deal with black clients. This issue is addressed in

---

3. EDITOR'S NOTE: References here are to material presented in Dr. Cheek's book, from which this chapter is reprinted.
4. Ibid.
5. Ibid.
6. Ibid.
7. Ibid.

the "Before You Work With Blacks" questionnaire, which suggests the minimum level of familiarity with black subject matter which is necessary to be of real service to a black client. However, if the assertive training facilitator has the willingness to depart from the conventional mode of being assertive and a real acceptance of the importance and value of the Black Experience, then the utilization of the suggested steps can make this approach emotionally and psychologically beneficial to a large segment of the black population.

Of crucial importance in modifying assertive training techniques to fit the needs of black clients is our willingness and ability to revise and broaden our ideas about what is the "right thing to say" in an assertive message. The *right* thing may only prove to be the *white* thing. And this would immediately take away the value of assertive training for blacks (remember the Jim Crow Halo Effect).[8] Now I realize that for many facilitators the assertive training process includes having clients concentrate on particular situations and develop their own "natural style" of being assertive. But if assertive training techniques are to become truly beneficial to the wide range of cultural attitudes and social differences that are represented in black people, some basic assumptions must be re-evaluated. Most therapists have worked so long with one type of middle-class-oriented client, that they accidentally fall into some habits of thought, convenient jargon and old assumptions. It is easy to forget that there are many who think, function and respond differently to the identical words and methods that previously brought success with a white subject. Thus, in teaching assertiveness to many blacks and non-middle class oriented groups, the therapist must be prepared to leave behind a format that uses procedures, expressions and cliches that were meaningful in past situations. Asking a client to concentrate on a particular situation and develop a "natural assertiveness" assumes, among other things, that the person will allow the therapist into his/her world of reality. When that same person is asked to watch someone as an effective model, it is assumed that the components of the model's style, and to a lesser degree the model's words, can be of value. To tell the person not to be loudly aggressive or offensive, again assumes commonly accepted interpretation of what is "loud" and what is "offensive." I am

---

8. "We suggest that this inability or unwillingness of whites to examine their own behavior and the effects of their behavior on the behavior of their black clients is the fundamental problem from which other problems arise in the counseling of black students." William A. Hayes and William M. Banks, "The nigger box or a redefinition of the counselor's role" in *Black Psychology*, Reginald Jones, Ed., pp. 225 and 226.

refering to such cautions as those offered by my colleagues Alberti and Emmons who suggest that the client be asked to consider alternative responses that are "less offensive."

Thus, to place a young black person, like the driver of that car, into an assertive training group without attention to these issues, may be to fail to prepare him properly to deal effectively and assertively with his peers. Likewise, a *book* which would provide that young black person with attainable and useful guidance must take into account the Black Experience.

WHY A WHITE APPROACH CAN FAIL

The reasons for failure in white-oriented assertive training when used with black clients can easily be traced to one or all of the following:
1) The facilitator's lack of preparation for dealing with the black client's high resistance to self disclosure.[9]
2) The facilitator's unawareness of the relationship between the client's exploration of self and the effects of the therapist's race.[10]
3) Ignoring the many problems involved in having a white facilitator function as a model for a black client.[11]
4) Ignoring the possibility that aggressive actions in terms of being "loud" or "offensive" may be defined or labeled differently by conventional whites and non-conventional blacks.
5) A general unawareness of the real world of the black client in which race, social barriers, survival and bi-dialectic speech

---

9. The hesitancy of blacks to fully disclose themselves has been consistently demonstrated in research. See Jourard and Laskow, "Some factors in self-disclosure," *Journal of Abnormal Psychology*, 1958, 56, 91-98. See also George H. Wolkan, Sharon Moriwaki and Karen J. Williams, "Race and social class as factors in the orientation toward psychotherapy" in *Journal of Counseling Psychology*, 1973, Vol. 20, No. 4, pp. 312-316. They found that since blacks are unwilling to reveal themselves even to each other, the lack of disclosure on the personal level could indicate more need for professional help.
10. Carkhuff, R.R. and Pierce, R., "Differing effects of therapist race and social class upon patient depth of self-exploration in the initial interview." *Journal of Counseling Psychology*, 1976, 31, pp. 632-634.
11. It should be somewhat obvious that a black client using a white counselor as a role model will encounter many dangers. Such a relationship could contribute to an identity crisis as well as conflict in the expression of racial attitudes. The black counselor is less likely to present such a conflict in the expression of racial attitudes. The black counselor is less likely to present such a conflict for the black client since usually they have lived a similar experience. This problem has been commented upon frequently by black observers like the late Edward J. Barnes. See Edward J. Barnes, "Counseling and the black student" op. cit. p. 219.

(talking black or talking white) have high priority and concern.

One of the promises of assertive training especially for blacks, is in helping young (and old) people resist their peers and the pressure of "going along with the crowd." It seeks to help provide and strengthen their right to choose, allowing them to resist drugs, alcohol, smoking, stealing cars, and fear of being called "square" or different. In addition, it can be used by black adults who fail to express their real selves for fear of being labeled "Tom," "Bourgeois" or "oreo." Of course, lack of assertion also functions for those blacks who fear the labels "militant," "activist" or "radical."

We, therefore, again face the critical question: "What form of assertive training did the young, black driver need to experience that could enable him to be assertive?" The answer is both complex and simple. The simple part is, that the young man needed exposure to a facilitator who had the ability to implement the five basic preparation steps which would automatically include a respect for the use of black language. Because of the particular situation, an effective assertive message would have to be couched in terms of a black message that could be properly understood (decoded) by his black peers. "Talking white" at that particular time would have been disastrous.

What is white talk and what is black language and what are the rules that guide appropriate usage? This part is complex; the Jim Crow Halo effect has kept blacks and whites separated to the point of each using the same language, English, but using it differently. Black language patterns make use of words in everyday situations that mainstream whites consider offensive—although the "less offensive" terms like "cool," "funky," "hip" and "right on" have been conveniently borrowed. But if a facilitator is to really get into the black world that is produced by closed eyes in a period of concentration, then the earthy "at home" words of the black experience may appear: "Nigguh," "mothafucka," "lighten up," "heavy shit," and "Honkey" plus a variety of filler words such as "you know," "like" and "I mean" which are part of *signifying, cappin* and *rappin* in the black tradition. It is this reality that blacks hesitate to reveal to white facilitators, assuming, in view of past experiences, that "they ain't ready to deal with it." The black person "knows" that the dominant white group has already judged black people, their values, speech and life-style as inferior. The black client's attitude frequently questions why he or she should re-experience the shock, dismay and patronizing comments of a white facilitator. More on language styles in Chapter V.[1]

I hope that through the use of the basic steps presented, assertive training can be so structured that a black client will be exposed to someone who is both black-oriented and already familiar with the black reality and black language styles. This type of facilitator can more easily elicit the participation of black clients (since they are not revealing something foreign, unknown and potentially shocking) in developing assertive alternatives. This type of facilitator will be less judgmental about the words of an assertive message and be more capable of modeling assertive responses, *appropriate* for the target person (the individual to whom the message is directed). If our young driver participated in such an assertive training session we could easily imagine him saying, "Hey, man, why you want to jump in my car and start all that old bullshit? Why don't you just lighten up, let me finish diggin' on this—cause you know it is my car and you can always get you ass out and walk—you dig?" I am sure the passengers would get the message and no doubt be cool—at least for awhile.

12

GROUP ASSERTION TRAINING FOR SPANISH SPEAKING MEXICAN-AMERICAN MOTHERS

Paula Landau, Terry Paulson

When a psychological approach becomes as popular as assertion training is currently, there is always some danger of it being regarded as merely the newest shiny toy of the middle class. This would be an unfortunate misconception because assertion training has been found to be a remarkably effective and even more sorely needed treatment modality for such non-traditional training populations as minorities, the politically powerless, delinquents, psychotics and prisoners.

The Mexican American is this nation's second largest disadvantaged minority. This population is severely handicapped by consistently low levels of education and a correspondingly high incidence of poverty. These factors combine to impede the Mexican American youth from meeting personal needs in socially acceptable ways. For many, life experience is a gradual process of alienation and eventually cycling out of the system. Thus, a large number of youths are turned loose on the streets of the tightly packed barrios without the requisite skills for coping with the social competition of the Anglo world—getting and keeping a job, making and maintaining productive relationships, active decision making, etc. Lack of prosocial competitive skills and the paucity of resources in their environment often foster the development of socially deviant methods to satisfy their needs. Aggression provides an immediate payoff, and the consequences, if any, are usually delayed.

Parental control is often weakened by a large number of children in the family and, in a number of cases, the frequent absence of the father. Even when present, the father is often not involved and regards child-rearing as the mother's responsibility. Thus, the mother often occupies the pivotal position in the poverty level Mexican American home.

Behavioral analysis of mothers who seek help for marital and child discipline problems has shown that they frequently lack interpersonal skills and exhibit inadequate and inappropriate responses, such as anxiety, withdrawal, somatic complaints, explosive anger, accusations, self-neglect, inability to make reasonable requests or refusals, or to generally express their feelings and wants. Many Mexican American mothers, particularly monolingual, Spanish speaking women at the poverty level, typically not only exhibit nonassertive response patterns, but express feelings of having little or no impact on their environment. This sense of helplessness often results in the mother feeling she has little or no control over the behavior of her children. The erosion of the mother's influence as her children become more independent is compounded by her lack of management and communication skills.

Frequently discussed issues in Chicano mental health have been the underutilization of mental health facilities and the inadequacy of traditional "talk-therapies." A problem and action-oriented approach, which focuses on present circumstances and concrete activity, offers the promise of greater effectiveness with low income clients than intrapersonal and "insight" approaches.

Group assertion training is designed to facilitate the shaping of adequate interpersonal skills in individuals whose general behavior is characteristically either overly passive or aggressive. Assertion training groups are active, structured and supportive, with primary emphasis on initiating change outside the confines of the group. The procedures are structured to provide clear client expectations, training in assertive techniques and specific problem focusing. They include cognitive restructuring, behavioral rehearsal, modeling, homework and group support. An innovation used by some trainers has been the use of poker chips for token discriminative feedback, to help group members distinguish between the three response styles: white for assertive responses; blue for withdrawing; and red for aggressive. These procedures can be easily learned and implemented by paraprofessionals in the community.

One of the practical advantages of assertion training as a treatment vehicle is its applicability to immediate problems. Given the pervasiveness of poverty in the Mexican American community, and the lack of necessary skills to satisfy many social and economic needs, traditional psychological approaches may have little or no relevance. While mental health clinics report that the most frequent problems brought to them are depression, somatic complaints, low self-esteem, decision making problems and family relationships, these problems are frequently subordinate to a greater need for such auxiliary services as medical, welfare, legal, and job training. Assertion training deals with concrete problems of getting one's wants and needs met, whether it be requesting aid or services, going on a job interview, refusing requests, etc.

AN ACTION-ORIENTED INTERVENTION PROGRAM

Attempting to deal clinically with these problems in poverty level Mexican American families, we developed a group procedure and manual for Spanish-speaking mothers utilizing the basic assumptions and strategies of assertion training. The primary focus was on facilitating the development of communication and management skills in Mexican American mothers and to decrease their anxiety and frustration in social interactions, particularly those involving their children.

Sixteen Spanish-speaking mothers were referred by welfare or probation programs from the La Colonia community of Oxnard, California, a poverty level section of the city that is populated almost entirely by minority ethnic groups, including a very large segment of Mexican Americans and newly arrived immigrants from Mexico. All but one of the mothers were monolingual in Spanish. Many reported not going past the third grade in school; two were semi-illiterate.

To provide a controlled study of the effectiveness of AT with this population, the mothers were randomly assigned to one of two groups, an assertion training group and a wait group that received no immediate treatment. The treatment group had weekly two-hour sessions for twelve weeks. Both groups were pre- and post-tested on the measures of assertiveness.

In-group training variables were divided into (a) didactic material, (b) behavioral focusing, and (c) modification strategies. The didactic presentations included lectures, video tape, and written material that were offered to the participants over the course of the 12-week program. The initial focus of the material was primarily to structure expectancies towards change and identify the disadvantages of their present unassertive response styles. For example, one of the mothers found all of her days tied up with babysitting for two friends who insisted that she was "the only one their children would stay with," in spite of the fact that she did not need the money nor want to babysit. Her inability to say "No" made it extremely difficult for this woman to find the time to pursue interests she had.

Subsequent sessions focused on content areas relevant to the majority of the mothers, such as giving positive messages, giving and receiving criticism, setting limits, and taking distance. Particular emphasis was placed on the areas of setting limits and taking distance to set the stage for future sessions in which the women began to focus increasingly on short and long-term goals and positive steps they could take to get and do more of the things they wanted. "Setting Limits" included limiting both what they agreed to do for others and their expectations of themselves in terms of what they thought they "should" do. "Taking distance" is taking time out from an interaction with another person, either in order to get more information and time in which to decide what to do, or in an emotional confrontation, to gain "breathing space" when one feels pressured or upset. The written material took the form of a 12-chapter manual written by the Assertion Training Institute staff.

After appropriate cognitive and perceptual sets were established, *behavioral focusing* was explained in terms of Alberti and Emmons' (1970) tripartite comparison of assertive, aggressive and withdrawing (non-assertive) response styles. The content and consequences of these styles were discussed and criteria for each response category established. In order to facilitate this discrimination acquisition, a video-taped response discrimination film entitled "¿Y Como Responderia Ud?" ("And How Would You Respond?") was used to show the three response styles to typical situations confronted by Mexican American mothers, such as family problems, school and getting services.

A primary *modification strategy* was the shaping of appropriate responses through the use of discriminative tokens (poker chips) given by the trainers and group members to each other as immediate positive or negative feedback both for in-group statements and for reports or statements or actions outside the group. The use of token feedback in groups has been subject to previous research (Flowers, et al., 1974; Paulson, 1974). Shoemaker and Paulson (1973) discussed its clinical use with anglo mothers in assertion training to teach the discrimination between assertive, aggressive and withdrawing responses. The advantages of token feedback in assertion training to facilitate interaction and immediate inter-member feedback was described by Paulson (1976). The tokens were used to reinforce the discrimination taught in the training film, to increase the immediacy of feedback, and to set the stage for in-group differences. White tokens were given for an assertive statement, defined as an explicit or implied first person statement which varied from the expression of requests, opinions, likes, dislikes, and disagreement to members asking for clarification, initiating problem solving, or doing something for themselves, such as taking time to do something they enjoyed. Though the principal focus of the token feedback was the content of the verbalization, nonverbal behavior, such as eye contact, voice, tone and posture, were also taken into account.

Blue tokens were given for withdrawing statements, which are inhibited or avoidance communications that deny the feelings, desires, and/or opinions of the speaker. Inappropriate overapologizing, habitually saying "I'm sorry," overjustifying, self-denial, frequent self-criticism, and "don't rock the boat" statements were included in that category.

Red tokens were given for aggressive statements or reports of such statements in outside interactions. Aggressive statements are usually expressed in the second or third person and often take the form of a threat, insult, or sarcasm. They commonly result in "put-down" feelings, hurt, hostility, defensiveness, and/or humiliation on the part of the recipient. The recipient is typically blamed for the conflict, whether for willful behavior or for stupidity or incompetence.

Modification procedures also include other learning approaches, modeling, rehearsal, and positive reporting. The term "modeling" is used here to describe a process of role-playing performed by a group member or facilitator for a specific verbal response to be observed by another specific group member. Rehearsal is the practicing of a specific verbal response or sequence of verbal responses by a group member. Token feedback was given throughout all these procedures. Positive reporting consisted of the group-go-around procedure, providing an opportunity for each participant to report all assertions recorded during the previous week.

Extra-group activities included readings in the manual, behavior assignments to be completed between sessions, and continued recording in their weekly notebooks. The assignments were made to facilitate both in-group material and response generalization to the natural environment.

Bilingual community workers were trained prior to the start of the program to assist in the training. Their input was used in the development of the training film, and the skills they learned are now being used in independently running assertion training groups for the community.

TECHNIQUES OF MEASUREMENT

The principal measures used in the present investigation were two behavioral assertiveness tests (BAT) in Spanish modeled after the work of McFall and Lillesand (1971), but adapted to make the situations culturally relevant to this group. The role-playing tests, in which participants were presented with tape-recorded stimulus situations requiring a verbal response, were used to establish both an assertive refusal and an assertive request rating. In both the BAT-request and the BAT-refusal tests, the mothers were instructed to respond verbally to each situation as if it were happening to them. The responses were taped and rated by two independent "blind" judges, with the average of their judgments used as an index of assertive refusal and request. Each test was broken into three equal sub-tests, each with four critical incidents. The order of the tests admininstered to subjects was varied to balance the use of each test in the treatment and control groups during the testing periods.

An evaluative questionnaire was used only as a post self-report measure to assess the impact of the training for the participants receiving assertion training. Likert scale ratings were provided so that the mothers could rate their improvement in specific interpersonal skills, improvement in their children's behavior, and improvement in specific key relationships. Room was also given for spontaneous comments about what they liked and didn't like about the training experience.

RESULTS OF THE AT PROGRAM

The Mexican-American mothers who received assertion training significantly improved on measures of assertive request and refusal when compared to the women who did not receive training. Unfortunately, circumstances, such as distance, time and lack of another bilingual therapist, prevented running a placebo group. The self-report questionnaire completed by the mothers receiving training also indicated their perception of improved ability to deal with relationships more assertively.

The mothers verbally expressed their enthusiasm for the group and appreciation for the relevance of assertion training to their specific life problems repeatedly throughout the course of the group: "It's more than just talk." The facilitator was also told that a prior group specifically oriented towards teaching mothers contingency management techniques with their children was terminated at the end of six weeks because the women no longer wished to continue. Because of time pressures the facilitator suggested concluding this group after ten sessions, rather than the originally proposed twelve. However, the women insisted they wanted to continue for the full twelve meetings. Several of the mothers in the original group also asked to enter a subsequent assertive training group being led by the community workers because they felt it was "so helpful."

In addition to the positive evaluative reports and data, there were reports by the community workers of behavior changes on the part of the women involved. They exhibited increased involvement in both employment and educational opportunities and verbally reported great improvement in their family relationships and in the behavior of their children. One woman, deemed "hopeless" by the social worker who referred her, got a job immediately after the group terminated. Two others began taking English classes; others took classes in adult education. An interesting sidelight was a crucial change in the relationship between two women who were sisters-in-law. During one of the later sessions both were able to express previously suppressed resentment over never feeling able to say "no" to each other when they didn't want to do something. One, for example, always felt she had to drive the other whenever asked unless she had a "good excuse." After the discussion, which was accompanied by some nervous laughter, both reported feeling much more comfortable with each other. During the last session they said that feeling free to say "no" without excuses and to give each other honest feedback had made them "better friends."

An unexpected development centered around decreases in somatic complaints during the course of the group. Women reported being able to sleep better, less frequent headaches, fewer gastric upsets, backaches, and an increased sense of energy. Besides the decrease in somatic complaints, the women, two in particular, showed definite improvement in self-care and personal appearance as the group progressed.

OBSTACLES, HUSBANDS AND GOALS

Prior to starting this program the researchers were warned of the "inherent difficulties" in group work with this population. Absenteeism, tardiness, lack of motivation and interest, high drop-out rates, and resistance from husbands were cited as probable problem areas. These difficulties did not materialize in our present study. Most participants were there promptly with assignments and notebooks completed. When women did miss sessions, it invariably involved a family emergency of some kind. These were poverty level families; when a child was ill they were not able to pay babysitters. The two who dropped from the program did so for emergency reasons, one's mother became ill with what was found to be terminal cancer, while the other left to secure seasonal employment (returning to join a later group run by the community workers).

In anticipation of problems with the husbands, the sessions focusing on positive assertions and complimenting were given early with assignments focusing on giving positive feedback to family members. Many of the members reported that their husbands were enthusiastic about their attending the group—they liked the positive feedback they were getting and the benefits from wives who were becoming able to say "no" to others, i.e., neighbors borrowing items, salesmen, and their children. Very little attempt was made by the therapist to have the women say "no" to their husbands. However, one of the women successfully experimented with "small no's," such as not wanting to go with him to the store or to get ice cream, without adverse effects. Another reopened the subject of applying to the Housing Authority for another house, which her husband had refused, after role-playing in the group. He agreed. In general, more emphasis was placed on making requests of their husbands for what they wanted than on saying "no." When the group finally progressed to the areas of negative feedback, there were no reports of adverse consequences and two women reported significant improvement in communication with their husbands.

One unanticipated difficulty that became quickly evident before the groups even began was the difficulty of participants in identifying their own problem areas and establishing specific goals. A self-rated goal attainment rating measure designed for use as a dependent measure proved only to frustrate both the women and the researcher. They appeared to attribute most of their problems to circumstances and actions by others over which they felt they had no influence. These women were not "therapy wise" and were not accustomed to focusing on themselves—their feelings, wants or goals. A major task of the early stages of the group was on training the members to focus on specific goals. This was facilitated by the emphasis on dealing with daily life problems and the constant discriminative token feedback.

A NOTE ON TOKEN FEEDBACK

The advantages of token feedback became increasingly evident. The use of tokens provides a tangible means of providing feedback without waiting for a speaker to finish. Nonassertive individuals have a difficult time interrupting the flow of conversation to provide verbal input, often choosing to wait until their comments would no longer be relevant. In addition, courtesy is a heavily emphasized cultural value in this ethnic group. The immediacy of feedback was stressed and the use of tokens provided a tangible means of giving it without having to interrupt the speaker verbally.

The tokens provided a clear discriminative cue for learning the differential meanings of assertive, aggressive, and withdrawing responses. Group members became increasingly adept at the discrimination in both their own behaviors and those of others in and outside of the group. They would frequently talk of wanting to give a "blue" to someone outside the group. A member would sometimes precede her account of an incident with "here come the reds!" One member began giving herself white tokens when she felt particularly proud about something she had done. As a group, they began to act and appropriately label more and more according to the discriminations learned. The importance of the therapist as a model is often lost because of the inability of members to focus on significant therapist behavior; the token feedback given by the therapist served as a simple initial focus for client modeling.

The reinforcing value of token feedback cannot be ignored; a pile of white chips in their laps or on the floor around them became tangible evidence of group support and approval. The value of social reinforcers in group has been well established (Liberman, 1970). Laughter and humor are important components in most assertion training groups; the tokens elicited humorous comments and laughter. It is possible that the high attendance of the group, especially in the beginning, was partially attributable to the fact that the members were enjoying themselves and having fun. The mothers would frequently say they loved the group and the tokens and looked forward to coming.

One of the premises of assertion training is that each individual has a perfect right to express differences of opinion, perceptions, feelings, and likes and dislikes. What several of the group members perceived as an assertive response was often experienced as aggressive by the more nonassertive members. Token use provided an unavoidable forum for such encounters. Once tokens were in flight, there was no way they could be brought back. Disagreements in token feedback provided ample opportunity to affirm the freedom to be different. There was no one right answer when it came to feelings, wants or opinions. Token use helped members express their individual differences and to acknowledge that such individuality was ok.

Token feedback also provided a tangible and easily learned motoric response as a first step in shaping the desired verbal interaction skills; a nonverbal comment in the form of a token "signal" is less anxiety evoking than making a verbal comment or criticism.

CONCLUSION

A duplication of our results would be difficult without the invaluable involvement of trained Mexican-American community workers. Not only were they helpful as co-trainers, but they were an important liaison between the researcher-leader and the group. It took many group sessions before group members felt able to give negative feedback directly to the leader; prior to that time the only source was the community workers who were already known and trusted. One of the most gratifying results of the project is that two of the community workers later completed a successful group of their own, and planned to continue offering these groups to the community. These encouraging results indicate that training bilingual paraprofessionals would be a productive and parsimonious method of reaching a larger number of this population which is currently not receiving mental health services proportionate to its need. Assertion training is particularly appropriate for such an extension of services because of its highly structured format, easily taught procedures and concrete "here and now" approach.

13

ASSERTION TRAINING FOR ASIAN-AMERICANS

Philip O. Hwang

Several years ago, a young student of Asian descent committed suicide at a mid-western university campus. He left behind a note which read: "The Anglos here don't understand me." Persons with oriental heritage in this country are probably the least understood group of all the minority segments. They are often perceived by the dominant society to be passive, quiet and non-complaining. In fact, Asian-Americans (Japanese, Chinese, Filipinos and Koreans, etc.) are frequently cited as the "model" minority group that has "made it" within the American system.

These and other similar negative stereotyped characteristics of Asian-Americans have been around for years and have unfairly boxed them in a category from which it is extremely difficult to break away. Lately, however, there are signs that this artificial "mold," whether self-imposed or imposed from outside, is cracking and breaking away at a rather fast pace. The First National Conference on Asian American Mental Health, held in San Francisco in 1972, perhaps served as the best example. Officials of the sponsoring National Institute of Mental Health expecting a quiet, orderly and routine conference, were surprised and shocked to experience a stormy and volatile meeting. The pre-conceived image of Asian-Americans being passive, reserved and non-complaining was shattered even before the meeting got started. Instead of the eighty-one invited participants more than 600 concerned Asian-Americans showed up (Huey, 1972).

Since then, the Pan Asian Coalition has been formed, the Asian-American Mental Health Research Center established, and several community based counseling and mental health agencies have come into existence. These and other significant events point toward an awakening of America's most silent, passive and ignored minority group. Many factors have contributed to this group's seemingly sudden courage and strength in expressing Asian-American concerns, feelings and experiences more freely and openly. First, there seems to be a trend within the American society slowly moving toward a more tolerant acceptance of cultural diversity and individual differences. Second, the success and accomplishments of other minority groups in this country have motivated the Asian-Americans to voice similar demands for personal rights. Third, many Asian-Americans themselves, especially the younger generations, are critically re-examining, questioning and forming their own values and systems of beliefs.

At this point, the Asian-Americans of this country seem to indicate that they want to break away from the stereotyped image of being passive, quiet and non-understood. As a group, they are becoming more and more vocal in asserting their basic human rights, and are achieving a minimum degree of success. As individuals, the critical question remains: how to be assertive in an aggressive-prone American society. There exists a need to teach and train these individual Asian-Americans who need and want to be more assertive in their daily lives. Consider the Filipino who wants to overcome his *hiya* and learn to return defective merchandise to the store without feeling shame; the Chinese who desires to overcome his *lien* and learn to say "no" without feeling guilty; the Japanese who wants to overcome an exaggerated sense of humility and modesty and learn to speak about abilities and accomplishments when applying for a job or asking for a raise: these and many others can be trained in responsible assertion skills which are considered by many to be necessary personal characteristics for freedom, happiness and even survival in American society today.

It is in response to this urgent and critical need that this paper is written to explore the possibility of setting up a loosely structured program to train Asian-Americans on how to act and react assertively. However, the task of writing an assertion training program for Asian-Americans is extremely complex and difficult. Some of the more apparent road blocks are: 1) as a group, the Asian-Americans are really not homogeneous; they have many distinctive characteristics among themselves. Thus, the Chinese-Americans may need and want assertion training more in social situations than the Filipinos; 2) the communication patterns of Asian-Americans within their respective ethnic group is rather different compared with interactions with the dominant white majority; 3) there are very few reliable and useful research studies to draw from in formulating a semi-structured, psychologically-based training model for Asian-American assertiveness.

Since the above problems and limitations exist, the following procedures for training Asian-Americans in responsible assertion should be viewed as guidelines, suggestions and exploratory ideas to generate further discussion, research and study. The first section deals with self-assertion, which is defined here as the ability to say "yes" and "no" to self. With many of the Asian-Americans, the imbalance lies in excessive degrees of self-denial. This is followed by a discussion on the necessity of building a rational base for assertion through the rejection of "oriental myths." Finally, the "how" and "what" of assertiveness as they relate to Asian-Americans are explored, and specific training techniques given.

SELF-ASSERTION

In the most commonly accepted definition, assertion is always taken to be inter-personal. It usually involves the interaction of two or more persons. In the training of Asian-Americans, the best way seems to start with self. There seems to be quite a high degree of self-denying and self-effacing among the majority of people of oriental descent. It appears that there exists a constant saying of "no" to self. This, of course, narrows the person's vision and limits his/her personal life experiences. Perhaps this is based on the fact that oriental cultures tend to stress the formulation of collective identity and group responsibility rather than individual identity and personal responsibility. Thus, the self-assertion training set up for Asian-Americans should utilize structured exercises which focus immediately on self-worth, self-awareness and self-experiencing, a more personal valuing of self and a richer and broader existential living. In short, the person becomes a "freer self" who says "yes" more often to self without any "yes . . . but . . ." As a student, instead of staying in the library to study while half of the student body is at the football stadium on a Saturday afternoon, go and join them, yell and scream like everybody else and have fun with it. Sometimes allow oneself to taste and enjoy exotic foods of other cultures instead of the daily oriental cuisine. Finally, try to spoil oneself occasionally. Instead of saving money from the paycheck which just arrived, go and buy something which one desires, but has held back because of other needs.

One technique which has been used with a certain degree of success in training Asian-Americans to a greater degree of self-assertion is an adaptation of Fritz Perls' bipolarities of the topdog and the underdog (1969). In this exercise the counselee is asked to think of the latest personal conflict during a decision making process. He/she is then to imagine the topdog saying constantly "no" and at the same time giving all kinds of reasons why he/she shouldn't. The client then takes on the role of the underdog who says "yes" and responds to each and every criticism of the topdog. The bipolar dialogue continues for a while, after which a discussion takes place with regard to how the client feels about the whole dialogue between the topdog and the underdog. Some of the most revealing responses from the clients have been: "I never knew that I could say yes!" "I didn't know that I was allowed to speak back." "I just said yes and I feel good."

ORIENTAL MYTH

One of the major goals of assertion training is to build a personal belief system which will help the person to support and justify the decision to act assertively (Jakubowski-Spector; 1973). For the Asian-Americans this goal can be attained only through the rejection of the so-called "oriental myth." This perhaps is the most difficult aspect of the entire assertion training process. Two reasons are clearly apparent. One, centuries of oriental culture and heritage are still very much a powerful influencing factor in the thought process and behaviors of the various Asian-American communities in this country. Two, the majority of the dominant society expects the Asian-American to act non-assertively. Thus, oriental assertiveness within the American culture has not received the positive reinforcing responses for its cultivation and growth. In addition, events from history (e.g., the relocation of Japanese Americans during World War II) have re-confirmed their irrational belief that to survive within the American society, it is better to be quiet, anonymous and non-assertive (U.S. Commission on Civil Rights, 1975).

Within a large training group, one of the simplest techniques can be employed to achieve astounding results. Divide the large group into small groups of about six to eight persons. Each group is given newsprint and color markers and asked to brainstorm about the myths of oriental non-assertiveness. Each small group draws up a list and reports to the entire group for further discussion and summation. In a one-to-one situation, the client may be given a pre-drawn list of myths

and asked to react to each one of the myths on the list, then is to choose one which applies to him/her personally. One such list could be this:
1. It is a myth that Asian-Americans have to be passive, quiet and non-assertive in the American society.
2. It is a myth that the best way to act in this country is to be submissive and non-complaining.
3. It is a myth that oriental modesty and humility demands our rejecting or discounting complimentary remarks.
4. It is a myth that the best way to obtain a raise is to give in to the boss's excessive demands for hard and long hours of work without asking for monetary compensation.
5. It is a myth that one way of communicating "no" is to say "yes" in a soft voice with head bowed.
6. It is a myth that the best way to act is not to "create waves."
7. It is a myth that shame or loss of face should prevent one from expressing sincere, honest and true feelings.
8. It is a myth that authority is always right.
9. It is a myth that it's best to keep one's sufferings, pains and emotional distress within oneself.
10. It is a myth to endure blatant violations of personal and human rights as the decrees of fate and that there is nothing one can do about it.

SKILL ACQUISITION

The third element of AT for Asian-Americans deals with skill acquisition. Here the practical training centers around specific and concrete inter-personal conflicts wherein the clients experience anxiety because they lack the necessary skills. It deals with practical aspects of how to do it and what to say. The "how" is extremely significant as this, to a large extent, deals with the non-verbal messages communicated during the process of interaction. Looking directly at another person and maintaining eye contact is one way of communicating straight, honest and assertive messages (Alberti and Emmons, 1974). Yet, most Asian-Americans are not accustomed to looking directly at someone's eyes. It takes some effort and training to demonstrate the efficacy of eye contact and to help the client become more comfortable with it. The same holds true for body postures, gestures and facial expressions. To say "no" with a smile is just not convincing. The conventional oriental deferential posture of bowing or even a few degrees of stooping coupled with flat tone and low voice will seldom convince the other person that one means every single word he or she has just spoken.

What is said, of course, is just as important as how it is said. For many Asian-Americans this is another big hurdle to overcome, especially for those who do not speak the English language fluently. Assertive messages are perceived and understood quickly and clearly when proper words are used at the appropriate moment. Many Asian-Americans, as stated earlier, have the problem of saying "yes" to self, but when it comes to inter-personal relationships the problem is just the opposite—the inability to say "no" to unreasonable requests and excessive demands, especially from authority figures. Another problem to overcome in this area will be that of teaching clients to freely express their sincere and honest feelings in a given situation. The acquisition of such a basic skill in assertiveness will not come in one session. It takes long hours of practice and a constant fostering of a new belief system. The client must be convinced that it is all right to speak in a sincere and honest way and that in the end he/she will be happier for it.

One of the most powerful instruments to be used in training Asian-Americans in acquiring assertion skills in the "how" and "what" is through the extensive use of closed circuit video equipment. Here the client can clearly see his or her non-verbal behaviors and can practice the appropriate behavior. Specific situations, too, which have been known to often cause non-assertive behavior in Asian-Americans, can be put on video tape and then shown to the client as an exposure to alternative behaviors. Finally, the client can go through role playing and role reversal situations with great profit. The use of video equipment here will provide immediate feedback to aid the process of re-learning. One last word: in the practice of role playing and for the production of model tapes, it seems best to have an Anglo as a partner to interact with, since this will help the client feel more accurately the realism of the situation.

To assert is to communicate. But communication clearly involves the sender, the message and the receiver. This loosely structured assertion training for Asian-Americans focuses on the sender and the message. Hopefully, one who communicates freely his or her sincere and honest feelings will be better understood, and future tragic incidents such as the one mentioned at the start of this paper can somehow be prevented.

14

ASSERTIVENESS AND ANXIETY: A CROSS-CULTURAL AND SOCIO-ECONOMIC PERSPECTIVE

Brian S. Grodner

The growth and popularity of assertive behavior training in recent years has paralleled a growing emphasis in the mental health movement on dealing more effectively with the needs of minority, ethnic, and lower socioeconomic class groups. The often-found lack of effectiveness of psychotherapy with ethnic and lower socioeconomic class clients has spurred the search for different delivery systems and psychotherapeutic modalities. This emphasis on *delivery* of mental health services to minority groups has resulted in the relative neglect of the groups' specific psychological characteristics, patterns, and needs.

Since a lack of assertiveness may result in being taken advantage of and losing opportunities, assertive training may be especially appropriate with many minority and/or lower socioeconomic group members who are having emotional problems. In order for assertive training to have maximum benefit, it is vital that it be utilized in accordance with the *actual*, not imagined or stereotyped, needs of the client population. Thus, in applying AT with minority ethnic and/or lower socioeconomic populations it is important to substantiate or deny, on the basis of careful research and observation, the descriptions, interpretations, and myths about members of these groups.

Before suggesting an increase in assertiveness and conventional assertive training for those individuals or groups found to be lacking in assertiveness, certain questions must be answered. Are there culturally or socio-economically linked factors influencing the level of assertiveness and the relationship between assertiveness and personality, beliefs, and anxiety? Are some behaviors too culturally ingrained to be changed? Hopefully we will look at a person's assertiveness, or lack thereof, through his or her phenomenological perspective, and not make assumptions based on generalities and push solutions based on a majority cultural view.

This paper examines the levels of assertive behavior of Anglos ("White") and Chicanos ("Mexican-Americans")[1] of different socio-economic classes, and the nature and effects of cultural and socio-economic traits (as well as anxiety) which influence the level and development of assertiveness. Also included is a practical discussion of the implications of these factors for high quality and appropriate assertive behavior training for all people.

Psychological and sociological characteristics of an ethnic group as well as socio-economic class may effect levels and types of assertiveness. It is important at the outset to realize that while we may focus on group differences, it is dangerous to generalize uncritically about any group. Groups divided on any criteria have greater commonalities than differences and most important, show great intra-group scatter.

CHICANO CULTURE

Among the problems with research into the Mexican-American culture are the different degrees of acculturation, the influence of recent change, age, urban and rural demographics, and language. Much of the older research done on rural Mexican-Americans (e.g., in south Texas) may no longer be valid, especially for Chicanos living in California, New Mexico, or other areas where patterns of migration and culture are markedly different.

Chicanos who speak only or mostly Spanish appear very different from Anglos on many studies. Edgerton and Karno (1971) found the

---

1. EDITOR'S NOTE: Although the terms "Chicano" and "Mexican-American" are used almost interchangeably in this chapter to refer to a particular subculture of Latino people, it should be noted that they do not have identical meaning to all people so described.

Spanish-speaking had many traditional traits and attitudes, such as fatalism, strong attachment to family, authoritarianism, and a conservative morality. An English-speaking Chicano group, in contrast, held attitudes very close to those of Anglos.

Marquez (1972) believed that the Chicano is more intensely emotional and linguistically expressive than the Anglo, giving greater priority to human relations with neighbors and friends as well as with nuclear and extended family. Schwartz (1967) found Chicano adolescents from blue collar families had a higher expressive orientation than their Anglo counterparts. This expressiveness may aid in the production of assertive behavior.

Guttentag (1971) reviewed the literature on general group cohesiveness and the effects of ethnic group cohesiveness. She felt, "protected by the cohesiveness of their group, low status people feel freer to express hostility directly," (p. 39).

The family is usually the most important social unit in a Chicano's life. "It is usually at the core of his thinking and behavior and is the center from which his view of the rest of the world extends," (Murillo, 1971, p. 102). The family provides emotional and material security for a person's entire life. The extended family also gives support and nurturance. Ramirez (1967) found middle class Chicanos scored much higher than Anglos on a scale of authoritarianism and a scale measuring Mexican family values which correlated very highly with the authoritarianism scale.

While close relationships in and out of the family may give Chicanos both the experience in interpersonal relationships and the security to be assertive, the emphasis on submission and obedience, and the closeness in family relationships may make assertiveness less likely than in the Anglo culture. Assertiveness in the form of positive feelings, however, may be more likely to occur in the Chicano culture (Johnson & Sikes, 1965; Logan, 1971; Ramirez, 1973; Schwartz, 1967).

The concept of "machismo" has dominated the study of the Chicano family, dating from early psychoanalytic studies of Mexican "character" Montiel (1970). Based on a sense of inferiority and worthlessness, this hypothetical male builds up "virility" to support a deflated ego which, when threatened, acts out with revenge and hostility. With poor methodology and outdated theory, the jump was made to the "true Mexican national character," then the Mexican male, the Mexican family, and finally to the Mexican-American family. This "macho man" and corresponding masochistic, yet dominating and controlling woman, are presented as hopelessly neurotic and the underlying cause of Mexican and Mexican-American problems.

The scope of machismo, especially in its extreme form, has been overestimated for Mexicans and overestimated and distorted for Mexican-Americans. Male dominance and masculine superiority are a part of Mexican-American culture (as it is among many lower socio-economic class groups), but not commonly to the extent suggested by the machismo concept. Although this could exert a force towards assertiveness among Chicano males, the extreme form of machismo is generally shown by hostility and aggression, not necessarily assertiveness.

Reyes (1972) pointed out that there is a strong Indian input in the Chicano culture. Communal rather than an individualistic way of life, subservience to leaders, elders, priests, and dependency on tribe have an effect on willingness to stand up for one's own rights in relationship to the rights of society or one's reference group. The Indian's conduct, resourcefulness, and industry were geared to benefit the tribe. Cooperation as it is now in the Chicano culture and family was highly valued. Experimental studies (Kagan & Madsen, 1971) have confirmed this observation.

A language reflects the attitudes and values of the people who speak it. The Spanish form for "I missed the plane" translates in English as "the plane left me." The relatively greater use of the reflexive in Spanish may produce feelings of less responsibility, power, and activity in those who use the language.

SOCIO-ECONOMIC CONSIDERATIONS

The greatest problem in the differentiation of Chicano behavior and cultural traits is the confounding of ethnicity with the variable of socioeconomic class. Casavantes (1971) believed that "with rare exception, every time scientists have studied Mexican-Americans they have ended up describing poor Mexican-Americans, . . . ignoring Mexican-Americans who are middle class. The net result of this extraordinary scientific oversight is the perpetuation of very damaging stereotypes of the Mexican-American" (p. 46). The few studies of Anglo and Chicano differences which controlled for socio-economic class reached different conclusions than those that did not make that control.

Casavantes listed eight qualities which have been *invalidly* attributed to Chicanos as part of their ethnicity. Casavantes believed they are really attributes of the culture of poverty. They are:

1. Spending a larger portion of social time with relatives and neighbors.
2. Not joining voluntary associations.

3. Preferring the old and familiar.
4. Demonstrating an anti-intellectual attitude.
5. Demonstrating machismo, "manliness" (the male).
6. Using physical force to settle arguments or punish children.
7. Being unable to postpone gratification.
8. Being very fatalistic in the view of the world, feeling little control over nature, institutions, people or events.

These qualities are understandable attempts to deal with the environment of economic deprivation.

Reisman (1964) pointed out that the poor are oriented more to the present; future orientation being too much of a luxury or chance. Due to their experience and lack of opportunity, they do not see, expect, or sometimes feel comfortable with change. They are also likely to "adjust" rather than "overcome," and to value dependence or interdependence with family or neighborhood rather than "rugged individualism."

The fatalism, authoritarianism, dependency, and fear of change frequently found may limit the assertiveness of lower socio-economic class members.

Toughness, action orientation, intolerance, and difficulty in delaying gratification may add to the likelihood of assertive behavior. These last characteristics, however, may more likely find expression among lower socio-economic class members in aggressive rather than assertive behavior.

One difficulty in interpreting much of the literature of the psychology of lower socio-economic class members is the inconsistency and lack of clarity of exactly *who are the people studied*. They have been called underprivileged, poor, culturally disadvantaged, culturally deprived, disenfranchised, blue collar, and working class. The common treatment and understanding of both lower class and working class is clinically incorrect and leads to many distortions and misconceptions.

While there is much in common, blue collar-working class members live under less difficult conditions, have more access to middle class goals and means to get them (e.g., labor unions), have more stability in jobs and neighborhoods, and most important, have less of the mental set of continued poverty and the fatalism which goes with it. We assume from this that working class members will be as a group more assertive than lower socio-economic class members. The factors influencing the assertiveness of the lower socio-economic class are less culturally implied and more in the nature of responses to their environment.

We have discussed some cultural attributes and ramifications of these attributes which may lead Chicanos to be both more or less assertive. It must also be remembered that assertiveness may be exhibited in a variety of different situations and by a variety of different behaviors. Therefore, individuals and groups may show great variability in their assertive behavior.

To recapitulate, some characterizations of Chicano culture are accurate; some should be attributed to the variable of socio-economic class; some should be attributed to both culture and class; and some are myths, perpetuated by prejudice, lack of information, and poor research. It must be remembered that Chicanos are not a monolithic group, and individual, as well as geographic, demographic, age, and acculturational variables make valid and reliable general statements difficult. Differences between groups are more often a matter of tendency and degree than polarities. Every culture, however, interprets reality from different vantage points, and through their customs. Even when values are shared, they may be placed in different orders of importance and priority.

ASSERTIVENESS AND ANXIETY

Our next step is to examine how cultural influences on assertiveness may interact with anxiety, supposedly the major influence on and inhibitor of assertive behavior. The behavioral theory for lack of assertiveness stated by Wolpe and Lazarus (1966) is: A person who is unassertive ". . . has unadaptive anxiety-response habits in interpersonal relationships, and the evocation of anxiety inhibits the expression of appropriate feelings and the performance of adaptive acts" (p. 38). This behavioral theory of assertiveness, therefore, characterizes assertive responses as "reciprocally inhibiting" to anxiety and suggests that the assertiveness and anxiety in a person should correlate negatively. Salter (1961) described the unassertive person as having an "inhibitory personality," suffering from too much foresight, always analyzing and planning and worrying about the future.

Perls (1969) called anxiety "stage fright," which occurs when a person leaves the here and now and worries about catastrophic expectations, i.e., what will happen, what response will come.

Wolpe (1969) believed assertive training to be "required for patients who in interpersonal contexts have unadaptive anxiety response that prevent them from saying or doing what is reasonable and right" (p. 61). Wolpe (1973) also noted that nonassertive people, when angry in a situation, have impulses to assert themselves but stop because the counteracting impulse of anxiety is greater than the impulse to assert. Neuman (1969) described assertive training as "arranging environmental situations with the client so that certain impulses previously inhibited by anxiety can be expressed in overt behavior" (p. 433).

Laws and Serber (1971) and Hersen, Eisler, and Miller (1973) suggested some people are unassertive at least partially because assertive responses have never been learned. The genesis of this deficit in learning has never been clearly explained. It may be due to anxiety inhibiting the initial learning of assertive behavior as well as its expression (in which case, anxiety remains the prime determinant of the lack of assertive behavior). It may be due to never learning or having been exposed to a skill, such as a boy from an isolated rural area or country not learning how to play basketball, in which case cultural and demographic variables, as well as lack of learning opportunities, may be considered.

Finally, the deficit in learning may not be a real deficit at all. It may be the skill is possessed, but a choice is made (not due directly to anxiety) to abstain from its use. Examples would be a Mormon who does not drink liquor, an Orthodox Jew or Moslem who does not eat pork, or a Chicano who would not allow a young man to get ahead of him in line but would never oppose an older person. While there may be anxiety if the moral or cultural codes are broken, the behavioral deficit is predicated on cultural values and learning, not on anxiety. The impact of cultural traits on assertiveness, therefore, may weaken the relationship between assertiveness and anxiety in Chicanos.

A COMPARATIVE STUDY

The effect of cultural differences and socio-economic class on levels of assertiveness, and the relationship between assertiveness and anxiety were investigated in a sample of 90 Anglo and Chicano psychiatric patients at the Albuquerque, New Mexico Veterans Hospital. Subjects were given: the Adult Self-Expression Scale (ASES) to measure total level of assertiveness; the Taylor Manifest Anxiety Scale (MAS) to measure anxiety; and a questionnaire was used to ascertain ethnicity, socio-economic class, and additional variables.

The categorization of people in terms of social stratification is an extremely complex issue. The method used in this study involved a simplified version of the two factor Index of Social Position (ISP) (Hollingshead & Myers, 1968). Participants were classified into three socio-economic levels on the basis of a weighted combination of their years of formal education and their occupational level. A trichotomy of middle, working, and lower class was used.

"Chicanos" were defined as those subjects who considered themselves Chicano, Mexican-American, Spanish-American or Hispanic.

The subjects were divided into 12 major groups and subgroups and a wide variety of statistical analyses was performed. The groups were: (1) total group, (2) total Chicano, (3) total Anglo, (4) total lower class, (5) total middle class, (6) total working class, (7) Chicano lower class, (8) Chicano middle class (9) Chicano working class, (10) Anglo lower class, (11) Anglo middle class, and (12) Anglo working class.

There are several important limitations in assuming the results of this research hold true for all Anglos and Chicanos of different socio-economic classes, including possible differences in assertiveness and anxiety: between psychiatric (outpatient and inpatient) subjects and a "normal" population; between men (only males were subjects in this study) and groups of both sexes; and between Chicanos from New Mexico used in this study and those from elsewhere in the country.

Results of the study are summarized only briefly here. The following material is distilled from extensive correlational analyses of the research findings.

Relationship Between Assertiveness and Ethnic and Socio-economic Differences

The results showed that both the working and middle class groups were significantly higher in total assertiveness than the lower class group. The middle class group scores on the subscales of expressing opinions, initiating conversations and dealing with others, global interaction, and interaction with friends were significantly greater than those subscale scores for the lower class group. The great variability of the levels of assertiveness of behavioral and interpersonal situational components show that assertiveness is a multifaceted trait.

These results show that not only is the middle class more assertive than the lower class, but that the working class is similar to the middle class in levels of assertiveness and must be differentiated in this area from the lower class. At this point of discussion, social class but not ethnicity seems to be an influencing variable in the level of assertiveness. In brief, the lower the social class, the less assertiveness was shown.

Interestingly, however, ethnicity had a small but insignificant partial correlation with anxiety; socio-economic class had a somewhat larger significant partial correlation with anxiety. Thus, the lower the social class, the more anxiety was shown.

Relationship Between Assertiveness and Anxiety

The "reciprocal inhibition" theory of assertiveness states that as assertiveness increases, anxiety decreases, or as assertiveness decreases, anxiety increases. The study results support the position that levels of assertiveness generally have a negative relationship with levels of anxiety (for most groups). Specific assertive subscale behaviors and situations may differ both within and between groups in their relationship to anxiety. In most of the groups, "taking the initiative in conversations and in dealing with others" has the greatest relationship with anxiety, and "expressing negative feelings" the least. This means that a lack of this type of initiative probably is related to anxiety, while not expressing negative feelings is not. It is interesting to note that the expression of negative feelings is one of the major assertive behaviors associated with the behavioral theory of assertiveness. Another behavior receiving much attention by the behavior therapists is "standing up for legitimate rights," which was next to last in the total group in its relationship to anxiety. Possibly people make careful choices in these two areas on whether to be assertive or not.

The results showed the Chicano combined lower and working class have a significantly lower negative correlation than the Anglo combined lower and working class on the correlation between anxiety and: (a) total ASES; (b) "refusing unreasonable requests;" (c) assertiveness "with authority figures;" (d) "expressing personal opinions;" (e) "expressing positive feelings;" and (f) assertiveness "with intimate relations."

Table 14-1 offers a comparison of Anglo lower and working class and Chicano lower and working class in the relationship between assertiveness and anxiety:

Table 14-1

Ethnicity, Assertiveness, and Anxiety

Scale		ANGLO Lower & Working Correlation With Anxiety	CHICANO Lower & Working Correlation With Anxiety
ASES	(Assertiveness)	-.5809***	-.1978
A	Expressing	-.4103*	+.0527
B	Refusing	-.6524***	-.1974
C	Favors	-.1890	-.1666
D	Initiating	-.6262***	-.4554***
E	Positive	-.5892***	-.2340
F	Negative	-.2558	+.0021
G	Rights	-.2637	-.0954
AA	Global	-.5005**	-.3175*
BB	Parents	-.5422***	-.4702***
CC	Public	-.3107	-.0773
DD	Authority	-.5164**	+.0336
EE	Friends	-.4482	-.1620
FF	Intimate Relations	-.5148**	-.1583

Anxiety measured by Taylor Manifest Anxiety Scale (MAS)
  * Significant at the .05 level (significant)
 ** Significant at the .01 level (very significant)
*** Significant at the .001 level (extremely significant)

The following chart may aid in an understanding of the relative importance of (a) anxiety and (b) volitional choice and/or cultural traits in the determination of levels of assertiveness:

Ethnic Group	Anglo			Chicano		
Socio-economic class	Middle	Working	Lower	Middle	Working	Lower
Relative level of assertiveness	Higher	Higher	Lower	Higher	Higher	Lower
Anxiety as determiner of level of assertiveness	Lower	Higher	Higher	Higher	Lower	Lower
Volitional choice and/or cultural traits as determiner of level of assertiveness	High	Low	Low	Low	High	High

It is important to remember the subscale variations for all groups. For instance, even the Chicano lower and working class may have anxiety associated with being assertive to their parents and taking the initiative in conversations.

This information suggests that, for lower and working class Chicanos, assertiveness is not related to anxiety. An increase or decrease in anxiety does not seem to be related to an increase or decrease in assertiveness. For Anglo lower and working classes, assertiveness is related to anxiety. For lower and working class Chicanos, the lack of assertiveness may only be infrequently related to excessive anxiety; and anxiety may not decrease when assertive behavior is shown.

CONCLUSIONS

Based on the findings of the study, the following conclusions appear to be warranted:

1. Psychiatric patients appear to be less assertive than subjects who are not psychiatric patients.
2. Assertiveness is a multifaceted behavior with large differences in assertiveness levels among behavioral and situational components as measured on the subscales of the ASES, both within and among groups.
3. Chicano and Anglo psychiatric patients of comparable socio-economic class level appear to be similar in their level of assertiveness.
4. Middle class psychiatric patients are more assertive than lower class psychiatric patients. This is especially true when working class patients are not included in the study.
5. Socio-economic class and not ethnicity has a significant relationship with levels of assertiveness.
6. In most psychiatric patients, as assertiveness increases, anxiety tends to decrease; and as assertiveness decreases, anxiety tends to increase.

IMPLICATIONS FOR THEORY AND PRACTICE OF AT

Many traits (and ramifications of these traits) attributed to the Chicano culture are better explained by socio-economic class influences. Traits such as fatalism, dependency, and fear of change, commonly found among the lower class and discussed in this study, may be a cause of low assertiveness. Traits such as courtesy, emphasis on family cohesion, obedience, human relations, and expression, commonly found among Chicanos are not collectively important influences on assertiveness, in the sense that they serve to balance each other.

The data suggest that, in general, assertiveness and anxiety may be partially, reciprocally inhibiting to each other. Reciprocal inhibition between assertiveness and anxiety is prevalent among Anglo lower, Anglo working, and Chicano middle class group members and not prevalent among Chicano lower, Chicano working, and Anglo middle class group members. There is support for the theory that cultural values and/or volitional choice as well as anxiety have much to do with the assertiveness of some people and groups.

The working class cannot simply be placed with either the lower or middle class in terms of assertive behavior. In levels of assertiveness, the working class closely resembles the middle class, but in the relationship between assertiveness and anxiety, the working class of each group closely resembles the lower class of that ethnic group.

In the diagnosis and treatment of emotional disturbances in general and problems in assertiveness specifically, it is important to be aware of and take into account patient variables relating to culture, socio-economic class, and interaction between culture and socio-economic class. This includes the subtle differences within categories such as differences in acculturation of special groups and differences between lower and working class patients. This does not include the myths and prejudices which many groups are saddled with or blocking the chosen goal of a patient to transcend or overcome his or her cultural, socio-economic or familial norms.

Assertive training may be particularly important and useful for lower class individuals, beyond the alleviation of anxiety and the increase in general interpersonal effective functioning. The assertive behavior of "standing up for rights," the most germane to issues of powerlessness, inequality, and discrimination did not at all differentiate between middle and lower class individuals, however. Assertiveness with friends, but not with authority figures, was significantly lower among the lower class. It appears that an increase in levels of assertiveness may aid, but not completely change the societal and psychological existence of the lower class.

The evaluation of the possible benefits and detriments of assertive training for lower class Chicanos is a complex issue. Being lower class, they may gain particular benefits from the results of assertive training. For lower class Chicanos, unlike lower class Anglos, a low level of assertiveness is not necessarily associated with a high level of anxiety or discomfort. Therefore, with Chicano lower class individuals, special care should be taken before encouraging or embarking upon a course of assertive training.

It should not be assumed that each patient or client is uncomfortable about his or her lack of assertiveness. The possibility of increased assertiveness bringing about cultural conflict and increased anxiety should be thoroughly explored. If assertive training is decided upon, either with or without the alleviation of anxiety as a goal, goals should be specific and the ramifications and working through of cultural conflicts should be attended. A low level of assertiveness due to cultural inhibitions may have generalized to produce a low level of assertiveness with no cultural component. If this occurs, assertive training of selective behaviors and situations may be accomplished without bringing about cultural conflict. As always, the practitioner's ethical responsibility is to offer alternatives and allow the client to make the choice.

Finally, it should be noted by the practitioner that the behavior of *individuals* does not conform to the average behavior ascertained for their *group*. The assertive behavior trainer should be aware of the wide range of behavior exhibited and attainable for all people.

Part Four: APPLICATIONS OF ASSERTIVE BEHAVIOR TRAINING

15

THE ASSERTIVE WOMAN: DEVELOPING AN ASSERTIVE ATTITUDE

Stanlee Phelps, Nancy Austin

Because assertion is a very personal, rather than mechanical, learning experience, it is necessary for you first to know yourself so that you can adapt assertion to your own particular needs. Assertion is only one tool that you may choose to employ to better your life. It is not the answer to every question; it is not the solution to every problem. As you explore your attitudes and deepen your awareness you will be better able to identify the ways in which assertion can be valuable to you personally.

Developing an awareness of what is normally accepted as feminine, as well as an awareness of the transition that women are going through today, is part of the "consciousness raising" process experienced by the assertive woman. This process usually occurs in small groups in which women examine traditional values and stereotypes in a very supportive atmosphere which is conducive to helping women to grow and change. Many of these discussions motivate women to action and to attempt to assert themselves.

In Chapter XIII "Women Together" [*The Assertive Woman*, Impact, 1975],[1] we talk more about the consciousness raising group

---

1. From *The Assertive Woman*, pp. 31-46, Stanlee Phelps and Nancy Austin. Copyright © 1975. Impact Publishers, Inc., San Luis Obispo, California. Reproduced by permission.

as a special resource, and mention sources of further information.

Apart from group experiences, a woman can increase her own consciousness raising with such techniques as our "consciousness razors" provided here for your use. The concept of consciousness raising certainly has merit; it describes the process of increasing one's awareness level and heightening one's perceptions. Yet we especially like the pun on the word "razor," because it implies that each razor has a sharp edge to help you cut through some attitudes that may inhibit your assertiveness.

USING CONSCIOUSNESS RAZORS

Following are a list of razors. Try to answer each item as honestly as possible. After responding to each item, review your comments carefully.

- Have you ever felt different from other women?

- Have you felt competitive with other women?

- Were you treated differently from your brother(s) as you were growing up? How?

- Have you ever felt pressured into having sex?

- Have you ever pressured yourself into having sex?

- Have you ever lied about orgasm?

- Have you ever felt like a sex object?

- Do you ever feel invisible?

- Do you often feel insignificant?

- What was your relationship to your parents?

- What was your parents' relationship to you?

- How was your education affected by your being female?

- How was your interest in sports affected by your being female?

- How was your career choice affected by your being female?
- How do you feel about getting old?
- How do you feel about your mother's aging?
- What do you fear most about aging?
- What goal have you wanted most to achieve in your life?
- What, if anything, has stopped you from achieving this goal?
- Do you see yourself operating in a dependent and/or in an independent way? How?
- How do you relate to authority figures? (Clergy, doctor, police, etc.)
- Have you ever felt powerful?
- How do you feel about your body?
- Have you ever punished yourself? When? How?
- Have you ever forbidden yourself a pleasure, a meal, or some gratification?
- Have you ever pinched or slapped yourself?
- Do you often feel a sense of aloneness or loneliness?
- Do you have some attitudes that could inhibit your being more assertive?
- What are they?
- Which affect you the most?
- Which affect you the least?

As you review your comments on the consciousness razors, look for:
- Patterns or habits that seem to repeat themselves over and over in your life.

- Rationalizations about why you do or don't do something instead of expressing your honest feelings.

Explore your feelings in depth, trying to avoid an intellectual exercise in pursuit of the "right" answer. The goal of consciousness raising is to know yourself better and to accept who you are as well as to undertake the changes that you decide to make.

GETTING OUT OF THE COMPASSION TRAP

We believe that one particular attitude or "trap" prevents women from acting in more assertive ways: The Compassion Trap. We give it special attention here because it affects all women in our society on one or more levels. Your recognition and understanding of the Compassion Trap and how it affects *you* personally is an important part of developing an assertive attitude.

In her article, "The Compassion Trap" (From *Woman in Sexist Society: Studies in Power and Powerlessness*, edited by Vivian Gornick and Barbara Moran, New York, Basic Books, Inc., 1971.) Margaret Adams defines the Compassion Trap as a trap exclusive to women who feel that they exist to serve others, and who believe that they must provide tenderness and compassion to all at all times. This attitude is very difficult to throw off, but avoiding the Compassion Trap is essential for the assertive woman.

Years ago, it was a very important job for Doris to "keep the family together" through her self-sacrificing and compromising, while the man of the house endured many hassles outside the home in the industrial world. Overall, the totally compassionate woman benefitted society by making things comfortable, so that men could tend to the "more important concerns" of work, business, science, and politics. Now, although women have begun to move out of the home, they still tend to cluster toward the "helping professions" (social work, nursing, teaching, domestic services, etc.) in which they may extend their roles in providing care and compassion for those whom they serve. However, many a Doris becomes frustrated and confused as she tries to follow her own individual preferences while still looking out for the needs of others. She is torn between expressing herself directly and thus reaping firsthand rewards, and supporting others, thereby receiving vicarious pleasure from the accomplishment of others.

Because the Compassion Trap dictates that a woman express herself through meeting the needs of others, it frequently prevents a woman

---

2. EDITOR'S NOTE: References to "Doris," "April," "Iris," and "Agatha" relate to the chart on page 162.

from being assertive. The assertive woman feels the freedom to be direct, and to act on her own behalf, while at times she may *choose* to be compassionate. She rarely feels, however, that she *must* always be compassionate to the exclusion of her own feelings. In this area it has been very difficult for some women to burst through traditional barriers. Women often have colluded with each other and reinforced one another for being devoted and dedicated to others, perpetuating the Compassion Trap to the utmost degree. Women in the Compassion Trap place greater importance on taking care of other's feelings than on meeting their own needs.

Getting out of the Compassion Trap does not mean that, like Agatha, you must become insensitive to others' feelings. Instead, it means valuing your own feelings and being responsive to them with the same care that you give to others, as April does.

Generally, we find five areas in which Doris, Agatha, or Iris may find herself in the Compassion Trap:

1. She may see herself in a protective role, as a mother with children who is afraid to act on her own behalf for fear that there will be negative repercussions toward those whom she is trying to protect.

2. A woman who is single may give up career opportunities to take care of her aging or sick relatives.

3. An employed woman may be reluctant to leave an unsatisfactory job for fear that her clients will suffer in the short run, even though she may benefit in the long run.

4. When no one else is concerned about a problem situation, a woman may enjoy being seen as the one who has special understanding or compassion.

5. Whenever a crisis arises, a woman may be willing to push aside a creative project to give her full attention to the crisis; she feels indispensable.

On a practical level it is important for us as women to look at the consequences of what we do. April asks: are we *really* helping other people so much by always pampering them and taking care of things that cause them discomfort? What price do *we* pay as individuals when our giving and compassion is done at the expense of our own happiness? What price does the *receiver* of our compassion pay when we have felt obligated and resentful? Many times, just as much or more can be accomplished if we allow others to be assertive and take responsibility for themselves, while we pursue what is best for us. Whenever you are assertive, you make it possible for yourself to grow and change without cramping anybody else's style. Consider the implications of both men and women taking turns playing the compassionate role. Nothing is a trap as long as you know that you will exercise your right to do or not to do according to what feels best for you.

THE COMPASSION TRAP QUIZ

Gauge the extent to which you are in the Compassion Trap by taking our quiz below. Answer each question *honestly*. If you have not personally experienced some situations, choose the response that most closely approximates the way you think you would respond. After you have finished, turn the page and add up your score. The corresponding key will help you to determine how "trapped" you really are.

1. You have been seeing this man socially for several weeks, but you are beginning to feel bored and disinterested in continuing the relationship. He likes you very much and would like to see you more often. Do you:
    a) tell him you'd prefer not to see him, feeling you've been honest with yourself?
    b) feel a sudden attack of the Hong-Kong flu coming on?
    c) continue to be the object of his affections, because leaving would really hurt his ego?
    d) tell him that he bores you to tears, and that even if you were both marooned on a desert island, you would camp out on the opposite shore?
2. You invited a friend of yours who lives out of the state to spend her/his two week vacation with you at your home. It is now one month later, and your friend shows no intention of leaving, or reimbursing you for food and telephone bills. You would like your friend to leave. Do you:
    a) not mention anything about your expenses or feelings, because you don't want to damage the friendship?
    b) leave a note saying that you're terribly sorry, but your mother has decided to live with you and you'll need the room?
    c) tell your friend that you really value your friendship, and that her/his extended visit is putting a strain on it. You ask that your friend make plans to leave?
    d) put all of your friend's belongings out on the doorstep with a note: "Don't call me; I'll call you?"
3. You are enjoying one of your rare visits to San Francisco, and you are staying with your brother and sister-in-law. One of your favorite things to do in San Francisco is to sample the fine restaurants. Your

brother and sister-in-law are terrible cooks, but they insist on "treating" you by cooking for you themselves. You would much prefer going out to eat. Do you:

a) decide to have dinner at your brother and sister-in-law's home because you don't want to disappoint them by refusing their offer?

b) tell them that you appreciate their thoughtfulness, and explain that one of the reasons you come to San Francisco is to enjoy the restaurants? You suggest that all of you go out to eat instead.

c) loudly tell them that you're not there for *their* food?

d) call and claim that you are unavoidably detained, and tell them not to wait dinner for you—then sneak out and eat by yourself?

4. You are working on a project that is very important to you. Some friends drop by unexpectedly. You'd really like to continue working on your project. Do you:

a) shelve your project, prepare hors d'oeuvres, and apologize for your cluttered living room?

b) loudly berate your friends for not having called first?

c) explain that you're in the middle of an important project and arrange to see them at a mutually convenient time?

d) ignore your friends and continue working on your project while they are there, hoping they'll get the message.

5. Your ten-year-old daughter customarily walks to school, but today she wants you to drive her. You have driven her on rainy days, but it is not raining today. She continues to ask you to drive her, adding, "Besides, everyone else's mothers drive them." Do you:

a) tell your daughter she can walk to school today, as usual?

b) begin by telling your daughter that you won't drive her to school but after a short time you give in and drive her, feeling guilty that you hesitated?

c) reply "Oh, okay, I'll drive you," thinking of all the other children whose mothers faithfully drive them? You will feel like a neglectful mother if you don't drive your daughter to school?

d) threaten to call the truant officer and report on your daughter if she doesn't leave for school immediately?

Key

1. a) An assertive choice. (3)
   b) Honesty is the best policy here. (0)
   c) Don't forget *your* feelings. (0)
   d) Don't forget *his* feelings. (0)
2. a) You'll feel resentful later. You're trapped. (0)
   b) This may get her/him out, but how do you feel about trapping yourself with *that* one? (1)

    c) Right. This will also get her/him out, and
       leave you with your self-respect. (3)
    d) This will get your friend out of your life, also. (0)
3. a) This Compassion Trap will result in your
       disappointment and indigestion. (0)
    b) The assertive thing to do. (3)
    c) Better look for a hotel room—your brother and sister-in-law
       won't want to have you as a guest for some time. (0)
    d) You'll soon run out of excuses. Then what? (0)
4. a) The Compassion Trap. (0)
    b) Only if you *never* want to see them again. (0)
    c) Ain't it the truth? (3)
    d) You're wasting time; it may take hours for
       them to get the hint! (0)
5. a) You've got it! (3)
    b) A good start—but you're in the Compassion Trap here. (1)
    c) Are you really neglectful? The Compassion Trap again. (0)
    d) You avoided the Compassion Trap, but stepped
       into the Aggression Trap! (0)

Add up your total points and gauge the extent of *your* Compassion Trap:

14+: We couldn't ask for more. You can choose what to do without being trapped. Be on the lookout, though, for other situations that may trap you.

9-13: You can avoid the Compassion Trap most of the time, and you're moving in the right direction. Give some extra attention to the people/situations that continue to trap you, and attempt more assertive ways of handling them.

2-8: Consider the price you are paying when you do things at the expense of your own happiness. With some practice, you *can* leave the Compassion Trap and *enjoy* what you *choose* to do. Be an assertive woman and be loved for it.

CHOOSING YOUR OWN LABELS

Developing an assertive attitude is an important part of becoming an assertive woman. If your attitudes and feelings about being assertive are positive and supportive, you can *reward* your assertive behavior. However, if you feel you are being "impolite," "bossy," or "bitchy" when you assert yourself, you can inhibit your assertive behavior and seriously weaken your assertive attitude. You can strengthen or minimize your assertive skills by the *labels* you place on them.

Do the labels *you* apply to your assertive behavior encourage or prevent you from being assertive? Use *positive* self-labels to support and encourage your assertive behavior. ("I'm really being assertive—I love it") *Negative* self-labels can only serve to inhibit and prevent your assertiveness. ("What a bitch I am!")

Other people can mislabel your assertive behavior also. Because women have been expected to behave passively for so long, becoming an assertive woman seems to be an extreme contrast. Other people's expectations of how you behave are being thwarted if you have been consistently passive with them, and are now being assertive. They will be quick to label your behavior as aggressive in an attempt to inhibit it, fearing they may have to change, too. This is particularly true for people close to you (family members, other relatives, close friends, employers) who have in some way benefited from your passivity, as with the Compassion Trap. On the other hand, if you have been consistently aggressive in your interactions with others, moving to a more assertive way of relating will usually be encouraged, and given positive labels by those around you.

Be aware of the negative self-labels you attach to your assertive behavior, and work toward replacing those labels with more positive ones. If you do this, other people can follow your example and work at changing their labels also. Use the following exercise to see how *you* label your assertive behavior by comparing your responses with the responses of our four women, Doris Doormat, Agatha Aggressive, Iris Indirect, and April Assertive. Each of these situations were handled assertively, but it is the label each woman has attached to the assertive behavior that varies here. How would you label each assertion?

"Thanks, but no thanks..."

You have been telephoned by a solicitor who is trying to sell you a magazine subscription. You say you aren't interested in receiving the magazine and end the conversation. Do you think to yourself:

Doris Doormat: I really didn't *want* the magazine, but wasn't I impolite and irritable to say so? The next time I'm asked to subscribe, I'll be more polite and do it.

Iris Indirect: Well, I certainly was easy on him! I should have said yes, and then refused to pay the subscription to teach them a lesson about bothering me.

Agatha Aggressive: I wish I'd given that solicitor a piece of my mind! What an insolent person! The next time that happens I won't be so mild-mannered and meek.

April Assertive: I was really assertive with that solicitor. I feel good about being honest and direct, and I didn't fall into the Compassion Trap.

"Get ready for dinner"

Your children are playing outside and you want them to come in for dinner. You go outside and tell them it's time for dinner and to come in now. They protest that it's not that late and couldn't they play for a while longer? You firmly tell them again to come in, and they do. Do you think to yourself:

Doris Doormat: I'm glad they came in, but wasn't I nagging and bossy? I don't want to nag, so I think in the future I'll ask once, and if they don't come in, I'll just try to keep dinner warm.

Iris Indirect: I'm sure they would have come in sooner if I'd not been so polite. Instead of asking twice, I should have just said okay and waited until dinner was burned for them to come in. Then they'd feel bad.

Agatha Aggressive: Was I quiet and passive! What a softie! Next time I'll teach those kids who's boss around here. I'll really give them a lecture!

April Assertive: I'm glad they came in when I asked them to. I'm really being assertive and honest with them.

"You're late."

You are scheduled to meet a friend for an important meeting. She is an hour late when she arrives. You tell her that you are upset because she is so late, and you would have liked more time to spend with her. She acknowledges your feelings and says she will try to be on time in the future. Do you think to yourself:

Doris Doormat: I'm really pleased that she will make an effort to be on time in the future, but wasn't I awfully aggressive and mean to say anything about it? I hate being so aggressive, so I'll stop demanding things and just hope they work out from now on.

Iris Indirect: She might be on time in the future, but I shouldn't have said anything about it today. It's so embarrassing to have to go out of my way to say something about it. I should just be late next time and see how *she* feels.

Agatha Aggressive: I sure let her off easy. What an inconsiderate woman to be late! I should have really told her off.

April Assertive: I'm really glad that our meeting will be on time in the future, and I'm pleased that I was assertive and mentioned it today. I was really honest and spontaneous, and I really like that.

If Doris' responses sound all too familiar to you, you have been mislabeling assertive behavior as aggressive, bitchy, impolite, nagging, bossy, etc. You are also inhibiting your own assertive behavior by attaching an inappropriate, undesirable label to them. Remember that *aggressive* behavior such as Agatha's could be labeled "nagging," "Bossy," or "bitchy"—*not* assertive behavior.

If your labels are more like Iris', you are looking for revenge or trying to elicit guilt rather than rewarding your assertive behavior. You are mislabeling your assertive behavior as too easy or too direct, or as embarrassing. If Agatha's labels resemble yours, you are mislabeling your appropriate assertive behavior as weak, passive or meek. Assertive behavior may seem mild in comparison to your aggressive behavior, but you are inhibiting your assertive responses by mislabeling them. The assertive woman, April, correctly labels her assertive behavior as direct, spontaneous and honest. She rewards her own assertive behavior. Attach appropriate labels to your assertive behavior, and make a conscious effort to tell yourself you've been assertive. Rewarding your assertive behavior will give you support to attain a very desirable goal—being an assertive woman.

SELECTED TYPICAL CHARACTERISTICS	DORIS DOORMAT	AGATHA AGGRESSIVE	IRIS INDIRECT	APRIL ASSERTIVE
Point of view	I'm not OK	You're not OK	You're not OK, but I'll let you think you are	I'm OK and you're OK
Dominant role	Inhibited underdog	Underdog in bear suit	Mad dog in lamb's suit	Top-dog
Sample games	"If it weren't for you," "Kick me" and "Why does it always happen to me?"	"Now I've got you!"	"I'm smiling while stabbing you in the back"	"Let's play tennis"
Self-sufficiency	Low	High or low	Looks high but is usually low	Usually high
Decision-making	Others choose for her	Chooses for others and they know it	Chooses for others and they don't know it	Chooses for herself
Significant other	Agatha, Iris, or April	Doris	Agatha, April, and/or Doris	Herself
Feedback she gets from others	Guilt, anger, frustration, disrespect	Hurt, defensive, humiliated	Confusion, frustration, feels manipulated	You respect me and I respect you
Social pattern	Puts herself down	Puts herself up by putting others down	Appears to put others up while putting them down	Puts herself up
Defensive pattern	Flees or gives in	Outright attack	Concealed attack	Evaluates and acts
Action pattern	Under-reacts	Over-reacts	Acts indirectly	Acts directly
Success pattern	Lucks out	Beats out others	Wins by manipulating others	Wins honestly
Potential for	Suicide, alcoholism, drug abuse, other withdrawals	Committing crimes, homicide	Being murdered, provoking retaliation	Peaceful, active life

The idea for this chart was modified and adapted from the "Characterological Lifechart of Three Fellows We All Know," by Gerald Piaget presented at the Institute on Assertive Communication, American Orthopsychiatric Association Convention, San Francisco, April, 1974.

16

ASSERTIVE BEHAVIOR AND CLINICAL PROBLEMS OF WOMEN

Patricia A. Jakubowski

As therapists we all have an implicit, if not explicit, model of emotional health which guides our therapy. Although it is beyond the scope of this article to present a full theory of emotional health, I believe that one aspect is central: *Emotionally healthy, fully functioning people believe that they can make an effective impact on the people in their environment. They do not feel that they are helpless victims of life's events or of other people's demands. Instead they feel in charge of themselves because they believe that they can engage in direct behavior which will effect other people in constructive ways.* White (1973) stresses the importance of a similar concept, interpersonal competence, for healthy functioning.

When people do not feel that their behavior can make an impact on others—in other words, when they do not feel interpersonally effective—their resulting feelings of anger, helplessness, and hurt may evolve into a wide variety of psychological problems. Although a person needs many skills to be interpersonally effective, one essential skill is the ability to be assertive . . .

---

1. From *Psychotherapy for Women* edited by Edna I. Rawlings and Diane K. Carter. Courtesy of Charles C. Thomas, publisher, Springfield, Illinois 62717.

I will examine . . . the relationship of nonassertive behavior to various psychological problems . . .

In the following section various psychological problems will be discussed which may be related to a client's failure to assert herself. Since clients rarely conceptualize their problems in terms of assertion, it is primarily the therapist's responsibility to make this clinical assessment. In discussing each of these clinical problems I have clarified the conditions under which assertive training would be an appropriate treatment strategy.

CLINICAL PROBLEMS

Depression: Experimental Analog Data

Depression is probably the most common client problem. Although there are many theories of depression, Seligman's (1973) is particularly compelling and has the most implications for women and assertion. His theory is that laboratory observations of the cause, cure, and prevention of the laboratory-induced "learned helplessness" phenomenon (Seligman & Maier, 1967) can be applied to *reactive depression* or what Wolpe (1971) has called *neurotic depression*.

According to the research of Seligman and his associates (Seligman, Maier & Solomon, 1971; Thorton & Jacobs, 1971), an organism learns to be helpless when it is repeatedly exposed to stress conditions in which no behavior in which the organism engages reduces the stress. When the organism is later placed in a different stress situation where it could act to eliminate the stress, it fails to do so and instead under-eats, does not fight back when attacked, exhibits sexual disturbances, and has decreased norepinephrine levels in its brain.[2] Seligman (1973) theorizes that clinical depression, like learned helplessness, occurs when individuals are unable to control important events in their lives.

Laboratory-induced learned helplessness is reversed when the organism is compelled to engage in behavior which enables it to escape the shock (Seligman, Maier & Greer, 1968; Seligman, 1969). Depression may be similarily cured through therapeutic strategies

---

2. . . . many people have associated lowered norepinephrine levels with clinical depression. The tricyclic antidepressants are known to definitely enhance the action of injected epinephrine and norepinephrine at peripheral sympathetic receptor sites; whether or not the tricyclic antidepressants actually release endogenous stores of epinephrine and norepinephrine is still unknown (Goodman & Gilman, 1970, p. 188).

which are designed to get the clients moving and acting on their environment. The therapeutic goal would be to demonstrate to depressed clients that their behavior can effect others and that they are not helpless and controlled by external events and other people.

Organisms who have had prior experiences in mastering stress do not become helpless when they later experience inescapable stress situations. This finding has implications for prevention: Seligman (1973) theorizes that people who have had extensive experiences in mastering their environment and have developed a wide repertoire of coping responses may be less vulnerable to neurotic depression.

Seligman's theory, based on his experiments, has at least four important implications for women, depression and assertion: *First*, it helps to explain why women are more likely than men to become depressed. Women are usually socialized to be more passive, dependent, and nonassertive than men (See Table 16-1); this means that they are more likely than men to learn to depend on other people to take care of them. This, in effect, denies women an opportunity and a need to acquire a wide repertoire of coping skills. Furthermore, women are more likely than men to be told that there are certain situations which they cannot handle; women may avoid these situations and never learn how to master them. *Second*, the theory suggests that when a woman's failure to act assertively has made her feel powerless and subsequently depressed, assertion training would be a useful treatment for the depression.

Third, Seligman's (1973) theory puts women's feeling of fatalism into perspective. It helps to explain why it is so difficult to convince generally nonassertive individuals that it is both desirable and possible to act assertively. If they learned directly or vicariously that they could not positively effect other people or their environment, then when they are in a new stress situation where they could be effectively assertive, they are likely to react with learned helplessness—rejecting the notions that assertion could be effective or that they could act assertively. It is common for them to simply say: "I couldn't do that (perform an assertive behavior) because it's *not me* to act that way!" Finally, the theory suggests that assertive training could be a preventative to depression. People who know that they can assertively handle a situation feel in control of themselves and feel that they are governing their own lives and that they are not victims of other people's expectations or demands.

Depression: Case Study Data

Various case studies have been reported which provide suggestive evidence that assertive training can be helpful in treating depression: Bean (1970), Cameron (1951), Katz (1971), Lazarus and Serber (1968), Piaget and Lazarus (1969), Stevenson and Wolpe (1960, case #3), and Wolpe (1958, case #2).

Depression: Clinical Examples

Newly Married Blues

Upon getting married any couple faces a certain period of adjustment during which their personal habits and preferences become synchronized into some mutually satisfying pattern. In some marital relationships the wife becomes depressed during this adjustment period.

Assertion training could be used to treat this depression when the following conditions are present: *One*, the wife feels that she must place her husband's needs and preferences above her own in order to be a good wife. She need not be sacrificing important preferences. As a matter of fact, she is usually sacrificing minor preferences, for example, giving up the side of the bed that she slept on before her marriage or changing her normal sleeping times to fit his pattern. Objectively minor changes may acquire major significance when they represent a loss of some part of her own identity or a feeling of loss of power. In the early stages of marriage, particularly, a woman may be vulnerable to some identity loss if part of her identity has been attached to her birth name or to a loss of power if she must get her new husband's signature in order to keep her credit cards. *Two*, she resents making sacrifices, but feels guilty about feeling resentful. *Three*, she is afraid that if she were assertive the resulting conflict would be destructive to her marriage, but fears that if she is nonassertive that she will be submerged by her husband's personality. When these conflicts are seen as insurmountable, depression results and assertion training is needed.

Super Mom Syndrome

Bart (1971) has cogently noted that super moms often become depressed in middleage. In their youth they were extremely active—rushing to cart their children to dancing and music lessons, participating in community affairs, giving parties for their friends and their husband's business associates. When the children left, so did the energy and vitality. Assertion training would be appropriate when depression is caused by having expended so much energy in caring for other people that a woman has neglected her own development and needs and does not feel she has the right to care for herself.

Mid-Life Depression

This depression may occur in the woman's life when her husband is preoccupied with his work. He may be worrying about whether he still has time to make the dreams of his youth come true, or struggling with the knowledge that he will never be as successful as he had hoped, or striving to keep success (Sheehy, 1974). The woman is worried about what she's going to do with the rest of her life when the children are grown and is questioning her ability to change and to satisfy her new, emerging needs.

For those women who are searching for new directions in their lives but who don't know how to be constructively assertive with husbands and friends about desires to go back to work or school or to fulfill long-neglected needs, assertion training would be highly recommended. Among the many assertive problems which this type of woman is likely to encounter are: Telling her husband of her new developmental needs which must have consideration, counteracting her husband's fears of her new development and his objections to her new assertiveness, being assertive in the work world, and accepting her own legitimate assertive rights.

Depression Due to Loss

A widow or divorcee depressed over the loss of her husband may feel overwhelmed by new responsibilities. If she has not learned how to deal with banks, tax accountants, and unsolicited advice from friends and children, assertion training would help to decrease her sense of vulnerability and inadequacy. It would also give her skills she will need to take care of herself.

Dating

Women who are unable to form meaningful relationships because they lack effective interpersonal skills or who avoid getting emotionally close to a man fearing they would be completely dominated by him, are in need of assertion training. Some common areas in which these women need to develop assertive skills are initiating or limiting sex, asking for consideration or tenderness, expressing opinions different from their dates', initiating and refusing invitations, and expressing their own preferences for dating activities. Assertion training also would be appropriate when a woman feels that she can keep her boyfriend only by sacrificing her integrity and allowing her personal rights to be violated or when she is unable to ask for a more firm commitment in the relationship.

Job-Related Problems

Assertion training would be appropriate for a variety of work problems: being unjustly criticized, being the target of unwarranted backbiting and sexist remarks, receiving a discriminative salary, being unable to get her ideas accepted in meetings, being automatically rejected for higher positions merely because she is a woman. When the woman does not have effective assertive skills, she is likely to feel that no matter what she does there is no way that she can make a positive impact on the people in her work environment. For case studies giving examples of assertion training for work situations see Geisinger (1969), Wolpe (1958, case #1), Wolpe and Lazarus (1966, case #2).

Child Abuse

Assertion training may be a useful adjunct to therapy when a mother ricochets between nonassertive and aggressive behavior with her child—nonassertively denying her own needs by sacrificing herself for her child and, when she's drained, aggressively over-reacting to her feelings of helplessness and inadequacy that are triggered when the child cries or is disobedient and seems to be demanding yet more of her.

In such cases, a mother will need help in learning how to accept and assert her own needs, and how to express constructively her anger and disappointment with her child. She may also need training in assertion with her own parents and husband who may be highly critical of her and who, therefore, contribute to her feelings of inadequacy.

Couple Counseling

Therapists would generally agree that couples who fight aggressively or who pathologically avoid conflict would benefit from both learning how to express their requests and irritations assertively and how to listen with empathy. However, an accurate diagnosis of the situation is also needed: for example, when a wife has assertively told her husband that she is irritated about his repeatedly coming home late from work, her assertion will be for naught if her husband cannot assertively tell his employer that he is over-worked and needs some additional help! If the therapist does not help the husband to realize that he has an assertive problem, she is apt to interpret his coming home late as an indication that he loves his job more than he loves her and that he is a thoughtless person. Assertion training may be used for two purposes in couple counseling: to establish a more healthy communication pattern between the partners and to help the partners change those nonassertive or aggressive behaviors which contribute to the marital conflict.

Fensterheim (1972) reports a case study in which he has successfully used assertive training for marital problems and provides a relatively clear description of his procedures.

Psychosomatic Problems

When the psychosomatic problems are caused or exacerbated by tension, assertion training may be useful if the situations that arouse the anxiety and tension are ones in which the woman fails to assert herself and instead inhibits her spontaneous reactions and supresses her feelings of hurt, anger, or humiliation. There is some suggestive case study evidence that under these circumstances, assertion training in combination with other procedures, such as relaxation training, can benefit tension headaches (Dengrove, 1968), a variety of chronic dermatological problems (Seitz, 1953), some cases of asthma (Gardner, 1968; Wolpe and Lazarus, 1966, case #3), and abdominal spasm (Lazarus, 1965).

Drug or Alcohol Dependence

Assertion training could be used with clients who are dependent on drugs or alcohol when these are used primarily (1) to escape from conflict situations with other people who overpower them; (2) to indirectly express hurt and anger towards significant others; or (3) to disinhibit themselves so that they may be able to say things that they would ordinarily have been too afraid to express. In addition, assertion procedures would be appropriate with clients who have overcome their dependence problem but who still have trouble refusing drugs or alcohol. Salter (1949) has reported success with problems of alcoholism (pp. 200-201) and drug addiction (pp. 213-214).

Agoraphobia and Irrational Fears

Agoraphobia appears to be mainly a woman's problem. According to Fodor (1973), the majority of agoraphobes are women. Typical agoraphobes are married women whose phobias peak after approximately five years of marriage. While these women may appear to be self-sufficient and independent before marriage (Symonds, 1973), after marriage they become, gradually or suddenly, extremely afraid to be alone or to leave home. While nonassertion may not be the cause of this phobia, there is some suggestive case study evidence that assertion training in combination with other procedures may help to reduce it (Lazarus, 1966). (See also Hardy, Chapter 28.)

Rimm (1973) has some case study data which suggests that his *covert assertion* procedure may be helpful in reducing irrational fears. In this procedure the client is taught how to stop her obsessive thoughts and make forceful and assertive statements when she is in the actual phobic situation.

Aggressive Problems

Although assertion training procedures are most often used for problems of nonassertion, these procedures also show promise for modifying aggressive behavior (Gittleman, 1965; McNamara, 1970; Rimm, Hill, Brown and Stuart, 1974; Rimm, Keyson and Hunziker, 1971 cited in Rimm & Masters, 1974; Sarason, 1968; Sarason and Ganzer, 1973; Wallace, Teigen, Liberman and Baker, 1973). Rimm and Masters (1974) and Kaufmann and Wagner (1972) describe some special methods that therapists could use in working with aggressive problems.

CONCLUSION

Healthy, fully functioning people feel that they can make an effective impact on their environment; they engage in assertive behavior which makes them feel in charge of themselves and which effects other people in constructive ways.

Women's sex-role socialization decreases the likelihood that women will act assertively. When women are nonassertive, they usually feel a loss of personal power and self-esteem and an increased sense of anger and hurt. Various psychological problems may be caused or exacerbated by women's failure to act assertively. This view is supported by the clinical case study literature which suggests that assertion training is of help for a wide variety of psychological problems. Some of these problems were briefly discussed and the conditions under which assertion training would be an appropriate therapeutic strategy were presented.

I encourage therapists to help women achieve more fulfilling lives and reclaim their basic human rights by using procedures which will free them to develop assertion skills. Women need to learn that they can be *strong* and *effective*, as well as sensitive.

Table 16-1

How Socialization Messages May Negatively Affect Assertion

Socialization Message	Effect on Rights	Effect on Assertive Behavior	Healthy Message
Think of others first; give to others even if you're hurting. Don't be selfish.	I have no right to place my needs above those of other people.	When I have a conflict with someone else, I will give in and satisfy the other person's needs and forget about my own.	To be selfish means that a person always places her/his needs above other people's. This is undesirable human behavior. All healthy people have needs and strive to fulfill these as much as possible. Your needs are as important as other people's. When there is a conflict over need satisfaction, compromise is a useful way to handle the conflict.

Be modest and humble. Don't act superior to other people.	I have no right to do anything which would imply that I am better than other people.	I will discount my accomplishments and any compliments I receive. When I'm in a meeting, I will encourage other people's contributions and keep silent about my own. When I have an opinion which is different than someone else's, I won't express it; who am I to say that my opinion is better than another's.	It is undesirable to build yourself up at the expense of another person. However, you have as much a right as other people to show your abilities and take pride in yourself. It is healthy to enjoy one's accomplishments.

Table 16-1 (continued)

Be understanding and overlook trivial irritations. Don't be a bitch and complain.	I have no right to express anger or even to feel anger.	When I'm in a line and someone cuts in front of me, I will say nothing. I will not tell my boyfriend that I don't like his constantly interrupting me when I speak.	It is undesirable to deliberately nit pick. However, life is made up of trivial incidents and it is normal to be occasionally irritated by seemingly small events. You have a right to your angry feelings, and if you express them at the time they occur, your feelings won't build up and explode. It is important, however, to express your anger assertively rather than aggressively.

Help other people. Don't be demanding.	I have no right to make requests of other people.	It is undesirable to incessantly make demands of others. You do have a right to ask someone else to change their behavior if their behavior effects your life in a concrete way.
	I will not ask my friend to reciprocate babysitting favors.	
	I will not ask for a pay increase from my employer.	A request is not the same as a demand. However, if your rights are being violated and your requests for a change are being ignored, you have a right to make demands.

Table 16-1 (continued)

Be sensitive to other people's feelings. Don't hurt other people.	I have no right to do anything which might hurt someone else's feelings or deflate someone else's ego. I will not say what I really think or feel because that might hurt someone else. I will inhibit my spontaneity so that I don't impulsively say something that would accidentally hurt someone else.	It is undesirable to deliberately try to hurt others. However, it is impossible as well as undesirable to try to govern your life so as to **never** hurt **anyone**. You have a right to express your thoughts and feelings even if someone else's feelings occasionally get hurt. To do otherwise would result in your being phoney and in denying other people an opportunity to learn how to handle their own feelings. Remember that some people get hurt because they're unreasonably sensitive and others use their hurt to manipulate you. If you accidentally hurt someone else, you can generally repair the damage.

17

ASSERTIVENESS TRAINING FOR MOTHERS AND DAUGHTERS

Iris. G. Fodor, Janet L. Wolfe

Mother's Day: Bittersweet

> *Liberation. Extrication. Our mothers grow old and we watch them becoming us, and ourselves becoming them and whom do we extricate from what? And how: And do we pass this dear murderous entanglement on to our daughters with the family silver? Often I wonder if this is not some ultimate form of liberation: the most painful and the most elusive.*
>
> Martha Weinman Lear
> Mother's Day, 1975

Next to husbands, lovers, and bosses, women coming for assertiveness training appear to complain most about problems with parents, especially mothers. Unlike most other relationships (marriage, for example—where divorce provides some sort of terminus for an abrasive relationship), problems with one's mother can be life-long. And if not worked out, some of these problems may linger long after the parent's death.

Generational difficulties provide fertile ground for painful clashing and communication difficulties. Interacting with generational/cultural conflicts to further confound the difficulties, are life cycle shifts. The same two women, for example, may essentially reverse roles during their lifetime: for the first dozen or so years, a dependent child may be in conflict with an autonomy-striving mother, while ten or twenty years later, that same daughter, striving for her own independence, may be in conflict with her now dependent mother who is in the throes of an empty-nest syndrome. The parent-child conflict seems particularly emotionally-charged between mothers and daughters, their same-sexedness creating possibilities for competition and identification not normally present to nearly the same degree in the mother-son dyad. Painfully lacking are the cultural supports for dealing with these conflicts and life cycle shifts, and guidelines to help two women to be friends and care for each other as adults—the relationship they will have for most of their lives.

Traditional psychoanalytically-oriented psychotherapy involves women's spending years on the couch, discussing their mothers and ultimately getting the message that—whatever their particular disturbance—mother is to blame for it. With assertiveness training, mothers and daughters can both escape the flagrantly sexist assumptions inherent in Freudian psychoanalytic theories and move directly to learning newer and more effective ways of communicating and relating. And there is some evidence that these improved communication skills begin to generalize to other situations in which some of the same dynamics involved in the mother/daughter interaction are also evoked—for example, with work colleagues or spouses.

ASSERTIVENESS TRAINING FOR MOTHERS AND DAUGHTERS

Mother/daughter assertiveness issues can be handled in a variety of settings: 1) in individual counseling sessions, with one's "partner" absent; 2) in mother-daughter "couples" sessions (we often think of arranging for spouses to come in; why not mothers or daughters?); 3) in a general assertiveness group, with women of different ages; or 4) in a special mothers-and-daughters group, specifically geared toward mother-daughter interactions.

We shall focus here chiefly on AT sessions with mother-daughter couples and mother/daughter groups, in which an ongoing situation is worked on directly with both partners present. What emerges in these sessions are recurrent patterns of assertiveness problems which occur at key life cycle junctures. The mother/daughter conflicts are intensified at these times by the beliefs that each holds about her role and that of her partner. These beliefs arise from sex role socialization of parent/child roles, and serve (1) to create anxiety and guilt when mothers and daughters engage in assertive behavior, (2) to perpetuate demanding, commanding behavior, or (3) to inhibit assertive responding altogether. One is dealing, in other words, less with a social skills deficit than a problem in uprooting psychological blocks to assertion and other forms of interpersonal communication.

Assertiveness training with mothers and daughters involves five key steps:
1) Identification of the life cycle issues each party is dealing with;
2) Identification of the underlying beliefs that inhibit assertive responding;
3) Helping mothers and daughters figure out what their rights and goals are;
4) Helping mothers and daughters identify the emotions that interfere with pursuing their rights and goals (anxiety, hostility, depression, guilt), and the key "red flag" words that tend to trigger these feelings;
5) Reworking new scripts, trying out new ways of behaving and new patterns of communicating, and providing support and reinforcement for change.

The focus of this chapter will be to illustrate some of the recurring themes common to assertiveness problems between mothers and daughters, and to identify the goals seen as being most relevant for the successful resolution of each kind of conflict. Some of these issues also relate to general parent/child interactions.

MOTHERS' COMPLAINTS

The mothers of adolescents or older children who are still living at home comprise a large percentage of the mothers who come to assertiveness groups for help in dealing with their daughters. There are two main classes of problems: 1) Conflicts between a parent's mothering function and her need for time for herself (more common when children are young); and 2) power/control conflicts between the parental role and the increasing autonomy of an older child or adolescent who is seen as rebellious (more common in daughters from the ages of 13 or 14 through the ages of 60 or 70!)

Conflict Situation 1:

Mothers discounting their own needs to serve their families

As women who are also mothers are becoming more aware of the world outside and the ways in which they have made their own self-growth subordinate to that of their families, they are coming for help in dealing with the resistance of their family to change and ways of dealing with their own guilt and anxiety.

The counseling goal in working with the mother involves teaching her to learn to help tolerate the passive resistance or interpersonal conflict that results from her asserting her rights with a family that would rather have her continue her servant functions. Mother has to learn to be comfortable asserting her rights and putting what she desires openly on the table. She must not be intimidated into silence when other family members express displeasure at having long-accustomed services pulled out from under them.

Case Illustration

In an ongoing mother/daughter workshop, Marjorie, a divorced woman in her mid-40's who is just beginning her social life again, and Dominique, her 18-year-old daughter who works after school, babysits for her mother, and does many household chores, report many recent conflicts and bad feelings between them.

With the encouragement of the leaders, the pair selects a recent situation to role play in which mother was rude to a woman who called to ask Dominique to babysit on Saturday evening. During the first role-play—in which it was extremely difficult to get either of them to express how they were feeling—their pattern of poor communication became clear. M. did not tell D. how upset she was that D. might babysit for someone else when she wanted to go out; and D. did not tell her mother how angry and upset she was about her rudeness. When questioned about their self-statements, D. stated that she was afraid to upset her mother, while M. reported feeling guilty because she felt she should take care of her daughter and might be robbing her of her "teenagehood." Each woman was denying her own feelings, taking emotional responsibility for the other's feelings, then feeling angry and resentful because her own goals weren't getting met. Assertiveness training for these two women involved direct training in feeling talk. We started with M. and D. practicing positive feeling talk: e.g., M. told D. how pleased she was that she did the dishes and D. expressed how much she appreciated a special treat; and gradually worked up to letting these women express upset and angry feelings toward each other. The group was helpful in giving the pair feedback and support. The issue for these two women was to shift from the mother-daughter

Conflict Situation 1	Socialization Message	Mother's Self-Statements That Inhibit Assertive Responses	Mother's Feeling	Mother's Behavior
Mother asks for help from her youngster for what is considered a "mother's" job: e.g., help with household chores, shopping, babysitting for younger children; wanting children to provide own transportation, to move out, or be more economically independent.	Mothers are self-sacrificing. The highest feminine duty is to care for children. One's own needs don't count.	My family needs me; I have no right to ask her to help me. It's my job to please my family; I'm being selfish.	Conflicted, guilty, anxious, self-hating. **Life Cycle Issue:** For mother: Shift from mothering role to more autonomous person.	Plays the martyr, is nagging or demanding; and periodically explodes.

role to that of two friends living together; sharing responsibilities and concern about the other, but still in touch as well with what each wanted for herself and able to put what she wanted on the table for discussion. (In family settings where such a favorable balance is more difficult to obtain—e.g., where mate and youngsters "gang" up on the "defecting" mother—separate participation by the mother in a women's group as a means of receiving ongoing support is strongly encouraged.)

Conflict Situation 2:

> *"I'm still the boss and you have no right to question my authority or the rules;"* or, *"How dare you speak to me in that tone of voice!"*

It has long been acknowledged that mothers and daughters often have particularly stormy times together in the adolescent-parent power struggle. Mothers will come to clinics dragging reluctant daughters with the mothers reciting a long list of complaints, while the daughters either sulk, fume, or occasionally disagree in a highly vocal way. Usually, it is the stubborn holding on to power or enforcing of rules that becomes the central area of conflict, with both parties digging in and taking sides. These situations often erupt into stormy battles, long periods of silence, and a nerve-jangling tension level for the entire family. Occasionally, the culmination may be the teenager's running away from home. Issue 2 somewhat relates to issue 1 in that the control battle often involves the daughter's being ordered to take over what she really considers to be the mother's chores.

Case Illustration

In an ongoing assertiveness group for mothers and daughters, Mary, a suburban mother in her 40's, arrives with her sullen 16-year-old daughter, Dorothy, in tow.
M: Her attitude isn't the way I'd like it to be. I ask her to clean up her room and she eventually does it, in her own good time! But I'd like her to do it without my having to keep nagging her.
D: The way I look at it, I'm going to bitch all I want, 'cause I get the work done.
They role play a recent problem interaction:
M: How come you haven't folded the laundry yet?
D (with exasperated tone): How many times do I have to tell you I'll

Conflict Situation (from mother's viewpoint)	**Socialization Message**	**Mother's Internal Beliefs**	**Mother's Feelings**	**Mother's Behavior Toward Daughter**
My daughter is impossible; she won't do anything I ask her without a fight (situations: coming home on time, doing chores, homework, etc.	I'm the boss. Mothers must be respected: honor thy mother.	My daughter's treating me nastily degrades me. How dare she treat me this way? What a rotten ingrate she is.	Hurt, rejected, angry.	Critical, commanding, yelling.

	Daughter's Internal Beliefs	**Daughter's Feelings**	**Daughter's Behavior**
	How dare she treat me like that, order me around, make me do her dirty work.	Anger, resentment.	Silent treatment, hostile voice tone. sarcasm, non-performance of work.

Life Cycle Issue

For mother-daughter: power shift from authoritarian, protective parent of a small child to more egalitarian relationship of older woman to younger one.

do it after Star Trek? Why do you always have to keep interrupting my favorite TV programs?
M: It's been four hours already. (Aside: In real life I would get upset and blow my top and have a really unpleasant fight, then leave feeling guilty.)

The other group members, some of whom have similar problems, are very helpful at this point. They point out that M. insists that things must be done according to her timetable, and that D. should behave and feel differently than she does. D., with her own set of shoulds, is demanding that her mother absolutely not treat her like a child, order her about, and deny her the right to take care of her room in her own fashion. The group helps D. and M. to construct alternative scripts to yelling and blaming/sulking and cursing, with another mother/daughter pair with similar problems modeling an alternative way of handling the same situation:

M: D., I'm really feeling uncomfortable with what's been going on between us—the tangles we get into over chores. I'd really like it if we could sit down and figure out some better way of setting things up. How do you feel about that?
D: That's just fine with me ... I get so annoyed when you cut into my time, then I snap at you and feel cruddy afterward. To tell you the truth, I guess I feel the more you tell me to do something, the less I want to.
M: I think I know how you feel—I used to get bugged when my mother kept reminding me, too. But I also hope you can appreciate how I feel: I'd like some leisure too, but it's really hard to get the time just to sit and unwind, unless there's more sharing. How about us making a deal: I'll really bend over backward this week to stop reminding you ... and in return you really try to get the laundry folded some time before the end of the day? Deal?
D: O.K.

Out of the group problem solving arises a solution in which M. and D. sit down together to assign chores in general, and D. assumes the responsibility for setting her own timetable. "Should-ing" and blaming eliminated, there is space for mother and daughter to quietly share with each other what it is like to be 16 with a need to express oneself as she wishes; and what it is like to be 40 and to have responsibility for running a household with minimal support.

DAUGHTERS' COMPLAINTS ABOUT MOTHERS

Generally in assertiveness training workshops, adult daughters seem to complain more about their mothers' behaviors than vice versa. They report that the mother is more effective in asserting her rights and wants and that they, the daughters, are often paralyzed at these times into non-assertiveness. It appears to be a collusional system, in that both mother and daughter believe that what mother wants is more important than what daughter wants.

Common to most of these situations are the following beliefs on the part of the daughter:
1. If I don't do what my mother wants, I'm a bad daughter.
2. I can't show anger toward my mother.
3. Her needs are more important than mine.
4. What's the use, she's older and has always been this way; she'll never change, so why try?
5. If I really tell her how I feel she'll die, reject me, disown me.
6. If I move to Hawaii or China to avoid my mother, it will all go away.

There are at least three major types of situations that are very frequently brought up by women having difficulties asserting themselves with their mothers. All of them involve issues of autonomy and the right to adopt independent lifestyles that are often in direct conflict with the *mother*s wishes and lifestyle. The following three cases will illustrate these conflict situations.

Conflict Situation 3:

"My mother treats me like a kid."

The goal in this type of mother/daughter system is to shift the dominance-dependency relationship to one involving two separate adults.

Case Illustration

May, a 50-year-old public relations executive, accompanied her 26-year-old daughter Dee to an ongoing mothers-and-daughters assertiveness workshop.
D: My mother takes over my life . . .
M (interrupting): *That* isn't the problem!
(The group laughs at what is clearly a live example of the problem the daughter has presented. The leaders suggest that the pair select a recent problem situation and role play it as it occurred. The situation is

Conflict Situation 3	Daughter's Internal Dialogue/Beliefs	Daughter's Feelings	Behavior Toward Mother
Daughter is living away from home, but mother is still interfering in her life: e.g., buying her clothes, demanding to be consulted on major decisions interfering with rearing of grandchildren.	I am still a child and need my mother vs. How dare she still continue to treat me like a child.	Helpless, weak, insecure, anxious, angry, resentful.	Compliant, seeks mother's approval. Attacks mother when her independent striving is not approved of.

Mother's Socialization Message	Mother's Internal Dialogue/Beliefs	Mother's Feelings When Daughter Asserts Own Needs	Mother's Behavior Toward Daughter
A mother's job is to care for her children throughout life.	My daughter is helpless, needs me to take care of her. She doesn't do anything right. The world is a cruel place and I must save her from catastrophe.	Hurt, rejected, angry.	Overprotective, overbearing; hypercritical, attacking; punishing.

that D. has just gotten a new apartment and phones to tell her mother about it.)

D (sounding very excited): I just signed a lease for a nifty apartment in Greenwich Village!
M: How long a lease?
D: Two years.
M: Two years! Why such a long lease, dear? You don't know what you may be doing in two years. Also, that's an unsafe neighborhood for you to be living in by yourself and it means you'll also have a long subway ride to work. Did you look around enough?
D (now close to tears): But, Mom...

When M. questions D.'s motives for moving, D. reports that she feels her competency is being questioned and that she is unable to defend her reasons for the move to her mother. It is clear that she feels insecure in dealing with her authoritative and very competent mother, yet is feeling needy of her approval. M. appears to have difficulty listening to her daughter without questioning and criticizing.

Mother needs help in seeing how undermining her behavior appears to her daughter, while the daughter needs support from the group for her view of the situation, as well as some guidelines for alternative ways of behaving with her mother. Several young women volunteer to role-play D.'s situation, with her mother playing herself. These daughters are helpful in articulating those aspects of the mother's behavior which interfere with D. being more assertive in dealing with her. In addition, one of the young women is skilled in presenting some autonomous behavior. Out of these role-plays, a discussion emerges about some of the boundary problems that M. and D. appear to have. M. appears too ready to step into D.'s life and D., who keeps asking for her mother's approval, sets herself up for these "takeover" situations. Using the scripts from the other role models, M. and D. do a role reversal as a way of putting them in touch with the other person's feelings and perspective. During the role play, they follow one group member's suggestion that as a step toward recognizing each other as adults, they use first names instead of "mother" or "dear." In the final role-play sequence by M. and D., we see a change:

D: I just signed a lease for a nifty apartment in Greenwich Village.
M: How long a lease?
D: Two years. I'm delighted to find such an attractive apartment at this price, so close to my friends and to the places I like to go to.
M: I'm really pleased for you! I'm looking forward to visiting you in your new place.

At the end of the workshop, when each member was asked what she had learned, they replied:

M: I learned to cut the umbilical cord and to recognize emotionally and intellectually the right for D.'s inner sanctum; and I'm going to do my best from now on to try and not invade it.

D: I think I'm going to try to stop and ask myself, before I pick up the phone, why I'm calling my mother. And then when I've decided I really want to communicate and talk to my mother, I will call just to talk.

Conflict Situation 4:

"I must be a good girl."

For young adults in our rapidly-changing culture, some of the major assertiveness problems often revolve around value differences between the older generation of parents and the younger adult. Nowhere in our history has there been so much social change in so brief a time period. Many assertiveness difficulties in young women center around such issues as telling their parents that they want a career rather than marriage; informing them that they are living with their boyfriends; or that they no longer subscribe to family moral and/or religious beliefs and practice.

Women in particular are pressured into following familial wishes. Often the issues involve resistance to being channeled into the traditional sex role choice.

Case Illustrations:

In many workshops with young women, a recurrent issue involves telling mothers of untraditional choices. This is often perceived as very disappointing to the families, who usually hold more traditional sex role expectations for their daughters. The following illustrates such an interaction during a role play in a women's AT group (Wolfe & Fodor, 1975):

MOTHER (role-played by group member): I hope you've gotten that Ph.D. nonsense out of your head by now . . . father and I have been so upset. We lie awake at nights, worrying about you.

HELAINE: I'm sorry—I really didn't mean to upset you so much. But I really *do* want to go; it would mean so much to me. I saw my old professor and he's really encouraging me to go, and is sure I'll have no trouble getting in. I'm really excited about the possibility of going into biology.

Conflict Situation 4	Mother's Socialization Message	Daughter's Internal Dialogue/Beliefs	Daughter's Feelings	Daughter's Behavior Toward Mother
Daughter informs mother of a life choice that is not parentally approved: e.g., moving out of parents' home; deciding not to marry or have children; going to grad school; living with boyfriend; choosing to be gay; getting a divorce.	Mother's job is to instill good morality; to guide her daughter to the correct decision and thus avert disaster.	I have to be and do what my mother wants or I'm a rotten daughter. If I tell her I'm living with my boyfriend, it'll kill her. How dare she tell me how to live.	Guilt Anxiety Anger	Hiding of facts; avoidance of communication. Continued seeking for approval; occasional bursts of anger.
Life Cycle Issue:		**Mother's Internal Dialogue/Beliefs**	**Mother's Feelings When Daughter Asserts Self**	**Mother's Behavior Toward Daughter**
Daughter is autonomous from family; family has to accept her going away and her differences in life-style choices.		My daughter must do what I want or else she (and I) are failures. She must benefit from my experience.	Put down, rejected, angry, self-righteous.	Gets ill, sulks, withdraws. Lectures, threatens. commands, ridicules,

MOTHER: Look, we're not telling you this because we want to interfere or anything. But I really think you should go out, get a job, and concentrate on your social life, meet some nice guy. You know, you're not getting any younger. It really hurts us to see you sitting here on weekends, writing papers, when you could be going out and having a good time. I just don't see how there's any future for you in this... getting a Ph.D.
HELAINE: (close to tears at this point, she stops the role-play.)
THERAPIST: What's going on now? What were you just feeling?
HELAINE: I was feeling really put-down. I guess I was thinking, "she's right; I'm really not cut out to finish a doctorate." There probably is something wrong with me, that I'm not married or at least in a relationship.
THERAPIST (to the person playing the role of the mother): Joyce, what was your reaction to Helaine's dialogue with you?
JOYCE: Well, she did stick somewhat to her guns and let me know she was excited about the possibility of going to grad school. And she did look me in the eye. But to tell you the truth... I felt that if I kept up badgering her just a little more, she'd finally begin to feel guilty enough that she'd probably back off. She already apologized for upsetting me so much!

A very similar script was elicited by another client who felt intensely anxious to the point of nausea, at the thought of telling her mother that she was gay. In both these situations, there is an overconcern with what the mother will feel, a prediction of a catastrophic response, and enormous guilt over being responsible for upsetting the mother. To deal with these situations, group support in script writing and modeling responses must be supplemented by cognitive response. First the client must see that she is not responsible for the mother's emotions; and that if the mother chooses to upset herself, that is unfortunate, but not awful or catastrophic. In the beginning role-plays, the clients often cry in confronting their mothers around these issues, but behavior rehearsal seems to help them to acquire the strength to see that their own needs count.

In the above situation, when the daughter finally had the conversation with her mother after the group, she met with a mother who expressed distress, puzzlement, and some hurt, but who was willing to discuss the situation with her daughter. As is frequently the case when people convey some difficult communication, the anticipated catastrophe did not occur; rather, mother and daughter were on the road to a newer, more egalitarian and more communicative relationship.

Conflict Situation 5:

"I must take care of my mother."

Women in our culture more frequently have the responsibility for caring for aging mothers and mothers-in-law than do men. From young adulthood on, a common situation brought up in assertiveness groups concerns demands on the part of a mother to spend holidays with her children, or to be taken shopping or to the doctor's or dentist's, or to spend long visits at the hospital or at home with an aging parent, when such demands conflict with the daughter's own plans or preferences. The dilemma is strikingly similar to that of a mother of young children trying to decide how much time she is willing to give up and attempting to deal with the ensuing guilt. In this case, the daughter must deal with the guilt resulting from the belief that a daughter's role is to cater to her mother, particularly as she gets older. The dilemma is a difficult one, compounded by how much time one has to devote and lack of clarity as to what mother's and daughter's rights are at such a developmental stage, and by the realities of the problems of an aging parent. Assertiveness training sessions dealing with this conflict situation generally involve a good deal of clarification of rights and responsibilities, with the group exchanging experiences and attempting to help the woman raising the problem to become comfortable with whatever amount of time or caring she is willing to give her mother.

This is often a painful and difficult situation, particularly if the mother is alone, elderly or sickly. In the case of mothers-in-law, the situation may be compounded by additional pressure from the woman's husband. Often, the assertiveness problem is not so much with the parent, as with other relatives (e.g., sisters or brothers) who do not hold up their share of caretaking duties. The solution ideally involves the woman sitting down with other persons who might have some share in the responsibility for the parent, deciding how much time each is willing or able to give, and working out assignments. Since this is often a common problem for many women in the group, other members frequently share experiences and the session becomes a group problem-solving experience.

Case Illustration

M: I'm making Easter dinner Sunday, and I would like you and Jim to come over.
D (postponing): I'll let you know.

Conflict Situation 5	Socialization Messages	Daughter's Internal Dialogue/Beliefs	Daughter's Feelings	Behavior Toward Mother
Mother wants daughter to spend holidays with her; take her shopping or to dentist; visit relatives; spend all week visiting in hospital with her; take her into her home to live.	Family ties must always come first. Mother and daughters especially must be close.	I have no right to my own life; it's selfish. Daughters should cater to mothers. That rotten woman—she always gets her own way.	Guilty, conflict-ridden. Resentful, angry	Complies and resents it. Avoids dealing with it (e.g., by moving far away). Asserts self or explodes.

Life Cycle Issue		Mother's Internal Dialogue/Beliefs	Mother's Feelings When Daughter Asserts Self	Mother's Behavior Toward Daughter
Aging parent asks for more caring and attention at a time daughter is busy pursuing own goals.		You're a rotten, selfish daughter not to do what I want. After I've sacrificed the best years of my life for you, it's awful if you don't reciprocate. Who else can I depend on?	Rejected, depressed. Anxious, threatened. Angry.	Demanding, guilt-tripping (calls her selfish, ungrateful). Crying, clutching. Attacking, blaming.

(later that week):
M: I'm shopping for everything today and I'd like to know now if you're coming for dinner.
D: I'll have to let you know later.
M: You know we have practically no family, and I'm really counting on you to be with me for the holiday.
D: O.K., I'll be there.

In this situation, the daughter and her husband wished to take a weekend trip over Easter, but felt she could not tell her mother how she felt. Instead, she gave up her own plans, went to her mother's, and, resenting being there, had many angry exchanges with her as a result.

The following role-play of this same kind of situation (this time, dealing with Thanksgiving dinner) provided a group solution to this very typical situation.

M: I'm planning on you and Jim coming for Thanksgiving. I so look forward to having the family all together.
D: As you know, Jim and I have very few long weekends off from work, and so we decided we would like to take a trip. There are some wonderful charters available. I know this is disappointing to you, but perhaps we can plan our own private Thanksgiving celebration when we come back the following weekend. I know it's hard for you to have some of the family absent, but in this way, we can have a special celebration on our own later.

A therapist colleague of ours recently described her handling of such a situation. A week before Christmas, when she was feeling depressed because her daughter would not be spending the holiday with her, she met another woman in the same situation who was very depressed and agitated. She invited this woman to be with her that Christmas, and they discovered that they had much in common. A friendship developed and they enjoyed their unusual celebration more than if they had been sitting with offspring who resented spending the time with them. Women frequently have a hard time realizing that by being at their dependent mother's beck and call, they are not being entirely nurturant, but in fact may be robbing their mother of the freedom (or necessity) to develop other friendships and interests and thus extricate themselves from what is often a neurotic dependency.

Even more guilt-arousing situations involve ill or lonely elderly parents who are making what seem unreasonable demands for time or care. There are few guidelines for these exceptionally difficult situations. Particularly sad is the fact that the daughters often have the support of friends or counseling groups, while the elderly parent is more alone. Since these situations are recurring more and more, there is a need to incorporate some group problem-solving around these very difficult issues involving a person's relating to an aging parent into community mental health programs. Thus, while one group may support a daughter and help her to become more comfortable telling her mother (for example) that she doesn't want her to live with her, more supportive work can be done with the elderly parent, helping her find alternatives to being alone or in a hospital.

SUMMARY

As is increasingly found to be the case in assertiveness training where reduction of anxiety, anger and guilt are crucial, assertiveness training for mothers and daughters often involves more cognitive restructuring than skills training. The goal of these workshops and sessions is to help mothers and daughters construct new "scripts" and learn to talk openly about their wants and feelings, so that they may evolve a relationship based on friendship between two adult women who enjoy a special bond of sharing and closeness. Assertiveness training can help these women to increase their self-esteem and ability to function independently; and give them the ability to choose lifestyles and ways of relating derived not from outmoded obligations and duties set forth by society, but on newer, freer, and more individually-determined bases.

18

DEVELOPING ASSERTIVENESS IN CHILDREN

Judith S. Thoft

The use of assertiveness training as a means of helping young children develop effective social skills has been explored by the author using a group approach.

Justification for helping children alter their social skills is provided by a variety of theoretical positions. Theoreticians such as Erikson (Maier, 1969), R. W. White (Mussen, Conger, and Kagan, 1963), Bronfenbrenner (1970), and Havighurst (1953), have stressed the importance for the middle-age child to successfully master key developmental tasks, including those of getting along with his/her age mates and achieving a sense of belongingness in a peer group, in order that future social development not be endangered.

Since the acquisition of social skills is particularly critical for the middle-age child, fourth, fifth, and sixth grade students from a middle-class elementary school were screened to identify children who lacked effective social skills. On the basis of the screening results, an Assertiveness Training Group was formed which consisted of ten 4th, 5th, and 6th grade male and female students who represented both extremes of an assertiveness continuum. Some of the children's lack of peer acceptance seemed due to their minimal level of social activity, while others seemed to lack the acceptance and support of their peers due to the aggressive quality of the social interactions.

The assertiveness group met once a week for 14 weeks and was led by the author and a male, first year doctoral student. Both the leader and the assistant leader had had experience in behavioral counseling. Children in the group were taught to: (a) define, and give examples of assertive, non-assertive, and aggressive behavior, (b) examine their own and others' behavior in terms of specific assertive components, and (c) engage in systematic behavior rehearsals of modeled assertive components. Audio-tapes, videotapes, and role-plays were used to aid children in observing and practicing new assertive behaviors.

Since the literature has provided little information regarding assertiveness training with children, the assertiveness program described herein was based upon common elements from several adult assertiveness training models. For example, assertive behavior components such as "greeting talk" (i.e., initiating social contacts), "feeling talk," "asking why," etc., described by Rathus (1973) provided the topics around which several of the meetings were organized. In addition, modeling and behavior rehearsal procedures, such as those described by Wolpe (1969), Jakubowski-Spector (1973), and Alberti and Emmons (1974), often coupled with corrective video-tape feedback such as that described by Serber (1972), were adapted for use with children. During the first several group meetings the assertive situations and role-play scenarios which formed the core of the program were developed by the leader and were based upon several years' observations of the kinds of non-assertive/assertive/aggressive behavior situations in which middle-age children are typically involved. The assertive situations and role-play scenarios used during the last several meetings were presented by the children from their personal experiences. At the end of each meeting specific tasks which were an extension of the group meeting were assigned as homework activities for the following week. The following is a general outline.

A FORMAT FOR ASSERTIVENESS TRAINING WITH CHILDREN

Week 1

During the first meeting of the assertiveness group the leader defined and gave examples of assertive and aggressive behavior. The children viewed the animated film, "Hopscotch" (Churchill Films, 1972) which portrays a young child trying out both assertive and aggressive behaviors in his attempt to make friends. The children learned very quickly to pick out examples of aggressive and assertive behaviors in the film and to note the consequences of those behaviors.

Week 2

During the second meeting the concepts of assertive and aggressive behavior were reviewed, and the concept of non-assertive behavior was introduced. In addition, two assertive behavior components designated as: (a) making contact or greeting an individual, and (b) eye contact, were discussed and modeled and the children given an opportunity to practice them. The following sequence of activities was used to help the children learn to make more assertive contact with others:

1. The leader asked the children, "What would you say when—?", and described a number of situations in which the children would be required to make a greeting statement. The children responded to each of the situations.
2. An audio-tape was presented in which highly social children from another school modeled assertive responses in replying to the same situations which had been presented to the group.
3. The leader repeated these greeting situations to give the children in the group an opportunity to respond again in ways which they considered more assertive.

During the first presentation of these stems, the children tended to respond very softly and either haltingly or with a minimum of words, as exemplified by the following:
"What would you say when you knock on your neighbor's door trying to sell a school magazine subscription?"
Martha: "Would you like to buy umm—would you like to buy umm—a magazine, umm—a newspaper, a magazine subscription?"
The group then listened to the audio-taped models of spontaneous responses to this same stem which were as follows:
Liane: "Hello, Mrs. Hartley, would you like to buy a subscription to the *Reader's Digest* for the Coffin School?"
Kirsten: "Hello, Mrs. Milligan. I'm selling subscriptions to *Time* magazine. Would you like to buy one?"
Following presentation of the audio-taped models, the children in the group were asked to respond to the "greeting" stems a second time. In general the children responded more fluently and more fully. For example, the child mentioned above altered her response the second time in the following way.
Martha: "Would you like, would you like to buy a subscription for a magazine?"

Week 3

During the first part of this meeting the children's cooperative and competitive behaviors, which emerged during their participation in activities requiring teamwork, were videotaped in order to provide useful material for the children to study at a subsequent meeting.

During the second part of the meeting the assertive behavior component of "feeling talk" was defined and modeled by the leader. The leader asked members of the group to discuss their "least favorite" or their "most favorite" subjects as a means of eliciting spontaneous examples of "feeling talk." When these occurred, the leader pointed them out and reinforced them, as in the following transcript in which Meg had been describing the Eskimo practice of killing fish:

Meg: "The next morning when they wake up they have—blood soup" (verbalized slowly, in an ominous way).
Anthony: "Oh! Sickening! Blood!"
Leader: "Did anyone notice how Meg and Andy spoke then? Those were good examples of 'feeling statements.'"

The children responded by noting Meg's and Andy's tones of voice, facial expressions, and the fact that Meg had drawn her words out. This segment was also videotaped to provide children with examples of their own "feeling talk" or lack thereof, which they could study at the next meeting.

Week 4

The video-tape which had been made the previous week was shown during this meeting. The children were asked to pick out those children on the tape who demonstrated assertive eye contact and "feeling talk." The tape was stopped in instances where eye contact and "feeling talk" were noted, and the child who had been exhibiting them was complimented. During the presentation of this videotape Tom exclaimed that he wished Anthony, who was absent, were there so that he could see himself and become more aware of how he was acting and talking. The members of the group then agreed that it was interesting for them to see themselves behaving with other members of the group. Alice emphasized,

"It doesn't seem like you (herself) talking. If you were taping me right now, like if I was watching myself, I don't look like myself."

Leader: "You mean you don't have a sense of how you look while you're talking to other people and how they see you. And when you see this, you're seeing yourself as other people see you?"

Alice: "Yeh! Right!"

The assertive component "accepting compliments" was examined by means of a sequence of activities similar to those described under *Week 2* in regard to "greeting" statements. Audiotaped responses of children from another school were again used as models for group members' behavior rehearsals.

Week 5

During this meeting the component of "talking about oneself" (i.e. being able to appropriately sustain the focus of a conversation on oneself) was introduced. A videotape was shown in which the leader had conducted individual interviews with children from another school who were considered highly social. Group members were instructed to observe the models' ability to respond to the interviewer's questions fully and to sustain the focus of the conversation on themselves.

The concept of "body posture" was then explained with demonstrations given by the group leaders. The leaders emphasized that body posture reflected how one was feeling in a given situation, and had an effect on how one was perceived by others. The interview tape was then replayed without the sound, and the children discussed the impressions which the models' body posture conveyed.

Week 6

This meeting was devoted to continued practice in sustaining the focus of conversation on oneself, and, also, to the introduction of the assertive component of "asking why" when unreasonable requests are made.

The children paired up and role-played interviews similar to the ones they had seen on the training videotape the preceding week. Children who were not currently engaged in a role-play were instructed to observe and comment on specific assertive behavior components of the interviewer and interviewee including: eye contact, body posture, honest expression of feelings, and the ability to sustain the focus of conversation.

The leader introduced the assertive technique of "asking why" by eliciting from the group requests that might have been made of them in the past, which they felt were unreasonable but did not know how to respond to. During the remainder of the meeting the leader described, and the children role-played, a series of situations in which an unreasonable request was made. The child of whom the request was being made was instructed to stand up for his/her rights and respond to the request in a way which he/she considered equitable for both parties.

Week 7

During this meeting the leader introduced the concept of "assertive talk," i.e. not letting others take advantage of one, and the children practiced making appropriate responses in this type of situation.

In introducing the concept of "assertive talk," the leader gave examples of situations in which one person was being taken advantage of by another, modeled responses which were either nonassertive or aggressive, and then contrasted these with responses which were assertive. The children were instructed to role-play several scenarios devised by the leader. As had happened on several other occasions, these scenarios prompted many of the children to recall similar incidents which had actually occurred and about which they felt disappointment or anger at their own lack of assertiveness. For example, the leader had described the scenario: "A child is being denied his/her turn in a game. How should that child respond?" After this scenario had been role-played Martha volunteered a similar personal situation in which she had been appointed Captain of her class softball team a few days earlier and had wanted to be first at bat. But Terry, a very popular girl in the class, had argued with her about it and Martha had backed down and batted third. Martha was then given an opportunity to role-play this situation. The children who were not participating in the role-play focused on Martha's eye contact, body posture, and expression of feeling; commented on what aspects were assertive and which ones were not; and made suggestions about how her responses could have been more effective. Martha then re-enacted the role-play making an effort to incorporate the observers' suggestions in her responses.

Weeks 8, 9 and 10

The purpose of these meetings was to give the children additional practice in conceiving and role-playing assertive responses in a variety of interpersonal situations.

The children were aided in writing descriptions of personal social situations in which assertive behavior was needed. Each child role-played his/her situation with the other children taking the role of the antagonists. Allen, for example, described being invited to a classmate's house to spend the night and not knowing how to say "no." The situation was so convincingly enacted by Billy, who played the aggressive friend and Allen, who became entangled in a series of inadequate excuses, that the other children began calling out responses to Allen which they felt would be more effective. This particular role-play prompted Allen and Meg to describe personal situations in which they had difficulty saying "no" to a particular classmate who insisted upon joining them frequently or visiting them at home. Again the other children suggested useful responses. At this point several children expressed concern about hurting others' feelings and suggested that perhaps they oughtn't to disappoint or risk hurting others by declining invitations even when they wished to. The leaders re-emphasized that the members of the group also had feelings and rights, and that they were not being fair to themselves in denying these rights.

Weeks 11 and 12

The procedure followed during the 11th and 12th meetings consisted of modeling, behavior rehearsals, and peer and video-tape feedback.

During the eleventh meeting each child was video-taped as he/she role-played a personal social problem with one of the leaders, received suggestions from the other children about what he/she might do to make his/her responses more assertive, and then re-enacted the role-play in an effort to incorporate those suggestions. If a child had difficulty incorporating the suggestions, the child who had made them participated in the role-play with the leader in order to model the suggested behavior.

During the twelfth meeting the children viewed the previous week's video-tape in order to see their own and other children's repeated attempts to behave more assertively in a particular situation. After viewing each child's video-taped situation the group members filled out "Assertive Role-Play Rating Sheets" devised by the leader. The behavioral components on which each of the children were rated were: a) eye contact; b) body posture; c) what the person said and the manner in which he said it; and d) the overall assertive impression created by the person.

The children were perceptive about which behavioral cues created an impression of assertiveness and which did not, and continued to give one another appropriate suggestions for improving social interactions. The reliability of the independent ratings given by the children was surprisingly high, and in most cases their ratings coincided with the leaders'. The children were extremely attentive and enthusiastic during the eleventh and twelfth meetings, and in most instances were able to appropriately modify their role-play behavior. Their response during these meetings and subsequent group evaluation statements suggests the need to incorporate the procedures of these two meetings earlier and more extensively in future assertiveness group programs.

Weeks 13 and 14

The final two meetings were devoted to evaluation procedures, discussion of various aspects of the course, and termination of the groups.

SOME OBSERVATIONS AND SUGGESTIONS

The children were enthusiastic about most of the activities and materials used throughout the course and seemed able to respond to them appropriately. Activities which involved videotape feedback and the opportunity to rate oneself as well as others, seemed particularly appealing and beneficial.

It had been thought that presenting group members with video-tapes of highly social children interacting spontaneously in their natural settings would be an effective modeling technique. However, this was found to be a more cumbersome and less practical means of achieving appropriate modeling than video-taping children who had rehearsed specific responses to narrowly defined situations. The latter approach, while it seemed less "natural" increased the likelihood that the children in the group would attend to the behavior components which the leader felt were critical and not be distracted by behaviors which were not to be imitated. The use of children's carefully rehearsed behavior sequences rather than more complex *in vivo* responses as models for the group is, therefore, recommended for future children's assertiveness programs.

Another change which will be implemented with future groups will be to create a more homogeneous group with respect to the kinds of skills which are lacking. The current group consisted of several children who were non-assertive and several who were aggressive. Had the group consisted entirely of children identified as predominantly one or the other, both modeling and behavior rehearsals might have been carried out more effectively.

At the conclusion of this assertiveness training program the group leaders, the children's teachers, and the children themselves were able to provide numerous examples in which the children's classroom and playground behavior had become more assertive. In addition, however, several instances were observed in which children's attempts to behave more assertively were either ignored or responded to negatively by teachers or other children. These observations suggest that some restructuring of the child's environment is necessary to insure that skills learned and rehearsed during training are transferred to the natural environment. Ideally, future children's assertiveness groups should provide for this purposeful restructuring by 1) more out-of-group practice assignments, to improve the transfer of assertive skills, and 2) instructing teachers, parents, and peers in appropriate responses to new assertive behaviors. This would increase the likelihood that the child's initial *in vivo* attempts to engage in assertive behavior, rather than being ignored or punished, will be reinforced and strengthened, thereby increasing the probability that they will become an integral part of the child's behavioral repertoire.

19

CASE STUDIES IN ASSERTIVE TRAINING WITH ADOLESCENTS

William D'Amico, Jr.

Modification of covert events has been receiving increased attention in the literature since being discussed in a benchmark article by Homme (1965). Since that time, the thoughts, images, memories, sensations, perceptions, and cognitions of the client have become legitimate phenomenae for the behaviorist in both research and treatment strategy. Central to this work has been a regard of covert events as intervening, mediating behavior between the behavioral contingencies of stimulus-response and response-consequence. Where regarded as stimuli, as discussed in the work of Barber and Hahn (1964) and Waters and McDonald (1973), these events have been shown to effect the arousal state of an individual. Where regarded as responses, as discussed in the work of Homme (1965) and Bandura (1969), these events have been viewed as antecedents to subsequent overt and covert responses. And finally, where regarded as consequences, as discussed in the work of Cautela (1969, 1973) and Kazdin (1973), these events have been shown to possess reinforcing properties to either increase or decrease associated covert or overt responses. The reader is directed to the above articles or to Mahoney (1974) or Meichenbaum (1974) for a more complete discussion of covert events.

Discussed below are two strategies involving the modification of both overt and covert behaviors that were applied to the procedure for acquiring assertive behavior reported in Alberti and Emmons (1974). The first strategy utilizes a counter-covert conditioning approach, the principles of which were derived from the work of Wolpe (1973) and Cautela (1969, 1973). This strategy fosters the acquisition of assertive behavior through the prior learning of an interpersonal anxiety management procedure. The second strategy utilizes a cognitive-behavioral approach, the principles of which were derived from the work of Meichenbaum (1974), Meichenbaum and Turk (1976), Meichenbaum and Cameron (1973) and Spivack and Shure (1974). This strategy fosters the management of interpersonal anxiety through the prior learning of a procedure for the acquisition of assertive behavior.

COUNTER-COVERT CONDITIONING STRATEGY

This strategy was implemented with a fourteen-year-old adolescent boy whose referral problem was a difficulty in maintaining any relationships with his peers. He was a successful member of his school's sports teams, though he was more known for his size and physique than for any specific athletic ability. He regarded himself more as an enforcer (whose role it was to inhibit the top scorers of the opposing team) than as a scorer for his own team. His athletic prowess had enabled him to meet quite a few of his peers, especially girls, but he had never been able to develop any lasting friendships with peers of either sex. Through pre-treatment role-play, it was observed that he possessed a limited repertoire of communication behaviors, all of which failed to take into account the perspective of the other person. When this stock repertoire ran its course, he could not think of many effective behaviors to keep the communication process open. This embarrassed him, which led to anger, which led to either his or the other person's withdrawal from the encounter. On more than a few occasions, this withdrawal was accompanied by specific verbal responses and non-verbal gestures intended to punctuate the termination of the encounter. Through a discussion of these observations with the student, it was learned that he felt it was "their" (his peers) problem. "If a kid doesn't want me as a friend, it's ok, because I really don't want that kid as a friend anyway." He would then proceed to "rank" or "put down" this person, which served to further underscore his desire not to want that person's friendship.

When confronted with his development of anger in these situations, he stated "Who wouldn't get angry, having to deal with clowns like that." He offered no evidence as to an understanding that his responses were inappropriate and that in being so, they might be contributing to the development of his anger.

A treatment plan needed to be developed that would enable him to acquire assertive behavior while also providing him with a means to manage his interpersonal anxiety. The anxiety management procedure would be dealt with first, for it was believed that, even if he knew how to give an assertive response, it would have a low probability of being given under the condition of extreme anger. After learning how to control his anger, his arousal state might be more favorably disposed to effect the occurrence of the desired assertive response.

Anxiety/Anger Management: Management of his anger was accomplished through adaptation of a relaxation design reported by Jacobson (1938) and by Wolpe (1973). The student was first taught to tense-relax specific muscle groups and then to associate the pleasant physiological sensations of relaxation with the thought/command "relax." Through practice of this relaxation procedure over a period of several weeks, the student would then be able to cue the sensations of relaxation to a desired muscle group by concentrating upon the word "relax." As with most adolescents, the student evidenced some resistance to the initial relaxation exercises, due to the inherent feature of making the person who is tensing several facial muscles appear to look, as said by the student, "pretty foolish."

However, after being told it was acceptable to look "foolish," and seeing the exercises modeled, the student lost this initial resistance and "really got into" the procedure, reporting that it was a "funky way to be high!"

A time-sampling procedure was then taught to the student whereby he was asked to rate himself for each half-hour (on a scale of 0 - 4) as to his current level of anger, using 0 as being calm, relaxed and using 4 as being anxious, angry, and ready to give one or more of his "punctuation" behaviors. For those times in which he felt the most upset, he was to write down whom he was with, what were his responses, what were the consequences of his responses, and then to initiate relaxation to calm himself. The results of this data showed him to have a high probability of becoming upset when he was exposed to both academic and social situations in which he did not know either what was expected of him or how to give the response that was expected of him.

In discussing these results with him, the student, again, stated his desire not to appear "foolish." It seems that when confronted with such a situation, he would try to shift the focus or demand of the situation away from himself through a 'put-down'' of either the situation itself or of the other person in the situation. As this occurred, it would cause the other person to become angry or frustrated with him, resulting in the withdrawal of this person from the situation.

However, through the effects of the self-monitoring and of the relaxation, both the frequency of his high arousal states and the magnitude of these states began to diminish.

Assertive Skill Development: It was felt that the second part of the treatment plan could now be implemented. This was accomplished by (1) having the student read *Your Perfect Right* (Alberti and Emmons, 1974), (2) discussing the differences between passive, aggressive and assertive behavior, and the feelings associated with these behaviors; (3) focusing upon the perspective and rights of the other person; (4) generating alternative responses, and (4) examining both the immediate and terminal consequences of these responses, and the effectiveness of an assertive response to provide a resolution of the interpersonal problem. In the earlier presentation of this assertive model, the student was quite consistent in his inability to determine alternative responses that took into account the rights of the other person and in his inability to determine the terminal consequences to many of these alternative responses. As his ability to state these terminal responses increased, so did his ability to generate both more alternative responses and more responses that took into account the rights and desires of the other person.

The student then observed a video-tape of more assertive peers who served to model responses in a variety of interpersonal situations. Role-plays were then presented to allow for the continuation of modeling, for rehearsal of specific behaviors, and for feedback as to the effectiveness of the behaviors.

At first, open-ended role-plays were used, where a demand for an assertive response would be presented. The video-tape would then be frozen while the student verbally scanned the situation for cues that would answer the questions posed by the assertive model. This scanning would then result in the student's choice of a particular assertive response and a discussion with the counselor as to the expected feedback to that chosen response as to its assertive effectiveness.

As the counselor became sure that the student was effectively scanning and responding in these role-plays, the role-plays became more closed-ended, calling for both more specific assertive responses and for decreased latency of the specific assertive response.

Covert Procedures: At this point most clients would be ready for a trial of their assertive behavior in an actual interpersonal situation. However, as a hedge against residual amounts of anger occurring, a covert conditioning procedure (Cautela, 1969) was introduced. Covert positive reinforcement (CPR) (Cautela, 1970, and Kazdin, 1973) was given to the occurrence of an assertive behavior within the context of an imaginary interpersonal encounter. The student was then asked to imagine himself:
a) in the problem encounter
b) becoming a bit anxious
c) coping with the anxiety
d) scanning the situation for cues that would lead to an appropriate assertive response
e) giving the response
f) reinforcing himself

The student had no difficulty in learning this covert design as it bore much resemblance to the previously learned positively reinforced relaxation design. It would seem that as the role-plays allowed him to rehearse both the process of determining an assertive response and the performance of the specific assertive response, the CPR allowed him to rehearse his coping with a situation that had previously been the occasion for much inappropriate behavior.

In Vivo Application: After some practice with the above scene, a target situation was selected by the student to develop the friendship of another member of the football team whom the student had either ignored or fought in the past. The student then described the responses that we could use to initiate and maintain this friendship, the initial and terminal consequences that these responses could effect, and the overall effectiveness of each response as to its probability of developing a friendship with the other student. He then was instructed to initiate this relationship and to provide the facilitator with feedback as to its effectiveness.

After a two-week follow-up, the student reported success with the target situation. He also reported that he was now better able to maintain conversations with most people, for he was now really "listening" to them, and in fact, he had even become more tolerant of other students who had previously "turned him off."

Although successful, this case left a few unanswered questions. Was the anxiety management really needed or was it just a nice thing to learn that enabled some positive relationship to be developed? Was the CPR really necessary or a case of a counselor making something too complex? Would the anxiety have decreased through the occurrence of assertive behavior alone, as suggested in Wolpe (1973)? These questions are further discussed through the presentation of the next case.

COGNITIVE-BEHAVIORAL STRATEGY

This strategy was implemented with a twelve-year-old adolescent boy whose referral problem was a difficulty in initiating any relationships with his peers. He was a recent transfer to an urban junior high school, where after a period of several months, it was noticed that he was still regarded as an outsider by his classmates. His teachers reported him to be doing well academically, but he seemed to be more of a follower, never initiating any work on his own, and never expressing his interests, opinions, or desires of his own accord. He was the kind of student whose absence from class would not be missed by either his teachers or peers, being verified only through the class attendance roster. Through pre-treatment role-play focused on his verbal and non-verbal communication behaviors with his classmates, it was observed that he, indeed, was quite boring. It was not so much what he said, but that he demonstrated reluctance, hesitancy, response latency, and emotional flatness when talking about himself. This had an effect of turning off the person to whom he was talking. This had easily developed into a self-fulfilling prophecy. As he found it difficult to express appropriate affect when talking about himself, he conveyed a boring or uncaring attitude to others. As long as he was so regarded by others, it became more difficult to get others to listen to him. This "punishment design" had the effect of decreasing any interpersonal initiating behavior. He became a follower by choice, for it was easier than having to become the center of attention, to which he would respond inappropriately, as demonstrated above.

Through a discussion of these observations with the student, it was learned that he had always found it difficult to talk to his peers, a difficulty that was compounded by his new environment. He reported the existence of an older sister, one who seemed to enjoy a great deal of success in both academic and social activities, and one upon whom a great deal of attention had always been focused by his family. In any comparison to his sister, he would always fall short. She had been able to adapt to the new environment with little trouble. He, however, had found the new sets of language and social behavior just a bit too much with which to cope. He was having problems with his communication responses in both their substance and style.

A treatment plan needed to be developed that would, as above, enable him to acquire more assertive behavior while also providing him with a means to manage any anxiety that might occur as he sought to increase interpersonal initiating behaviors.

However, as this student was more inhibited (passive) than impulsive (aggressive), in contrast to the client described in the case above, it was hypothesized that the acquisition of assertive behavior itself would serve to facilitate the management of any interpersonal anxiety. Meichenbaum and Cameron (1973) and Spivack and Shure (1974) argue that through the process of learning a cognitive strategy to effect the occurrence of specific behavior, the cognitive process itself serves to mutually exclude any inhibitory anxiety. Shure and Spivack (1972) report data that socially competent children differ significantly from less competent children as measured by decreased response latency and by the number of alternative responses generated towards the solution of an interpersonal problem. It seems that one who *expects* to succeed, will. That is, by expecting to be able to adapt to an interpersonal problem, perhaps through the knowledge of a cognitive process designed to foster this adaptation, inhibitory anxiety is managed and the probability of an occurrence of an adaptive response increases.

The treatment plan for this student was in two parts. The first part was focused on the procedure for acquiring assertive behavior reported in *Your Perfect Right* (Alberti and Emmons, 1974). This program was similar to that described above. However, as the treatment strategy for the first student was concerned with the *unlearning* of a previously existing behavioral repertoire (aggressive behavior), this second treatment strategy was more concerned with the *learning* of a behavioral repertoire (assertive behavior). Therefore, a great deal more time was spent with both covert and overt behavioral rehearsal to increase the probability that both the cognitive assertive model and the specific assertive behaviors (initiating, talking about oneself, etc.) would be learned.

Assertive Beliefs and Self Concept: Whereas the first student had difficulty taking into account the role/perspective of another person, this student had difficulty in believing that he, himself, was worth being assertive. Therefore, prior to the actual learning of an assertive behavior repertoire, some time was spent with the student discussing the Behavioral Model for Personal Growth (Alberti and Emmons, 1974), the Revised Rathus Assertiveness Scale for Children (D'Amico, 1976) and a Student Reinforcement Survey Schedule for Children (D'Amico and Gracia, 1975). These discussions focused upon the student's low frequencies of responses in personal growth activities, the need to increase these responses, and some activities available to the student, within his new environment, through which he would be able to develop these responses. In concluding these discussions, the student reported a feeling of increased self-worth and was now anxious to learn how to communicate this feeling with others.

The counselor now introduced the assertive model as mentioned above, noting that this student had more difficulty with the recognition and expression of emotion than did the first student. Both had difficulty with the generation of alternative responses, however, the second student had less difficulty with the examination of initial and terminal consequences of an assertive response than did his counterpart.

Assertive Skill Development: The second part of the treatment strategy was focused on the performance of these newly learned behaviors. This treatment strategy needed to consist of procedures that would allow the student to cope with the demands of an assertive situation, and thus serve to reinforce the student, increasing his newly established sense of self-worth. The counselor adapted a Stress-Inoculation Training model developed by Meichenbaum and Cameron (1973) for use with assertive training.

The stress situation in the Meichenbaum-Cameron model was equated to the demand for assertive behavior in an interpersonal situation. The adaptation of their four basic parts was then delineated as follows:

a) Preparing for the assertive demand:
    1) What is an adaptive response for this assertive situation?
    2) If I just follow the assertive model (verbal and non-verbal cues/expectancies, alternative responses, their consequences, and total response effectiveness) I can deal with the demand!
    3) Keep thinking about the model! It is better than getting upset!
    4) No negative self-statements about my not being able to deal with it! Just think of the model!
    5) Don't worry! It won't help at all!
    6) Maybe what I'm feeling is not anxiety, but just my eagerness to respond appropriately!
b) Confronting and handling the assertive demand:
    1) Hey! I can do it!
    2) One step at a time now, think about what I'm doing!
    3) Don't think about getting anxious, just about what is expected!
    4) That's it now, slowly, one step at a time!
c) Coping with the presence of interpersonal anxiety:
    1) Ok, now, I'm feeling some anxiety, I'll just pause!
    2) Now, I'll label it from one to ten and watch it change, first it will go up a bit, now, its going down.

3) Focus back on the situation and watch it go away soon!
4) That's it now, I'm coming up with the appropriate response!
5) Go ahead, now, give it!
d) Reinforcing self-statements:
1) Hey! I did it! It worked!
2) Boy, do I feel good about that!
3) That wasn't so bad!
4) The more I do this, the easier it will get!
5) Hey! I did it!

Through both treatment sessions and homework, this cognitive assertive strategy was learned and rehearsed in both overt and covert, role-play situations.

In Vivo Applications: At this point the student was instructed to select a target situation in which to apply his newly learned skills. He selected a situation from his Social Studies class where he would soon be expected to present an oral report and to lead a class discussion of this report. The next session was then concerned with the student's ability to generalize this cognitive-behavioral model to his selected situation. The student scanned the situation, selected an appropriate assertive response style through which to deliver this presentation, rehearsed this delivery, managed/coped with negative self-statements, and then reinforced himself for appropriately delivering the presentation and discussion through the positive self-statements. He then was instructed to covertly rehearse this scene as homework prior to the actual presentation and to provide feedback to the author as to his performance in the actual situation.

A two-week follow-up resulted in the student reporting success with his presentation. A check with the Social Studies teacher confirmed the student's observation. His response latency was now reduced, he was talking about himself in a manner that was more interesting, and he was initiating more conversations with his peers and teachers. The student reported the latter to be still an occasion for some interpersonal anxiety, but, after a one-month follow-up, he reported that he could no longer perceive interpersonal anxiety being present in these situations.

As in the first case, there remain a few unanswered questions. Was the innoculation design really necessary? Is there some qualitative or quantitative difference in interpersonal anxiety that would suggest against use of a cognitive strategy in favor of, perhaps, a systematic desensitization strategy? Are the two strategies really that different or, to put it another way, what do the strategies have in common?

SUMMARY

The "counter-covert conditioning" and "cognitive-behavioral strategies" were relatively successful with the two teenagers described here, however their general efficacy remains unproven. An experimental design is presently being completed by the author to compare these two strategies as to their effectiveness and appropriateness for use with groups of children and adolescents. It is hoped that this presentation will encourage others to both apply and to amplify these techniques with their clients, towards a goal of more effective assertiveness training designs.

DEVELOPING ADOLESCENT ASSERTIVENESS

Gail W. McPhail

For days after our first Assertive Training Workshop, my world fairly rang with excited comments from students; "I was assertive with my boyfriend last night. That stuff really works!" "Hi! I tried it again. I didn't get exactly what I wanted but I sure feel better," and more than once, the clenched fist salute accompanied by a smiling "Assertion, Right on!"

ADOLESCENT POWERLESSNESS

Since coming to the high school as a counselor, I observed with increasing concern that most of our students did not seem to have assertive skills; they did not know how to effectively stand up for themselves and negotiate for what they wanted, either at school—with teachers, counselors, administrators—or outside of school—with parents, family, friends, bosses, salespeople, other authorities.

Surely these students learned, from the very existence of compulsory school attendance, a feeling of powerlessness; they had many years of experience in traditionally structured classrooms which demanded and rewarded much passive behavior. I heard them chafe at the sometimes authoritarian environment they spent 4 to 6 hours a day in, but *few*—and I include the highly motivated, achieving and skilled students—ever learned more than a very limited repertoire for responding to the demands of the system. Typically, they have only two behavior styles from which to choose: 1) *the passive mode*, in which the student smiles, keeps quiet, and "goes along with the program;" and 2) *the aggressive mode*, usually chosen when the student feels "pushed" beyond endurance, feels "out of control," and almost always after accumulating a host of hurt feelings, anger and frustration. At school this aggressive behavior almost always happens in the least productive situation: the student chooses to confront the teacher in the presence of the class with the predictable consequence that both teacher and student lose.

In my counseling contact with students, they discussed their problems with relationships outside of school, often reporting feelings of powerlessness, anger and confusion. As in school, students described their behavior with parents, other family, friends, and employers as primarily passive and occasionally aggressive. For a rare few, the style was consistently aggressive in these relationships.

We decided to offer students what we saw as a key to living more happily both in school and out, assertive training. Our first assertive training workshop was billed as an opportunity for the students to learn how to get more of what they wanted in their lives, the beginning of a skill to help them get power with their world.

DEVELOPING A HIGH SCHOOL AT PROGRAM

In preparation, the plans were carefully described first to the building principal and then to the district administration, stressing the goal of teaching students new communication skills. This step included careful work to allay fears of both staff and administration, acknowledging their concern that any school activity that might be labelled a "sensitivity group" could easily draw disapproval in our conservative community. Preparation also included consultation time with the community mental health staff and other local professionals, drawing on their expertise and experience in presenting successful adult assertive traning workshops. Finally, administrators and teachers were invited and encouraged to observe and participate.

We began with a 1-day off-campus workshop with 25 volunteer

students. The success of that program led us to develop formats for teaching assertive skills in classrooms during the regular day, and for 1/2-day workshops offered on campus, with varying and increasing staff support and participation.

Clear and relatively limited goals were established for the AT program. Our basic group goals were to improve:
1. The ability to say "no,"
2. The ability to express both positive and negative feelings;
3. The ability to make requests, to ask for and accept favors;
4. The ability to initiate, continue and terminate general conversations.

ELEMENTS OF THE ADOLESCENT AT PROGRAM

1. Training typically was begun with a description of the characteristics, relative merits, and pay-off of the three types of behavior, passive (or non-assertive), aggressive, and assertive. The following summary charts were duplicated (with permission) from Bob Alberti and Mike Emmons, and used to help explain these behavior patterns to the students:

NON-ASSERTIVE (PASSIVE)
Self-denying, inhibited
Allows others to control
Goals not achieved
Not expressive of self / HURT
Emotional Distance from others

AGGRESSIVE
Self-enhancing at other's expense
Controls others
Goals usually achieved
Expressive of self / GUILT
Emotional distance from others

ASSERTIVE
Self-enhancing
Controls self / values others
Goals usually achieved
Expressive of self / GOOD FEELINGS
Emotional honesty and closeness

The styles were role-played clearly so students were comfortably conversant with the dimensions of each general type of behavior.

2. In the next step, the components or "nuts and bolts" of assertive behavior were presented, noting that these variables control the clarity and effectiveness of our communications with others:
- a. Eye contact
- b. Body posture
- c. Gestures
- d. Facial expression
- e. Voice tone, inflection, volume
- f. Timing
- g. Distance
- h. Content (what you say)

Adolescents find items a, f, and h to be key points, each for different reasons. *Eye contact* is the critical factor in communicating the importance of a message. Students discovered the possibility of immediately improving their interpersonal communication by looking directly at the person to whom they are speaking.

Timing was found a particularly important element of being assertive with both teachers and parents. Students learned to make appointments with persons in authority, usually choosing to meet in private rather than in front of a group. Students reported much greater success in communicating concerns when such appointments were made.

When asked to name the most important component of communicating a message, invariably students would assume that *content*—the words they said—would be most important of all. They seemed relieved to know that how they put their words together—how "hip" or "cool" their actual verbiage was—was not nearly as important as the other variables noted, particularly eye contact.

3. A third major step, often overlooked in AT programs and in the literature, is one which I consider to be the most important process in helping students to be assertive. In this procedure, which we call the quick "Two-Step Process," the student clarifies (1) What is it that I feel? (irritated, angry, hurt, confused, fearful, etc.); and (2) What is it that I want? (outcome, demand, expectation).

Often students are unclear about what they really are feeling and what they want from another person as they attempt to be assertive. In our workshops, we often begin role-playing with the rather common scene of having to deal with a very persistent door-to-door salesperson. Our first instruction is to ask the student to clarify his or her feelings about the situation. We encourage students to list words or short phrases that describe these feelings. Perhaps "I feel annoyed, powerless, angry, trapped, etc."

When a student has been able to describe feelings adequately and feels comfortable that these are the emotions he or she is feeling, we then proceed with the desired outcome. "What is it that I want to see happen in this situation?" These demands may range through "I want to tell you 'no, thank you;' " "I will listen to your sales pitch at the door but I do not want you to come in;" "I want to tell you that I am not interested and will not listen to your sales talk;" "I want you to leave immediately."

Once the feelings and demands are clear, we will replay the scene at the door, using successive approximations and feedback until the student feels that he or she has achieved the desired result, and feels comfortable about the degree of assertiveness shown.

It should be noted that Values Clarification and Decision-making exercises (Simon, 1972) are congruent with the goals of assertive training and are particularly helpful in aiding students in clarifying and naming feelings and demands in the two-step process.

It is very helpful for trainees to think of this step in terms of its carryover value to all situations which call for assertiveness. Valuing oneself enough to allow and respect one's own feelings and wants is a vital precondition to effective assertiveness. I think of it as "being assertive with myself."

4. **In the process of behavior rehearsal and feedback,** we initially used a video-tape but have concluded that it can be a very distracting device in an adolescent group; we preferred to instruct the group to function as the video—to report back to the person exact behaviors they observed, in terms of the specific components of assertive behavior we had covered.

In addition, students were urged to label observed behavior as assertive, aggressive or passive, and to be sensitive to the observation of more than one behavior. For example, "You started out sounding very passive. Your voice was very soft and had a slight whine to it. You were louder, more clear, and got very assertive when you said, ..."

It is stressed that learning a new behavior style—assertion—is much like learning to ride a bicycle. It requires patient, continuous practice.

ADOLESCENT ASSERTIVENESS PROBLEMS

The students are asked for real situations from their lives in which they reported "not getting" what they wanted. Below is a partial but representative sample of role-playing topics they gave us:

Friends

> I need to be able to tell a friend "no." For instance, a friend wants to come over to talk and I really have a lot to do and just don't feel like talking. How do I say "no" without being mean or feeling guilty?
>
> I want to be able to tell people who are visiting that I want them to leave because I have to eat dinner or go to a meeting.
>
> I want to be able to tell a good friend of mine what things about him or her *really* bug me.
>
> When I am with a guy at the show or something and the guy is trying to go too far. I like him a lot but I don't want to do anything. What should I do?
>
> My girlfriends and I only talk about boys but when we're with boys we have nothing to say. I want to be able to talk and keep a conversation going with any person of any age or sex.

Home—Parents and Family

> I would like to be able to talk to my parents when they're mad at me without being told, "Don't talk back to me, young lady."
>
> My grandmother is always asking me to do something while I am watching T.V. So, of course, I get up and do it even though I don't want to do it.

Work Relationships

> How do I tell the lady who asks me to babysit how much an hour I want?
>
> How do I tell people that I don't want to babysit? I feel guilty if I don't say yes, but I really don't want to do it.
>
> I'm afraid to call in sick at work because the boss seems to get mad. What can I do?

School Relationships

> How do I tell a teacher I think he or she is being unfair?
>
> I need to learn how to keep a conversation going with a new guy in school.
>
> I would like to be able to start and hold a conversation with girls of my own age.

General

How do I handle a person selling something at the door?

I get very embarrassed when someone compliments me. What can I do?

Students were urged to recognize that they could now choose *which* style of behavior they wished to use: passive, aggressive or assertive. We cautioned them against thinking they must act assertively in every situation, but instead, to be aware of how they were choosing to act and to acknowledge that they had a *choice*.

Finally, we acclaimed all of us—students, teachers, administrators, parents, everyone—had the right to ask for what we wanted 100% of the time, only we didn't expect to always get it!

EVALUATION AND FEEDBACK

When asked to evaluate the assertive training workshops, staff and administrators commented:

"This was an important opportunity for students to learn how to express themselves honestly and openly. All of us (teachers and students) felt very positive about the experience."

"One of the important outcomes seems to be that students can begin to see both sides of a mutual problem, whether it is one of parent-child, boyfriend-girlfriend, employer-employee, teacher-student, etc."

"I liked the atmosphere the assertive training workshops foster—a relaxing, trusting and sharing time."

Feedback from workshop participants was solicited to detect what behavioral changes students reported in their lives, as well as their suggestions for improvement of future workshops. Students reported the following personal statements about the result of their experience:

"It's helped me control my emotions."

"I feel better inside myself."

"I've learned that I should not constantly be putting my considerations second, that most of the time, they should be first."

"I feel I've been helped to say 'yes' or 'no' when I feel like saying it. Before I would say 'yes' about something and just ache inside because I had wanted to say 'no.' "

"I have learned to say what I mean and not hurt someone by doing it."

"I've learned how to be more firm with my boss (teacher, mother, boyfriend, salesperson)."

"I've learned how to achieve my goals in such a way as to preserve the feelings of others and still get what I want."

"I've learned to be firm without being mean at the same time."

"I now feel like I can deal effectively with other people in situations that I would generally avoid."

"I'm learning not to be so passive; I will say how I feel now."

"Thanks. I found out how I must sound when I am aggressive with someone."

And finally, the oft-repeated request, "The class was too short. Please, let's do it again."

Assertion—Right on!

21

ASSERTION TRAINING WITH JUVENILE DELINQUENTS

Lynne Garnett

Historically, it has been the common practice in dealing with juvenile delinquents to provide treatment in a setting (milieu therapy) considered therapeutically conducive to change from socially unacceptable behaviors to behaviors more adaptive to society's demands. The therapeutic climate has varied from setting to setting depending on the orientation of the therapist involved. In some instances, delinquency was considered characterological while in other settings the orientation was directed toward the social system.

As therapeutic methods became more refined, there followed an increase in the variety of approaches used in dealing with delinquents. Assertion training is one such method that seems applicable as an adjunct treatment in the therapeutic milieu. This paper reflects one such experience of assertion training with a group of court-referred delinquents.

STARTING THE PROGRAM

In 1973, an assertion training group consisting of eight court-adjudged juvenile delinquents, whose ages ranged from 13 - 17, was conducted by a co-therapist team. There were six males and two females, and their offenses ranged from truancy to armed robbery. All of the group members were on probation and were in a special correctional continuation school, having been expelled from the standard continuation junior high and high schools. In obtaining a history from each one of them, it became apparent that their behavior patterns were typically nonassertive for long periods of time, interspersed with aggressive behavior.

It was not easy, initially, to gain the trust of the eight students. Although I met with their teacher and probation officers originally to explain assertion training and its values, and I met with all of the students in the school to explain the process, the students remained very suspicious of us. As the group got under way, there was little attention given and a lot of "hassling" behavior (getting up and walking in and out, cracking jokes while we were talking, knocking each other's chairs over). When the behavior failed to extinguish by being ignored, we stopped the process and layed out a more formal contract with the group as a whole. We clarified again what we thought assertion training might offer them, and how it could increase their repertoire of behaviors and give them more choices. We discussed consequences to all behaviors, and how they could choose probable outcomes. We reminded them of our contract with the school and that their participation in the group was purely voluntary. The students debated among themselves for a moment and decided that "being in a group beat being in class," and they would agree to the contract. This proved to be the turning point. After that, whenever a student was disruptive in the group, the other group members reminded him or her of the contract.

AT TECHNIQUES WITH THE JUVENILE GROUP

The assertion training intervention included such behavioral techniques as modeling and role-playing. *Modeling* is the process whereby the facilitator (or another trainee) plays the trainee's role in a specific situation in order to *model* or demonstrate ways in which the trainee might appropriately respond in that situation. Modeling was used in various situations where students responded inappropriately with passive or aggressive behaviors (such as silence, physical withdrawal, or verbal abuse) to frustrating or uncomfortable situations. The facilitator would model more appropriate responses within the role-playing situation, such as mother-child or student-teacher encounters. For example, when a student was confronted by an angry mother who returned from work and found the chores not done, the response of the student was to become defensive and claim he was not loved nor appreciated. This response served to continue a directionless argument. The modeled response by the facilitator was to acknowledge that the mother was tired and upset, and then proceed to tell his mother how much he liked it when they could really sit down and talk (thereby reinforcing more appropriate behaviors). Once the mother was calm, the suggestion was to carry out an appropriate task, such as taking out the trash. This reinforced the mother to deal with her son in a calm, direct manner.

Role-playing included a repertoire of responses including behavioral rehearsal (practicing behaviors), role-reversal (the process whereby the facilitator or another student plays the student while the student plays the antagonist), and modeling. In the process of assertion training, the student began role-playing (practicing) small assertions which were likely to be reinforced (rewarded). In other words, the student's behavior was shaped (changed through the process of successive approximations to the task) from non-assertive or aggressive responses to appropriately assertive responses. The students chose their own situations to practice and created their own assertive hierarchies (least threatening to most threatening assertive situations).

The eight students, one county probation officer (cleared by the group), and two co-therapists in the group met in a circle on folding chairs. Role plays were conducted in the center of the circle or in facing chairs around the circle.

Besides the traditional techniques of behavioral rehearsal, modeling, etc., the therapists consistently checked out the appropriateness of any assertions with the student's personal frame of reference and their peer group. If any particular assertion was offensive or inappropriate within their frame of reference, it was evaluated and either restructured or dropped totally.

One of the most important aspects of my approach to assertion training in groups is that I deal with each group member on a one to one basis, as well as interacting with the group as a whole. Rather than teach assertive techniques and skills in a general (and perhaps unrelated) context, I prefer to utilize the individual's own personal situations. There are times, of course, when it is appropriate to create a context; for example, having each group member compliment another in order to practice giving and receiving compliments. I feel, however, that assertive skills or assertive behavior is most appropriately learned within the context of one's own personal interests and life experiences. I believe that this approach also helps to mitigate against people just learning "scripts" or "tricks" of control or coercion. By relating assertive skills and assertion training to their own personal lives, they can learn to monitor and alter their own behaviors as they grow and change.

PROCESS OF THE AT GROUP

The first role-playing session for this group of court-ruled delinquent youths started with a subject close to all of their hearts, the police. It was decided that a typical situation might be trying to talk an officer out of a ticket. In the first sequence the roles came out stereotypically, with the parts of the policeman and the driver being played by males and the passenger played by a female. Initially, the players were a little raucus and embarrassed, but this was quickly dissipated as each student got into his or her role character. Too, the effect that their beginning assertive responses had on other people seemed to have the desired impact. They were amazed that they could find alternative ways of responding to the police other than kow-towing or "wising off."

The first behavior to be restructured was language. The first response to the "officer" was "What do you want, pig?" With that the student playing the officer grabbed the "driver" and proceeded to pretend to club him with his night stick. At this point the laughter appeared nervous and a little stilted. But, we used humor to help reduce general anxiety and to clarify or demonstrate ideas. We asked the "officer" how he felt being called a "pig." He replied that it angered him and he wanted to "get back" at the "driver." The group decided, however, that since cops acted like "pigs" they ought to be called "pigs." This provided the opportunity for didactic approaches (cognitive restructuring) and some modeling to demonstrate how it might be possible that if you call a "non-pig" a "pig," he might *act* like a "pig." We ran through several sequences of the same role-play situation, varying the participants, including female police. There was ample allowance for laughter and fun within the context of the role-play. The students were, with practice, able to stay on task (in character) while gaining experience with several new ways of responding to police, and they still had fun with it. They also learned that you can respond to individuals rather than jobs, that some people will abuse their authority, and some people won't.

During the course of the five week training period (5 sessions, one hour each, one per week) the main thrust of the assertion training centered around problems related to authority conflicts. The authority figures included policemen, parents (particularly mothers, as there were few fathers around), teachers, and probation officers. There were a number of practice sessions on reinforcing mother for the things she did that they liked, dealing with specific complaints that she had in regard to their behavior, and ignoring non-specific complaints. Two of the students in particular had significant success with these techniques. The events centered around greeting mother when she returned "dead-tired" from work, acknowledging her tiredness, ignoring her non-specific complaints (e.g., "you never do anything around here"), agreeing non-defensively with specific complaints ("you're right, Mom, I didn't take out the trash; I'll do it before we sit down to dinner"), and, of course, meeting that contract. At first, the students were reluctant to put out any extra effort for mom, but through some directed discussion (cognitive restructuring) and role-playing (including role reversal), they were able to give the new behaviors a try. The students were truly surprised and gratified by their mothers' and their own responses.

Although most of the role-play sessions were variations on authority problems, we also dealt with the students' own authoritarian behaviors. One 15-year-old boy wanted to get his 10-year-old sister to "behave," that is, for the sister to stop smoking and swearing. In the role-play sequence he tended to behave in a patronizing manner, telling his sister what was "good" for her, or he experienced frustration and called her a "punk kid." When asked if they ever had comfortable or enjoyable interactions he was unable to identify any. Although the interaction in the role-play did finally approximate civility, he never did find a comfortable level with her. In reporting on his homework assignments the next week, however, he did mention that she wasn't such a bad kid after all, and in subsequent sessions, he reported that the tensions between them had somewhat subsided. One of his original antagonisms toward her was that she got "everything" from mother and he got "nothing." We did some reality testing regarding his statements using the terms "everything" and "nothing," and he admitted some exaggeration. This led to a more realistic expectation for positive feedback and attention from his mother.

STUDENT-STAFF RELATIONSHIPS AND AT

The final session proved to be more *in vivo* practice than the role-playing format we had followed in previous sessions. The group had left the prior week's session on a very high note. The feedback was that the members were finding the assertion training helpful in their lives and they were looking forward to the final session. At the start of the meeting, however, the students behaved in a moody, angry manner. Some whispered to each other, two stretched out on the floor and fiddled with notebooks or keys, and one female was in tears while talking with her parole officer. In questioning the group, we discovered that all of the individual group members were having difficulty with a particular staff member. We were able to pinpoint particular incidents that were amenable to role-play, but the feedback from the students was that "he will never listen to us." Because of my prior contact with this particular staff member, his enthusiasm for the program and training, his own perceptions of his interactions with the students, his recognition of the need for change, and his understanding of assertion training principles, I decided to approach the staff member with the group's suggestion that they practice their assertions together, with the staff member playing his own role. I discussed the idea with the staff member, apprised him of the dynamics of the present situation, offered several reasonable and ethical alternatives, and offered as much information as I could about potential outcomes. In light of his commitment to his students and his desire to improve communication with them, he decided to join the group for some *in vivo* assertion practice.

Based on the following feedback from the staff member and the students, the outcome of the group session was considered to be positive (four of the students were able to make direct, appropriate assertions with the staff member). However, I would not suggest this process as standard procedure because of the power relationship and the possible ramifications. Although we were pleased with the outcome in this case, it may have been more appropriate to have set up another series of sessions in which the staff member could have become a working member of the group, rather than become the sole target of the group members' assertions during a single session.

SUMMARY

Although many observers have held that juvenile delinquents often behave in aggressive ways, and that these modes of behavior are learned (Bandura & Walters, 1963; McCord & McCord, 1958; Bateson, 1936; Whiting, 1941), it appeared in our training sessions that these behavior patterns were really of the non-assertive—aggressive types rather than just learned aggressive modes of behavior. Not only were they more likely during the course of the training to choose a learned assertive response over a learned aggressive one, they also reported and demonstrated by their behavior that they would choose non-assertive responses before they finally would aggress.

Given the opportunity to develop skills of appropriate assertiveness, the aggressive behaviors were minimized. The students' desires to be heard and complimented appeared to be just as strong as those of non-delinquents. For whatever antecedent reasons (parental modeling, peer expectations, etc.), before this assertion training experience they simply did not possess the skills to get appropriate feedback, behave productively, and get the social payoffs that most of the non-delinquent population is able to manage. It is encouraging to note that delinquents can learn new ways of behaving just as readily as anyone else.

22

ASSERTION TRAINING IN MARITAL COUNSELING

Robert E. Alberti, Michael L. Emmons

Imagine the following scene: John's day has been exhausting: he has washed windows, mopped floors, completed three loads of wash, and continuously picked up and cleaned up after the children. He is now working hurriedly in the kitchen preparing dinner. The children are running in and out of the house banging the door, screaming, and throwing toys.

In the midst of this chaos, Mary arrives home from an equally trying day at her office. She offers a cursory "I'm home!" as she passes the kitchen on her way to the family room. Dropping her briefcase and kicking off her shoes, she flops in her favorite chair in front of the television set, calling out, "John, bring me a beer! I've had a helluva day!" John's response is . . .

How will John express his anger? Throw a mixing spoon across the kitchen? Yell "go to hell!" at Mary? Kick the perennially underfoot cat? Burn the broccoli? Scream at the still noisy children? Tell Mary to get her own beer? Take the beer to her?

---

1. From the *Journal of Marriage and Family Counseling*, January 1976, pp. 49-54. Copyright © 1976 by the American Association of Marriage and Family Counselors. Reprinted by permission.

The style of John's response to Mary may be characterized according to our Non-assertive/Assertive/Aggressive paradigm (see Table 22-1). We have observed in counseling couples that marital conflict often results from selection of an inappropriate style for expression of strong feeling. Inadequate communication styles are often established during "courtship and honeymoon" days, when partners were still trying to "impress" each other. Thus hurtful aggressiveness or self-denying non-assertiveness may develop as destructive of communication in an intimate relationship.

Table 22-1 helps to clarify the differences among *nonassertive*, *assertive*, and *aggressive* response styles. Unfortunately, it is commonly assumed—alas, even by many counselors!—that "assertive" and "aggressive" are synonymous. We believe the differences are very important, and suggest that marriage and family counselors note the differences when assisting clients toward greater positive self-expression.

Assertion is not "constructive aggression" nor "successful intimidation." Assertion is not designed to foster hostility or combativeness between couples. The ultimate goal of assertion is to have both marital partners become more self-expressive in a positive, non-hostile style, bringing them closer together as a cohesive unit rather than driving them apart.

Because "assertive" and "aggressive" are frequently confused terms, we suggest that counselors take special care to encourage appropriate assertiveness by actively demonstrating the differences, utilizing the procedures described later in this paper. Many clients are reluctant to assert themselves because they see aggression (self-expression at someone else's expense) as the only alternative. The assertive style can become "real" through effective modeling by the counselor.

Effective intervention by the marriage counselor requires accurate identification of the inadequacies of the existing communication/behavioral patterns in the relationship, and assistance to the partners in establishing new and more positive styles. It is neither necessary nor sufficient for the counselor to determine "why" the inadequacies exist. Suffice it to say that we are all human, and imperfect. Valuable counselor contributions result from interventions which take clients from where they are to where they want to be.

It is often assumed that attitudes, *before* behavior, must be changed. In our experience the attitude-behavior cycle may be interrupted at any point, but we find behavior much more amenable to short-term therapeutic intervention. Moreover, following a behavioral change (such as exhibiting more adequate assertive behavior), the client

Table 22-1

NON-ASSERTIVE BEHAVIOR	AGGRESSIVE BEHAVIOR	ASSERTIVE BEHAVIOR
As Actor	**As Actor**	**As Actor**
Self-denying	Self-enhancing at expense of another	Self-enhancing
Inhibited	Expressive	Expressive
Hurt, anxious	Depreciates others	Feels good about self
Allows others to choose for him (her)	Chooses for others	Chooses for self
Does not achieve desired goal	Achieves desired goal by hurting others	May achieve desired goal
As Acted Upon	**As Acted Upon**	**As Acted Upon**
Guilty or angry	Self-denying	Self-enhancing
Depreciates actor	Hurt, defensive, humiliated	Expressive
Achieves desired goal at actor's expense	Does not achieve desired goal	May achieve desired goal

*From Alberti, R. E., & Emmons, M. L. *Your Perfect Right*. San Luis Obispo, California: Impact, 1970, 1974. Used by permission of the authors and publisher.

begins to notice a change in the manner in which others respond to him/her. Positive feedback from others is heady reinforcement for the formerly non-assertive, self-denying person. Attitudes toward self begin to change significantly as a result of the awareness that "I am responsible for bringing about the positive response I am getting from others!"

Thus effective assertive behavior, begun as a wish on the part of the client, and accomplished via facilitation by the counselor, has strong self-reinforcing benefits. The client becomes more effective in interpersonal situations, gets positive feedback, and feels better about him/herself.

The process of facilitating assertiveness, we have found, is best achieved in a systematic fashion. The procedure we use, developed as a result of our own work and that of a number of researchers on assertiveness (Wolpe, 1969; Bandura, 1965; Serber, 1972; McFall & Marston, 1970; Cautela, 1970; Fensterheim, 1970), is described in the balance of this paper.

COMPONENTS OF BEHAVIOR

The importance of non-verbal as well as verbal dimensions of communication has received extensive attention in the literature. In defining and facilitating assertive behavior, we have found systematic attention to the following components particularly useful:

1. Eye contact: Does one person non-assertively avoid looking at the partner when strong feelings are expressed? Is the expression of the eyes consistent with the verbal message? Does one partner use an aggressive "glare" to intimidate the other?

2. Body posture: Do the partners make contact while communicating? Do they lean toward or away from each other? Is the "listener" turned in the direction of the "talker?" Does one stand taller and "look down" on the other?

3. Gestures: Does one partner threaten with a clenched fist? Is capitulation signaled by turned open palms? Are hands thrust in pockets in resignation?

4. Facial expression: Is anger so difficult to express that one partner smiles while trying to say, "I'm mad at you"? Is one partner expressionless, regardless of strong feelings? Does an aggressive sneer interfere with open communication?

5. Timing: Is communication of feeling relatively spontaneous—occurring at the time of the incident? Or is resentment allowed to build and "fester"?

6. Fluency: Can each partner speak up openly without undue pauses or hesitation in speech? Do unfinished sentences leave much communication to assumption ("You know what I mean . . .")?

7. Content: Does "I am angry with you" come out as an aggressive "You're an SOB"? Do hurt feelings gain denied expression via "Oh, that's ok"?

Observation of each partner's behavior in terms of these components, and counselor efforts directed at systematic improvement of each component of the client's behavior (according to the *client's own* goals for his/her effective communication) can pay big dividends in increasing the value of counselor interventions.

FACILITATING ASSERTION

Keeping in mind these specific components of behavioral expression, we utilize a step-by-step process for assisting each client to become more adequately assertive and to avoid non-assertive self-denial or aggressive intimidation (Alberti & Emmons, 1974):

1. **Assessment**: Role playing the "John and Mary" scene described above, with careful observation by the counselor (including videotape whenever possible), provides an excellent starting point for identifying what is typically happening between the partners. Such assessment must include a very systematic and specific examination of each partner's behavior, with careful attention to each of the important components of behavior. A variety of such scenes may be used to demonstrate to the clients the inadequacies in their patterns of relating. A similar system, identified as "situational role playing" was described by Maass (1972).

2. **Situation definition**: At this point it is necessary to get very specific about individual situations which are sources of difficulty in the clients' relationship. John and Mary again provide us with a good example. We ask clients to go into considerable detail in defining just "what happens" in such a conflict situation.

3. **Covert rehearsal**: Working with John first, we would here ask the client to close his eyes and visualize the scene as he would typically respond to it.

4. **Modeling**: At this point, the therapist roleplays the scene, taking John's part, and demonstrating *one* effectively assertive response. It is important at this step to point out to the client that this is only *one sample* of an assertive response to Mary, not "*the* preferred" way to handle the situation. John should be encouraged to carefully observe the counselor's behavior in terms of the components noted above (i.e., watching more for the "how" than the "what" of the counselor response).

5. **Feedback**: The clients are now invited to review the modeled response: in what ways did the counselor's behaviors effectively carry his/her message? Counselors must be open to honest feedback about how they came across, and help clients to see the value of such feedback, specific to the components of assertiveness. Videotape playback of the modeled behavior is, of course, invaluable here. Also, continued emphasis upon discriminating among the non-assertive, assertive, and aggressive qualities in each behavioral component is important.

6. **Covert rehearsal**: Having reviewed their own behavior and observed the model presented by the therapist, clients are now asked to repeat step 3, but visualize a successful assertion and positive response.

7. **Client role play**: John is now ready to role play himself in the

scene, to try his "wings" at a new and more assertive response to Mary's demand. While many clients are "embarrassed" about role playing at first, simple encouragement from the counselor is usually sufficient to involve them in the process. For clients who are unable to allow themselves to role play, desensitization or other therapeutic procedures may be in order.

8. **Feedback:** Providing specific directed feedback to the client regarding each of the components of his/her behavior is the key step in the process of shaping effective assertive responses. Good feedback will let John know exactly what it is about his behavior toward Mary which dilutes the strength of his message (e.g., his downcast eyes, his whining voice, his "little boy" pout, his helpless gestures). Again, videotape is the most valuable resource for this step, when available.

9. **Coaching:** Repeating steps 6, 7, and 8 will give John practice toward achieving the self-expression he hopes for himself. Although we generally prefer to work jointly with both partners, such learning on John's part may be facilitated more readily without Mary present. In any event, it is important to inform her of what is taking place, and what she may expect in John's new behavior.

10. **In vivo rehearsal:** At this point John is prepared to direct his newly developed assertion toward Mary in their "natural" environment. It is best to encourage him to initially select situations in which the likelihood of success is great. Moreover, if Mary is supportive of the goal of increasing John's assertiveness, she can cooperate by reinforcing his efforts. Clearly, the counselor's effectiveness in preparing Mary will be a significant variable at this stage. Also important at this stage is that the client be sensitized to reinforcers for assertiveness in his/her own environment (e.g., the way others respond, the good feeling from self-expression), since the counselor will soon no longer be a source of support.

11. **Follow up:** The counselor is urged to maintain contact with the couple as John practices his assertiveness in a variety of situations. The process described above will not, of course, resolve all of the issues in the relationship of John and Mary. Indeed, John's new assertiveness may *create* some difficulties. Nevertheless, our experience with couples indicates that a relationship between assertive near-equals is measurably more satisfying to the partners than one in which one partner is dominant and the other a compliant, non-assertive "servant."

OTHER CONSIDERATIONS

Our preference in marital counseling is to work with both partners together. In the dynamics of an intimate relationship, there are few changes which can be made by one partner without affecting the other. We urge the partners to encourage and to reinforce assertiveness in each other. John may have typically held his criticism of Mary inside, because early in the marriage she reacted to critical statements by pouting, hurt, and tears. John decided that open expresion of his concerns wasn't worth the price of Mary's pain. This inhibition, of course, could be on the part of either partner toward the other. Such a pattern needs to be brought to attention, discussed openly, and a foundation for greater honesty developed.

Both partners must share responsibility for the quality of the relationship. John has avoided criticizing Mary because he "didn't want to hurt her." Yet John has allowed *himself* to hurt, *without ever actually checking out what Mary feels!* Often the counselor's direct intervention, "Have you ever asked Mary?" with Mary present, will open a new door and help to expose such destructive assumptions.

Choice is the heart of the matter. If John *knows* Mary "cannot handle" his assertions, and if he thereby chooses not to express himself in particular situations, that is his right. And such a choice leaves John actively directing his own life. If, however, he is avoiding such assertions routinely, because he "cannot" assert himself, a therapeutic intervention is necessary. In either event, both Mary and John need to be aware of such patterns in their relationship.

APPLICATIONS IN COUNSELING

This discussion has focused principally upon "one-partner dominant" relationships. Clearly, assertive (positive self-expressive and not aggressive) behavior, as we have defined it, is called for in nearly all areas of interpersonal relationships. Consider the needs of: women who are shedding the stereotypic "wife" role; counselors and other nurturing types who are caught in what has been termed "the compassion trap" (Phelps & Austin, 1975); socially inept, withdrawn individuals; children who are denied human rights by overprotective and/or authoritarian parents; minority group members oppressed by a white male dominated society.

The potential is great for helping these and other denied (or self-denying) persons, and those who may be denying others by their aggressiveness. The techniques of assertive behavior development which we have described here are widely used in therapy, in schools, in industry, in hospitals, in churches, in individual lives to increase the sense of personal power which people have in controlling their own lives. We consider them a valuable addition to the marriage counselor's repertoire as well.

23

DIVORCE RECOVERY: ASSERTION TRAINING FOR THE DIVORCED

Terry L. Paulson, Paula Landau

Joe sits alone at the bar of a singles club. People mill around him as he stares down at his drink; everyone seems to know each other and he doesn't know how to break in. His divorce has left him free but unsure of himself. Jan sits across the room masking her frustration in a blank stare. After fifteen years of marriage she too has lost the skills of starting new relationships. Both leave as they came, alone.

Linda is still feeling the sharp pain of the divorce. Every familiar face, each innocent question, every forced explanation bring her tears closer to the surface. As she walks into the store she bumps into an old mutual friend and is faced again with: "Haven't seen you for ages—how are you and Sam doing?"

Tom finally left after three long years of trying to keep a crumbling marriage together for his son's sake. Visitation has become a nightmare. His son, confused, ambivalent, and sometimes angry, seems to make every request a test of his father's love. Tom finds himself too afraid of losing his son to set limits. He resigns himself to another weekend of constant entertaining and overspending.

The label "failure" hangs over Sharon like a cloud. "You should have . . ." "How can you even think of . . ." "If you hadn't . . ." "If you would only . . ."—the phrases ring in her ears; she hears them so often from her family, friends, and children. Each little conflict with her ex rekindles her frustrated resentment: "It's his fault, but he makes me feel it's mine!"

Divorce has become a serious mental health problem in the United States. It is estimated that more than one-third of the marriages in this country end in divorce and the rate is rising. Even when it is wanted, divorce inevitably brings some sense of failure and loss. It forces changes in living style—friends, places, habits, activities, finances—which contribute to feelings of disorientation, frustration, withdrawal and depression.

In spite of growing concern over the magnitude of the problem, few treatment approaches have been found that are effective in giving the divorced the skills, support, and emotional energy to both cope with the problems and feelings created by the divorce and to move on to exploring new ways of living.

Assertion training is an action-oriented treatment approach that goes beyond talking about problems to offer direction, support, and constructive feedback to help people begin to move beyond their self-blocks and to develop and maintain new or lost skills. It has become one of today's most widespread and popular therapy approaches because it covers the whole range of responses to other people as well as vigorously combatting self-defeating attitudes. Too often, the divorced withdraw in frustration, guilt, agonizing self-analysis and re-living of the past or get so tied up in hostility and resentment that they are unable to let go and move on.

"Divorce Recovery," a group assertion training program for the divorced, is extremely effective in providing the impetus for the members to begin to take active charge of their lives. The group structure provides reality testing and support. It's not just counselors giving advice and support; all of the members share their experiences, triumphs and defeats. Lectures, role-rehearsal, modeling and outside practice help the members take their first tentative steps toward beginning to handle things differently. For some, the challenge to "take charge" is terrifying. One participant said:

> It was terrible. I was really depressed. I wasn't sure I had it in me to decide whether or not to go back to school, sell the car, move, or ask for help. I had never really lived by myself before, making all the household decisions by myself. People were always telling me what I should do. I was really confused and just wanted to get away. The group gave me the support I need to let me know it was my struggle and I could make my own decisions. Things just took off from there.

It is our belief that many of the men and women confronted with the realities of divorce are basically high-functioning people caught in a crisis of external change and internal confusion. It is not so much a question of *knowing how* to assert themselves as it is a problem of *overcoming* the self-blocks, guilt, and negative self-evaluations that interfere with allowing them to assert themselves. Any successful assertion training program for the divorced must place a major focus on struggling with the irrational belief systems that block assertiveness.

Assertion training in the past has emphasized two basic treatment approaches, direct skills development training and cognitive restructuring. AT treatment procedures for skills development have been adequately described elsewhere. Cognitive restructuring involves the identification of irrational beliefs and the self-statements that maintain them, critical testing of those statements in group interaction, and the identification and practice of counter self-statements to combat those irrational beliefs. Cognitive restructuring has become the primary goal of the intensive divorce recovery workshops and ongoing groups. The major concepts and group interventions used to combat the principal problem areas which confront the divorced are the subject of this paper.

AT WITH PROBLEMS OF THE DIVORCED

1. Ex-Spouse—Bed Partner, Lost Love, or Enemy?

Being able to "let go" is much harder than the signing of the legal forms. Too many waste their time and energy continually looking back through the rear view mirror at the *whys, what ifs, if only I'd*, or *s/he'd* . . . . To some, the divorce almost literally spells THE END—"he was the only one for me; there'll never be anyone else!" or "I'm a failure; no one will ever want me." Others have no desire for reconciliation but invest their time and energy trying to "get even." Both are different ways of holding on to the past and evading the central question: "Where do I want to go from here? How do I want to spend the rest of my life?" A major thrust of assertion training is focusing on what I can control—myself. Whenever my goal becomes controlling someone else—making him return to me, having her crawl back and ask for forgiveness, making him pay for what he did—I've lost.

Here is an example of how directive interventions are used in group assertion training to counter non-productive thought patterns:

Ann: It may take me a lot of time, but I'm not going to let him get away with it!
Therapist: What does your lawyer say?
Ann: He says we'll never be able to prove it. But I'll make him pay even if it's only in the hassling!
Therapist: Where will that get you?
Ann: I'll feel better!
Therapist: Will it get you closer to what you want to do with your life?
Ann: No.
Therapist: You seem to be letting him continue to control your life.
Ann: He doesn't control anything anymore!
Therapist: Without even trying he's keeping you from spending your energy and time in building a new life for yourself. It doesn't seem like you're getting anything out of this but stomachaches and battles.
Ann: I can't just drop it. He'll think he won!
Therapist: I'm not concerned about him. I am about you. I don't want to see you lose by continuing—let go!

Assertion training is action-oriented because beginning to act differently in relating to others is a crucial element in beginning to think differently. John felt that dating would be just an exercise in futility because he'd lost the "only" woman he could ever love. But he did agree to increase his social contacts as a means of handling his depression. Though he wouldn't admit it, he gradually began to enjoy being with other women. When his ex-wife asked him to return he refused because he had found a more satisfactory relationship.

The "drop-by" syndrome is characteristic of many divorces and is a serious impediment to letting go. As one participant said, "The old shoe may not be very attractive but at least it fits." Some couples maintain constant or sporadic contact for sex, comfort, house repairs, or almost any excuse. Each contact fans the emotional fires. Vacillation is increased by the fact that the contacts are novel; they aren't confronted with the daily living problems that caused them to separate. "We couldn't live together, but . . ." is a recurrent phrase that keeps too many people from cutting the ties and moving in a new direction. Group members are told to expect such mixed feelings; they are asked to decide whether "you want to spend the rest of your life in that relationship?" If the answer is no, they are taught the skills to limit necessary contact. "Broken record" is used to focus provocative conversations: "I would rather not talk to you unless it's a business issue." The goal is not to abuse, but to limit. There is no need to antagonize the ex-spouse, but it is counter-productive to encourage lingering on.

For many, entertaining one's ex-spouse is out of the question—a raging battle emerges every time. Conflict and distrust are as much a part of divorce as lawyers' fees. Each side is armed with past evidence of wrongdoing and dives headlong into the battle over division of property, spouse and child support, custody, child visitation arrangements, etc., etc. Group efforts are focused on helping the members do their part to restrict arguments to important issues and avoiding the trap of just finding fault. After role-playing the interaction in group, one member reported the following interaction:

Phil (group member): I want to let you know that I feel very annoyed at the way my scheduled visits with Michael have been cancelled at the last minute.

Ann (ex-wife): I told you I couldn't help it. Things just came up and I felt it was important for him to be with me.

Phil: I just wanted to let you know I didn't like it. In the future I would like to have a strict schedule and stick to it unless it is an emergency.

Ann: Well, you never seemed to care about the kids before. After all it was you who wanted to leave. If you really cared about Michael you would have thought about it then!

Phil: I don't want to argue about that, Ann. I do want a commitment from you as to a schedule for visitation with Michael that I can depend on.

Ann: OK. When do you want him next. I want you to at least take him for a weekend; not just a day.

Phil: Fine.

Phil reported weeks later that the issue had been resolved and a fixed schedule was set up. Phil also reported going beyond complaining to actually expressing appreciation to Ann for her cooperation in the matter; there was less tension and much less conflict.

2. There Are More Important Things Than Money—Somewhere!

No divorce is cheap. Each experiences increased costs and loss of income and it usually seems that the other is getting the better deal. Double the rent, double the utilities, lawyer fees, custody and babysitting fees—all add up to headaches, frustration, and blaming. Assertion training groups help participants move past futile anger, blame, and self-pity to looking at what they do to make things better for themselves.

They are shown how they can choose among a range of options; how they can either decrease their responsibilities and/or expectations or increase their power in various ways. They can begin to say "no" to others and to some of their own expectations of what they need; or they can increase their ability to live the way they'd like by improving their skills, financial planning courses, or being able to assertively ask for help. Taking charge often means learning to say to others "I need help." Clear, direct communication of needs does much to mobilize existing governmental support programs, as well as friends, family, business associates, even therapists!

Too often non-assertive clients wait for the world to do things for them and fail to actively push for what they want. Martha was sure there was no way she could earn a living with no work experience for 22 years. At the urging of another group member who had seen some of her crafts, she started selling them at a local swap meet. The confidence created by her first sales set the stage for a career. She was able to earn enough money to put some away for a store of her own. Group support was crucial in getting the plan going.

Too many people get bogged down in negative, self-defeating thoughts. "I gave him 20 years of my life and now I have nothing." "There's nothing I can do—I don't know how to do anything." They are encouraged to move out and explore their own potential, not to sit home and bewail their fates or try to "find" themselves. The number of opportunities that exist today for re-education and new careers is pointed out.

3. The Children—Parenting Isn't Proving

In no area are "shoulds" more inappropriate and obvious than in parenting. In divorce, those "should's" are only further exaggerated. Children learn early how to play off both parents to get what they want. Youngsters that were a big job for two become an intolerable burden for one parent, particularly if he or she feels the constant need to prove love. One mother complained: "I feel like I'm dragging three parasites on my back trying to get ahead. They are clawing and scrapping and keeping me down. Every time I get my head above water, they demand more. They never understand that there are limits to what I can do!" *They* never learned because *she* never had taken the responsibility of setting consistent limits and assertively following through. Disappointing her children meant "bad mother"; "bad mother" meant "I must make it up to them by sacrificing more." Sacrificing more just sets the stage for more resentment and family conflict.

In her assertion training group, Pam was brought to an awareness that she counted as much as her kids; only when she was able to give to herself could she really be free to give to her children without resentment. Pam learned to be able to disappoint them. As she put it: "I was keeping them on my back by not standing firm; when I let them know where I stand and that my words mean what I say, they give me room. I don't have to prove my love anymore. You know, I think they are more relaxed now, too."

The parent with custody is not the only parent who feels a need to prove. Too often visiting parents take on the role of entertaining and continually try to win back the love they feel the divorce has cost them. He or she may spend the whole weekend running, buying, proving—being unable to say "no" while feeling a nagging resentment that only increases guilt. Divorced parents need to learn how to say "no" to their children to balance their relationship. Assertion training can provide the prompting, the mental ammunition, and the support for beginning to try that out on a consistent basis. On the positive side, that means not having to prove your love every time the child calls a contest—"If you loved me, you would . . ." It means taking the time to assertively share your positive feelings of love when you feel them, "I just wanted to let you know I really enjoyed being with you this afternoon."

4. Family and Friends—Support or Sabotage

Divorce is a shaky place and it's natural to turn to family and friends. Unfortunately, when they most need support and bolstering, the divorced are too often met with resistance, anger and disapproval. The people around us are upset by change and it's all too easy to be "moral" about someone else's life.

Too much energy is spent worrying about what others think; their negative comments only serve to further deepen the sense of failure that many already feel. AT provides group support for dealing with and countering guilt-evoking messages. One client reported the following conversation:

Ruth: I know it will be hard on the kids in the beginning, but I'd rather do it now than go on like this.

Her Mother: I thought we had brought you up differently. Every marriage goes through some bad times—you can't just break up your children's home.

Ruth: I don't want to hurt my kids, Fred or you, but I feel I'll do more damage to my children by continuing to live this way.

Mother: You're just being selfish and childish.

Ruth: I am looking out for myself. I feel it's about time. I understand how you feel, but I don't want to talk about it any further. (When her mother tried to pursue it, Ruth got up and left.)

Ruth felt emotionally drained but relieved that she'd been able to stick to her guns with her mother without feeling guilty. Her assertion was met by applause and echoes of support in the group. Prior to assertion training she had felt trapped and defensive whenever anyone suggested she might be selfish. In the group, she began to experience her right to be interested in taking care of herself.

Tom had been married for 27 years. He owned his own bakery and his clients had grown close to him and his family over the years. He was encouraged to confront the problem directly with a clear message: "Beth and I are separated and we may get a divorce; it's something both of us will have to work out. I don't want you to feel you have to take sides—both of us would like your support and friendship." Tom was pleased by the feelings of relief the message gave him in dealing with those he cared about.

5. Looking Beyond the Bars— Getting in Touch with People

Becoming single again can be bewildering, confusing and frightening. Too many sit back waiting "to be ready" because the water looks awfully cold. The decision to reach out again to start a new social life means risking. The emphasis on *people* as opposed to *"the" person* is important. Participants are encouraged to find activities and groups centered around things they're interested in, such as square dancing, hiking, school courses, arts and crafts, etc., thus forming a common ground for meeting people who share their interests. But depression prevents many from even being able to identify their "wants."

George: Great. Do what you want! Well, I don't *know* what I want. I don't seem to want anything.

Therapist: I wouldn't expect you to want a lot. You've been cutting yourself off from what you want for a long time. It doesn't just happen. You have to exercise wanting just like anything else. Can you think of anything you'd like to do?

George: First, I want to get my head together. That's why I'm here.

Therapist: People who sit back getting their heads together usually end up bouncing off the walls inside their heads. Getting your head together is a process of doing and reacting and changing—it's not a state you just arrive at. I'd like you to pick one thing you used to like or think you might want to do this week.

George: I used to enjoy camping, but I haven't been in years.

Therapist: Would you be willing to check into the Sierra Club this week and go to a meeting?

George: OK.

George went on to join the Sierra Club and began to make new friends. Many never knew or have forgotten how to interact with others. Skill development is an integral part of assertion training groups. In order to build confidence, participants are encouraged to take the first small step by starting "mini" conversations in elevators, restaurants, department stores, on movie lines, etc.

Fear of rejection is another block that interferes with making new contacts. Too many people get caught in the "outcome trap" in which their self-esteem depends on success—the other person saying "yes." The focus in assertion training groups is on separating the outcome from the performance. Participants are told there are only two things they can control: how they deliver their messages and how often they do it. The other person's response is not under their control and can be affected by many variables—mood, being already involved with someone—so they shouldn't feel inadequate when someone says no.

Assertion training reaffirms each person's individuality and right to choose. This is particularly important in a society where there is no longer a universal code or set of standards. Each person has to evolve his or her own standards in a world that is very different from what one may remember from the pre-marriage life as a single. Women have begun taking a more active role, the request for sexual intimacy with no strings is common, and more people are opting for a "single" life-style. It is important for everyone to not only feel the right to choose one's own life-style, but to allow others the same freedom. The following conversation is representative of that point of view:

Jan: I don't know what makes men feel they have the right to ask me to hop into bed after one drink! I can't believe it!

Therapist: It sounds as though you expect him to know you don't want to go to bed.

Jan: I don't expect him to know anything but better manners.

Therapist: I think we get trapped in that kind of thinking. I feel a person has the right to ask for anything he wants as long as he's willing to accept the consequences—in this case, a possible quick refusal and dislike. He can ask; you have the right to say "no."

Karen: That's how I feel. I had a guy ask me to sleep with him last week after a half hour conversation. I felt flattered, but not

	all that interested. I told him so, and it was no big deal. I suspect he was even a little relieved.
Jan:	Do you mean to say I have to like that kind of person?
Therapist:	You don't have to like him. I'm just asking you to accept his right to ask and your right to refuse. Being different doesn't make either of you wrong.

Jan went on to talk about how difficult it was for her to give a really direct *no*. We spent 20 minutes in group modeling and role-playing a clear refusal without having to put the other person down.

SUMMARY

For some, the Divorce Recovery group temporarily became one of the primary stabilizing forces in their rapidly changing lives; they feel the support of others' sharing similar problems.

The group also focuses on decreasing confusion by providing a secure structure to help them make sense out of their world. They become aware that they can be concerned about their own self-interest without abusing others—that middle ground, in the midst of turbulent upsets, is often very hard for the divorced to find. Identifying assertive, withdrawing and hostile ways of responding sets the stage for choosing how they want to respond in different situations. The importance of doing to change, choosing which "shoulds" they want to live by, the assertive rights and blocks to assertion all become a part of the cognitive restructuring of their assertion training experience.

ASSERTIVENESS AS AN AID TO WEIGHT CONTROL

Merna McMillan

If the old maxim is true, and inside of every fat person is a thin one struggling to get out, then the struggle appears to have been a losing battle (no pun intended!). Obesity continues to be one of the major health problems in the United States, and is linked to a variety of disorders including cardiovascular disease, diabetes, arthritis and kidney disorders. The United States Department of Public Health (1966) has taken the position that regardless of health implications, obesity (overweight) is an aesthetic problem and, thus, often a psychological problem for patients who live in societies where overweight people are regarded as unattractive (U.S. Department of Public Health, 1966, p. 29).

SOCIAL & BEHAVIORAL IMPLICATIONS OF OBESITY

Dr. Louis Dublin, statistician with the Metropolitan Life Insurance Company (1953), has written concerning overweight:

It often provides a handicap in the personal life of individuals.

It can be a factor in employment, either because of the self consciousness of the job-seeking overweight, or because of the preference employers may give to applicants who are of normal weight. It is also a handicap in social relationships and may give rise to emotional problems. The fat child is ridiculed by other children. He is, therefore, likely to shun them and seek satisfaction in sedentary recreation and in eating. The chances of marriage for the obese girl are less than for her thinner rival (p. 995).

Three factors are generally cited in considering the etiology of obesity: genetic, traumatic, and environmental. While the causative factors in overweight may be multiple (Mayer, 1953), all treatment must ultimately be concerned with the regulation of food intake. The final admonition of most diet programs has been for long term success the clients must change their "eating habits." But until recently no one has concentrated on teaching them how this could be done. Insight therapies, psychoanalysis, and medical treatment using drugs has not centered on this aspect of treatment; now, however, techniques of behavior modification offer a promising approach to weight control.

After conducting a review of current research in the field, Dr. Albert Stunkard (1972), head of the Department of Psychiatry at Stanford University, concluded:

> Both greater weight loss during treatment and superior maintenance of weight loss after treatment indicate that behavior modification is more effective than previous methods for the treatment of obesity (p. 398).

He also commented on the creativity and patient responsibility that can highlight behavioral therapy for both patient and therapist. While the behavior therapies appear to be the most effective way to deal with the problem of overeating, a review of the research indicates the problem is by no means solved. In a comparative study of behavioral techniques in the treatment of obesity (Romanczyk, Tracey, Wilson & Thorpe, 1973), it was found that a full behavior management program employing all of the elements described was significantly more effective than any of the elements in isolation, although self monitoring did produce substantial weight loss.

In discussing results, mention was made of one of the significant problems in weight reduction. It was noted that the subjects receiving the full therapy package tended to show increasingly greater weight reduction from the post-treatment to the second follow-up. This suggests that they had learned behavioral skills which they were able to implement on a continuing basis. Only long-term longitudinal studies will, in fact, determine if this is true. Most studies report not only high attrition rates, but also discouraging results in long-term follow-up.

The importance of external cues in the environment which promote eating in the overweight, in contrast to the internal cues relied on by normal weight persons, has been well documented (Schlacter, 1968). Many of the procedures used in weight control programs deal directly with controlling the eating environment or teach the client to use self-control procedures when confronted with the external stimuli. The accompanying list has been found useful with clients in weight control and illustrates these procedures. Little attention, however, has been paid to the influence of significant others in the client's environment.

SABOTAGE

The American Society of Bariatric Physicians (specialists in the treatment of obesity) conducted a study reported in *Readers Digest* (1974), in which 213 of the 236 physicians contacted reported their patients frequently met resistance to their dieting efforts, not only from friends but also from close family members as well. Spouses were particularly notable contributors to such "sabotage," and it was estimated that 30 percent of patients encountered resistance in one form or another in their efforts to lose weight, even though mixed messages of encouragement were initially given. Stuart and Davis (1972) alluded to the need to individualize treatment and to involve significant others in reinforcing the client's efforts.

Self-esteem statements, in addition to focusing on social behaviors in assertive training, are especially important where potential sabotage has been identified. One client reported having been successful on previous attempts to lose weight until her mother would visit. The mother would persist in fixing "goodies" and insisting the client eat them and be hurt if she did not comply, insisting her 200-pound daughter looked "peaked" from her dieting. In a group setting, behavioral rehearsals were held over a period of four sessions in which the client developed a repertoire of assertive responses and practiced using covert self-esteem statements in response to her mother's insistance. She proudly reported success through both Thanksgiving and Christmas season and subsequently achieved her desired weight.

Sabotage by a spouse can be especially destructive and it is important, when at all possible, to enlist the aid of the significant others in a client's life in weight control just as in any other behavior change. They can represent powerful reinforceres or deterrents to the client's progress.

ASSERTIVENESS TRAINING AS A TREATMENT STRATEGY

The application of systematic ways to assist a client in combating this type of sabotage has seldom been described in the literature. Procedures involving the learning of assertive responses have been used for *other* problem behaviors, and show promise for use in a weight control program to deal with the problem of sabotage from self and others. Rimm (1973), in the treatment of phobias, used procedures based on the work of Wolpe (1969) involving thought stopping and covert assertion to reduce anxiety, as well as teaching new ways of responding to cues which promote overeating.

In addition to covert self-assertion, learning assertive responses to others appears to have the potential to facilitate both weight loss and maintenance of a desirable weight. The use of assertive training specifically applied to eating behaviors may provide another technique for self-regulation which is so necessary when the therapist or group contact ceases. Assertive responses can be useful in situations involving attempts by others to sabotage the efforts of those in weight control programs.

Assertive training administered to groups using modeling and behavioral rehearsal has been cited in a variety of studies as an effective means of modifying social behavior (Alberti & Emmons, 1974), but at the time of the author's initial study (McMillan, 1975), it had not been widely reported as having been used specifically in any weight control research.

Since that time, assertive training, thought stopping, and covert assertion have been used in my work with groups and individuals for weight control. Some of these clients have been enrolled in other types of weight control programs or were seeing a medical doctor for treatment of obesity. Assertive training can be a powerful adjunct to any weight control program; for regardless of the treatment modality chosen, the ultimate task comes to be learning to say "no" to oneself and others concerning the consuming of excess food.

AT PROCEDURES IN A WEIGHT CONTROL PROGRAM

While initial weight loss may occur with any approach when the person is motivated, sustained weight loss appears to be best accomplished through combining assertive training with other behavioral procedures. The following procedures might be included in a program:
1. Discuss research findings related to overeating, behavioral methods, and assertive training;
2. Gather information from client (Figure 24-1);
3. Keep weekly graph of weight and weight loss;
4. Provide nutritional and exercise information;

5. Take "before" and "after" photos;
6. Prepare client's contract for weight loss with rewards including significant others when possible;
7. Practice relaxation technique;
8. Record and analyze eating behavior. Depending on analysis, any one or a combination of these strategies may be initiated:
   A. Identification of situations where assertive responding to another would be necessary in relation to refusing food. An example can be modeled by the therapist, behavioral rehearsal conducted in pairs, alternating roles. Each pair chooses an example to rehearse before the group for feedback. Responses also practiced covertly.
   B. Clients list two things that are reinforcing high probability behaviors occuring during the day (talking on the phone, reading, etc.). Choices discussed in pairs and with group. Each person chooses two eating behaviors to modify during the week from the list provided with additions from group included (Figure 24-2). Explanation given concerning the use of engaging in high probability behavior when a forbidden eating behavior stimulus occurs. Clients are instructed to make a positive assertive response regarding controlling their behavior (E.g.: "I can control my eating by doing other things I enjoy.")
   C. Practice in visualizing forbidden situation related to eating behavior (E.g.: snacking, or particular item). Instruction in thought stopping and assertive responding first vocally, then subvocally. Practice first under direction of therapist then covertly.
   D. Identify one positive and one negative statement from information forms that have special meaning to the client (Figure 24-3). Therapist explains pairing of these thoughts making a high probability behavior (except eating) contingent on thinking these thoughts with the negative aspect presented first (anti-overeating) and the positive thought (pro-noneating) second. Each client writes the two statements on a card to carry with them to practice during the week.
   E. Discussion of sabotaging by others and the use of vocal and subvocal assertion. Examples elicited and practiced.
   F. Practice thought stopping and covert assertion using *real* food items.
   G. Therapist explains use of fantasy statements described and recorded by clients (Figure 24-3). During relaxed state, instruction is given to visualize the fantasy as clearly as

possible and to conjure up this image just prior to eating any food.

OTHER BEHAVIORAL TECHNIQUES IN WEIGHT CONTROL

A basic behavioral approach will have the client first identify not only how much is being eaten, but when and under what circumstances. This information can be recorded on a tabular form. This self-monitoring alone will produce initial weight loss for some, but its main purpose is to identify the particular eating habits so problem areas can be identified and the program can be individualized and progress evaluated.

It is essential to determine if the client has medical approval for embarking upon a weight loss program. Nutritional and caloric information must be provided to ensure the patient has a clear understanding of the amount of food which can be consumed to produce the desired weight loss, and the role of nutrition in maintenance of health. These same methods can be used, of course, in conjunction with a physician to assist persons who need to alter their eating patterns for physical disorders such as cardiovascular disease, diabetes, etc.

Another innovative strategy consists of stressing a *positive* rather than a *deprivation* approach, by having clients compute how many calories (or carbohydrates, if this has been approved by their physician) they have to "spend" over a week or even a month, as opposed to stressing the limitations imposed by a 900 or 1200 calories a day "diet." Clients respond with enthusiasm to this approach which allows for decision making on a week long basis and recognize that utilization of food by the body is not confined to a 24-hour process.

Clients are also instructed to never say they are "*on* a diet" which implies they can "go off," but to say to themselves and others, if necessary, "I am changing my eating behaviors." They are also cautioned to never explain nor apologize to others about the methods and procedures they are employing. Practice during assertive training sessions specifically deals with responses to the inquiries of others. One client found strength in saying to herself, "Those that matter, don't mind; and those that mind, don't matter!"

Various behavioral methods can be employed using contingency management self-control procedures, and focusing on breaking existing behavioral chains of eating and establishing new ones. Clients are also asked to complete an information sheet about past efforts at weight control, and to describe some of their perceptions about being overweight and normal weight (Figure 24-3). This information is also used in therapy, and the same principles which are applied to external eating *behavior* are also utilized to control *thoughts* toward eating.

To allow for the fact that those who overeat seem to respond to environmental cues rather than internal cues, real food items are used whenever possible in simulating situations for assertive training.

COVERT ASSERTIVE METHODS

The modification of self-talk and learning covert assertiveness can take the same form as other assertive training methods. The client identifies a particular situation or stimulus which presents a problem, using the record of food intake as a guide. Using real food items, clients practice vocally, then subvocally, assertive statements (sometimes coupled with self-esteem statements) giving particular reasons why they want to be of normal weight. Some of these responses have been identified by the client on the form filled out at the initial session (Figure 24-3). Some clients use a fantasy scene of themselves being of normal weight to block thoughts of eating; such a visualization is used in addition to the assertive statements.

The use of a relaxation technique is helpful at the beginning session and is used subsequently as an aid and in combination with other procedures.

One client, whose overeating focused around mealtime preparation for her family, found particular help from her fantasy scene of herself walking on the beach in a bikini on a beautiful, sunlit, windblown day. Every time she had to open the refrigerator, she visualized the scene, coupled with the assertive statement, "NO! I can control my eating behavior."

This same statement is also reported by clients as being helpful to say when using thought stopping to block eating impulses. One client who had been a compulsive eater identified the anxiety associated with being lonely as a key factor in her behavior. She recognized that she was overeating when alone, which initially reduced her anxiety; this caused her to be more anxious because of her overweight, which promoted her to cyclically overeat to reduce the anxiety about overeating! She successfully stopped the eating binges through the use of relaxation, imagery, thought stopping and covert assertion. It is important to recognize the importance combining strategies and individualizing the program to fit the particular behavior of the client.

One woman overate following each meal when she cleaned the plates of other family members, not being able to see food "wasted." She was aided in her learning to save even small items for the next day by subvocally shouting "stop" and saying "No!, I am not a garbage can!"

While some of these responses may seem frivolous, they can be powerful aids to clients who have previously believed their behavior and thoughts, particularly about food, were beyond their control.

SIDE EFFECTS OF ASSERTIVE TRAINING

There are often sexual fears surrounding weight loss. Many women, in particular, feel a renewed sensuality and in becoming more attractive to the opposite sex will often regress in their weight control program unless specific measures are taken to identify and assist with this problem. This is another area where assertive training can play an important role by identifying real or feared situations where the client may have to acquire assertive behaviors as a means of reducing anxiety to deal with compliments, as well as real, or feared, sexual advances.

The use of assertive training in weight control programs is of particular importance because it provides a means for clients to reduce the anxiety which sometimes leads to overeating, it teaches them new ways of responding to attempts to sabotage their efforts at weight control, and also helps to individualize treatment. Another advantage is that it can also be administered in a group setting by para-professionals and requires a relatively short therapeutic period when compared with traditional psychotherapies.

Figure 24-1

Personal History

Name _____ Date _____

Address _____ Phone _____

_____ Age _____

Occupation _____ Education _____

Marital Status _____ Children _____

Parents Living _____ # of Brothers _____

# of Sisters _____ Position in Family _____

Present Weight _____ Height _____ Desired Weight _____

Weight range in adulthood: Year weighed least ____ Weight _____

Year weighed most _____ Weight _____

Weight during past 3 months: _____ _____ _____
                                    3 mos. ago 2 mos. ago 1 mo. ago

At what age did you first become overweight? _____

What do you think was the reason? _____

Health _____ (if currently under a doctor's care or taking prescription medicine, please explain on the back of this form.)

Do you (always, sometimes, never) eat breakfast _____
                                                  lunch _____
                                                  dinner _____
                                                  between meals _____

Favorite food _____ Do you have a problem with eating binges? _____ If so, what food is usually involved? _____

Can you identify a mood that brings this on? _____

What diets have you tried? _____

Have you sustained a permanent weight loss from any of these? ____

Which ones? _____ How much? _____

Please identify any members of your family that are overweight:

_____

Have you ever enrolled in a diet program or dieted under a doctor's supervision? _____ When? _____ Please name the program and explain:

_____

Did you lose weight? _____ How much? _____

For how long? _____

Have you ever used drugs to lose weight? _____
Please explain and note results:

_____

Do you consider yourself a competitive person? _____

Figure 24-2

Eating Behaviors to Be Modified

1. Pause for two minutes halfway through each meal.
2. Always sit down when eating, even a small amount.
3. Chew each mouthful 20 times, become aware of the texture and flavor of each bite . . . RELAX.
4. Completely finish the mouthful you are chewing before preparing the next bite. This means not putting the food on your fork nor cutting the next bite until you have finished the mouthful you are chewing. It is helpful to put the utensils down between bites.
5. Keep food separate from other activities (TV, reading, driving, etc.) which might prompt eating when you are not hungry.
6. Eat in the same spot, sitting down, with the table completely set.
7. Use a small plate; it will appear you have more to eat.
8. Keep food **only** in the kitchen and eat only foods that have to be prepared.
9. Always shop from a list and shop only after you have eaten a full meal.
10. Save one item from each meal for later.
11. Eat only foods that can be eaten with utensils.
12. Leave a small portion of every item on your plate (about 10%).

General Considerations

- Try to include at least a small portion of a favorite food at each meal so you will feel satisfied.
- Notice how other people eat their food. Notice what trim people eat and how they eat. Observe overweight people eating and note any differences.
- Some people lose more rapidly if they take the same amount of food in 6 or 7 snacks instead of the traditional 3 meals.
- Enjoy your food. Be aware of each mouthful you take. Make it last as long as you can. It takes your body at least 15 minutes to tell you it is full. Give it a chance.

Figure 24-3

Personal Reasons for Deciding To Lose Weight

Name_____ Date_____

Positive statements about being of normal weight (not overeating):

1. _____

2. _____

3. _____

4. _____

Negative statements about being overweight (overeating):

1. _____

2. _____

3. _____

4. _____

Circle the one positive and one negative statement above that mean the most to you.

The most pleasant scene I can imagine concerning my being of normal weight is: _____

Have you imagined this scene vividly? Never before _____
Sometimes _____
Always _____

Identify something about yourself that you would like to change:

_____

Identify something about yourself that makes you a special person, something that makes you feel good about yourself:

_____

25

ASSERTIVENESS AND THE JOB HUNT

Kathleen Wheeler

"How can I sell myself when I don't have any skills?"
"I know I can do the job, but I always fail miserably in interviews."
"I haven't worked in years. How can I possibly compete with all those college graduates?"
"I'm scared to death of looking for a job. I just don't know how to begin."

If you are someone who is involved in facilitating the development of assertive skills in others, you have probably encountered these and similar questions frequently. Perhaps you have even asked them yourself at one time or another. Where *does* one begin in looking for a job? And, more specifically, what does it mean to launch an "assertive" job hunt?

It is not uncommon to see individuals who are normally assertive in other areas of their lives become suddenly immobilized when faced with the prospect of job hunting. Many who make their own decisions with ease elsewhere will allow others to make their decisions for them when they are job-hunting. They may ask that a psychological test decide for them what they "should" be doing. Or they may allow the obscure "Employer" or the "Occupational Outlook" dictate where they will look for work. People who customarily establish independent goals and take assertive action will often passively wait for a job to turn up after mailing resumes to Personnel departments. Women who have learned to avoid trying to please their husbands at their own expense suddenly find themselves, in a very real sense, trying to please the employer—again, at their own expense. People who refuse to answer offensive questions in other settings will waive that right in the employment interview. Men and women of all backgrounds who usually have positive self-images may, when they are planning their careers, willingly accept external judgments of their qualifications and abilities. Regardless of the group—men, women, jail inmates, adolescents, homemakers—concerns surrounding the job hunt are universal, and their significance is real.

The goal of Assertiveness Training (AT), as described by Alberti and Emmons in *Your Perfect Right*, is to "help people to learn to exercise their rights as equals . . . and to assist them in developing an expanded repertoire of behaviors such that they are free to act in their own best interests." The goal of developing effective job seeking skills is the same—to learn to exercise your rights as a job seeker, and in doing so, to be able to *choose* where you wish to work. The assertive job-seeker, in effect, is as much a "screener" as is the employer.

The value of assertive behavior is in its tendency to greatly reduce feelings of personal powerlessness. In planning a career or pursuing a job search, there are many opportunities to feel personally powerless. What most don't recognize is that it doesn't have to be that way. Assertive job-seeking helps to eliminate those feelings and, what's most important, it works. The purpose of this article is to illuminate the relationship between assertiveness and the job hunt, and to enable the professional facilitator to make the best use of AT methods in the area of career planning and job seeking skills.

Many of the basic principles and assumptions of effective job seeking coincide directly with those of assertive training. It will be useful to clarify those here, and then to proceed by stating specifically how those principles can be translated into exercises or techniques for use with groups.

At the heart of behavior therapy and AT is the belief in the importance of individuals setting their own clearly defined goals and actively working to achieve those goals. The same is true of any workable job-seeking system. The individual must first define his or her goal. To chase job leads indiscriminately is to behave in a "reactive" rather than a "proactive" manner, and will probably lead to frustration.

AT emphasizes the use of positive reinforcers, along with gradual change. The use of a hierarchy of steps, beginning with low risk behaviors that are relatively assured of success, and then moving to more radical responses, is seen as a practical and desirable learning tool. Again, the wise job-seeker will employ a similar method in researching a new position, rewarding him- or herself along the way.

Assertiveness trainers emphasize, above all, the concept of choice. The goal is an enhanced repertoire of behaviors allowing for "self-fulfilling responses in a variety of situations." An assertive job seeker, too, begins with the assumption that there are more ways than one to behave, for example, in an interview.

Most importantly, effective job-seeking and assertiveness both require practice. They are both learned behaviors. The emphasis in both fields is on skill development. This conceptualization in itself is a freeing thought to many people. "I can *learn* how to get what I want and feel good about it," rather than "Assertiveness is something some people are lucky enough to have, and some aren't."

Assertive job-seeking involves not waiting for a "great job" to turn up or blaming the tight job market for one's occupational fate. It means planning a self-directed search aimed at landing a specific job. In addition, the behavioristic concept that behavior changes attitude, or that what you *do* will effect how you *feel*, is true of the job-seeking process. The ways in which one describes experience or approaches an employer will in turn effect the candidate's feelings about self and abilities.

STAGES IN THE JOB HUNT

A successful job search, according to John Crystal and Richard Bolles in their book, *Where Do I Go From Here With My Life?*, includes roughly three stages, which are described below. AT methods can be creatively adapted at each stage.

1) Self Assessment: An initial decision-making process, incorporating an evaluation of one's strongest and most enjoyable skills; an assessment of one's interests, and an analysis of what working conditions are most suitable to one's productivity and well-being.

2) Research: Self-generated, live research to identify openings and opportunities that will correspond to the personal criteria developed in Stage One; a time of crystallizing goals.

3) Communicating Potential: Having chosen a few select places where one might like to work, the final step involves getting hired—essentially by demonstrating to a potential employer how one's skills will match the employer's needs.

SELF-ASSESSMENT

In discussing the first stage of effective job-seeking there are two AT concepts which are particularly relevant, and which can be easily applied in either a workshop setting or on a one-to-one basis. The first is positive self-statements *a la* Albert Ellis, and the second is behavioral goal-setting. Consider the story of Ellen:

> Ellen was a recently divorced woman in her forties who found it necessary to re-enter the job market. Her experience consisted of several years of managing a household, in addition to occasional part-time work in an office. She was anxious about facing the prospect of job-hunting, stating that she "didn't know what she wanted to be," and that she "wasn't qualified to do much of anything."

It was suggested to Ellen that instead of thinking about what she wanted to be, she think about what she wanted to do, in terms of the skills she especially wanted to use. When she said she didn't have any, she was asked to write down the tasks she had performed in her various experiences, and to then identify the skills she had used in doing those tasks. For example:

Clerk-typist — organizing filing systems
editing reports
dealing with the public
writing procedure manuals

Cub Scout Den Mother — planning recreational activities
budgeting funds
selling new ideas
group leadership

Ellen was astonished at the variety of skills she could claim, and began to prioritize her skills to further define those she wished to use in future jobs. This activity provided the foundation for Ellen to: 1) make positive statements about her skills (not "I was only a housewife," but "I have skills in organizing, planning, writing, etc."), and 2) set special goals based on what she liked to do and what she was good at.

The process of skills-identification described in Ellen's story was developed by John Crystal, and is most effectively accomplished in pairs or groups of three:

1) Have each person make a list of tasks taken from both paid and unpaid experience.
2) Have each person pick one task and identify his or her own skills first.
3) Have the other person/s suggest additional skills which may have been left out.

Practicing making positive self-statements is a vital part of AT and has a notable impact on the employment interview. A fun and tremendously beneficial follow-up exercise to skills-identification is "I'm Good Ats":
1) Have each person in the group pick one of the skills which they have identified from their tasks.
2) Go around the group and have each person make a statement beginning with the words "I'm good at," and adding a skill of their choice.
3) Suggest these guidelines:
—Keep voice volume high
—Don't shrug
—No self put-downs such as "I'm good at writing, but I'm a lousy speller!"
—Don't giggle

An AT approach to behavior change begins with setting specific, behavioral goals. In most AT groups this is accomplished by first "targeting" the behavior one wishes to change. "I want to be happier," or "I need more from my marriage" are vague statements which are indeed difficult to work with. On the other hand, "I would like to work on asking my spouse to spend time playing tennis with me" is a reachable goal, and one likely to meet with results.

A similar process becomes vital in career planning and job-hunting. "I want a fulfilling job," or "I want to make lots of money," or even "I want to work with people," are statements that are only rough approximations of goals and represent only a beginning. To target a behavioral goal in a career planning sense would mean to define how one actually wishes to spend one's time on a job. **How** do you want to work with people, using which skills, and under what conditions? Only then is it possible to mobilize efforts in a direction that has payoffs.

It is also wise to set behavioral goals in terms of the hunt itself. Examples of such goals might be: "I will make three contacts this week," or "I will ask so and so for a letter of reference." These goals are much more "do-able" than "I must work harder to find a job."

RESEARCH

The second stage of effective job-seeking involves skills in actively making contacts and seeking information concerning places to work. Here, too, there are a number of AT tools which can facilitate the development of those skills.

It can be frightening to make cold calls to businesses or to talk to employers face-to-face. It can also be difficult sometimes to get in to see those one wants to speak with, particularly in large bureaucracies. The

AT concept of using a hierarchy of risk, beginning with small, manageable amounts, can be suggested as an assignment for job-hunters. As a way of "getting your feet wet," John Crystal suggests "interviewing for fun." This aids in getting a feel for talking to people, and it provides beneficial practice for the employment interview. Viewed from an AT stance, it can also be almost a means of *in-vivo* desensitization. It is also a means of building reinforcement into a job campaign. Talking to people in a low-risk situation about one's genuine interests is reinforcing and confidence-inspiring. This is how one workshop participant went about it:

> Steve was reluctant to visit any employers. Instead, he pored over the want ads, mailed out countless resumes, scouted bulletin boards in personnel departments and employment agencies and made phone calls to potential employers. He balked, however, at the idea of talking to employers in person. Nothing came of his job search and he became increasingly discouraged. It was recommended to him that he try Crystal's *field survey method* for getting over his fear of talking to employers.
>
> First he chose one of his hobbies, skiing, and went to a ski shop to talk to them about their business. This was easy for him since he was enthusiastic about this subject and was not looking for a job. He asked them how they got into the business of skiing, what they liked about it, what they didn't like about it, and where there were others making a living doing ski-related activities.
>
> Next he went to talk to someone who did the kind of work he wanted to do—not to ask for a job, but to seek information which would help him in a later interview. He continued in this way and soon had developed several contacts in his chosen field, gained self-confidence and eventually got a job in the area he wanted—by talking to the employer face to face.

The facilitator can suggest that individuals try the field survey either alone or with a friend until they are more comfortable.

Another common concern brought up by clients during their research efforts is that of not being able to get in to see the hiring official in an organization, not being able to get some information they want about an agency, or having difficulty presenting new innovations into old systems. The "Broken Record" technique—calmly repeating a request over and over without apology or over-explanation—often brings results in such situations. The following is an example of how this technique might be appropriately applied:

> Bill and Lorraine wanted to share a job (where each would

work half-time on the same job). They approached an employer together and wanted to make a proposal showing the value of their complementary skills. This concept is a new one and has yet to catch on in many organizations. The personnel department of this employer would not accept a joint application for employment. The first clerk they spoke to refused to accept the application because there was no rule providing for it. Bill and Lorraine persisted in their intent to apply in this manner by repeating over and over that they wanted to talk to someone about their proposal. Soon they were talking to the clerk's supervisor. This process continued for some time until they had gone through five or six levels in the hierarchy and found someone who was in a position to discuss the topic with authority.

Both the field survey and the broken record technique can be practiced in role-play sessions ahead of time:

1) Have the job-hunter write a paragraph describing the situation to be rehearsed. For example, "I am in a ski shop, and the owner asks if he can help. My task is to initiate a conversation with him about his work." Or: "I am in an office facing a somewhat cold secretary who wants to know why I'm here. My task is to request to see the boss assertively until I get what I want."
2) Set up the situation with a variety of players from the group, so that a variety of behavioral patterns are explored.
3) Watch for anything that sounds like a self put-down, an unnecessary apology, or over-explanation.
4) Give feedback on body language.

COMMUNICATING POTENTIAL

The final stage of an effective job search is that of communicating skills in a positive manner to the employer. Here, the AT concepts of choice, practice, and non-verbal assertiveness contribute greatly to feelings of self-respect and a sense of equality with the employer.

In the context of the AT or Career Planning workshop, a variety of behavioral options can be practiced with minimal risk and much support. The interview situation lends itself beautifully to role-play practice. Even the resume can be written in an assertive manner, by eliminating "self put-down" language, and by putting selected positive self-statements into writing.

The notion of choice is a powerful one. It is very easy to make the assumption that in an employment interview we must answer any and

every question that is put to us. One tool that increases personal freedom by allowing for alternatives to immediate answering is that of "fielding" questions, a concept developed by Irene Dempsey, a learning consultant in Davis, California. This can easily be practiced in a workshop in pairs or small groups. Begin with participants asking each other any question that comes to mind. (It doesn't need to be job-related). The task of the person who is "fielding" is to respond to the questioner without answering the question.
For example:

Question:
How much do you weigh?

Options for fielding:
Speaking of weight, I was reading an article . . . .

Enough.

I prefer not to answer that.

I'll forgive you for asking that question if you'll forgive me for not answering it.

The guidelines for fielding are: Take your time. You don't need to respond quickly. The important element is choice. You are free to answer or not, as you please.

An often-expressed concern in Career Planning or AT groups is how to deal assertively with awkward or even illegal questions in an interview. Examples of such questions range from "Do you plan to have children?" to "What does your husband do?" Fielding these questions seems to be a superior alternative to passively answering or aggressively saying "It's none of your business." Consider how fielding worked for Sara:

Sara had been through a series of frustrating interviews in her job search. She expressed resentment at being asked questions which she felt had nothing to do with her potential job performance. Her responses to such questions had normally been either passive or aggressive. Her typical responses had been to answer them apologetically or to over-explain. Once she responded with "That's a male chauvinist question and I don't intend to answer it." This ended the interview and she left with bad feelings and no job.

In a workshop the possibility of fielding questions without actually answering them was discussed. Sara practiced fielding a variety of questions with the help of the group. As a result, she felt more in control because she knew that she was in charge of what information she would reveal to the interviewer. In future interviews she spoke positively about her abilities and skillfully fielded the questions she chose not to answer. A few weeks later she found a job she wanted and shared some examples of questions she had fielded. Here are two of them:

Interviewer: "Are you divorced, separated or what?"
Sara: (with a twinkle in her eye) "Is this a proposal?"

Interviewer: "Why did you leave your last job?"
Sara: "I'll be glad to answer that but first I'd like to know why the last person left the job I'm applying for."

Sara felt that her responses were humorous, assertive, and set the stage for an atmosphere of equality and mutual respect. She felt that her assertive style had helped her in getting hired.

In addition to recognizing the range of choices for verbal responses open in the interview, it is also helpful to practice non-verbal means of taking charge:

> John felt intimidated by the panel interview situations he encountered in applying for work in large organizations. Most of the rooms were confining and the experience of three people questioning and judging him was overwhelming to him. It was suggested that one option for taking charge of the situation was to use assertive body language in claiming space for himself. He practiced a variety of behaviors including shaking hands, commenting on the environment and moving his chair to a spot that was comfortable for him.
>
> John's next interview went well. He made time at the beginning to get his bearings which paid off in self-esteem.

The facilitator may want to encourage practice of effective body language in the context of role-play interviews. This can be done in small groups or in trios—with an interviewer, an interviewee, and an observer. It is often helpful if the facilitator or another member of the group "models" a particular behavior before the job hunter practices it him or herself. Feedback can be given on voice volume, eye contact, speech fluency, use of hand gestures, and speech content. This exercise goes more smoothly if people first identify specific interview questions they would particularly like to work on. Examples might be: "What is this gap in your employment?" or "What makes you think you're qualified for this type of work?" and so on.

SUMMARY

There are innumerable opportunities for creatively asserting oneself at each stage of the career planning and job-seeking process. The theoretical conceptualizations and practical techniques of the field of AT have tremendous application for job-seekers. If you are a professional facilitator of AT, you are in a unique position to encourage individuals to re-think their assumptions regarding themselves and the world of work, and to expand their awareness of their choices. And that is what effective job-seeking is all about.

26

FOUR MYTHS OF NONASSERTIVENESS IN THE WORK ENVIRONMENT

Sherwin B. Cotler, Susan Morgan Cotler

This chapter describes four myths (myth of anxiety, myth of modesty, myth of the good friend, and the myth of obligation) which encourage people to act non-assertively, not only in their personal lives (Cotler & Guerra, 1976), but in their working environment as well. It is recognized that the behaviors described here do not inevitably occur with each and every individual; however, their occurrence has been frequent enough to merit an awareness of when and where these behaviors can interfere with job success and satisfaction. It is also recognized that men and women may be affected somewhat differently by these four myths in the working environment; consequently, it may be helpful to look at certain variances within each of these myths in order to understand and work more satisfactorily with both sexes.

A *myth*, as used here, is simply a popular belief which is erroneous. Thus, the *myth of anxiety* suggests that a person *should* not feel anxious in social situations, when the fact is that *most* people *do* feel some tension in certain social conditions. The *myth of modesty* would lead us to believe that one should *never* talk about, or allow others to talk about, oneself in positive terms.

The very pervasive *myth of the good friend* tells us that a ''good friend'' always knows exactly what one wants and needs, even if one has not said a word. Similarly, the *myth of obligation* drives individuals to agree to *any* request of another person, regardless of personal cost.

Let's take a closer look at each of these four destructive beliefs, in the employment context:

THE MYTH OF ANXIETY

Individuals who subscribe to the myth of anxiety believe that it is a sign of weakness and inadequacy to have, or even worse to show others, tense or anxious feelings. Furthermore, this individual often believes that if this anxiety is detected, the other person (be it an interviewer, a supervisor, or a fellow employee) will ridicule, reject, and/or take advantage. As a result of this belief system, the person accepting the myth of anxiety will go to great extremes in order to cover up signs of anxiety in front of others. Unfortunately, trying to cover up and "power through" feelings and overt symptoms of anxiety does not work very well at times. Consequently, when some of the symptoms of anxiety begin to show (e.g., sweating, flushing, cracking voice, trembling), the individual, trying desperately to cover up these symptoms, may become increasingly anxious as a direct result of the cover up itself! Obviously a self-defeating effort.

During the job interview, if the individual spends a considerable amount of energy or becomes increasingly anxious in trying to cover up signs of tension, then he or she is likely to become less able to think clearly and to answer the questions being asked. Instead, this person is likely to spend increasing time making internal statements to himself or herself such as, "I wonder if he sees the sweat spots under my arms," "I am really screwing up again." "I would sure like a glass of water, but my hands would shake so much I couldn't drink it."

There are several alternatives to reduce the feelings and symptoms of anxiety when one interviews for a new job. A first step in relieving the pressure in a job interview (or for that matter in a presentation, confrontation, etc.) is to acknowledge that anxiety *is* what one feels when confronted with a situation one would prefer to avoid. Similarly, the awareness that others may also feel much the same way in similar circumstances, may enable one to verbalize to oneself (and/or to other "safe" individuals) that this anxiety is not something to be ashamed or embarrassed about.

If the interviewer can be perceived as a "safe" individual, and the interviewee, therefore, can share his or her feelings of discomfort and anxiety, the individual no longer need expend large amounts of energy trying (often unsuccessfully) to cover up the tension symptoms.

MYTHS OF NONASSERTIVENESS IN WORK ENVIRONMENT

Consequently, the tension level is very likely to subside within a relatively brief period of time. If the anxious individual can recognize that it is very normal and, in some cases, even helpful to have a certain level of tension (e.g., in taking a test or being interviewed for a job, some mild tension will improve task performance), then it may be more acceptable to share these feelings with the other individual.

An example may help to clarify:

Job Interviewer: Hello, my name is Bob Bigwig.
Prospective Employee: Hello, I'm Jason Maloy.
Job Interviewer: Mr. Maloy, I see that you are applying for a job as a district salesperson.
Prospective Employee: Yes, that is correct. I have heard some very favorable things about this company, and I believe I would very much like to work here.
Job Interviewer: What kind of background do you have for a sales position?
Prospective Employee: I have had three previous jobs in sales, and although I am aware of the fact that I am feeling a little anxious right now, I typically do quite well in sales.
Job Interviewer: If you are well qualified, there is no reason to be nervous here.
Prospective Employee: I believe I am well qualified; however, I also know that I sometimes feel a bit tense at first in new situations or in situations where there is alot at stake for me.
Job Interviewer: Maybe you are right. I suppose it is much less stressful for me than for you!

It is important to note that the prospective employee did share how he was feeling fairly early in the job interview, and came back with a clear, assertive statement when the interviewer said something to negate the presence of any stress. As such, this may go a long way in helping to feel more at ease in this situation. If, however, the tension became increasingly apparent and was not acknowledged by the prospective employee, the interviewer may conceivably form a number of erroneous conclusions (e.g., the person is lying about his qualifications, the person does not interact comfortably with others and, therefore, would make a poor salesperson). Similarly, it is often helpful to acknowledge anxiety when making a presentation to a group of colleagues or even clients: "I always feel a little nervous when I stand in front of a group like this, but after a few minutes my voice stops squeaking and I feel a lot more comfortable!"

It is, therefore, our belief that openly acknowledging feelings, including feelings of anxiety, is not inappropriate in most job related situations. In fact, this process may be one of the simplest and most direct ways of reducing the anxiety itself to the point where it does not interfere with the task at hand.

Both men and women feel stress in various job situations; however, from our experience, women seem to be socialized to expect and accept their anxiety to a slightly better degree than men. Being slightly anxious and expressing these feelings seems to be easier for women than men. However, the expression of very high degrees of anxiety may be as difficult for women to express as it is for men. One hypothesis, developed while working with women from various life styles, is that as women progress professionally to higher management levels they begin competing with men to a greater degree and, therefore, begin to lose their willingness to share their feelings of anxiety. Consequently, they develop the belief that they must be as "tough" as the others they work with (who most often do not *seem* to be anxious) and they then begin covering up and denying feelings that quite naturally occur.

Another alternative found to be successful in reducing stress related to a job interview is to have the person role-play the prospective job interview while a therapist or "coach" teaches the use of certain breathing procedures, biofeedback apparatus, and/or muscle relaxation exercises (Cotler & Guerra, 1976). However, this procedure, which follows a systematic desensitization paradigm (Wolpe, 1969) usually involves considerably more time and training on the part of the once-anxious individual.

There can be some negative side effects at times to feeling relaxed and comfortable in a situation where others are expecting you to feel tense and uncomfortable. A while back, I (S.B.C.) was being interviewed for a new job in a mental health center by a group of professional peers. Having trained others for the previous eight years on how to relax in potentially stressful situations, I quite automatically began to utilize some of these relaxation skills during the interview. Consequently, I was able to maintain a relatively low level of tension throughout the interview. However, in some feedback on the interview at a later date (after the job had been offered to someone else), I was told that the committee felt that anyone who could appear that relaxed in such a situation was either covering up their feelings (which they thought should include at least some anxiety), or else the individual was just not that interested in the job (which was not true)! Certainly, in this situation the expression of some anxiety was permissible and, in fact, was seen by the interviewers as a very appropriate reaction to the situation at hand.

THE MYTH OF MODESTY

A second false belief which often comes into play during the job interview, the myth of modesty (Cotler & Guerra, 1976), is actually comprised of three separate parts: the inability to acknowledge or say nice things about one's self; the inability to accept compliments from others; and the inability to give compliments to others.

An individual who subscribes to the first part of this belief feels that one who says *anything* positive about oneself or one's past achievements (even in a job interview!), will be seen as vain, pompous, or overly boastful. Unfortunately, such individuals do not see the difference between an accurate representation of accomplishments and over-exaggeration. Furthermore, individuals adhering to this belief in extreme modesty may feel that once they *say* they can do something, they can never again fail or do poorly at that task. Therefore, rather than say something positive about themselves that may not hold up 100% of the time, they choose to say nothing at all.

Individuals who adhere to the first part of the myth of modesty may be able to get away with this response style if they have an outstanding reputation (or a good agent!) that preceeds them to the job interview. However, more commonly the individual may need to help sell himself or herself to the interviewer, or later to obtain a promotion or raise. As such, the ability to reflect one's strengths and positive attributes can be a powerful asset. For example, the question may arise, "what makes you believe that you are qualified for this job?" In answer to such a question, a person needs to be able to describe his or her past experiences in a positive manner, rather than play these experiences down or, worse, to deny their existence on the basis of having been just "lucky" in the last job. This does not mean that the person needs to exaggerate, brag at great length, and/or put others down in the process of complimenting oneself. What it does mean, however, is that it is an advantage for the person to be able to put himself or herself in a favorable light based upon past accomplishments or future expectations (e.g., "From what you have said about the job description, I believe I have both the skills and the motivation to do this job well;" "Here is the finished project, boss—I'm really pleased with the way it turned out!").

The second and third parts of the myth of modesty (i.e., the inability to receive and to give compliments) are often more apparent after the individual has been working on the job. The individual who has trouble believing and accepting praise from others will often "throw away" a compliment by saying something to neutralize and negate the compliment given. A compliment such as "That certainly was a nice piece of work you did on that project," may be responded to with: "Oh, the project turned out to be alot easier than I thought," or "Yea, but I certainly didn't do anywhere near that well on the last assignment you gave me."

After a number of negative replies have been given to someone expressing a genuine and honest compliment, the person giving the compliments becomes less likely to give this particular individual further words of praise. At the same time, the individual who is compliment-anxious now begins hearing fewer and fewer compliments from others. After awhile, the lack of praise (a situation which the person helped to create in the first place) now begins to bother the individual, who, therefore, may increase the frequency of negative self-statements and, in turn, feelings of inadequacy, insecurity, and depression.

It is recognized that some individuals use insincere compliments as a way of manipulating others to do what they want ("I really enjoy having you as my friend and co-worker—by the way, will you loan me $20.00?"). For some, a compliment is almost always followed by a criticism or demand, ("You've done a good job in getting these reports out on time; how come you don't usually do such a good job?" "Great! Now here are two more projects."). However, to assume that all or even most compliments given to us are insincere, manipulative, or misleading can be a mistake. If we do that, we then forego one of the most powerful ways of feeling good about ourselves: the sharing of positive feelings by others. As such, this can severely restrict a person in all of his or her relationships with others (business and otherwise).

The third and final part of the myth of modesty involves the inability to compliment and praise others. In business settings, one will sometimes hear a supervisor defend the position of not praising others on the grounds that: "It will go to her head and then I won't be able to get any work out of her," or "He knows that he is doing well—as long as I don't talk to him, he should assume everything is alright," or "I never got pampered when I was working in their job, why should they?"

Unfortunately, many supervisors, bosses, and fellow employees do not realize just how powerful verbal recognition and praise can be to job performance and satisfaction (in some cases even more important than monetary incentives). For some, there is an ignorance as to the potential positive effects of verbal praise. For others, it is a feeling of uneasiness that keeps them from complimenting others even though they feel the other person genuinely deserves this praise. Perhaps this uneasy, tense feeling occurs because the individual deserving of the praise is someone who throws away compliments, perhaps it is because the supervisor never received praise him/herself, or perhaps there is a fear of establishing a closer and potentially more vulnerable relationship which the prospective complimentor is trying to avoid.

For whatever the reasons, we feel that the myth of modesty (in all of its forms) does not enhance or promote a better working environment. Consequently, in working with others, we spend a considerable amount of time reducing feelings of guilt and self-consciousness so that individuals can more easily hear praise, accept praise, and give praise both to themselves and to others (Cotler & Guerra, 1976).

THE MYTH OF THE GOOD FRIEND

Essentially, the myth of the good friend (Cotler & Guerra, 1976) assumes that the other person can accurately read one's mind. In the business world, a person subscribing to this myth believes that "the boss should *know* I deserve a raise after all of the hard work I've been doing," or that "Barbara should know I need that report before I am able to continue with this contract write up." However, most of us are not very good at reading minds; consequently, we must often be told things (sometimes more than once) before we are able to effectively respond to another person's needs.

Unfortunately, an individual who believes in the myth of the good friend does not feel that such communication is necessary. This individual may believe, for example, that the job specifications are quite clear and require no further explanation or that "common sense" and "common courtesy" would dictate the "proper" response expected. Failing to recognize that "common sense," "common courtesy," and even written instructions may mean different things to different people, they tend to become angry and frustrated with employees and co-workers when their needs or expectations are not met as anticipated. Much of this anger and frustration could be alleviated if the person falling into this myth could accept the premise that individuals do not all feel or respond alike in the same situation. For that matter, the same individual may respond very differently from one time to another in what appears to be very similar circumstances (Promptness at the time clock doesn't necessarily mean promptness in completing work assignments!). Consequently, when one would like something specific to occur, it may be necessary to ask for it directly (especially when the job or relationship is a relatively new one).

Unfortunately, some bosses do not take the time to clearly specify what they want from their employees, making statements to themselves such as: "You can't change someone like that—he was just born lazy and will never succeed," or "If I have to tell him what I want, that just means he doesn't know enough to be in the position." Likewise, the employee might covertly resent the fact that a raise has not been forthcoming, that a promotion was given to someone else, or that no mention was made of the long overtime hours put into completing a special project, but may never tell the supervisor.

In any case, when one buys into the myth of the good friend, the end result is likely to be feelings of anger, resentment, withdrawal, misunderstanding, and, if carried to extreme, perhaps an end to the job itself. Simple as it may sound, the solution to the pitfalls of this myth lies in keeping one's mouth in gear and telling the other person (be it boss, employee, or co-worker) specifically what it is that one would like to see done in order to make existence on the job more enjoyable and more effective.

THE MYTH OF OBLIGATION

The fourth and final myth, obligation (Cotler & Guerra, 1976), leads the employee to disregard personal feelings and needs, and to feel obliged to meet all the requests of supervisors and/or co-workers, rather than run the risk of losing the job or the relationship.

It is recognized that in working and relating with other people, we do not always get our personal needs met and that we sometimes do things which are not our first choice (e.g., staying late to work in the office when you are tired and would rather be home relaxing). However, individuals who seldom seem to be able to say "no" (even though they would like to), and who frequently feel imposed upon by others' requests are those who believe the myth of obligation. Most large businesses usually have one or more individuals who seem to *always* put in late hours when requested, stop whatever they are doing in order to complete a task for someone else, and, in general, never say "no" to a request that is made of them. Some of these individuals may be making these choices quite willingly in order to advance the company; however, others may just be unable to refuse requests because of their unassertiveness. Consequently, they may be sacrificing their job satisfaction, their home life, and/or their health in their inability to tell others how they are feeling. Often times, these individuals are smiling and compliant on the outside; however, internally they may be feeling angry and resentful at others for making requests, and at themselves for not being able to refuse.

Another side to the myth of obligation is that the individual does not make requests of others because the person feels that others, like himself or herself, will be unable to refuse such a request. Consequently, since this prejudgment has been made, many requests go unasked and many needs go unsatisfied.

In our personal experience, it is always a delight to work with someone who does not suffer from the binds of this myth. In such cases, anything can be asked for because one knows that the other person is capable of saying "no." Likewise, when a "yes" response is given, it is assumed to be a genuine "yes" and not one which is likely to be followed by anger and withdrawal.

GUIDELINES FOR ASSERTION TRAINERS

In order to reduce the negative effects of the four nonassertive myths described in this chapter and enhance more assertive behaviors, the following guidelines are offered for facilitators who may be focusing their attention in this area:

1. Teach individuals how to identify anxiety symptoms within their body both at low and moderate levels.
2. Have individuals experience different ways of reducing their anxiety and tension such as by self-disclosure to others, relaxation training, meditation, biofeedback, and so forth.
3. Have individuals describe why the feel behaviors such as acknowledging anxiety in front of others, complimenting self, complimenting others, saying "no" or "yes" to a request, are inappropriate. Avoid ridiculing their feelings; however, at the same time, show that there are other alternatives to the situations they describe. This can be accomplished most successfully via a group process.
4. Set up situations within the sessions whereby the client can role-play some of the "other alternatives" described above. Provide positive feedback, ways in which the individual can lower anxiety, and prompting as the role-played situation calls for this (see Cotler & Guerra, 1976).
5. Give between-session assignments (on a graduated basis) to clients so that they can begin to practice and generalize the behaviors that were role-played and discussed.
6. Carefully evaluate with the client the possibility for the person to be rejected or fired before making an outside assignment. Discuss risks

and potential benefits with the client. In some cases, the reality may be that the risk is too great.
7. If possible, have the client maintain a written, anecdotal record of his/her assertive and nonassertive experiences and feelings outside of the group.
8. Give positive feedback and support for *effort* as well as *success*.
9. Remember that each individual is unique and his or her job situation may be very unique. Consequently, assertion goals and strategies need to be tailored to the job and to the person. Nothing *always* works!

DEBUNKING MYTHOLOGY

Just as nobody gets his or her needs met 100% of the time, likewise no one is assertive 100% of the time. Even so, some individuals are much more assertive than others (at work and elsewhere) and, as such, are able to more openly express their feelings and get more of their needs met a greater percentage of the time. To the extent that an individual falls into the four nonassertive myths described in this chapter and/or fits the description of a nonassertive, indirect aggressive, or aggressive person (Alberti & Emmons, 1974; Cotler & Guerra, 1976; Phelps & Austin, 1975), that individual may experience more difficulty in carrying out satisfying interpersonal relationships, both at work and elsewhere. However, these four myths rest upon what we feel are erroneous beliefs, and given that assertive behaviors can be successfully learned (and taught to others) in a wide variety of settings, it is now possible to enhance one's self-evaluations as well as benefitting interpersonal relationships with others.

Assertion training can be a powerful tool in overcoming the effects of these destructive myths: by helping "believers" to achieve an acceptance of their humanness; by teaching more effective, direct forms of self-expression; and by facilitating feelings of self-worth and personal dignity.

27

ASSERTIVENESS: ONE ANSWER TO JOB DISSATISFACTION FOR NURSES

Sonya J. Herman

Nursing, as other helping professions, has certain technical aspects which can be mastered by progressing through a curriculum. Once basic theories and sciences are learned, the next question is—how can the individual grow interpersonally and maintain personal satisfaction while at work? This option for nurses appears unlimited. Any interaction with a patient, physician, or another nurse has the potential to be an assertive experience with positive consequences in terms of morale and self-image. Opportunities which are avoided, however, limit behavior to a professional minimum. Most often this ignores relating on a person-to-person level and is dehumanizing not only to professionals but to patients and others.

Nurses lament that they are disappointed in their choice of careers. Instead of feeling fulfilled and enhanced as persons, they feel that they have no control over what they do, that they are not listened to, and, in general, that they are exploited. Nursing research has shown high job turnover rates, and has demonstrated that job dissatisfaction continues to be of concern to hospitals and the nursing profession (Lysaught, 1970; Altman, 1971). This situation is not only a disruptive force in the nursing staff but contributes to a morale which is so low that many even leave the profession. Furthermore, it is inconsistent with contemporary nursing education and practice which has a focus of primary care involving a high degree of self-confidence, responsibility, and accountability.

The research literature (Lyon and Iranevich, 1974; Everly and Falcione, 1976) shows interpersonal relations to be a primary correlate of job satisfaction for nurses and more rewarding than salary (McCloskey, 1974).

Despite these facts, and scientific evidence which indicates that much purpose and meaning in life arises within honest, sincere interpersonal relationships, many nurses do not relate in an authentic manner to obtain personal satisfaction at work. What are the constraints which prevent nurses from effectively relating to patients? There are many: (1) The very nature of the job, (2) the origin and history of nursing education, (3) nurses' belief and value system, (4) socialization of women, and (5) the mythical evaluation of people in the bureaucratic setting.

THE NATURE OF NURSING

The nursing job itself, particularly in hospitals, is unique. While a hospital admits people who are ill, the major twenty-four hour responsibility for patient care is carried by the nursing service. Although nursing has the *responsibility*, the major *authority* for giving patient care rests with the physician. This splitting of responsibility and authority for a job not only promotes powerlessness, ambiguity and tension, but limits nurses' control over patient care. This reinforces the helplessness and dependence nurses feel, and adds to the confusion regarding to whom they are responsible: the patient, the physician, or both. An example of this splitting of responsibility from authority occurred recently in a maternity ward in a well-known hospital.

A patient who was nine months pregnant was admitted in active labor. After one of her labor pains she said to the nurse:

Patient: "I am so glad I took the natural childbirth classes. The breathing is helping me control the pain and I am certainly not afraid and look forward to seeing my baby born naturally."

Nurse: "That's great. I'm happy for you."

Several labor pains and 10 minues later a doctor enters and says to the nurse:

Doctor: "Prepare Mrs. X. for a caudal."

Nurse: "Alright." (She gets tray, prepares patient and

doctor does the caudal [a spinal anesthetic]. Patient never questions treatment nor does the nurse nor does anyone explain to the patient what is happening.)

After the procedure the patient says to both, "Will this procedure interfere with me having natural childbirth? Earlier I told the nurse how excited I was to be able to give birth naturally."

The nurse, by her silence and passiveness, became an agent of the doctor and discounted what the patient had said previously. As the physician's authority was not questioned, the nurse behaviorally colluded with him, giving up previously acknowledged responsibility.

This situation is complicated by the additional stress and anxiety nurses experience as a result of working in an environment which deals not only with people who are physically ill or injured, but with life-threatening situations as well. Since the recovery of patients is not certain, the threat and reality of suffering and death is a daily occurrence—one most lay people do not face.

NURSING EDUCATION

Another constraint which inhibits relating to patients effectively has been nursing education. For over a hundred years nurses were taught to be subservient, obedient, quiet, and personally uninvolved with patients. Functionally, nurses were to follow the physician's orders and soothe patients emotionally as well as physically, but remain uninvolved. This, however, is an impossible task. Because nurses were taught not to relate directly when conflicts arose, nurses were unable or did not confront them, thus perpetuating their own self-denial. Nurses who did integrate the above mixed values managed to "not rock the boat," but at personal costs to themselves, i.e., headaches, anxiety, and low self-esteem. Although this was congruent with the subservient behavior *expected* of nurses, it prevented them from being decisive, therapeutic role models who could have helped patients learn to deal with conflicts regarding decisions about their health problems.

Currently, in contemporary nursing education, emphasis is placed on concepts such as independent practice, accountability, leadership, holistic care of the patient, and assertive communication. Much remains only lip service, however, as little energy has been invested in constructively implementing such behaviors, by either the nurses themselves or the health system. The growing feminist movement in the health fields may help stimulate more action in nursing, as it promotes awareness of the changing value system of women.

THE VALUE AND BELIEF SYSTEM OF NURSES

A further restriction on the effectiveness of interpersonal relationships in nursing results from the fact that dichotomous values have been perpetuated throughout nursing history, causing anxiety and frustration for nurses who cannot live up to the roles they perceive for themselves. From the time of Florence Nightingale, who established sacrifice and humility as a nurse's supposed virtues, the nurse's role has been viewed as one of subservience and obedience.

In reality, however, even Ms. Nightingale, with a group of nurses, demanded food and supplies to take to the Crimean War, and insisted upon proper shelter and sanitation facilities for the sick and wounded soldiers. Thus her behavior demonstrated initiative, and independent thought and action. These values have not been stressed in practice. Consequently, in hospital situations where such initiative and independence is required to adequately care for patients, the nurse's ingrained belief in her subservient role, reinforced by physicians and other nurses, hinders her from fully accepting her responsibilities.

Nurses often limit what they say in terms of refusing requests, asking for change in behavior, giving information or handling criticism. When asked, nurses say they practice this behavior for fear of not being perceived as competent to give patient care, fear of hurting patients' feelings when they are ill, fear of being criticized by either supervisors or physicians, and fear of making physicians or their colleagues angry with them. These fears perpetuate traditional values of servitude and dependence, which do not reinforce the nurse's respect for herself nor reinforce autonomous behavior. Other nurses are afraid of stating their thoughts or feelings because patients or staff will label them as aggressive. Since aggressive behavior is incongruent with nurturance and caring, to be labeled as such would present an insurmountable conflict to nurses who are taught to be considerate of others at all times.

These fears or beliefs are incompatible with the patient advocate role. On the one hand, the nurse is taught to utilize expert communication skills and constantly provide clarity while at the same time the values to which the nursing profession clings as passivity, powerlessness, "existing for others," oppose this behavior. Consequently, when three or more people, i.e., patient, nurse, and physician, are involved in a communication system, confusion is often the result. This is not helped if nurses keep themselves (or are kept) so busy taking care of patients that a habit of ignoring one's own rights becomes established. This leads to isolation from thoughts, feelings, opinions, and beliefs, and interferes with the nurse's functioning in an independent manner.

THE SOCIALIZATION OF WOMEN

Early socialization messages from society to women are constraining and are similar to the manner in which nurses have been trained. Since the overwhelming majority of nurses are women, the profession has inherited these messages almost "automatically." Some examples of these messages are: (1) Think of others first, even if you are hurt, angry, or tired; (2) be humble—never brag or tell others positive things about yourself; (3) always listen and be understanding—never complain; (4) always find out what the other person is thinking or feeling (don't ever hurt others); and (5) be willing to give to others. In recent years, the women's movement has reinforced nurses in overcoming these messages, but clearly many internal conflicts still exist. The more external conflict for nurses can be seen between (1) the interpersonal rights of nurses, and (2) acceptance and integration of these rights in light of the historical, educational, and cultural system of which they are a part. Such conflict, as has been illustrated, may be professionally and personally devastating.

THE MYTHICAL EVALUATION OF PEOPLE IN HIERARCHIES

There is a strong tendency in nursing to evaluate humans on scales in which some persons are seen as "better" than others (Alberti and Emmons, 1974). In the nursing profession, the following is often perceived: physicians are better than nurses, head nurses are better than staff nurses, supervisors better than head nurses, and nurses better than patients (Herman, 1976). Acting as if some people have more or less value than others, however, is not only unrealistic in the nursing profession but complicates the main task—that of patient care. Individuals who occupy the roles of patient, nurse, administrator, and physician are still human beings.

This is not to say that human beings do not occupy hierarchical roles in a bureaucratic system, as a hospital, which carries differing kinds of authority, nor that the authority of a supervisor in the system does not carry power and weight. What is of more value and equal importance is that nurses, as individual human beings, have their own authority and right to be respected, much as the larger hierarchical bureaucracy has a right to be respected. In other words, individuals have as much right to be heard as does the institution. This at times seems more complicated in a hospital service institution, which takes care of living and dying persons, because of the general pervasive constraints of uncertainty and anxiety surrounding illness, as well as the myth that silence is golden in heavily emotional situations.

Not only are patients faced with uncertainties which require decisions, but also the staff, nurses, doctors, and administrators who work to resolve these uncertainties. This combined emotional and intellectual complexity of working in a health setting, fraught with anxiety because of life-threatening situations and death occurrences, can only promote conflict, thus making mutual respect between people even more important. Nurses have reacted by "not rocking the boat" and absorbing the tension, utilizing behaviors such as smiling or denial, and depersonalizing situations which may arise.

THE ASSERTIVE RESPONSE

The common denominator in the constraints mentioned is the inability to communicate thoughts, opinions and feelings in a personally satisfying and effective manner. Assertion training encourages direct, sincere, honest and appropriate expression of one's thoughts, feelings, opinions, and beliefs without infringing on the rights of others. This can be helpful in dealing not only with fears, frustrations, and conflicts which occur in nursing practice, but with actualization of personal fulfillment on the job. Further since interpersonal satisfaction comes from genuineness, respect, and empathic understanding, nurses utilizing assertive behavior skills can build their own self-esteem which has so long been put down by themselves and others. Hospital administrators, supervisors and physicians usually respect colleagues who are able to speak up, whether in agreement or not. A short, direct discussion moves work along more rapidly, and involves people at humanistic levels, saving time and energy spent in gossiping about a situation, or avoiding talk.

Although assertiveness training is being implemented in government and business settings, it has lagged in the health fields and particularly nursing. Besides the constraints already mentioned, nurses occupied in work caring for others and not thinking of themselves resist the change. This is not without reason, as there are certain risks involved. In one situation a director of nurses in a large hospital, who was not being respected by a group of physicians, spoke up in an assertive manner and was relieved of her position. The doctors were unable to respond to her thoughts and feelings, felt threatened, and so arranged for her to be fired. In this instance she could no longer tolerate the nonassertive behavior skills she had utilized and made a decision to be honest regarding her thoughts and feelings. Even though this cost her a job, she said she made the decision to stop contributing to ineffective, non-direct ways of communication. Although situations like this one may occur, they are not usual and most physicians and nursing administrators would rather be confronted directly. Utilizing assertive behavior does include risk-taking, which may be uncomfortable but it is growth-producing and generally reinforces one's self-esteem. Practicing assertive behavior skills increases the likelihood that nurses will express their own thoughts, feelings, beliefs and opinions more spontaneously.

ASSERTIVENESS IN NURSING PRACTICE

The following nursing examples demonstrate the applicability of assertive behavior skills to nursing practice. Differences in responding in an assertive, nonassertive, or aggressive manner are illustrated, and assertive behavior skills such as refusing a request, making a request, asking for change in behavior, giving and receiving caring assertion, and accepting criticism, can be observed in the examples of work situations:

A. Assertive Behavior Skill—Refusing a request

Example—Work Overload
Amputee patients require much emotional and physical assistance. You like working with them and appreciate being recognized for your competent work, however, eight patients is unrealistic for one morning's work assignment.

Head Nurse to Staff Nurse, "You work very well with paraplegic patients. I am assigning you to bathe and care for the patients in wards A and B this morning" (Four patients in each ward).
1) You look down at the floor, sigh, and begin the morning's work.
2) In a tense, high-pitched voice with some giggles you reply, "You must be kidding," (Laugh) and make a put-down nonverbal gesture rolling your eyes to another nurse.
3) In a firm, pleasant voice, with a serious look on your face you reply, "I cannot accept that assignment because four of the patients are so seriously ill they need constant attention. I can take the responsibility for four of the patients, however."

Remarks:
1) If you chose this approach, you will be doomed to fail automatically, first with yourself and then with your head nurse. On the one hand you feel flattered that the head nurse realizes you do good work with paraplegic patients, but you realize that in the past you have only been able to care for a few because of the complexity of patient care. Your sigh cannot be interpreted by the head nurse, and your nonassertive acceptance of the assignment may end in your feeling depressed or angry at the end of the shift.

2) You can't believe this head nurse has such bad judgment in making patient assignments. It is infuriating to you and you feel helpless. You indicate this by rolling your eyes at another nurse, hoping for support. She remains quiet.
3) It is obvious to you, based on your experience in this specific patient area, that you cannot handle eight patients. You realize the ward is a little short of help, but compromising quality of care isn't the answer. You clearly assert yourself in stating your limitations and offer to do what is reasonable.

B. Assertive Behavior Skill—Asking for Change in Behavior

Example—Lateness

The evening nurse who administers medications has been late to shift report for the preceding three days. This has caused much delay for the evening shift as the charge nurse had to repeat the patient report.
1) In the shift report the charge nurse says to others, "Well, I wonder if Ms. X will even show this evening. She's late every day."
2) In a sweet voice with a smile on her face the charge nurse says to Ms. X, "It must be convenient to make your own time schedule."
3) In a firm, calm voice the charge nurse says, "You have been coming in fifteen to twenty minutes late this week. I am frustrated as I have to repeat the patient report and many patients are asking for their medications. I would like you to be on time."

Remarks:
1) If you tell others, this is only a waste of time toward resolving the issue. The lateness can only be corrected by the person utilizing this behavior.
2) By masking over your irritation with a sweet voice and smile, a clear message is avoided; again the issue is avoided, but hostility may be felt.
3) By describing the behavior, the charge nurse directly states her feelings and thoughts about the lateness. This allows the other person to say what she is thinking.

C. Assertive Behavior Skill—Accepting Criticism and Asking for More Information

Example—Unclear Work Orders Involving Patient Care

You do not understand the order for medication as written, so you page the physician who wrote the order. He does not respond for 45 minutes and when he does come he yells, "What's the matter with you? Why are you looking for me?"
1) You look at the chart in your hands and in a low, shaky voice say, "This order seems a bit strange."
2) You snappily respond, "Who are we supposed to look for when an order is whacky?"
3) In a firm voice with no smile you say, "I don't like to be yelled at. I was looking for you as I do not find this order clear. Do you want the medicine given in the morning and evening, in divided doses, or just in the morning?"

Remarks:
1) You look down and are afraid he will again yell at you. The fact that he raised his voice and you then avoid the issue may give him permission to do so again.
2) You are angry that he yelled at you, and return similar behavior to him. Your anger causes you to forget to verbalize what was confusing about the order.
3) In a self-confident manner you let him know your feeling when yelled at; also, you specifically mention what is unclear in regard to the medicine order.

D. Assertive Behavior Skill—Giving and Receiving Caring Assertion

Example—Dealing with Pain and Setting Helpful Limits

Ms. F. (patient) is suffering from painful metastatic cancer. In order to control the pain, she was given a large amount of narcotic medication and has become addicted. Since she was not in the last stage, the physician, patient and nurse discussed the situation and together decided to alleviate the narcotic to relieve periods of depression with the hope the patient would be able to resume some of her previous activities, despite some painful intervals. The nurse is to help the patient tolerate and deal with the pain to implement this plan agreed upon by patient, physician and nurse.
Patient: (screaming), "Nurse, I have tolerated this pain all morning and I can't any longer. Do something!"
1) In a tense voice you say, "Well—it will get better. I'll go get you some juice, then we'll talk about something else."
2) In a brisk voice you reply, "You agreed to the plan of helping you

cut out the narcotic—didn't you mean it? You know it will require self-discipline and time.''
3) In a calm voice you say, ''I understand how difficult it must be to tolerate the pain—let's explore some of your thoughts about it as this may help you deal with it. When did it begin this morning?''

Remarks:
1) You feel upset and uncomfortable that the patient is in pain. As a nurse you want to relieve her pain medically immediately, as it increases your feelings of helplessness. You agreed to the plan but now feel anxious, so you offer juice instead and walk away.
2) By reacting and putting all the responsibility on the patient and adding ''didn't you mean it?'' you inflict additional stress as guilt on a person who is already dealing with the stress of pain. In addition, the patient remains unaware that you realize the difficult situation. This, in fact, may make it worse as you offer no sympathy. Instead you return your frustration, which may increase the patient's.
3) In a calm voice you allow the patient to realize you are able to understand this very difficult situation she faces. You also will talk about it more and be assertively involved in helping the patient deal with the pain. The conversation may then have proceeded:

Nurse: (calm voice), ''I understand how difficult it must be to tolerate the pain—let's find out about the pain as this may help you deal with it. When did it begin this morning?''
Patient: (tense), ''Oh, I don't know—how can you be so heartless to want to do nothing but talk?''
Nurse: ''It may sound heartless, but this is one way of helping relieve the pain. By pinpointing when it occurs, we can then look to see what circumstances provoked it. Now, when did it start?''
Patient: (calm), ''Right after breakfast—when I used to get my shot of narcotic.''

These examples help to make clear how nurses utilizing assertive behavior skills in their work performance may acquire a greater sense of authenticity, thus developing their own self-esteem while experiencing mutual respect in their interactions. This will help promote job and interpersonal satisfaction that many are missing. Assertiveness is no ''cure'' for the problems of conflict and dissatisfaction in the nursing profession, but it can certainly provide a ''facilitative condition!''

28

ASSERTIVE TRAINING IN THE TREATMENT OF PHOBIAS

Arthur B. Hardy

The treatment of phobias and anxiety reactions has been greatly overlooked by the psychiatric profession. There is very little emphasis on phobias in medical school or in the psychiatric residency.

Individual phobic reactions are usually identified, such as a fear of snakes, but Agoraphobia, which is more like a pan-phobia, often goes unrecognized by both the medical doctor and the psychiatrist. As a patient told me: "I went to my doctor, thinking I was having a heart attack. He did all sorts of tests and finally told me it was just 'nerves' and sent me to a psychiatrist. I went through psychoanalysis for seven years, tried TA, TM, encounter groups, Est, and they were all useful, but I still have my phobias. Why don't more doctors understand?"

The seriousness of this affliction is not generally appreciated when, in fact, it is a devastating and debilitating problem. Likewise, it is far more prevalent than the general public realizes. It is estimated that 1 out of every 100 people suffers severe enough anxiety to greatly affect his or her life adversely. Agoraphobia in particular prevents people from living normal lives. Those who suffer from this problem are almost as confined as if they were in prison. It is more debilitating and heartbreaking than arthritis, it absorbs more family time and consideration than multiple sclerosis, and if the sufferer is the head of the house, it can pauperize the family; yet it is less understood and less treated than the common cold.

Early in my study of the condition I formed the concept that phobias occur in people who would be classified as having excitable personalities. These people do well as long as they have a release for their feelings, but they develop fears, anxieties, or phobias when they become inhibited: they operate to a considerable degree on an "either-or" or "all-or-nothing" principle. So it is as though *either* they go all out for release of tension *or* they hold it all in and develop symptoms. They are easily intimidated by others and therefore they easily become inhibited. They develop intense fears of aggression with subsequent strong avoidance reactions to arguments, dissention, or disagreements. This tends to isolate them from others, which compounds the problem of dealing effectively with others. A phobic patient said to me, "My mother is excitable. But she is so scattered and so constantly emoting, demanding, crying, feeling hurt, that it made everyone around her uncomfortable. So I decided that I would try to never be like Mother. Now I'm so inhibited I'm full of symptoms." She had closed up completely.

It became obvious that therapy would have to include some training, instruction, and practice in how to release tension in a socially acceptable way. This included all tensions caused by unexpressed feelings: love, fear, anger, sadness, wanting, etc. We used a lot of psychodrama and behavioral rehearsal and found these methods extremely beneficial. More than just giving people a technique, the process changed their general attitude. This attitudinal change was often reflected in their tone of voice, body language, and other non-verbal expression to the degree that many situations improved without conscious effort of direct verbal exchange.

In our phobic program we have homework. Here is an example from the homework following assertive training, and a request for doing unconventional things to break taboos and overcome their inhibition. "I told the girl at the credit card company what I wanted and I got it. I complained about the performance of my new vacuum attachment and was put off once but got a reasonable response the second time. I expressed my feelings directly to my mother about her griping to me about my father and she quit. After this, I found I could drive the car with no problem. I also found I was able to sign my name on the safe-deposit slip at the bank without shaking or worrying about what the people in the bank were thinking."

The phobics have been so inhibited and have become so dependent upon others that they have long forgotten how to ask for what they want. In fact, they feel that asking for what they want threatens their survival. Like children, they cannot tolerate the rejection, the "no" answer, because they feel they will disintegrate. They need a way to practice and test out a small situation in a safe, supportive environment in order to find out that, whether they get what they want or not, they are not devastated.

This moved us naturally toward an early form of assertive training. There was very little emphasis on assertive training, and very little published, so our pioneer efforts were somewhat unorganized. We did emphasize (1) having it very clear in your mind what you want; (2) adopting an attitude that it was appropriate to ask for it; (3) that the verbal message should be positive and definite; (4) that the message should be short and to the point; (5) that you should not be led or distracted from the subject; (6) that your non-verbal expressiveness must show through and be appropriate to the verbal message. "What has helped me," said one patient, "was the feeling that I had rights, I had a right to talk back, to ask questions, to want things, the right to say no, the right to say I don't care. I have a choice now."

Since those earlier beginnings, others have gone forward to organize and define specific procedures and to develop exercises which are much more efficient in teaching assertiveness.

The results of assertive training are immediate and very exciting. When a person understands a new method, he or she is more willing to risk the effort. For example, characteristically the phobics operate on an all-or-nothing principle so that they either clam up and say nothing, which makes them feel bad and accomplishes nothing; or they come on full blast which has a bad effect upon others and frequently ends up in failure again, which further reduces the self-image. For example, a patient practiced saying (on a play-back TV in the office) that she wanted to be able to leave a situation whenever she felt she had to. Otherwise she couldn't go into the situation. The other day she called me to report that "I was invited to a party and I told the hostess that I would love to come but that I wanted to be able to leave early if necessary. That was okay with her, I went to the party, and was able to stay the whole time. I felt great."

Assertive principles provide the phobics with a higher rate of success, thereby improving the self-image. They become more satisfied with themselves and get more of what they want, while maintaining good relationships with others. The fears of criticism and rejection are reduced and are replaced with a feeling of competence and confidence in interpersonal relationships. With more self-confidence, they are able to take more risks; they feel more able to cope with the situations of day-to-day living and less need to obsessively worry about what might happen in the future.

Learning, understanding, and practicing assertiveness is one positive step out of the "trapped" feeling.

In summary, for phobics, assertive training and practice is a great step toward opening up, experiencing self-discipline, dealing successfully with others, building ego and self-confidence, achieving many small successes instead of continued failures, and learning to cope with the world. It is a real must in the therapeutic treatment of phobias.

29

ASSERTIVENESS TRAINING WITH ALCOHOLICS

Steven M. Hirsch

Alcoholism has long been a major health problem in this country, directly affecting an estimated 9 million individuals and their families. About one in ten of the 95 million Americans who drink are either full-fledged alcoholics or at least serious problem drinkers. In the last ten years this age-old problem has been taking a disturbing new turn for the worse as more and more of our nation's young people are becoming addicted to the most devastating drug of all—alcohol. The cost of alcoholism may be as much as 25 billion dollars a year, much of it due to lost work time in business, industry, and government. Moreover, it is estimated that treatment of alcoholic individuals with present methods would fill every existing hospital bed and require the utilization of all of our nation's physicians. Consequently, solution of this problem must ultimately lie in the development of improved prevention and treatment techniques.

In recent years there has been a movement away from a generalized "psychotherapy" treatment for alcoholism in favor of an approach which matches specific interventions with particular problem areas. Alcoholics who benefit from treatment often state that they have become less inhibited, more outspoken, and able to stand up for their rights. Most recently, a growing number of clinicians have recognized that various procedures subsumed under the heading of Assertiveness Training can be effectively utilized to help alcoholic clients achieve a greater degree of self-esteem and emotional freedom. Researchers have suggested that interpersonal situations requiring an alcoholic to respond assertively (i.e., direct expression of personal rights and feelings) are often stressful and frequently lead to drinking episodes. Alcoholics whose drinking behavior temporarily has been controlled are unlikely to remain abstinent for long if they lack the behavioral competencies for securing gratification while sober. Therapeutic attention, therefore, should most profitably be directed toward building up a repertoire of coping techniques for use in problem situations in the community.

It is generally recognized by practitioners in the field of alcoholism that since multiple factors seem to contribute to alcoholism, multiple approaches are necessary to prevent and treat alcoholism. From a social learning point of view, alcoholics are people who have acquired, through differential reinforcement and modeling experiences, alcohol consumption as a widely generalized response to aversive stimulation. Therapeutic attention should, therefore, be most profitably directed toward reducing the level of aversive stimulation experienced by individuals, and toward eliminating alcohol stress responses either directly or, preferably, by establishing alternative modes of coping. Given more effective and rewarding means of dealing with environmental demands, alcoholic individuals will have less need to resort to self-anesthetization against everyday life experiences.

THE RELATIONSHIP OF ASSERTIVENESS TO ALCOHOLISM

Those of us who work in the alcoholism field know that there are vast differences among individual alcoholics and that these differences depend upon a wide array of factors such as social, psychological and cultural backgrounds, the stage to which drinking behavior has progressed, etc. However, we also know that there are certain personality characteristics or patterns of behavior that occur more frequently among alcoholics. Catanzaro (1968) has enumerated certain characteristics that appear to be quite common in a majority of alcoholics. These traits are not universal in all alcoholics, but are common enough to warrant description. Some of the characteristics mentioned by Catanzaro include (1) anger over dependency; (2) inability to express emotions adequately; (3) high level of anxiety in interpersonal relations; (4) emotional immaturity; (5) ambivalence toward authority; (6) low frustration tolerance; (7) low self-esteem; (8) feelings of isolation; (9) perfectionism; (10) compulsiveness.

Several of these characteristics appear to be directly related to the need for assertive training with alcoholics:

> *Inability to express emotions adequately* is common in alcoholics, and is also rather prominent in people suffering from depression. Alcoholics are in general very sensitive people. Consequently, they tend to build up feelings of anger at even minor rejections or frustrations. In addition, they find it very hard to deal adequately with their great wealth of angry feelings. They often find it difficult to talk of their feelings, and therefore either hold them inside or explosively let them out in an argument or fight. One of the main aims of therapy is to help the alcoholic learn to express his feelings verbally. (Catanzaro, 1968, page 16.)
>
> Alcohol's ability to reduce a high level of *anxiety in personal relations* has caused Dr. Jellinak to dub alcohol "a social lubricant." Many alcoholics, early in their disease use alcohol as a drug for calming anxious and insecure feelings which arise at social gatherings. Thus, as their inability to deal with people effectively becomes more pronounced, they need increasing amounts to blot out their increasingly unpleasant realities (p. 17).
>
> *Feelings of isolation* are the natural outgrowth of his inability to get along with people. As the alcoholic continues drinking, his behavior and conversation become less acceptable to those about him and consequently, his family and friends begin isolating him from their social circle (p. 18).

By providing alcoholics direct training in precisely those interpersonal and social skills typically lacking in their behavior, it is felt that they will have less need to resort to alcohol.

Drawing on ten years of research into the psychological meaning of alcohol consumption, McClelland, David, Kalin, and Wanner (1972) have developed a theory of alcoholism which in many respects gives added validity to the idea of using assertive training with alcoholic patients. They attempted to explain some of the variations in rates of heavy drinking in terms of their "power concern" theory. For example, why should middle-aged men drink more heavily than younger or older men? They answered this question with the following explanation:

> Generally speaking, more strength and assertiveness is expected of middle-aged men with heavy family and work responsibilities than of either younger or older men. Yet this increase in responsibility is associated with a regular physical decline in potency both in the sexual and aggressive sense of the term. What is more likely than that men faced with high demands for assertiveness and a lessening capacity should turn more often to the artificial sense of increased potency that drinking produces (p. 296)?

McClelland and his associates reported on a pilot attempt to help alcoholics by socializing their power needs. Although they arrived at their theory of drinking behavior quite independently of a behavioristic model, it is interesting to note that several of their specialized treatment approaches utilized role-playing and social, interpersonal situations and other strategies which are not uncommon to assertive training.

Miller, Hersen, Eisler, and Hilsman (1974), evaluating the role of stressful interpersonal encounters on the etiology of alcohol abuse, showed that when confronted with situations necessitating assertive behavior, alcoholics increased their rate of responding to obtain alcohol more than did social drinkers. The social stress conditions consisted of everyday life experiences in which the subjects were to act assertively. After the subject responded, the experimenter would tell the subject that his performance was very poor compared to other patients and that he apparently had let people boss him around and that he didn't stand up for his rights. The subjects were then confronted by two experimenters with their social, parental, or vocational inadequacies. Pulse rates were obtained immediately prior to and following these interactions. Both alcoholics and social drinkers significantly increased their pulse rates as a function of the stress condition. Exposure to stressful interpersonal encounters requiring assertive responses increased alcohol consumption in the chronic alcoholic subjects, but not for the social drinkers.

> These data corroborate findings in that alcoholics do not seem to have a lower tolerance for social stress than non-alcoholics. Rather, as a function of his prior experience, the alcoholic has learned to respond to stressful situations by consuming alcohol whereas the non-alcoholic has learned a variety of more adaptive responses (e.g., being appropriately assertive), (p. 71).

Eisler, Miller, Hersen and Alford (1974) reported the effects of assertion training on marital interaction. Three couples were video-taped while discussing their marital conflicts before and after husbands received training in assertive expression. In the context of role-played interpersonal encounters, assertive training consisted of instructions, behavior rehearsal, coaching and feedback. In all three cases, behavioral tests revealed substantial improvement in the husband's assertiveness. In two of the three cases, increased assertiveness produced marked changes in the couple's marital interactions. One of the most interesting aspects of this study was the fact that one of the husbands had a 6-year history of heavy, sporadic drinking following episodes of intense marital conflict. Breath-alcohol levels taken weekly for 6 weeks prior to assertive training ranged from .01% to .20% with a mean of .08%. For six weekly intervals following training, the levels ranged from .00% to .04% with a mean of .02%. Thus it appears that training the husband to be assertive in simulated marital encounters did generalize to actual marital interactions. Not only did changes in the husband's assertive behavior transfer to the interaction with his wife, but they also led to a decrease in the amount of alcohol he consumed. Although this finding relates to only one case, it is indicative of the potential effectiveness of assertive training with alcoholics.

A CONTROLLED STUDY OF AT WITH ALCOHOLICS

To demonstrate that assertive training can be an effective technique in modifying unassertive behavior in alcoholics, the first controlled research study into the effectiveness of assertion training with alcohol-dependent individuals was developed and implemented (Hirsch, 1975). The design of the study attempted to show that not only unassertive thoughts and attitudes could be changed but that an alcoholic's actual behavior in situations requiring assertive responses could be modified. The subjects for the study consisted of a group of 102 chronic state-hospitalized alcoholics. An equal number of subjects were randomly assigned into a Control group, a Minimal Assertive Training group, and an Assertive Training group based upon a subject scoring in the lower 50th percentile in the Rathus Assertiveness Scale (1973).

The Control group received the regular state hospital treatment program. The Minimal Assertive Training group, in addition to the regular state hospital program, received two hours of didactic presentation and group discussion on how each person could behave more assertively. This treatment group was an open-ended group, i.e., patients came into the group and stayed for only two sessions. Patients were given a common sense explanation of why they behaved unassertively and they were taught how to discriminate between assertive and unassertive behavior. They were strongly encouraged to behave assertively.

The patients in the Assertive Training group, in addition to the regular state hospital program, received 10 hours of assertive training, utilizing all of the component techniques of assertion training such as modeling, coaching, role-playing, instructions, behavior rehearsal and homework assignments. This treatment group was also an open-ended group. Patients entered the group and stayed for a total of 10 sessions. Each patient was asked to discuss situations in his/her own life which were problematic. Much of the focus of this group was to develop skills in precisely those aspects of unassertiveness in which the client was having difficulty. Patients were given a theoretical rationale for the treatment and they were strongly encouraged to begin behaving assertively.

At the end of two weeks, all patients were post-tested with the Rathus Assertiveness Scale. In addition, they were also post-tested with a tape-recorded situational test of assertive behavior, called the Behavioral Assertiveness Test (BAT). This instrument was similar to devices used by other researchers in the area of assertion training and aimed to assess patients' reaction to tape-recorded, role-played threatening or irritating social or interpersonal situations. These situations involved a combination of standing up for one's rights, expressing one's feelings honestly and directly, and showing anger in a provoking situation. Patients were presented with 10 tape-recorded stimulus situations requiring assertive responses. They were instructed to respond to each situation as if it were actually happening to them. The patients' BAT responses were tape-recorded by a second tape-recorder and analyzed at a later date by three "blind" raters. Responses were scored in terms of Response Latency, Response Duration, and on a 6-point scale of overall assertiveness.

Since all the previous behavioral role-playing tests had been constructed either for college students or psychiatric populations, it was necessary to construct a behavioral test that was appropriate for an alcoholic population. The following is an example of one item which appeared in the final version of the BAT.

Narrator: You are talking with a friend who the night before embarrassed you at a party by revealing a very personal and confidential story you had told her sometime ago in private.

Friend: "Sorry I embarrassed you, but I just had to tell them, I mean it was such a funny story and, well, sometimes I think you are too darn sensitive.''

(Bell sounds and subject begins responding.)
20 seconds

Narrator: Stop if you have not finished responding!

The third measure used in this study was an unobtrusive rating scale of assertiveness called the Assertive Behavior Index (ABI). This instrument attempted to measure a number of verbal and non-verbal components of assertiveness, such as eye contact, facial expression, body movement, loudness of voice, and fluency of voice. All patients, after completion of two weeks in the study, were individually interviewed regarding their plans for returning home after discharge from the hospital. These interviews generally lasted about 15 minutes and were conducted by psychologists, alcoholism counselors and social workers not directly related to the study. Upon termination of the interview, the staff member completed the ABI, rating the patient's behavior during the previous interview.

The outcome of this study was totally congruent with what had been expected and clearly demonstrated that group assertive training is an effective therapeutic technique for modifying unassertive attitudes and behavior in alcoholics. The results showed significant pre-post-test changes for the Assertive Training group on the RAS, but not for the Control or Minimal Assertive Training groups. On the tape-recorded situational test of assertive behavior, between-group differences revealed a similar superiority for the Assertive Training group over the Control group in terms of Response Latency, Response Duration and ratings of assertiveness. Patients in the Assertive Training group spoke more rapidly, spoke longer, and responded more assertively to the 10 role-played interpersonal situations they encountered. In addition, the Minimal Assertive Training group significantly improved their assertiveness over the Control group in their ratings of assertiveness. Their improvement, however, was much less dramatic than the Assertive Training group.

The results of the Assertive Behavior Index also demonstrated the superiority of the Assertive Training group over either the Minimal Assertive Training or Control groups. The data showed that patients receiving assertive training behaved more assertively on a number of non-verbal and verbal variables, such as eye contact, body language, voice loudness, etc. While patients in the Minimal Assertive Training group showed a significant increase in assertiveness over the Control group on the total assertiveness score of the BAT, they did not demonstrate the superiority in an unobtrusive rating situation. In fact, the ABI means for the Minimal and Control groups were identical. This suggests that what the Minimal Assertive Training group learned was a modification of the content of their responses and not what Serber (1972—See Chapter 6) calls a "command of style." He defines lack of style as the inability to master appropriate non-verbal as well as verbal components of behavior. Thus, a person may say the right thing but come across in an unassertive manner.

The feed-back, modeling, coaching, role-playing, and behavioral rehearsal received by the Assertive Training group made a significant difference in the way patients came across during the interviews in which they were rated. The fact that this group was rated more assertive has important significance. Although the time-lag between the assertive training and the interviews was relatively short (several days), the data are suggestive of transfer of training in assertive skills. It should be mentioned that although the ABI raters were not directly connected with the research study, the possibility of "experimenter bias" cannot be totally ruled out. All the ABI raters were full-time staff members on the Alcoholism Units and took part in the staffing of clients. It was not always possible for the rater to remain unaware of which group a patient was in. The degree to which the rater knew the client treatment group and the extent of bias that this knowledge may have had on the attained results cannot be accurately determined.

Although this study did not directly address itself to the issue of transfer of assertive skills once the patient leaves the state hospital, and to the effect such skill training has on future alcohol consumption, the results are extremely suggestive of the potential usefulness of assertive training in the treatment of alcoholism. The positive findings of this study were highly encouraging, but only on the basis of continued investigation and outcome studies can one expect to develop an effective and efficient treatment for alcoholism.

One aspect of the assertive training which was not revealed in the reported statistics of this study was the manner in which alcoholic patients reacted to the Assertive Training group. The patients frequently stated that the Assertive Training group was their favorite group on the Unit. The alcoholics responded well to the training, could readily identify with the need for assertive training, and understood the relevance of the group to their lives. The quality of the Assertive Training group was markedly different from most of the other groups on the Unit. Not only were they interested and excited about being in the group, there was a tremendous amount of *esprit de corps* among members and the quantity and quality of interpersonal relationships in the group remained consistently high. Members would frequently volunteer to role-play situations, and the amount of "risking" behavior on the part of the patients was extremely atypical for this chronic population. It is noteworthy that when the members of the Assertive Training group at one hospital learned that the group leader would be terminated at the conclusion of the study, they petitioned the hospital superintendent to keep the group leader on permanently.

ASSERTIVE TECHNIQUES WITH AN ALCOHOLIC POPULATION

Utilizing assertive training with an alcoholic population is potentially different than with other types of patients. The pattern of many alcoholics during their recovery period shows that they strive for perfection to make up for their past unacceptable behavior. They often cannot allow themselves to make a mistake or to be human. They frequently set goals that are too high and are unrealistic—insuring that they will fail, thus adding to their already deep sense of inadequacy. In developing role-play situations and homework assignments, the therapist needs to be cognizant of this tendency and to help the alcoholic set reasonable and obtainable goals.

Frequently in initial stage of treatment the alcoholic may be reluctant to participate in the behavior rehearsals and role-plays. In order to counteract this, the therapist must explore all areas of difficulty—the situational and personal variables that raise anxiety and decrease the patient's ability to behave assertively. Second, the therapist should help the patient build a personal belief system that will help support and justify acting assertively. This is important so that the alcoholic believes in the right to act assertively even when he or she may be unjustly criticized. The acceptance of certain basic interpersonal rights helps counteract irrational guilt that often occurs. Thorough didactic explanations are very useful in developing these belief systems.

Third, the therapist needs to set an example of openness and of willingness to risk in a group. In being the first one to risk role-playing, the therapist sets a safe atmosphere for interpersonal exploration. Often a real-life, humorous situation which the therapist has confronted is the only ice-breaker the patients need to begin sharing their own personal unassertive behaviors. Finally, extremely withdrawn alcoholics may benefit from non-threatening warm-up exercises such as greetings, learning each other's names, small talk or exchanging compliments. It also may be useful to begin role-playing less personal situations such as refusing a drink at a party with a persistent host.

In conclusion, here is a parental message to the novice who may be excited about using assertive training techniques in their alcoholism program: During the author's research project we encountered an unexpected, although not surprising result. The patients who participated in assertive training did not confine their newly acquired assertiveness to just that group. They also began behaving assertively in other treatment groups. We began to find some of the other staff threatened because for the first time patients would "stand up, speak out and talk back" in their groups. When people know they have the necessary skills to assert themselves, they do—and that just might create problems for others!

Part Five: ISSUES AND ETHICS IN THE PRACTICE OF ASSERTIVE BEHAVIOR TRAINING

30

ASSESSMENT PROCEDURES FOR ASSERTIVE BEHAVIOR

John P. Galassi, Merna Dee Galassi

The purpose of this paper is to discuss procedures for assessing assertive behavior which are useful to the assertion training practitioner. As is the case with other methods for modifying human behavior, progress in developing and refining the technique has outstripped progress in developing measures of assertive behavior and in evaluating the effects of the technique. The importance of assessment in the development and evaluation of an assertion training program is unquestionable.

Unfortunately, a number of methodological and conceptual difficulties exist in current assessment procedures. Among these difficulties are the lack of a commonly accepted definition of assertive behavior, the problem of differentiating aggressive behavior from assertive behavior, the relationship between anxiety and assertion, the lack of well-validated, paper-and-pencil measures of assertive behavior which are composed of subscales to measure different aspects of assertion, the cultural and situational relativity of assertion, our

---

1. Parts of this chapter have been reproduced, with permission from *Assert Yourself! How to Be Your Own Person*, Merna Dee Galassi and John P. Galassi. Copyright © 1977. Human Sciences Press.

incomplete knowledge of the nonverbal components of assertion, and the lack of adequate *in vivo* behavioral measures. Since the above issues have been discussed in detail elsewhere (Bodner, 1975; Galassi & Galassi, 1976; Hersen, Eisler and Miller, 1973; Jakubowski & Lacks, 1975), the focus of the paper is on answering the following question: Given the current state of the art, what assessment procedures are most useful to the assertion training practitioner? In order to answer this question, it is important first to adopt a common definition of assertive behavior and to recognize that the function and scope of assessment may vary depending on whether it is being used prior to, during, or after training.

NATURE OF ASSERTIVE BEHAVIOR

Assertion consists of a number of verbal, nonverbal, and paralanguage (tone of voice, inflection, etc.) behaviors. These behaviors are learned, and their purpose is to communicate an individual's wants, needs, opinions, etc. to others in a socially acceptable manner. Assertion is not conceptualized as a general or unitary personality trait (i.e., something that one has) but as a series of learned situation-specific behaviors (i.e., something one does). More specifically, assertion involves expressing a variety of behaviors (e.g., refusing requests, giving compliments, etc.) verbally, nonverbally, and through paralanguage to a number of people (e.g., friends, bosses, etc.). Table 30-1 illustrates this point in greater detail. Assertion occurs within a situation (e.g., private, public, etc.) that is embedded within a cultural context. One's behavior and therefore what is assertive and socially acceptable is affected by all of the above factors. Change in any one of the factors influences whether a given set of verbal, nonverbal, and paralanguage behaviors is judged to be assertive.

ASSESSMENT PRIOR TO TRAINING

Assessment for screening prior to training is designed to answer several questions. First, given a particular cultural context, what complex of behaviors (verbal, nonverbal, and paralanguage) does the potential trainee either have difficulty expressing or express infrequently, to what persons, and in what situations? Secondly, given the cultural context, what complex of behaviors does the potential trainee express in an aggressive manner, to what persons, and in what situations? Finally, what are the reasons (controlling variables) for the trainee's difficulties in assertion, and what components (e.g., modeling, behavioral rehearsal, cognitive restructuring, etc.) of an assertion training program would be most helpful to him/her?

Ideally, the first two questions are most adequately answered through behavioral observation of the trainee(s) in real life or in simulated (role-played) situations. Either the trainer or trained observers can rate the trainee's behavior in a variety of situations, either real or simulated (e.g., Galassi, 1973; MacDonald, 1974; McFall & Marston, 1970), which call for assertive behavior. In the typical role-played or behavior performance situation, the trainee is given a description of a situation which calls for assertive behavior. Then, he/she is asked to respond to statements that are delivered live or on tape by another person. The situation may require the trainee to initiate a statement or simply respond to the other person. In addition, the trainee may be asked to give one response or several responses. A typical simulated situation[2] is provided below.

> You've gone to lunch at a restaurant. You've ordered a chef salad with thousand island dressing. However, when you get your salad, it has blue cheese dressing on it. You prefer thousand island. The waiter/waitress is approaching your area now.
> Waiter/Waitress: Is everything okay?
> Trainee:
> Waiter/Waitress: I distinctly remember you ordering blue cheese dressing.
> Trainee:
> Waiter/Waitress: I have it written down right here on my slip—blue cheese.
> Trainee:
> Waiter/Waitress: All, right, I'll be back in a few minutes.

In such situations, a baseline of the trainee's behavior can be recorded and deficiencies in the verbal, nonverbal, or paralanguage areas can be noted. The value of behavioral observation in pinpointing a trainee's strengths and weaknesses in self-expression is undeniable; however, it often is impractical to rely solely on behavioral observation as an assessment strategy, especially when the practitioner is concerned with screening large groups of trainees for assertion training.

---

2. Excerpted from Galassi, M.D. and Galassi, J.P. *Assert yourself! How to Be Your Own Person*. New York: Human Sciences Press, 72 Fifth Avenue, 1977.

ASSESSMENT INSTRUMENTS

As a result, many trainers find it useful to employ self-report questionnaires or inventories as preliminary screening devices in conjunction with one or more behavioral assessment interviews and/or observations. Most of the self-report inventories developed to date provide information only on the frequency with which a trainee believes that he/she asserts him/herself in situations which require such behavior. Some of the inventories provide information about the level of discomfort (anxiety) which accompanies self-assertion. Few of the inventories provide information on whether the self-expression is aggressive or not, the reasons for the lack of assertiveness, and the verbal, nonverbal, and paralanguage behaviors that are present or absent in a particular assertion. For the most part, the best of the currently developed inventories attempt to provide the practitioner with a general survey of the presence or absence of assertion with a variety of behaviors (e.g., refusing a request, expressing justified annoyance, etc.), persons, and situations. Assuming that the trainee's self-report is reasonably accurate, these inventories can provide the trainer with information on the frequency of the trainee's assertions and on the behaviors, persons, and situations which might be included in the trainee's program. Subsequently, interviews and/or behavioral observation of the trainee's performance in real life or simulated situations could be used to "flesh out" the content of the program.

The authors are aware of at least 17 inventories in various stages of development with the majority having been intended for use with college students and/or adult populations. The existing inventories and questionnaires include: the Action Situation Inventory (Friedman, 1971), the Adolescent Assertion Discrimination Test (Shoemaker, 1973 as cited in Bodner, 1975), the Adolescent Self-Expression Scale (McCarthy & Bellucci, 1974), the Adult Assertion Scale (Jakubowski & Wallace, 1975 as cited in Lange & Jakubowski, 1976), the Adult Self-Expression Scale (Gay, Hollandsworth & Galassi, 1975), the Assertion Inventory (Dalali, 1971), the Assertion Inventory (Fensterheim, 1971), The Assertion Inventory (Gambrill & Richey, 1975), the Assertiveness Inventory (Alberti & Emmons, 1974), the AQ test (Phelps & Austin, 1975), the College Self-Expression Scale (Galassi, DeLo, Galassi, & Bastien, 1974), the Conflict Resolution Inventory (McFall & Lillesand, 1971) which was designed explicitly to measure refusal behavior, the Constriction Scale (Bates & Zimmerman, 1971), the Lawrence Assertive Inventory (Lawrence, 1970), the modified Rathus Assertiveness Schedule for the junior high level (Vaal & McCullagh, 1975), the Rathus Assertiveness Schedule (Rathus, 1973), and the

Wolpe-Lazarus Assertiveness Questionnaire (Wolpe & Lazarus, 1966).

We are not aware of any published, standardized, paper-and-pencil inventories for the assessment of assertive behavior with children from elementary school through adolescence. Although Vaal and McCullagh (1975) demonstrated that a modified version of the Rathus Assertiveness Schedule (RAS) possessed a lower readability level than the original RAS and that it possessed acceptable test-retest reliability for junior high school students over a two-month period, validity data have not been presented for the inventory.

For older populations, Jakubowski and Lacks (1975) and Lange and Jakubowski (1976) have stated that the Adult and College Self-Expression Scales appear to be the most useful for measuring a wide variety of different types of assertive behaviors. Both measures were conceptualized according to the behaviors and person's model of assertion described earlier. Although neither of the scales provides subscale scores for assertion with particular behaviors or particular persons, inspection of individual items can provide the practitioner with useful information concerning which behaviors and persons to focus on during assertion training.

The 50-item College Self-Expression Scale (Galassi, DeLo, Galassi & Bastien, 1974) was designed to measure the frequency or degree of difficulty of engaging in a variety of assertive behaviors with such persons as same and opposite sex peers, parents and relatives, authority figures, business relations, and strangers. The behaviors tapped include asking favors, complimenting, initiating conversations, expressing positive feelings such as love and affection, refusing unreasonable requests, expressing justified annoyance and anger, and standing up for legitimate rights. A variety of situations were represented. Norms have been collected for almost 4,000 college students. Two-week test-retest reliability coefficients of .89 and .91 have been reported for two samples. Significant positive correlations have been found between the College Self-Expression Scale (CSES) and the Dominance, Intraception, Heterosexuality, Achievement, Defensiveness, Self-Confidence, Exhibition, Change, Favorable, and Autonomy Scales of the Gough Adjective Check List, while significant negative correlations were obtained between the College Self-Expression Scale and the Unfavorable, Succorant, Abasement, Deference, and Counseling Readiness Scales (Galassi, et. al., 1974). The scale has been found to have little or no overlap with a measure of aggression (Galassi & Galassi, 1975).

In addition, Galassi and Galassi (1974) found that college students who seek personal adjustment counseling rate themselves as less assertive than both vocational-educational counselees and non-counseled college students. Significant but small correlations were obtained between student teachers' scores on the CSES and ratings of assertiveness by their supervisors and between dorm residents scores on the CSES and ratings by resident hall assistants. Students who score low on the CSES have been differentiated from high scorers and from a combination of moderate and high scorers in a behavioral role playing test of assertiveness (Galassi, Hollandsworth, Radecki, Gay, Howe, & Evans, 1976). The ability of the scale to demonstrate change following assertion training has been demonstrated by Galassi, Galassi, and Litz (1974). Additional research by Lacks and Connelly (cited in Lange & Jakubowski, 1976) indicates that the items are not significantly correlated with social desirability, that the scale takes a minimum amount of time to complete (average of 8.1 minutes, range 3-15), and is favorably received by respondents.

The 48-item Adult Self-Expression Scale[2] includes four original and 29 rewritten items from the College Self-Expression Scale. The items were designed to tap the expression of seven behaviors (expressing personal opinions, refusing unreasonable requests, initiating conversations, expressing positive feelings, standing up for legitimate rights, expressing negative feelings, and asking favors) in six interpersonal situations (with parents, the public, authority figures, friends, intimate relations, and in global situations in which the person is not specified). Reliability and validity studies (Gay, Hollandsworth, & Galassi, 1975; Hollandsworth, Galassi, & Gay, 1976) were conducted with a community college population (age 18 - 60), psychiatric patients, male prisoners, and adult students enrolled in evening classes at a technical institute and a university. Findings comparable to those for the College Self-Expression Scale were obtained. The relationship between the Adult Self-Expression Scale and behavioral performance measures of assertive behavior has not been investigated to date.

With respect to the question of the quality and appropriateness of self-expression (aggressiveness), the existing instruments do not seem to tap this in either a systematic or comprehensive fashion.[3] Similarly, the inventories provide almost no information about the reasons for nonassertive or aggressive behavior. Nonassertive or aggressive behavior in a situation may occur for at least three reasons: appropriate responses are blocked due to the presence of anxiety in the situation; the trainee does not know what an appropriate response is for the situation; and

---

2. A sample copy of the scale is available from ASES, P. O. Box 17174, Charlotte, North Carolina 28211.
3. We have used the Buss-Durkee Inventory (Buss, 1961) to tap this dimension of self-expression. Although we have found this inventory to be somewhat helpful, it, like other measures of aggression, appears to lack the situational specificity which is so helpful in assessment and in planning a training program.

the trainee is unsure of his/her rights or does not believe that he/she has the right to respond assertively in the situation.

The Assertion Inventory (Gambrill & Richey, 1975) is an exception to the last statement and does provide information concerning reason one. The Scale attempts to differentiate the frequency of engaging in assertive behavior from the degree of discomfort which is involved in asserting oneself. For each of the 40 scale items, trainees indicate their degree of discomfort or anxiety as well as their frequency of engaging in the designated behavior. Of course, the presence of anxiety could be tapped through other paper-and-pencil inventories and the use of physiological measures. However, the equipment needed to measure many physiological responses would be costly and impractical for the practitioner, and existing paper-and-pencil measures of anxiety either lack the necessary situational specificity and/or are too time consuming to administer.

INDIVIDUALIZED ASSESSMENT

Given the methodological weaknesses and the lack of diagnostic information provided by existing inventories, the assertion training practitioner may find it advantageous to construct his/her own inventory. Described below is a procedure for constructing such an inventory. By having the trainee complete all of the steps, the practitioner can learn the frequency of the trainee's assertion with a variety of behaviors and persons, the situations in which the trainee is aggressive, the presence of debilitating anxiety, the trainee's knowledge of appropriate behavior, and whether or not the trainee feels that he/she understands his/her rights in given situations. This assessment procedure is designed to provide the practitioner with maximum flexibility in assessment, in the sense that behaviors and persons can be added or deleted at will; questions that are not of interest (e.g. aggressive behavior) can be omitted; and specific details of a situation can be added if desired (e.g. Do you express justified annoyance to your parents when you are alone with them at home? versus Do you express justified annoyance to your parents?). The assessment procedure, the Assertion Self-Assessment Table, and instructions for presenting it to trainees is provided in the following section.

ASSERTION SELF-ASSESSMENT TABLE[4]

Assertive behavior involves directly expressing your feelings, preferences, needs, rights, and opinions without undue anxiety and in a manner which is neither threatening nor punishing to others. Assertion consists of numerous behaviors (e.g. refusing requests, giving compliments, etc.) directed toward various people (e.g. bosses, friends, etc.). Individuals differ in their ability to express these behaviors and in their ability to interact effectively with these persons.

Before learning more about behaving assertively, it would be helpful to determine how you presently express yourself. As with other skill training programs (e.g. speed reading), assertion training is enhanced if an assessment of the participant's skills is conducted prior to beginning the program. This assessment provides information that will be helpful in tailoring the program to meet your specific needs.

Now turn to the Assertion Self-Assessment Table. Notice that the row headings list a variety of behaviors which represent three major categories of assertion: expression of positive feelings, expression of self-affirmation, and expression of negative feelings. The column headings list persons to whom those behaviors may be addressed. The persons represented are not inclusive of all people with whom you may interact. Some columns contain more than one person. In these instances, you should choose the person who is most relevant for you. For example, if you are married, you will be answering (in most cases) questions about your behavior with your spouse, rather than boyfriend/girlfriend. The darkened cells indicate situations which are unlikely to be relevant for most people. There may be other situations which are not applicable to you. Simply ignore those cells which do not apply.

The Assertion Self-Assessment Table will be used to evaluate frequency of assertions, presence of anxiety, areas of aggression, knowledge of appropriate behavior, and knowledge of personal rights. By completing Steps 1-6, you will determine how frequently you assert ten different behaviors with eight different persons. Your responses to Steps 7-12 will indicate whether or not you experience undue anxiety while expressing yourself, and Steps 13-19 will help you evaluate whether you are aggressive while expressing particular behaviors with given persons. Steps 20-22 will help you to determine your knowledge of situationally appropriate responses, and Steps 23-25 will enable you to determine your knowledge of personal rights that are involved in the situation.

---

4. Excerpted from Galassi, M.D. and Galassi, J.P. *Assert yourself! How to Be Your Own Person.* New York: Human Sciences Press, 1977. A training program based on this assessment procedure is presented in the workbook.

Frequency of Asserting Yourself

Step 1. In reading the table, use the following question with each row and column heading:

Do I (*row heading*) to/from/of/with (*column heading*) when it is appropriate?

For instance, if you begin with the upper left hand cell, you would form the following question: Do I *GIVE COMPLIMENTS* to *FRIENDS OF THE SAME SEX* when it is appropriate?

Step 2. In answering the question for each cell, write in the word which best describes how often you engage in the behavior in that situation. Choose your answer from the words USUALLY, SOMETIMES, or SELDOM. For example, if you SELDOM give compliments to friends of the same sex when appropriate, you would write the word SELDOM in the upper left hand cell of the table.

Step 3. Now complete each cell in the table in the manner described in Steps 1 and 2.

Step 4. Look at the table and find the places where you answered with the words SELDOM and SOMETIMES. Are there one or more behaviors (e.g. making requests) for which you have given a number of SELDOM and SOMETIMES answers? If there are, list those behaviors here.

_____

_____

We suggest that you devote special attention to these behaviors in your assertion training program.

Step 5. Again, look at the places where you have the words SELDOM and SOMETIMES. Are there one or more persons (e.g. intimate relations: spouses, boyfriends, girlfriends) for whom you have given a number of SELDOM and SOMETIMES answers? If there are, list those persons here.

_____

_____

TABLE 30-1
Assertion Self-Assessment Table

BEHAVIORS	PERSONS							
	Friends of the same sex	Friends of the opposite sex	Intimate relations, e.g. spouse, boyfriend, girlfriend	Parents, in-laws, and other family members	Children	Authority figures, e.g. bosses, professors, doctors	Business contacts, e.g. salespersons, waiters	Coworkers, colleagues, and subordinates
Expressing Positive Feelings Give compliments								
Receive compliments								
Make requests, e.g. ask for favors, help, etc.								
Express liking, love, and affection					/////	/////		
Initiate and maintain conversations								

Self-Affirmation Stand up for your legitimate rights	Refuse requests	Express personal opinions including disagreement	**Expressing Negative Feelings** Express justified annoyance and displeasure	Express justified anger

We suggest that you devote special attention to these persons in your assertion training program.

Step 6. As you look at your SELDOM and SOMETIMES answers, you may find that they do not group into any particular behaviors or persons. This is not uncommon since people often have difficulty expressing only certain feelings to only certain people.

Presence of Anxiety

Step 7. To assess whether you experience any discomfort or undue anxiety when you express yourself, use the following question with each row and column heading:

When I (*row heading*) to /from/of/with (*column heading*), do I become very nervous or unduly anxious?

For instance, if you begin with the upper left hand cell, you would form the following question: When I *GIVE COMPLIMENTS* to *FRIENDS OF THE SAME SEX*, do I become very nervous or unduly anxious?

Step 8. For each cell, answer the question with either a YES or NO. If you answer YES, write YES in the cell. If you answer NO, it is not necessary to write NO in the cell. For example, if you become very nervous when you compliment a friend of the same sex, write YES in the upper left hand cell.

Step 9. Now complete each cell in the table in the manner described in Steps 7 and 8.

Step 10. Look at the table and note where you entered the word YES. Are there particular *behaviors* for which you have given a number of YES responses? If there are, list those behaviors here.

Step 11. Again, look at your YES answers. Are there particular *persons* for whom you have given a number of YES responses? If there are, list those persons here.

Step 12. You may find that your YES answers do not group under any particular behaviors or persons. This is not uncommon since people often experience anxiety only when expressing certain feelings to certain people.

Evaluation of Aggressive Behavior

Step 13. If you are considering assertion training because you feel that your behavior is aggressive at times, complete Steps 14 through 19. If this is not a concern of yours, skip to Step 20.

Step 14. As you may be aware, aggression can be expressed directly and include such behaviors as threats, hostile remarks, name calling, and ridicule, or it can be expressed indirectly and include such behaviors as sarcasm and malicious gossip. To determine whether you behave aggressively, at times, use the following question with each row and column heading:

Am I aggressive when I *(row heading)* to/from/of/with *(column heading)*?

For instance, if you are reading the lower right hand cell (last cell in the table), you would form the following question: Am I aggressive when I *EXPRESS JUSTIFIED ANGER* to *COWORKERS*?

Step 15. In answering the question for each cell, *shade* in those cells for which you report behaving aggressively in that situation.

Step 16. Complete each cell in the table in the manner described in Steps 14 and 15.

Step 17. Look at the table and note the cells you have shaded. Are there one or more *behaviors* for which you have shaded a number of cells? If there are, list those behaviors here.

_____

_____

We suggest that you devote special attention to these *behaviors* in your assertion training program.

Step 18. Again, note the cells you have shaded. Are there particular *persons* for whom you have shaded a number of cells? If there are, list those persons here.

_____

_____

We suggest that you devote special attention to these *persons* in your assertion training program.

Step 19. You may find that your shaded cells do not group under any particular behaviors or persons. This is not uncommon since people often are aggressive only when expressing certain behaviors to certain people.

Knowledge of Appropriate Responses

Many times people experience problems in expressing themselves because they do not know what would constitute a socially appropriate response in a particular situation.

Step 20. Look at those cells which you have *identified* as ones in which you infrequently assert yourself, you feel unduly anxious, or you have a tendency to behave aggressively. For these cells *only,* answer the following question:

> Do I know what would constitute an appropriate and assertive response when I (*row heading of identified cell*) to/from/of/ with (*column heading of identified cell*)?

For instance, if the last cell in the table were one of your identified cells, you would form the following question: Do I know what would constitute an appropriate and assertive response when I *EXPRESS JUSTIFIED ANGER to COWORKERS?*

Step 21. Complete each identified cell in the manner described in Step 20.

Step 22. List those cells in which you feel uncertain about what constitutes an assertive response.

We suggest that you devote special attention to *learning to discriminate appropriate responses* for these situations in your assertion training program.

Knowledge of Personal Rights

Problems in self-expression also can result when people are not sure that they have the right to assert themselves in a situation or are not sure of their rights in general with respect to the other individual(s) involved.

Step 23. Look at those cells which you have *identified* as ones in which you infrequently assert yourself, you feel unduly anxious, or you have a tendency to behave aggressively. For these cells *only*, answer the following question:

> Do I know my rights in those situations in which I (*row heading of identified cell*) to/from/of/which (*column heading of identified cell*)?

For instance, if the last cell in the table were one of your identified cells, you would form the following question: Do I know my rights in those situations in which I EXPRESS JUSTIFIED ANGER to COWORKERS?

Step 24. Complete each *identified* cell in the manner described in Step 23.

Step 25. List those cells in which you feel uncertain about your rights.

_____

_____

We suggest that you devote special attention to *learning about your rights* in these situations in your assertion training program.

This completes the Assertion Self-Assessment Table.

A Footnote for Trainers

Assuming reasonable accuracy of the trainee's answers, the Assertion Self-Assessment Tables alone or in conjunction with behavioral observation and/or clinical interviews should provide ample information about the most relevant content to include in an assertion training program for a given trainee as well as suggest the components of an assertion training package that will be most beneficial to a given client (e.g. relaxation and behavioral rehearsal for anxious trainees, cognitive restructuring for trainees who are uncertain about their rights, etc.).

ASSESSMENT DURING TRAINING

Assessment during training is designed to answer at least three questions. First, what specific aspects of an assertive response (verbal, nonverbal, and paralanguage) does a trainee need to develop and refine during training? What progress is the trainee making with respect to these aspects from session to session? Finally, to what extent are the trainee's skills in assertion transferred to and maintained in his/her environment?

A behavioral observation method of assessment would appear to be of prime importance in answering many of these questions. Table 30-2 presents a set of criteria [5] that can be used in a behavioral observation assessment strategy. The criteria are designed to be used by both the trainer and the trainee to evaluate the adequacy of the trainee's performance in the role-played or behavioral performance interactions that typically are included in assertion training programs. The use of these criteria has been discussed extensively elsewhere (Galassi & Galassi, 1977). As a result, only a few important points will be restated.

First, the criteria are designed to facilitate the assessment of the verbal, nonverbal, and paralanguage aspects of a trainee's response. The topography of these components will vary depending on the behavior being expressed, the cultural context, etc. For example, it is appropriate to raise one's voice when expressing justified anger, but a loud voice seems inappropriate when expressing love and affection. Trainers can adapt these general criteria to the requirements of the situation in which the trainee finds him/herself. Secondly, we have found it useful to evaluate the trainee's performance in four major areas: the degree of discomfort or anxiety experienced, verbal content of the response, the manner in which the message was delivered, and the satisfaction expressed by the trainee with his/her performance.

Question three can be answered by teaching trainees to use the criteria in everyday interactions and by teaching them to record their behavior between sessions. The trainee can record his/her behavior with respect to the frequency of occurrence and the quality of the behavior as

---

6. These criteria also can be used in any pretraining screening that may be conducted using behavioral observation of the trainee in real life or simulated situations which call for assertive behavior.

judged by the trainee using the assertive behavior criteria above. For example, if a trainee is practicing how to refuse requests between sessions, then he/she can record each time a situation occurred which called for refusal behavior.

Table 30-2

Criteria for Evaluating Assertive Behavior

1. Determine the anxiety experienced by the trainee in the situation:
    Suds score*
    Eye contact
    Relaxed posture
    Nervous laughter or joking
    Excessive or unrelated head, hand, and body movements
2. Evaluate the verbal content:
    Did the trainee say what he/she really wanted to say?
    Comments concise and to the point?
    Comments definitive, specific, and firm?
    No long-winded explanations, excuses, or apologetic behavior
    "I" statements and "feeling talk"
3. Evaluate how the message was delivered:
    Almost immediately after the other person spoke
    No hesitancy or stammering
    Appropriate loudness, tone, and inflection
    No whining, pleading, or sarcasm
4. Decide whether the trainee was pleased with his/her behavior.

*The Suds score refers to the Subjective Unit of Disturbance Scale score developed by Wolpe (1969). Trainees are instructed to rate the level of anxiety that they felt in situations calling for assertive behavior on a subjective scale which ranges from 0, completely relaxed, to 100, extremely anxious.

The trainee would record whether he/she refused the request as well as the adequacy of the refusal as judged on the criteria listed above. If a validity check on the trainee's recordings is desired, then help can be enlisted from a friend or relative of the trainee who has access to the trainee's behavior in situations which call for refusal. By reviewing the trainee's records at each session, a trainer can determine the progress that is being made and institute any modifications in the training program which might be indicated from the records and from a discussion with the trainee.

If a more scientific demonstration of change is desired, then a trainer could employ a single subject research design such as the multiple baseline design (Hall, 1971). Assume that prior to training, it has been established that a trainee has difficulty refusing requests, giving compliments, and initiating conversations. The trainee could be taught to record the occurrence/nonoccurrence of these behaviors for a period of time (e.g. one week) before training in order to provide a baseline or pretreatment level against which comparisons during and after training could be made. Training might begin by teaching the trainee only to initiate conversations. During this time period, the trainee would be encouraged to initiate conversations in real life but not be concerned about refusing requests or giving compliments. The trainee would continue to record the occurrence/nonoccurrence of all three behaviors. As soon as the trainer noticed an increase in initiating conversations that was maintained for a period of time (e.g. one week), he/she would initiate training on the second behavior. Once change was obtained on the second behavior, the trainer would proceed to work with the trainee on the third behavior. If changes occur in each of the behaviors only when training is introduced, then the trainer can assume that his/her training program was responsible for the change. A multiple baseline design also could be used with two or more subjects who had common behavioral deficits. In this usage, the training is instituted with one subject at a time rather than with one behavior at a time.

ASSESSMENT AFTER TRAINING

Assessment after training is designed to determine whether training resulted in changes in behavior that are being maintained in the absence of training. The ideal method for assessing such changes is through unobtrusive observation of *in vivo* trainee behavior. Some ingenious attempts (e.g. determining whether a trainee would refuse a magazine sales pitch on the telephone) to develop *in vivo* follow-ups have been made by McFall and his associates (McFall & Marston, 1970; McFall & Lillesand, 1971; McFall & Twentyman, 1973). However, such procedures are not without their problems (Galassi, 1973; McFall & Twentyman, 1973) and may be impractical on a large scale basis for the practitioner.

In the absence of direct behavioral observation of trainees in "real life," the trainer is left with several options. The first is to place the trainee, at one or more times in training, in simulated interactions which call for assertive behavior (e.g. with a live or tape recorded confederate) and observe the trainee's behavior. If large numbers of trainees are involved, this approach also may be impractical for the practitioner.

Some more practical approaches would involve asking the trainee to complete the paper-and-pencil inventories which were used for screening and to continue to record his/her behavior, with or without validity checks, and to give these records to the trainer at one or more times after training has concluded. A "buddy system" (see Shelton, Chapter 9) can be an effective method in group training. Based on these data and an occasional telephone call, the trainer and trainee can decide whether additional or "booster" assertion training sessions are desirable.

In summary, assessment should play an important role in assertion training. The type of assessment procedure which will be most useful to the assertion training practitioner will depend on the purpose of the assessment: for screening, for monitoring changes during training sessions or outside of training, or for determining the maintenance of gains after assertion training has concluded.

31

DEVELOPING ASSERTIVENESS: TRAINING OR THERAPY?

Martin E. Shoemaker

Twenty-five years ago the definition of the mental health practitioner was fairly simple. The clinical field was dominated by psychoanalytic theories of personality and the treatment of choice generally involved some form or variety of psychoanalytic psychotherapy. Today, the definition and practice of the therapist or counselor has been greatly expanded by the addition of new theoretical perspectives, e.g., humanistic-existential, behavioral, etc., and a number of new treatment strategies. In fact, the proliferation of new therapies is so apparent that recently a guidebook has been published to help even the professional find his/her way through the burgeoning forest of psychotherapeutic approaches (Kovel, 1976).

One of the major events which has significantly added to this diversity has been the acceptance of various active teaching strategies as a viable part of the therapeutic task. No longer is the therapist required to sit by or behind the client and passively reflect or interpret internal events. He or she can or often does give information or become involved in skill training.

There have been several determinants of these more "openly" didactic approaches to psychotherapy, but none so influential as behavior therapy, which uses modeling, behavioral rehearsal and out-of-therapy structured experiences to facilitate skill acquisition. As a predominantly behavioral approach, assertion training (AT), by its very name, demonstrates the commitment its practitioners have to instructional material and a "learn as you go" and "practice makes perfect" model.

Early in the formulation of AT, even before it had a formal name, Andy Salter suggested various "excitatory exercises" for his clients, aimed at changing inhibited feeling and thinking to excitatory verbal expression or motoric activity (Salter, 1949). Similarly, other pioneers, Joe Wolpe and Arnold Lazarus, asked their clients to role-play or rehearse various responses in therapy to explore inadequate behavior exhibited outside of the therapy setting (see Wolpe, 1969; Lazarus, 1968). Both of these men referred to this treatment as "behavior therapy," but specified selected training procedures for changing nonassertive responses, hence "assertive training." This basic model of AT was reaffirmed and elaborated on in Bob Alberti and Mike Emmons' big, "little" book, *Your Perfect Right* (1970, 1974) and later writings.

ISSUES IN DEFINING TRAINING VS. THERAPY

Following this first model, AT has been under a constant overhauling process, to the point that it may be unrecognizable to early writers and practitioners. Examples of the diversity can be found in books by Fensterheim and Baer (1975), Manuel Smith (1975) and Lazarus and Fay (1975) who each attempted to introduce AT to the layperson in extremely different ways, each emphasizing a few elements familiar to behavior therapists and labeling their contributions Assertiveness Training, Systematic Assertive Therapy, and Direct Assertion Therapy, respectively. To the average reader or mental health consumer, how the therapist or author decides to represent or identify his or her contribution is relatively unimportant. However, as elaborated elsewhere, assertion training therapy is itself in the midst of a rather "normal," adolescent identity crisis (see Chapter 4), with, on the one hand, a very technique-oriented, one-day training workshop approach (Smith, 1975), and on the other, an intensive therapy for individuals chronically disabled by passivity and anxiety (Fensterheim and Baer, 1975; Wolpe, 1969).

Such a disparity offers a wide range of applications to the trainer or therapist but at the same time poses such problems as: (1) *Competency and qualification.* Educational workshops with normal populations differ markedly from crisis or intensive therapy with clinical populations. (2) *Differing public expectancies*. Some people are more attracted to or less threatened by a psycho-educational course setting. Many of these "clients" either are fearful of or resent being led into highly personal or conflicted areas in the context of skill-training. On the other side are individuals who think therapy ought to be reserved for an in-depth experience led by qualified licensed professionals who abide by ethical guidelines for confidentiality and competency. Anything less than this leads them to skepticism and dissatisfaction. (3) *Public relations*. Advertising for licensed practitioners in the mental health disciplines is strictly controlled. Ethical guidelines require one to make careful distinction between an introductory course that teaches something *about* assertive behavior, and which can be "tastefully" promoted, and psychotherapy procedures which cannot be advertised to the public.

The above issues present particular problems for the professional in private practice, or one who is otherwise presenting services to the public for a fee. For instance, a training group is not usually covered by the client's insurance, but some forms of therapy would be. Similarly, the public expects to pay more for therapy than for some educational or training experience. Succinctly stated, using exclusively either the label assertion "training" or "therapy" to cover all that has been written and practiced in facilitating the development of assertive behavior has led to confusion, and sometimes outright misrepresentation to the public.

THE CONTENT-PROCESS MODEL OF AT

The model presented here conceptualizes the major differences between assertion training and assertion therapy according to both the content of treatment and the processes used to deal with the content. *Content* here is defined as the "stuff," subject matter, or topic of the AT group or individual sessions. *Process* is the style or structure imposed on the AT group by the leader. The primary concern here is with groups, but limited application to individual treatment is appropriate.

Commonly, but I believe mistakenly, the difference between therapy and educational training groups is more a function of who the clients and leaders are than of procedural variables. For example, if the clients are seen as in crisis, disturbed, or mentally ill, then the treatment is usually handled by a professional who calls his or her work therapy. If the same procedure is done in a non-traditional setting by a teacher, non-professional or friend it is something other than therapeutic.

It is my position that the *content* of the AT group and the *processes* developed or allowed by the leader ought to be the major determinants of whether the AT group is defined as "training" or "therapy." The model presented graphically in Figure 31-1 illustrates a convenient form for evaluating an AT procedure.

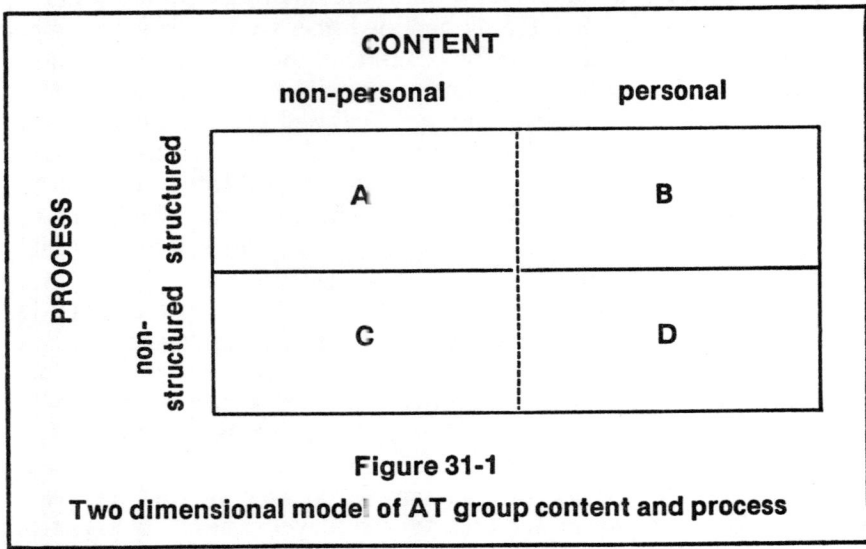

Figure 31-1
Two dimensional model of AT group content and process

Figure 31-1 presents these two variables as they are broken down into two dimensions each. *Content* is viewed as being on a continuum between non-personal subject matter, such as consumer issues, and highly personal areas such as sexual problems and interpersonal conflicts which require confidentiality and trust. *Process* is divided into structured and non-structured, with the former representing groups that are leader-directed and often pre-arranged in manual-guided or classroom formats. The non-structured approach allows for more interpersonal spontaneity and content is less controlled.

QUADRANT A—Leader Structured Process: Developing Assertive Behavior in Non-personal Areas

An AT group modeled after quadrant A is primarily an educational or course approach to developing assertive behavior. The leader takes a definite role in directing the group into primarily non-personal, non-clinical problem areas. The group often is large (15 people or more) and can make use of a one-day workshop approach. Group participants are expected to advance at somewhat the same rate and personalized attention is rare. Since the content areas are under the primary control of the leader, pre-arranged role-plays or rehearsal can be used as well as other structured materials, e.g., workbooks, manuals, etc. Confidentiality is not required, since highly personal material is discouraged, even when volunteered.

Quadrant A seems to take into account the plethora of self-help and adult education approaches to AT that are now evident in most large urban areas or university-related cities. Some CR groups led by interested non-professionals also seem to fall into this category. If properly run, these groups provide an invaluable service for individuals who would not or do not need to seek out mental health settings or professionals for a variety of reasons. Topical groups relating AT and consumerism, job-seeking skills, dating and social networks, consciousness-raising for both men and women, are providing excellent agents for self-growth. However, as therapeutic as these experiences are, they should not be billed or publicized as "therapy." Individuals seeking a more personalized, clinical involvement should be encouraged and referred to another type of treatment upon finishing such a training course, workshop or discussion group.

The key to the success of these groups is clearly upon the leader(s) and how creatively and enthusiastically the material is presented. From over a hundred workshop-type courses on AT in the past six years, the following guidelines have emerged:

(1) Keep a balance between didactic and experiential learning (50% talk vs. 50% doing).

(2) Keep the ideas and constructs simple and in a somewhat logical sequence. Try not to get too complicated or rushed.

(3) If you are teaching techniques, e.g., broken record, sheltering, etc., use rehearsal as often as possible to illustrate and provide practice opportunities. Also, caution participants about abuses and inauthenticity in the overuse of techniques.

(4) Above all, try not to shove assertiveness down people's throats. Being assertive is an option, therefore, laying on the "should" of always being assertive is an aggressive response style, violating the right of participants to choose their own behavior.

QUADRANT B—Leader Structured Process: Developing Assertive Behavior in Personal Areas

This quadrant is a structured approach aimed at developing assertiveness to remediate traditional clinical problems which are usually filled with emotional conflict and require group confidentiality and trust. Examples would be using AT to increase interpersonal intimacy, decrease marital tension, assist in divorce recovery, or deal with selected parenting problems. Group members are carefully screened for specific or related problem areas and groups are formed with a degree of homogeneity.

Such AT groups provide a short-term, intensive treatment experience structured by the leader(s). Content is focused and often pre-arranged rehearsals or other exercises are prepared by the leader(s) to help facilitate change. For example, in an AT group for mothers who were having difficulties controlling their children's behavior, various aspects of behavioral contingency management and requesting and refusal styles were presented. Specific assignments were given out to meet these target needs. This proved quite helpful to them as a parental figure, but may have not been appropriate for another type of group (Shoemaker and Paulson, 1976).

This type of group differs from quadrant A in that all the members are screened and the group size is usually limited to 4 to 8 members. Confidentiality is insured and usually a minimum of at least twelve sessions are planned along with follow-up procedures. In dealing with the clinical target areas of this type of group, motivational conflict toward change is often expressed and experienced and must be dealt with across time rather than in a workshop format, which often does not provide for much individualized attention or personal awareness.

This structured type of AT group, assembled for dealing with traditional clinical problems, seems to have both training and therapy components. The more the group is didactic and pre-arranged in some fashion, the more, according to this model, it approaches training. On the other side, the type of client placed in these groups often presents enough motivational conflict and emotional energy in the sessions that simple skill training is inadequate. In this case, forms of insight, cognitive restructuring, and spontaneous interaction between group members seem more necessary and the group approaches a "therapy-like" stance. Depending on the group, quadrant B seems to contain both elements. However, except for a very few instances such groups are best considered "therapy." This judgement is based upon the clinical content which requires individualized attention and confidentiality across a number of supportive sessions.

QUADRANT C—Spontaneous Problem-solving: Developing Assertive Behavior in Non-personal Areas

Quadrant C represents what is generally described as a discussion or "rap" group approach to AT. The leader takes a less structured, more group-centered approach, but limits the problem focus to specific non-personal areas. Examples of quadrant C groups might include adolescent rap groups dealing with dating behavior, and other normal development problems seen by a school counselor. Occasional role-plays or rehearsal can be set up, but the structure remains generally flexible. Group interaction offering advice and "focused intellectualizing" is encouraged.

Other examples of this type group are found in community agencies or in the business sector, particularly as a follow-up to workshops or quadrant A type of AT experiences. Involved personal problems away from the work setting are not encouraged in a quadrant C group for a number of reasons: (1) The contracting agency, e.g., business, school, etc., is not paying for "personalized therapy" but for a more communication-skill-building experience. (2) Generally, confidentiality is minimal. (3) The problem-focus tends to be agency or task related since certain types of personal self-disclosures in the work situation have high threat value or produce unresolved vulnerability.

A quadrant C group can contain up to fifteen members and usually meets across a three-to-six month consultation period. As mentioned earlier, this type of group is excellent as a follow-up to didactic training, where the concepts and strategies of AT are initially introduced. It is useful for the trainer to gradually fade the role of leader, and encourage other group members to take over the active leadership experience as a means of self-help and group/organization responsibility.

QUADRANT D—Spontaneous Problem-solving: Developing Assertive Behaviors in Predominantly Personal Areas

This last quadrant represents a highly personalized group therapy approach for the development of assertive behavior. Assertion therapy candidates are selected on the basis of several criteria:

(1) The client is experiencing a "here and now" crisis or crippling situation such as a reactive depression, some extreme form of substance abuse, marital separation, severe job dissatisfaction, disabling anxiety or fearfulness and other selected acute interpersonal conflicts.

(2) The client demonstrates a general passivity or avoidance pattern in interpersonal relationships; chronic nonassertiveness.

(3) The client demonstrates a pattern of aggression or violence of some form when faced with conflict or pressure. In many cases it is a combination of avoidance or withdrawing responses, culminating in guilt-inducing aggressiveness. An example would be a spouse who

generally avoids any family hassles until he or she has reached a boiling point. At that point the responses are overreactive, punitive and more often than not result in minimal conflict resolution.

(4) General interpersonal naivete, severe deficits in interpersonal functioning, and/or awareness of exaggerated feeling states created by relationships.

The assertion therapy group seems to function best when kept small in size (4-8 members) and run as open-ended. The open-endedness allows for the selection and addition of new members and the termination of current members according to client needs. A three-month client contract, focusing on particular target areas offers a helpful structure. At the end of the three-month period, the contract is mutually reassessed and the client terminated or reinstated with an expanded contract or problem focus.

Assertion therapy as conceptualized here is involved minimally with direct teaching and pre-arranged role-playing. At the first session, some printed materials or selected reading might prove helpful (e.g., explanation of different response styles, group expectancies, etc.), but a structured lesson format (quadrant B) is not attempted. Personalized rehearsal and spontaneous feedback is a major process, within the context of a flexible, responsive treatment environment. Open-ended discussion and intellectualization is not encouraged as it might be in quadrant C. Experience with assertion therapy points out the need for a therapist with a well-rounded clinical background and a working knowledge of interpersonal dynamic psychology along with the behavioral framework and strategies. This experience and psychological expertise is substantially more extensive than that required to run a quadrant A group.

DIFFERENTIATING TRAINING & THERAPY

Returning to the two dimensional model, a diagonal bisecting line may be added to the figure as a means of clarifying the training-versus-therapy confusion (see Figure 31-2). Groups that take on the non-clinical components and structure mentioned in quadrant A, seem to clearly involve a skill-training rationale, and require a different set of leadership skills and attributes than quadrant B or D. Groups or workshops so designed should be called *training* and not defined as therapy or necessarily require traditional therapist training or experience. Quadrant A groups can be very "therapeutic," but calling them therapy is a misnomer and very confusing to both the professional and consumer community.

Similarly, the model clearly differentiates quadrant D as a therapy

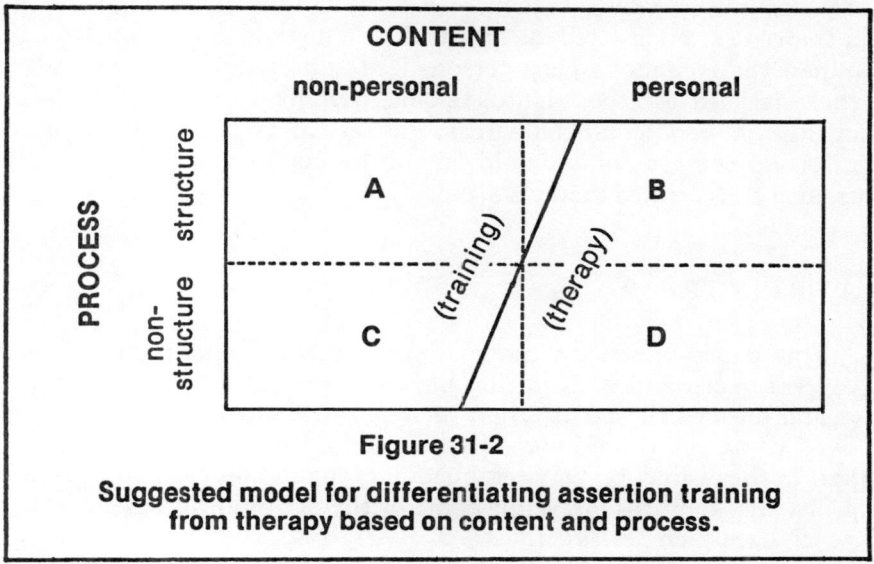

Figure 31-2
Suggested model for differentiating assertion training from therapy based on content and process.

rationale and a set of procedures aimed at helping a clinical population with nonassertiveness. To define this type of group as training seriously limits the public understanding of the group and opens the practice to non-therapist, inadequately trained leaders who piggy-back the AT movement. Many of these individuals can run or assist in running a quadrant A or C group, but professional ethics and responsibility to clients should restrict their involvement with critical clinical problem areas that require personalized ongoing treatment within a confidential, therapeutic setting.

Quadrants B and C, as Figure 31-2 suggests, cannot always be clearly differentiated as either training or therapy. However, most of quadrant C, or the more "rap" group approach to AT, is best referred to as *training* since it can be as a follow-up to a more structured training experience or as a place to air problems of nonassertiveness which are not too clinical or severe. In those instances when an qualified counselor or therapist sees the group moving toward a more personal content or focus, the process of a quadrant D type of group can be used. However, this movement needs to take into account the original contracting agency, the expectation of the group members, and the qualifications of the leader(s).

Quadrant B also has a mixed definition. It definitely has training components, since the group is often pre-structured for a focused and homogeneous membership. However, it has therapy components because often the members are experiencing critical emotions and conflict over a behavior change (e.g., leaving a marriage). In these instances a straight "tell me how to do it" methodology is inadequate. When the content is very personalized and confidential, and when there is need for special professional training to assist in behavior change in very conflicted areas, the group is best referred to as assertion *therapy*, and should be run by competent psychologically trained and certified therapists.

A FIRST STEP

This paper presents a model based upon AT group process and content to clarify the distinction between assertion training (quadrants A and most of C) and assertion therapy (quadrant D and most of B). Even if the AT community has difficulty differentiating quadrants B and C, the distinction between quadrants A and D is clear and presents a first step forward unraveling some of the definition problems of AT which have been described.

32

ASSERTION TRAINING WITHIN AN HOLISTIC-ECLECTIC FRAMEWORK

Michael L. Emmons

Most facilitators of the AT process are well aware that when an individual comes for help with problems of assertiveness that these problems are only a part of a total presenting complaint picture. Although the total nature of one's complaints will vary a great deal from person to person, the odds are that each will have more than one difficulty with which to deal. This statement seems to hold true whether one is a participant in a half-day workshop or an ongoing individual or group experience.

Despite our knowledge of this tendency toward plural difficulties versus a singular "problems-being-assertive" difficulty, it appears to be safe to conclude that most of us as mental health workers are not thorough enough in our assessment or treatment. The purpose of this paper is to attempt to provide a framework for a more complete therapeutic approach by placing assertion training into an "holistic-eclectic" scheme of therapy.

My approach will be to present some basic guidelines regarding an holistic-eclectic system, then to give specific examples relating directly to assertion training.

HOLISTIC

The word holistic when used in a therapeutic context means analyzing and treating the whole person: mentally, physically, spiritually. I have chosen the term *psychophysiospritulogical* to describe this threefold concept. To me, as a psychologist, this means dealing with all aspects of one's health, not simply one's psychological health. Most of us are familiar with the treatment of psychosomatic disorders, but we need to extend this line of reasoning further. If it is true that "mental problems" show themselves as physical difficulties (psychosomatic), why can't we install the reverse terminology and say that physical problems show themselves as mental difficulties (somatopsychic)? And, although our present state of knowledge is not complete enough, the next line of reasoning suggests that there are spiritual problems showing up as bodily complaints (spiritusomatic) and as mental complaints (spiritupsychic). Finally, we complete the picture by adding the terms psychospiritual and somatospiritual.

I personally prefer to avoid all of these categorizations, and not attempt to classify a problem as "psychosomatic" or what have you. The reason is because we are *whole* persons whose functioning is always interdependent and not easily segregated into pieces. A human being always functions *psychophysiospiritualogically*, and assessment and treatment designs need to be chosen to recognize this fact.

ECLECTIC

An eclectic treatment approach refers to the idea that therapists should select their psychological treatments from a wide variety of methods and systems. Generally speaking, it is vital that a therapist use more than one method within a system and also that methods from various systems be employed. If a therapist employs only one method such as assertion training, or only one system such as Gestalt, he or she suffers from "therapeutic narrowmindedness" and needs to expand his or her repertoire. My feelings are that one should be able to utilize therapies along three bipolar lines: (1) *directive-nondirective*, (2) *inner-outer*, and (3) *talk-nontalk*. Following this line of reasoning, if a therapist only uses, for instance, a regular talk therapy, whatever variety, he or she will be functioning at less than optimum.

I will not attempt to present a compilation of therapies for each of these bipolar areas because, in addition to being nearly impossible, my main point here is to stimulate one's thinking in order that one's choice of methods and systems will be more global. To illustrate my thinking I will simply show what I have personally done in this area.

My choice of a nondirective therapy is the client-centered method of

Rogers. The directive method is assertion training. Either of these classify as talk methods. For the inner method I have chosen *Meditative Therapy* (Emmons, in press). The outer method, again, could be any of the talk methods given above. Essentially, I have obtained the bipolar goals by using three methods. These are not the only methods that I utilize because I am constantly searching for other tools that will be helpful in eliminating symptoms, or in helping one in one's stride toward complete health. It is my philosophy to try experimentally any type of somewhat reasonable approach in order to see if it will do what it claims to do.

In addition to being diverse in one's choice of psychological methods and systems, one must also choose methods and systems that are holistic. This doesn't mean that the therapist refers clients to a medical doctor or a minister and lets it go at that. Rather, one needs to be knowledgeable about the client's total functioning and be familiar with what areas the eclectic psychological system may not be adequate to treat. It seems to me that it is useful to know something about osteopathy, chiropractic, acupuncture, traditional medicine, massage, physical therapy, naturopathic medicine, herbal medicine, and other "non-traditional" approaches to healing.

COMPLETE HEALTH

Complete health is a term I have chosen for the goal of an holistic-eclectic therapy system. If one was at the height of mental-physical-spiritual well being, there would exist complete health. I am not sure how much agreement there is in the definitions of terms such as *self-actualization* and *enlightenment* but there should be a great deal. From my viewpoint, if one were truly "self-actualized," or truly "enlightened" (or truly whatever word is used) he or she would necessarily need to be completely, psychophysiospiritualogically, healthy. I will not attempt a further explanation of what complete health is, or to verify if there are individuals who are completely healthy. Complete health has to be different for each unique individual, developing along these threefold lines to more and more closely approach complete health. I believe each person knows inherently what his or her personal complete health is, and even though one may not know the ultimate goal at certain points in time, the initial steps to take to begin the journey are known. As more and more growth takes place, new steps will be apparent and the ultimate complete health goal becomes clearer. Progress along these lines is quite tangible and can be judged by symptom removal or the appearance of mental, physical, and spiritual traits of self-actualization, enlightenment, cosmic consciousness, and/or liberation.

ASSESSMENT

If the individual should be *treated* holistically-eclectically, it follows that he or she should also be *assessed* in that manner. In other words, a *thorough* analysis of one's difficulties should be undertaken within a psychophysiospiritulogical framework. When an individual enters a workshop, group, or individual counseling, he or she typically will have a presenting complaint or complaints of some kind. Most therapists will look beyond presenting complaints to some extent, but often only for further psychological implications. For example, if the individual is depressed, the therapist will usually try to determine if the depression is triggered by a lack of assertion or problems with feelings of rejection. What I am suggesting is that the individual's life should be totally analyzed in order to treat the client as a whole being.

The degree of assessment will depend upon the particular setting in which one is working and also upon the client's expectations. A therapist will not spend several hours of thorough assessment when there are thirty participants in a half-day workshop, or if a client comes to individual counseling to find out about careers. However, it is my contention that individuals in these situations should be appraised of other possibilities for help than those offered by these specialized treatments.

In an initial individual assessment session the primary objective should be to allow the client an unencumbered opportunity to present his or her problems. My preference is to be as nondirective as possible in the early stages of counseling in order to give the client the chance to thoroughly explain his or her view of the problem without therapist interference. This step of listening facilitates rapport and trust between therapist and client. The therapist should also pursue topics which have been brought up by the individual but which need more explanation. Additionally, the therapist needs to ask about areas which have not been brought up by the client in his or her explanation. The client may need to be prepared for this type of questioning by a statement such as, "Would you mind if I ask you some questions about other areas? I like to be as thorough as possible and check everything out. I may even ask you some questions you wouldn't expect a psychologist to ask, if that is OK." After this type of statement, most clients are willing to proceed.

Physical

The first line of questioning I typically employ is in the area of physical functioning. One could say, "Imagine you are talking with a medical doctor, and simply describe anything that bothers you physically. Start at the top of your head and go down." The therapist may have to lead the individual step by step throughout his or her body. The head, including ears, eyes, and teeth, should be checked out for any difficulties. The neck, back, chest, including heart and lungs, and on down the line should be covered by appropriate questioning. Sleeping patterns, bowel movements, and sexual functioning should especially be checked out.

A thorough analysis of diet and exercise patterns should be included. I take an initial "typical day" sample of food intake, and then usually request that the person keep exact track of his or her diet for one week. That is to keep a log of everything eaten or drunk, including snacks, meals, vitamins, alcohol, and medications. The type and frequency of physical exercise is determined. If one jogs or lifts weights, a determination should be made as to what actually takes place in terms of time per exercise period and per week.

In addition to this line of questioning, it is a good idea to check out the client's past experiences with any form of physical illnesses and injuries. Once again, the more thorough the analysis the better. The therapist should find out if the client has been involved in auto accidents, falls, or any other type of stressful "physical" experience.

The reason for checking out the person's physical functioning is in order to derive an holistic treatment strategy. Of course, the therapist should not ask questions about diet, physical functioning, and exercise, without a treatment design of some kind in mind, if the client has a need. Such a design could be simply referral to other professionals, such as nutritionists or medical doctors or physical educators, or it could be that the therapist is prepared to handle these areas. I will not develop my own particular approach in this short paper, but will only mention that I follow the basic ideas of Fredericks and Goodman (1969), and Abrahamson and Pezet (1971) on dietary matters. Also, the recent material by Reuben (1975) looks promising. In the area of physical exercise I feel that the material by Cooper (1970) is excellent, and I also recommend Yoga-type exercises.

More and more I have been coming to the conclusion that an individual arriving for therapy should be medically screened. I believe clients should be given an initial battery of medical tests which would be a thorough analysis of current physiological functioning. A recent example will illustrate the reason for this statement: the case involves a young woman, age 22, whom I sent to an M.D. because she had been off of birth control pills for two years, had not been using birth control during that time span, and had not become pregnant. In addition, she had abdominal cramping during, as well as between, her menstrual periods. The first physician, because of preliminary findings, sent the young woman to a gynecologist who diagnosed endometriosis. Presently, she is being medically treated to see if surgery can be avoided. Two other women clients decided to go off birth control pills altogether, after which a good many of their anxiety symptoms disappeared.

I have become more careful about appropriate medical referrals partly because of experience in cases where referrals were not made by me, but the individual decided to seek medical help independently. I treated a 26-year-old woman for a period of three to four months, using a variety of methods. She continued to complain of excessive fatigue. Finally, she decided to go to our University Health Center where, after appropriate testing, a diagnosis of mononucleosis was made. In another case, a young man who experienced dramatic mood swings, uncontrollable eating binges of junk foods, and headaches decided to be checked out medically, and it was discovered he had very low blood sugar. Needless to say, a therapist could treat someone psychologically for years and never make a dent in these disorders. Now, rather than allowing such cases to slip by me, relying on "chance," I try to be as thorough as possible with each person.

Psychological

In addition to a physical analysis, a thorough analysis of psychological functioning is undertaken. Most therapists are knowledgeable when it comes to this step, but it is worth mentioning that *all* areas of functioning need to be checked out. I utilize the Fear Survey Schedule and Willoughby (Wolpe, 1969) and various assertion inventories in order to be thorough in my assessment of the psychological status of the individual.

Spiritual

The client should also be assessed in terms of spiritual functioning. A history of religious upbringing in terms of home and church can be taken, and also involvement after leaving home can be analyzed. The therapist may wish to look into how the individual feels about God, about guilt, about prayer, about meditation, about sin. This area seems to be more "touchy" to deal with than diet and exercise or mental functioning, but as mentioned above, it is crucial to treat the person as a whole. My own thinking along spiritual lines in terms of assessment and treatment is just in its infancy, but it is an area I feel stronger about, in terms of need, as I develop.

Spiritual aspects can be brought out in therapy or not, depending upon one's frame of reference. Take the example of physical exercise for a start. One can look at the reason for exercising simply as being to keep in good condition, to feel good, physically fit and mentally alert. On the other hand, if one wants to, a spiritual significance can be placed on physical exercise. The body can be looked at as the "temple of the living God," one of the places where one communes with God. If the temple is not kept in balance by appropriate exercise, how can the God-force work to its full potential through the person? The same logic can be applied to dietery considerations. If one has faulty eating patterns, it could be said that one is clouding up the full expression of one's spiritual self. Assertion training could also be talked about along these lines. One could say that assertion has a spiritual base in that one of the basic premises of assertion is to "do unto others as you would have them do unto you." Another religious precept which could be applied here is "what ye sow ye must reap;" in this context, the more you manifest assertion to others the more you foster assertion back towards yourself.

Much more could be said about analyzing the spiritual importance of these and other approaches, but at this point, it should be noted that all of these therapies work quite well without speaking of them in these terms. It is my feeling that therapists should, however, have a basic openness to spiritual lines of thinking because there will be clients who will need and want to deal with matters of this nature. Here again, referrals to appropriate consultants is important. If a client has a strong leaning toward a particular religious denomination, the appropriate clergy should be kept in mind as a referral source.

Summary

The overall purpose of an holistic-eclectic assessment procedure is to derive a complete picture of the presenting complaints. The phrase "presenting complaints" may not be an accurate one in this context because the client may not have been aware of some important areas of need when he or she entered therapy. One who comes to a mental health worker is usually not geared for anything but a psychological approach. However, an overall determination of the client's functioning is important because the material can then be translated into a specific list of complaints. This list should be referred to by the therapist and client at various points during therapy in order to check on progress. If a therapist utilizes a certain therapeutic approach such as AT with the intention that it will reduce or eliminate certain presenting complaints, then it is vital that he or she check out that assumption as therapy progresses.

CASE EXAMPLES

Let us now briefly analyze two individual clients. The first signed up for an AT group, and the second came to individual counseling first.

Client One

This client came to me of his own accord after about three weeks of an AT group and indicated that he could not grasp the material we were covering. He stated that the role-playing situations made him nervous and he couldn't successfully complete the homework assignments. I asked him a few questions about his anxiety and determined that it would be appropriate to see him individually in order to take a more thorough history and assessment. During his first individual session, he stated that his main difficulty centered around dating what he called "above-average-looking" women. He considered Friday and Saturday nights the worst nights of the week for him, dreading them because he couldn't ask out the women he wished to date. He continually excused himself as "being very tired" in the evening of each day (feeling that he was burned out from the day's activities), that he should be studying instead of dating, and that he hadn't dated much in the past so why should he now. His contact with women in the past had been negative because he would usually get turned down when asking for dates. If he happened to get a date, he didn't know how to act and would get "bottled up" inside.

This particular individual had previous contact with mental health workers. In junior college, three years before, he had seen a psychologist and he had seen one as recently as the previous quarter prior to seeing me. He also was being seen for academic counseling in our Learning Assistance Center (LAC). As part of that program he had been desensitized for test anxiety. In addition, within the past six months he had been through the Transcendental Meditation course and had undergone extensive medical testing, but with no significant findings.

Further questioning revealed that he had a minimum of three bad headaches, accompanied by pain in his eyes, per week, that his chest hurt at times for unknown reasons, that at times he would feel so weak that he felt like dropping to the floor, that his stomach would get sore or feel sick about once per week, and that he felt constantly pressured for time in school. An analysis by the LAC determined that he spent over 60 hours per week studying. Other complaints were frequent physical coldness, nervousness, tingling sensations, and extreme feelings of tiredness. In addition, he ate very little breakfast, drank excessive amounts of coffee, and was chronically underweight.

I believe that it is fair to say that this individual needed more treatment than an AT group or AT administered individually could offer. I make this statement realizing that AT can at times effect dramatic changes in complaints not seemingly related to difficulties with assertion. The only way to truly tell if AT will work with a certain difficulty such as nervousness or tiredness is to try it and observe the results.

The treatment program for this client consisted of dietary and physical exercise changes, Meditative Therapy, continuing in group AT, and situation-specific AT which focused on dating situations. Individual treatment consisted of approximately 15 sessions. Although no formal post-therapy assessment has been conducted at this point, informal self-report information indicates that there have been significant improvements in all key areas.

Client Two

Although only 21 years old, this young woman revealed a history of mental instability which included two suicide attempts around age 16 and three "nervous breakdowns," the first at age 18, the second at age 19, and the third at age 20. In addition, she presently felt on the verge of, as she described it, "flipping out" again. Despite her difficulties, she had not been to any type of mental health professional before. She and her husband had one child who was three years old.

Pre-testing with the Fear Survey Schedule and Willoughby revealed that many items were marked at the highest or next highest point on the scale. She also reported that she became depressed easily, had low energy levels, became easily upset, and felt nervous and restless a good deal of the time. Her father caused her a great deal of difficulty because she felt intimidated around him and unable to express feelings to him. She felt that he never made a mistake and it was "horribly frightening" for her to make one. As one might guess, she was very non-assertive.

Physical questioning revealed that she had developed bronchitis at age 3 and still had bouts of it at least twice per year. She also presently had acne, a problem of 10 years duration. Around the age of 18 she was involved in two auto accidents during which she experienced whiplash. She had received treatment, but reported having two vertabrae which were still quite painful. In addition, since the accident her kidneys caused her intermittent pain especially upon awakening in the morning. Other findings were that her bowel movements were irregular, taking place only once every two days or more, her diet and exercise patterns were not satisfactory, and she felt tired a good deal of the time and fell asleep easily during the day even though she slept a good amount each night.

Treatment totaled 17 sessions and consisted of a variety of measures, including systematic desensitization for fear of making mistakes, dietary and exercise changes, medical referral for her back difficulty, assertion training, and Meditative Therapy.

Results were evaluated after 11 sessions (three months from the start of therapy), prior to beginning the Meditative Therapy sessions, and again nine months after 11 treatments were completed. Evaluation was conducted through the administration of a follow-up complaint rating form and questionnaire, the Fear Survey Schedule (FSS) and the Willoughby. Her evaluation of specific complaints at the three-month and 14-month points are given below. The rating scale went from "no improvement" to "total improvement" on a 7-point scale.

Presenting Complaint	Evaluation at: 3 Months	Change	14 Months
Bronchitis	No new "bouts" at this time		Average Improvement
Kidney Pains	Total Improvement	(down)	Very Much Improved
Two Painful Vertebrae	Very Much Improved	(down)	Much Improved
Acne	Slight Improvement	(up)	Average Improvement
Nervousness	Total Improvement	(down)	Very Much Improved
Low Energy Levels	Total Improvement	(down)	Much Improved
Sleep Difficulties	Much Improved	(up)	Total Improvement
Bowel Movements	Much Improved	(down)	Average Improvement
Depressions	Total Improvement	(same)	Total Improvement
Fear of Making Mistakes	Much Improved	(up)	Very Much Improved

As can be seen by the table, she noted a great deal of improvement in her complaints and this improvement was maintained nine months following completion of all therapies. The FSS and Willoughby scores appear to confirm the same degree of improvement.

Her personal impression of the therapies, which was most helpful, was that the dietary suggestions and changes in her diet and assertion training were the most important.

SUMMARY

These cases and the other material in this paper have been presented in order to illustrate some of the possibilities inherent in an holistic-eclectic treatment program. Although it is difficult at times to decipher which treatment caused which result, the final outcome is the vital factor. From my clinical observations I know that the key therapy in treatment fluctuates, depending upon the individual being treated. At times Meditative Therapy will be the crucial treatment, at times AT will be, at times dietary approaches will be. However, despite the fact that one or two therapies may stand out for certain clients, I still maintain that an holistic-eclectic treatment system is necessary for each individual.

In conclusion, I feel that it is important that those involved in the facilitation of AT broaden their outlook in order that the whole person be taken into consideration. Assertion training is a very powerful tool to help one live life more successfully, but it is only one of many in a basic "carrying case" of tools. If we as mental health workers are to help individuals to change, and then to maintain and go beyond that change, then a variety of tools with which we can leave them is necessary. Hopefully, those tools will come from each of the areas: mental, physical, and spiritual.

SQUEAK UP!

Gerald Nachman

I wonder what happens when somebody who has read "Winning Through Intimidation" sits next to someone at a party who just finished "Power: How to Get It, How to Use It," and Mr. Power tells Mr. Intimidation to put out his cigar and make it snappy.

Assuming Mr. I doesn't say yes when he means no, it could end up with somebody in tears, or possibly dead, but I doubt it—not if I know my fellow mice.

No matter how many advice-to-the-hatelorn books they've read, people who hope to learn a little harmless Fascism to use around the office are sure to slip when shove comes to push. If you try doing Charles Bronson numbers on everyone when, underneath, you're still Charles Nelson Reilly, you are bound to (a) look pretty silly and (b) mess things up even worse as a semipro bully.

All the self-assertiveness best sellers claim that once you stand up for your rights, maitre d's will step aside with a flourish and say, "Yes, *sir*, Mr. Mitty, your table is ready!" and bosses will be so deeply moved by your sudden table-thumping skills they'll boost your salary

---

1. From *Newsweek* magazine, April 5, 1976, p. 13. Copyright © 1976 by Newsweek, Inc. Reprinted by permission of the author and his agents, Scott Meredith Literary Agency, Inc., 845 Third Avenue, New York, NY 10022.

that afternoon with a hearty, "By Jove, Milquetoast, I can see now you're a man on the move, whereas just two days ago I took you for a real shnook!"

In my own spotty experience of standing up for my rights, statistics show that about 83 percent of the time I'm wrong—a cruel blow to your up-and-coming Machiavelli. Whenever I call a waiter over to growl that the bill is $2.35 too high, he growls back that I forgot to add the onion soup. Exit scampering.

CRACKPOT RAVINGS

If, by some quirk, it turns out I'm right, I have to wait around for the manager to get back from lunch or fill out a twelve-page complaint form. Standing up for your rights involves much standing up.

When you *can* force someone to bend to your demands, they make it doubly rough on you. To quote the Mouse Manual: "Leave bad enough alone." In the classic case of sending back an undercooked steak, the chef always sends it right back out with sixth-degree burns, just to let you know who's really in control. (Most of the people who've benefited from aggression books seem to be waiters, chefs, desk clerks, etc.)

If you ask a hotel clerk for a nicer room, say with a view, you'll get your lousy room with a view, all right, but it will also have cold and cold running water. As the Mouse Manual notes: "You can't win."

All serious attempts to get my way are treated like crackpot ravings. A Manhattan Bakery that advertises "San Francisco sourdough French rolls" invites you to call the company president with any complaints. When I phoned him to say that his rolls would get him arrested in San Francisco for bread pollution, a secretary told me, "Gosh, nobody ever complained before."

SWAGGERING DEFEATS

In any given disaster, I'm always the "only one" to fuss. If I told the manager of the Leaning Tower of Pisa that his building appeared to be teetering, and I'd like to check out, he would just chuckle and say, "Funny—you're the first person to complain."

Conditions are never ideal for asserting myself. If my stereo breaks a week after it's been fixed, the man who did the job is in Lapland for a year. If I demand my way, I'm suddenly "causing a scene" and now everyone is mad at *me*; the mouse suddenly dwindles to pest.

Recently, I swaggered into Nathan's with free passes for two hotdogs and the henchperson said, "Ain't no good here. Next."

After I'd illustrated with sound logic (more sound than logic) that it plainly states "Good at any Nathan's," the manager grudgingly agreed to fork over the wieners. I felt I'd won my first clear-cut intimidation victory, good for at least a Gold Cluster from awed bystanders, but I'd somehow lost again, shot down from behind by an ex-ally: "Boy," said my wife, "were *you* obnoxious."

Look who's talking—little Ms. Power-Grabber herself, a born self-asserter who simply assumes she's always right and if not—well, she deserves it anyway. No matter how often I watch her in action in the ring, and hold her coat, I can't seem to get that attitude to rub off. Advises the Mouse Manual: "Marry into power."

Whereas I was born looking over one shoulder, she's always on the lookout for holes in the defensive line. One summer, we went to Clint Eastwood's outdoor restaurant in Carmel, Calif., but it was 3 p.m.—Patio Closing Time—and we were told to eat our avocado-burgers inside.

They hadn't figured on Mugsy, who pointed out that her watch showed 2:59, that we'd come clear from Egypt and that if we were not seated outside she would "take it up with Mr. Eastwood, a family friend." Well, it was a fistful of intimidation that Dirty Harry would have loved. We got a pretty patio table, overlooking a 2-inch-high manager.

Now if I'd tried this gambit (as if I can think that fast on my feet; mice tend to think best in the tub a day later), I'd have been arrested for impersonating a lion.

Not that we macho mice don't have our own cute little power plays—none of which works, but they make us feel lots better, and that's what counts. I go for moral defeats. One of my favorite tactics is WALKING OUT IN A HUFF, a swell way to assert yourself without risking a scar. When things get hot, I can be counted on to clench my fists and snort, "OK, if they don't serve us in *five* more minutes, we leave." (If anybody ever noticed us leave, they'd be destroyed.)

THE POWER OF PUNITIVE THINKING

Another pet ploy is known as GLARING. I have perfected an arsenal of withering scowls and triple whammies that wear me out but that noisy people behind me at the movies just take to be my normal scrunched-up expression.

Then there is my famed HEAVY SIGH OF DISGUST. This must be done with great melodramatic exhaling, enough so that outsiders can tell you're burned up as hell but not so extreme that people think you're having an asthma attack.

My last-ditch technique is LEAVING A NASTY NOTE. I used to live in an apartment under a man who liked to see how loud he could yell at 2 a.m. It was a hobby and he got awfully good at it. I could have marched upstairs and simply beat him up but I preferred to write a violent note that read "QUIET!!", slip it under his door, push the bell and run like crazy.

I don't recall if it worked, for I was so flushed with joy at my own ingenuity that I didn't care. And I was so tired from sitting up all night thinking of what I *might* do to him that I fell fast asleep.

As the Manual firmly whispers, "Better a drowsing mouse than a dead rat."

34

ISSUES IN ASSERTIVE BEHAVIOR TRAINING

Robert E. Alberti

Assertive behavior training has nearly "come of age." The preceding chapters have only begun to suggest the breadth of practice of the AT process. Moreover, increasingly sophisticated research has provided significant depth of understanding of those dimensions of the process which are of demonstrable value, and has called into question some early assumptions. It is no longer sufficient for the practitioner to claim to "do assertiveness training." An up-to-date, ethically responsible approach demands that the professional operate with an awareness of theoretical perspectives, current research, and issues of ethics and practice. Indeed, each responsible facilitator of assertiveness in others must continually seek to answer the question "What is it about my practice of AT which makes it *legitimate* for me to offer it as a service to clients?"

From the perspective of the editor's "last word," this chapter offers a reference point for the practitioner to develop an adequate answer to that question.

THEORETICAL ISSUES

The concept of assertiveness training has its roots in behavior therapy, notably in the work of Andrew Salter, Joseph Wolpe, and Arnold Lazarus, and was developed initially as a treatment procedure for clients with neurotic social anxiety.

In Chapter 2 of this book, Andrew Salter commented upon the potential of assertion training in offering help for a wide range of client conditions. His 1949 book *Conditioned Reflex Therapy*, now a classic in behavior therapy, presented detailed procedures for increasing "excitatory" behavior and decreasing "inhibitory" behavior. Salter introduced his then-revolutionary therapeutic concepts with the terminology of Ivan Pavlov, the Soviet physiologist who discovered *excitation* and *inhibition* as the key elements in the animal organism's capacity to be expressive emotionally.

Salter went on to present the essence of modern behavior therapy, including procedures for deconditioning anxiety, developing assertive responses, overcoming sexual dysfunction, treating addictions, freeing creative energy, and eliminating stuttering—all this in 1949! Although he never used the word *assertion* in his early work, AT clearly owes its foundation to Andrew Salter's *excitatory* model. He has remained steadfast in his dedication to Pavlovian principles, and his considerable success as a therapist—active in New York City today—has resulted directly from his consistently effective efforts to free clients of inappropriate inhibition.

Disinhibition, in the Salter-as-derived-from-Pavlov model, involves a *relearning* process directed toward deliberate *excitatory* behavior. Repeated excitatory actions result in increased freedom and awareness of excitatory *feelings*, and a corresponding decrease in inhibitory actions and feelings. Thus, Salter's behavior change procedures (using now-common AT methods of exhortation, behavior rehearsal, relaxation-and-suggestion) lead to changes in neural activity (per Pavlov's notion that excitation is a function of neural connections in the brain), which develops a new freedom of thought, feeling, and further behavior change. As Salter observes, Pavlov's term for "disinhibition" may be literally translated as "unbraking"—removing the brakes. Salter advocates unbraking behavior and freeing individuals to their fullest excitatory potential. An important criterion in Salter's definition of assertion is *honesty*.

First to use the term *assertive* in conjunction with openness in interpersonal behavior was Joseph Wolpe. His early work in deconditioning anxiety led to the concept of "reciprocal inhibition"—that the organism can unlearn anxiety through pairing of anxiety-evoking stimuli with anxiety-inhibiting responses. Key responses which inhibit anxiety are, according to Wolpe, relaxation and assertion. By teaching a client to relax while confronting stimuli which have produced anxiety, the anxiety response is weakened. Repeated confrontations of this type while relaxed can reduce the anxiety markedly—to effectively negligible levels. This is the paradigm involved in the *systematic desensitization* procedure.

Assertiveness, similarly, may be paired with an anxiety-inducing stimulus in order to inhibit and, eventually, overcome the anxiety, in Wolpe's model. By expressing non-anxious feelings—assertions of anger, pleasure, affection—the client weakens the anxiety response and thus encourages further assertions in the future. Sufficient practice of assertive responses—as all AT practitioners are aware—can effectively eliminate situation-specific anxiety, and often has carry-over into other social situations as well. Dr. Wolpe's work, like that of Salter, continues to be highly influential in assertiveness training and behavior therapy in general.

As we began our work with assertiveness training, Mike Emmons and I were heavily influenced by a humanistic value system, and by our own early training in the model of Carl Rogers (1961). Thus, we drew from Wolpe's behavioral concepts, and from the notions of human rights and potential, and were perhaps first to present AT as a behavioral-humanistic procedure for helping persons to gain their "perfect rights." The concept of assertiveness as a contributor to self-esteem, although only a clinical observation at that time, was an integral part of our contribution. Moreover, we have consistently opted for a non-manipulative view of assertion, as contrasted with hurtful aggression. Finally, in part thanks to the influence of Mike Serber, with whom we had the good fortune to work for a time, we expanded the notion of positive and caring expression as a dimension of assertiveness. In fact, it has been observed that we include nearly all "good" feelings and behavior. Thus, it may be said that the major Alberti-Emmons contributions have been (1) to move AT from a behavioral treatment for neurotic anxiety to a behavioral-humanistic approach to enhancing self-esteem; (2) to develop more systematic AT procedures, including emphasis upon non-verbal components in the feedback-coaching process; (3) to emphasize the notions of expanding the boundaries of human rights and expressing positive and caring feelings; and (4) to advocate ethical responsibility and standards for professional AT facilitators.

Arnold Lazarus, for a time a colleague of Wolpe, has more recently begun to develop an approach to AT and other therapeutic procedures which he calls "broad-spectrum behavior therapy." He has broken the barrier of "purely scientific" behavioral principles, and does a good deal of integrating of behavioral and humanistic approaches. Lazarus' conception of assertiveness is somewhat more limiting, in that he prefers to deal only with standing up for rights under the rubric "assertive." The expression of affectionate and other positive feelings are part of Lazarus' "broader" term *emotional freedom*, in which he includes expressions of all forms of affective thoughts, feelings and behaviors.

Among the more recent approaches to theoretical conceptualization of assertive behavior is that of Richard McFall, whose rigorous application of experimental criteria has led him to the conclusion that assertion must be viewed in a situation-specific manner, and must be defined in terms of its behavioral referents. *Measurability* of behavior and its effects are among the strict criteria which McFall considers essential. One of the signal research psychologists working with assertive behavior training, McFall is responsible for the first experimental study of AT (McFall and Marston, 1970). His current concern is for an adequate *behavioral competence* definition of assertion, noting that until we can adequately define the concept in terms which are observable and measurable, our treatment/training procedures are form without substance.

Herbert Fensterheim, himself a practitioner of AT (and perhaps reluctant to characterize himself as a theorist), has offered a pragmatic challenge to McFall. Fensterheim and McFall engaged in a lively discussion which the editor witnessed during the 1975 meeting of the Association for Advancement of Behavior Therapy. In a personal communication to the editor, Fensterheim (1977) followed up that AABT discussion with the observation that, although McFall's approach has the distinct advantage of "observable, recordable, measurable behaviors" and statistical objectivity, it has "nothing to do with Assertion or with life in general." Fensterheim also notes that he currently relates assertiveness to the *learned helplessness* paradigm of Seligman and his associates, with self-esteem as the major positive reinforcer—assertiveness gains self-esteem, helplessness loses self-esteem.

Another theorist who supports the hypothesis of a learned helplessness relationship with assertiveness is Gosta Andersson, whose doctoral dissertation at the University of Gothenburg, Sweden, was entitled "Toward a Unifying Theory of Assertiveness." Andersson undertook an empirical study of the concept of assertiveness because of a conclusion that the concept, as a personality trait, had not been adequately studied. The author wished to test the assumptions in the popular *typological* view of assertiveness—that some *people* are "excitatory" or "non-assertive"—against the notion of assertiveness as one *dimension* of the person.

Andersson developed a test of assertiveness, administered it to some

380 subjects of varying ages and life roles, then performed extensive factor analytic studies of the resulting data. Two principal factors were derived: *assertiveness inhibition*—an avoidance of the expression of opinions and feelings; and *assertiveness expression*—an expression of opinions, feelings, and refusal behavior.

Finally, Andersson proposes a theoretical model of *assertiveness deficiency* (a function of inhibition score minus expression score), and relates that concept to *helplessness*. Comparisons with standardized personality test data led Andersson to observe that assertiveness deficiency is positively related to depression, anxiety, pessimism, feelings of insufficiency, expectancy of inability to control reinforcement, needs of affiliation, needs of succorance, and needs of nuturance. Moreover, as might be expected, assertiveness deficiency is negatively related to self-confidence and autonomy.

The Andersson model offers strong empirical support for the concept of assertiveness as a dimension of personality. However, it should be remembered that Andersson's approach began by considering only a binary option: trait *vs.* type. Further examination of the Andersson data in terms of situation-specific criteria could prove enlightening.

In his discussion of a dimension of assertiveness essentially overlooked by other theoreticians (and most practitioners as well), Donald Cheek (1976) presents a strong argument for including the ethnic/cultural identity of the client as a component in AT theory. Noting that "there can be no therapy developed for someone you basically do not understand," Cheek challenges theoreticians and practitioners to discard theoretical assumptions developed from white-only populations. He considers the *intent of the communicator* to be the principal criterion for defining assertive behavior, and urges consideration of the social-cultural context in the labeling process.

How then do we reconcile these divergent theoretical positions? *Is there a "unifying" theory?* Is it important for the practitioner to have such a theory? The issues are complex, and the current state of the art/science of assertive behavior theory leaves them unresolved. As a general perspective from which to view the material presented in this book, perhaps we can agree that:
1) Assertiveness is a characteristic of *behavior*, not of *persons*;
2) Assertiveness is a *person-and-situation-specific*, not a universal, characteristic;
3) Assertiveness must be viewed in the *cultural context* of the individual, as well as in terms of other situational variables;
4) Assertiveness is predicated upon the ability of the individual to *freely choose* his/her action;

5) Assertiveness is a characteristic of *socially effective*, *non-hurtful* behavior.

RESEARCH ISSUES

Since research involves empirical investigation of theoretical hypotheses and variables of method and practice, the issues of research are nearly identical to those of theory and of practice. Nevertheless, it is useful to consider separately the concerns which are stimulating controlled studies of AT and its component constructs.

Preparation of this section has been made immeasurably easier by virtue of an excellent report of research issues in AT by Alexander Rich and Harold Schroeder (1976). Indeed, the interested reader is urged to study their very comprehensive paper for details, since only the barest outline will be presented here.

Definition of the concept of assertiveness again appears as a key issue. How shall we research a concept which is undefined? Indeed, how is it taught if undefined? Operational definitions which may satisfy our needs for training formats are simply inadequate as variables against which to collect quantifiable data. Without quantification, outcome studies are extremely difficult, at best. Yet, *can* we legitimately quantify human behavior? The debate goes on.

Trait vs. situation-specific concepts of behavior have been the source of another continuing controversy in the psychological literature for decades, and assertive behavior has recently been in the center of this dialogue. Greater specificity, of course, offers greater measurability, and contributes to objective evaluation. An increasing volume of research, moreover, concludes that no generalized trait of "assertiveness" exists.

Practitioners are skeptical, nonetheless. Too many clients appear with a broad constellation of non-assertive characteristics. And too many trainees emerge from clinical interventions with dramatically improved assertiveness in many areas of their lives. Perhaps resolution of this apparent conflict lies in two directions:
1) Experimental studies which evaluate behavior change are (of necessity in the current state of the art of behavioral **measure**ment) carefully controlled to allow as few variables as possible to contribute to the outcomes. It is tempting to speculate that the very nature of such measurement limitations in controlled *experimental* conditions *precludes* a generalization or transfer of training by trainees. Human behavior is subject to an axiom of the physical sciences, known as *Heisenberg's Uncertainty Principle*, which says, in effect,

that *the very act of observation or measurement itself CHANGES a phenomenom, so that exact measures are not possible*. Moreover, if training is restricted to a very narrow range of skills (as is typically true under experimental conditions) it is not likely that trainees will generalize as readily as those exposed to a broadly-based training experience.

2) We draw heavily from large-sample statistical treatment of experimental data in behavioral studies. Individual changes over time tend to regress toward group means when viewed in this way. It is entirely possible that some clients have the necessary learning skills to effect their own transfer of assertive behavior training to a variety of situations, while others are limited to skills learned in the training situation.

The reader may wish to leave the door open on this issue until more definitive research data are available.

Methodology of assertive behavior training is a persistent issue related to the preceding two. If we cannot clearly define assertive behavior, it is difficult to determine how we shall teach it! Thus many approaches are subsumed under the name "assertiveness training"—witness the variety reported in the chapters of this book—and this very variety makes definitive research virtually impossible. Questions raised by contributors to this volume are pertinent: Is AT primarily concerned with *verbal* or *non-verbal* procedures? Is it *training* or *therapy*? Who are the *clients*? What *settings* are appropriate? How *long* should interventions last? What *qualifications* are necessary for trainers/therapists?

The focus of training in AT is somewhat diffuse. Are we principally concerned with skill training? Anxiety deconditioning? Cognitive restructuring? All of the above? Once again the individual client is the key mediating variable, but most researchers are reluctant to perform $N = 1$ studies.

Measurement of assertive behavior and of training effects is itself a significant limitation for adequacy of research in AT. The general limitations of measurement of behavior and behavior change apply to AT, and are compounded by the shortcomings for other variables noted above.

Early research in assertive behavior training was primarily directed toward efficacy of techniques. Relative value of behavior rehearsal, video tape feedback, covert conditioning, homework, token feedback, bibliotherapy, scripts, coaching non-verbal components, were all evaluated in terms of the inadequate criteria of assertiveness which are available. Current and future research directions will undoubtedly lead us out of the current fluid state, as we develop firmer conceptual models for the content and process of assertive behavior training.

ISSUES OF AT PRACTICE AND ETHICS

Practitioners, after all, are principally interested in those issues which are of direct relevance to practice. The reader is urged to carefully consider the preceding sections of this chapter as well. However, as we view AT practice, a number of key concerns emerge:

Client self-determination is a fundamental value in any change-oriented intervention. As facilitators, we recognize and teach the importance of assertiveness. In our enthusiasm for encouraging and coaching clients to *be* assertive, we must resist the temptation to deny the client's right to *choose* to assert or not to assert! It is our responsibility to coach the client in assertive skills; it is the client's responsibility to decide whether and when to use those skills.

Client choice is, in my opinion, the primary criterion against which all interventions should be weighed. The fact is, we know assertion does not always work, and clients should not be pushed into risk-taking by zealous facilitators who do not have to live with the consequences of such assertions.

We may pause to reflect on the comment of Alfred Sams of Bangalore, India, who wrote in respose to his reading of *Your Perfect Right* that he liked our ideas, but in the "real world" *aggression works*! Alas, he is close enough to make us rest uneasily!

Facilitator understanding of what is happening is a key ethical issue. Indeed, one must characterize as unprofessional and unethical any facilitator who practices AT without at least a basic understanding of: 1) principles of learning and behavior, 2) anxiety and its effects upon behavior, and 3) limitations and potential dangers of AT. The professional *role* of the facilitator (e.g., teacher *vs.* social worker *vs.* psychotherapist) of course calls for both a differing *level* of intervention and differing facilitator skills. Clearly an important dimension of this issue is that the facilitator recognize his/her limitations and act accordingly.

Level of intervention, as noted above, is an issue which, like the others, affects all dimensions of AT. *Therapy*, the most intensive intervention, represents clinical efforts to assist persons who are severely inhibited by anxiety, or who significantly lack social skills, or who are controlled by aggression. *Training*, by contrast, is less intensive and is characterized by non-clinical interventions aimed at teaching assertive skills to those persons who require only encouragement and skill training. *Self-help*, of course, represents efforts by individuals to develop assertiveness on their own, and would include professionally prepared written materials or tapes designed to aid the process. Definition of these differences, identification of the level of intervention appropriate to each client's needs, and standards for the qualification of practitioners at each level are key issues in AT yet to be resolved. Marty Shoemaker's schema (Chapter 31) offers a highly useful model for differentiating the level of intervention, and should particularly be used as a guide for those whose qualifications may not prepare them for the interventions of greater intensity.

Monitoring facilitator effectiveness is a continuing problem for all types of change-oriented interventions. How do we know whether a facilitator is effective or not? How does one make appropriate referrals *without* knowing? *Certification* has long been considered a method for dealing with this problem. At least one task force of the Association for Advancement of Behavior Therapy decided that the problems of certifying qualified professionals outweighed the benefits. *Evaluative research* is always a desirable procedure, but may appear impractical for short term interventions, particularly in non-clinical settings. Notwithstanding difficulties in conducting adequate studies, *some follow-up is incumbent* upon the professional facilitator. *Educating consumers* holds perhaps the greatest promise, *if* we as practitioners would undertake to inform our clients sufficiently about the AT procedures we employ, the potentials, and the hazards. Clients themselves then become the best evaluators—as indeed they have always been—of our effectiveness. Nevertheless, we need to continue to look toward more adequate training programs (both pre- and in-service) for facilitators, continued research on dimensions of facilitator effectiveness, and a high standard of ethical behavior on the part of the facilitators.

Application to social issues is a dimension of AT which does not receive much attention (although a national magazine writer recently sniffed at my idea that AT is of significant value for oppressed groups). Recent efforts in this area are developing impressive gains. Part 3 of this book presents hopeful evidence for AT with ethnic minorities.

In a conversation with a group of professionals who apply AT in a variety of settings, I raised this issue. We wondered together whether a "law and order" society would respond favorably (reinforce) to assertive requests by minority citizens for equal opportunity in jobs, housing, education, and civil and criminal justice. A Black woman in the group answered for all of us: "Whether or not we think society will provide these things, ethically it is our responsibility as AT facilitators to teach the skills necessary for these denied citizens to *make the assertive request!*" And, I might add, to work assertively *ourselves* to bring about the changes we believe in.

Ethical guidelines for the practice of AT should be adopted. Practitioners of AT include persons in many professional roles (teachers, social workers, managers, personnel and training officers, physicians, correctional personnel, psychologists, ministers, counselors, women's group leaders, nurses, and on and on). Nevertheless, some broad set of ethical guidelines is needed, and I suggest wide dissemination of the statement presented in Chapter 35. Although many persons who practice some form of AT are not otherwise engaged in rendering a "psychological" service, it is nonetheless true that the encouragement and facilitation of assertive behavior is essentially a *therapeutic* procedure. When we, in *any* professional role, engage in helping persons to change their behavior, attitudes, and interpersonal relationships, we are, in my opinion, obligated to act within an ethical framework.

A multidimensional model for viewing assertive behavior training may assist the practitioner in evaluating the appropriateness of his or her AT interventions:

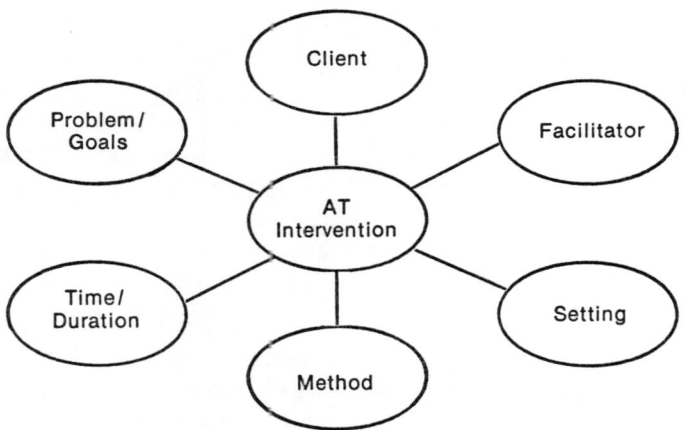

The dimensions may be characterized as follows:
Client: Who is seeking AT? Is the person a child or adult? Man or woman? Ethnic or Anglo? Hospitalized? Imprisoned? Aged? Is the client someone who can make an informed choice to try AT?
Problem/Goals: For what purpose is AT sought (or recommended)? Shyness? Severe inhibition? Supervisory skills? Anxiety reduction? Countercondition aggression? Are the goals appropriate to an AT intervention?

Facilitator: Who is conducting AT? Self? AT trained professional? Mental health worker? Teacher? Community group leader? Untrained person? Does the facilitator have the skills, understanding, and ethical principles effectively and responsibly to carry out an AT intervention?

Setting: Where is AT being conducted? Home? School? Clinic? Hospital? Prison? Business? Does the setting provide a facilitative environment, freedom of client choice, supervision/evaluation of the facilitator?

Time/Duration: How long does the AT intervention last? A few minutes? An hour? A few hours? A day? A weekend? Intensive sessions over several weeks? Does the length of the intervention provide for a brief encouragement, a facilitative workshop, or an intensive long-term therapeutic effort?

Method: How is the AT intervention conducted? Pep talk? Behavior rehearsal? Modeling? Didactic presentation? Covert sensitization? Memorize scripts? Desensitization? Self-management training? Does the method represent a "programmed" facilitator technique, or is it tailored to client needs? Is care taken to encourage small successful steps, or are punishing consequences likely?

Each AT intervention, from the most casual use of behavioral rehearsal to the most intensive therapeutic treatment of anxiety, may be viewed within the six-dimensional framework suggested above. In so doing, the professional facilitator may carefully examine the appropriateness and ethical responsibility of the intervention. It is evident that the dimensions are related, and largely interdependent (e.g., time duration of intervention depends upon setting, client, etc.), but may be examined independently in each case. Care in selection of AT interventions according to these six criteria may considerably enhance the level of ethical responsibility in the practice of an important tool for behavior change.

Chapter 35 represents a definitive statement of ethical principles against which the practitioner is urged to evaluate his or her application of AT.

A FINAL NOTE

In Chapter 1, I suggested that this book represents something of a "progress report" on the state of the art in assertive behavior training. Despite its impressive recent history and wide popularity, AT is still a very young and developing procedure. This chapter has raised at least as many questions as it has answered. It is my hope that readers who are actively engaged in assertiveness training, in any setting, will share their observations, experiences, comments, ideas, and opinions with others in the field. In particular, I would enjoy hearing your feedback on this book, and receiving reports of your work for possible publication in the *ASSERT* newsletter.

It is my hope that *Assertiveness* will be a significant contribution to the literature of assertive behavior training. It will be even more significant if it stimulates you to extend and to share your work.

A STATEMENT OF "PRINCIPLES FOR ETHICAL PRACTICE OF ASSERTIVE BEHAVIOR TRAINING"

As AT gained in popularity during the mid-1970's, an increasing concern developed among responsible practitioners for the misuse of the process: unqualified trainers, illegitimate purposes, contraindicated clients. At the December 1975 meeting of the Association for Advancement of Behavior Therapy in San Francisco, a group of nationally recognized AT professionals met to initiate work on a statement of ethical principles. The following statement is the result of their work.

Further discussion of this proposal occurred at the First International Conference on Assertive Behavior Training in Washington, D.C., in August, 1976, and at the Association for Advancement of Behavior Therapy in New York City, December, 1976. Although no amendments to the original statement have been formalized, considerable concern has been expressed about the academic credentials suggested herein for qualifying facilitators. It is likely that a competency-based criterion for qualification will emerge.

Moreover, AABT itself is preparing a statement of ethics for the practice of behavior therapy generally, which may have direct application to AT, although AT is not considered solely a "behavior therapy" by a considerable number of its practitioners.

Meanwhile, however, this statement remains the only public declaration by a group of professionals which is directed toward greater ethical responsibility in the practice of AT. Practitioners are urged to consider its implications for their own work.

PRINCIPLES FOR ETHICAL PRACTICE OF ASSERTIVE BEHAVIOR TRAINING

With the increasing popularity of assertive behavior training, a quality of "faddishness" has become evident, and there are frequent reports of ethically irresponsible practices (and practitioners). We hear of trainers who, for example, do not adequately differentiate assertion and aggression. Others have failed to advocate proper ethical responsibility and caution to clients—e.g., failed to alert them to and/or prepare them for the possibility of retaliation or other highly negative reactions from others.

The following statement of "Principles for Ethical Practice of Assertive Behavior Training" is the work of the professional psychologists and educators listed below, who are actively engaged in the practice of facilitating assertive behavior (also referred to as "assertive therapy," "social skills training," "personal effectiveness training," and "AT"). We don't intend by this statement to discourage untrained individuals from becoming more assertive on their own, and we don't advocate that one must have extensive credentials in order to be of help to friends and relatives. Rather, these principles are offered to help foster responsible and ethical teaching and practice by human services professionals. Others who wish to enhance their own assertiveness or that of associates are encouraged to do so, with awareness of their own limitations, and of the importance of seeking help from a qualified therapist/trainer when necessary.

We hereby declare support for and adherence to the statement of principles, and invite responsible professionals in our own and other fields who use these techniques to join us in advocating and practicing these principles.

Robert E. Alberti, Ph.D.
Counseling Psychologist & Professor
California Polytechnic State University
San Luis Obispo, CA

Michael L. Emmons, Ph.D.
Counseling Psychologist & Professor
California Polytechnic State University
San Luis Obispo, CA

Iris G. Fodor, Ph.D.
Associate Professor, Educational Psychology
New York University, Washington Square
New York, NY

John Galassi, Ph.D.
School of Education
University of North Carolina
Chapel Hill, NC

Merna D. Galassi, Ed.D.
Meredith College
Raleigh, NC

Lynne Garnett, Ph.D.
Counseling Psychologist
University of California
Los Angeles, CA

Patricia Jakubowski, Ed.D.
Associate Professor, Behavior Studies
University of Missouri
St. Louis, MO

Janet L. Wolfe, Ph.D.
Director of Clinical Services
Institute for Advanced Study in Rational Psychotherapy
New York, NY

May 1, 1976

1. Definition of Assertive Behavior

For purposes of these principles and the ethical framework expressed herein, we define assertive behavior as that complex of behaviors, emitted by a person in an interpersonal context, which express that person's feelings, attitudes, wishes, opinions or rights directly, firmly, and honestly, while respecting the feelings, attitudes, wishes, opinions and rights of the other person(s). Such behavior may include the expression of such emotions as anger, fear, caring, hope, joy, despair, indignation, embarrassment, but in any event is expressed in a manner which does not violate the rights of others. Assertive behavior is differentiated from aggressive behavior which, while expressive of one person's feelings, attitudes, wishes, opinions or rights, does not respect those characteristics in others.

While this definition is intended to be comprehensive, it is recognized that any adequate definition of assertive behavior must consider several dimensions:

A. **Intent**: behavior classified as assertive is not intended by its author to be hurtful of others.
B. **Behavior**: behavior classified as assertive would be evaluated by an "objective observer" as itself honest, direct, expressive and non-destructive of others.
C. **Effects**: behavior classified as assertive has the effect upon the receiver of a direct and non-destructive message, by which a "reasonable person" would not be hurt.
D. **Socio-cultural Context**: behavior classified as assertive is appropriate to the environment and culture in which it is exhibited, and may not be considered "assertive" in a different socio-cultural environment.

2. Client Self-Determination

These principles recognize and affirm the inherent dignity and the equal and inalienable rights of all members of the human family, as proclaimed in the "Universal Declaration of Human Rights" endorsed by the General Assembly of the United Nations.

Pursuant to the precepts of the Declaration, each client (trainee, patient) who seeks assertive behavior training shall be treated as a person of value, with all of the freedoms and rights expressed in the Declaration. No procedure shall be utilized in the name of assertive behavior training which would violate those freedoms or rights.

Informed client self-determination shall guide all such interventions:

A. the client shall be fully informed in advance of all procedures to be utilized;
B. the client shall have the freedom to choose to participate or not at any point in the intervention;
C. the client who is institutionalized shall be similarly treated with respect and without coercion, insofar as is possible within the institutional environment;
D. the client shall be provided with explicit definitions of assertiveness and assertive training;

E. the client shall be fully informed as to the education, training, experience or other qualifications of the assertive trainer(s);
F. the client shall be informed as to the goals and potential outcomes of assertive training, including potentially high levels of anxiety, and possible negative reactions from others;
G. the client shall be fully informed as to the responsibility of the assertion trainer(s) and the client(s);
H. the client shall be informed as to the ethics and employment of confidentiality guidelines as they pertain to various assertive training settings (e.g., clinical vs. non-clinical).

3. Qualifications of Facilitators

Assertive behavior training is essentially a therapeutic procedure, although frequently practiced in a variety of settings by professionals not otherwise engaged in rendering a "psychological" service. Persons in any professional role who engage in helping others to change their behavior, attitudes, and interpersonal relationships must understand human behavior at a level commensurate with the level of their interventions.

3.1 *General Qualifications*

We support the following minimum, general qualifications for facilitators at all levels of intervention (including "trainers in training"—preservice or inservice—who are preparing for professional service in a recognized human services field, and who may be conducting assertive behavior training under supervision as part of a research project or practicum):

A. Fundamental understanding of the principles of learning and behavior (equivalent to completion of a rigorous undergraduate level course in learning theory);
B. Fundamental understanding of anxiety and its effects upon behavior (equivalent to completion of a rigorous undergraduate level course in abnormal psychology);
C. Knowledge of the limitations, contraindications and potential dangers of assertive behavior training; familiarity with theory and research in the area.
D. Satisfactory evidence of competent performance as a facilitator, as observed by a qualified trainer, is strongly recommended for all professionals, particularly for those who do not possess a doctorate or an equivalent level of training. Such evidence would most ideally be supported by:
   1) participation in at least ten (10) hours of assertive behavior training as a client (trainee, patient); and

2) participation in at least ten (10) hours of assertive behavior training as a facilitator under supervision.

3.2 *Specific Qualifications*

The following additional qualifications are considered to be the minimum expected for facilitators at the indicated levels of intervention:

A. **Assertive behavior training**, including non-clinical workshops, groups, and individual client training aimed at teaching assertive skills to those persons who require only encouragement and specific skill training, and in whom no serious emotional deficiency or pathology is evident.
1) For trainers in programs conducted under the sponsorship of a recognized human services agency, school, governmental or corporate entity, church, or community organization:
   a) An advanced degree in a recognized field of human services (e.g., psychology, counseling, social work, medicine, public health, nursing, education, human development, theology/divinity), including at least one term of field experience in a human services agency supervised by a qualified trainer; **or**
   b) certification as a minister, public school teacher, social worker, physician, counselor, nurse, or clinical, counseling, educational, or school psychologist, or similar human services professional, as recognized by the state wherein employed or by the recognized state or national professional society in the indicate discipline; **or**
   c) one year of paid counseling experience in a recognized human services agency, supervised by a qualified trainer; **or**
   d) qualification under items 3.2B or 3.2C below.
2) For trainers in programs including interventions at the level defined in this item (3.2A), but without agency/organization sponsorship:
   a) An advanced degree in a recognized field of human services (e.g., psychology, counseling, social work, medicine, public health, nursing, education, human development, theology/divinity) including at least one term of field experience in a human services agency supervised by a qualified trainer; **and**
   b) certification as a minister, social worker, physician, counselor, nurse, or clinical, counseling, educational, or school psychologist, or similar human services professional, as recognized by the state wherein employed or by the recognized state or national professional society in the indicated discipline; **or**

c) qualification under items 3.2B or 3.2C below.
B. **Assertive behavior therapy**, including clinical interventions designed to assist persons who are severely inhibited by anxiety, or who are significantly deficient in social skills, or who are controlled by aggression, or who evidence pathology, or for whom other therapeutic procedures are indicated:
  1) For therapists in programs conducted under the sponsorship of a recognized human services agency, school, governmental or corporate entity, church, or community organization:
     a) An advanced degree in a recognized field of human services (e.g., psychology, counseling, social work, medicine, public health, nursing, education, human development, theology/divinity) including at least one term of field experience in a human services agency supervised by a qualified trainer; **or**
     b) certification as a minister, social worker, physician, counselor, nurse, or clinical, counseling, educational, or school psychologist, as recognized by the state wherein employed or by the recognized state or national professional society in the individual discipline; **or**
     c) qualification under item 3.2C below.
  2) For therapists employing interventions at the level defined in this item (3.2B), but without agency/organization sponsorship:
     a) An advanced degree in a recognized field of human services (e.g., psychology, counseling, social work, medicine, public health, nursing, education, human development, theology/divinity) including at least one term of field experience in a human services agency supervised by a qualified trainer; **and**
     b) certification as minister, social worker, physician, counselor, nurse, or clinical, counseling, educational, or school psychologist, as recognized by the state wherein employed or by the recognized state or national professional society in the indicated discipline; **and**
     c) at least one year of paid professional experience in a recognized human services agency, supervised by a qualified trainer, **or**
     d) qualification under item 3.2C below.
C. **Training of trainers**, including preparation of other professionals to offer assertive behavior training/therapy to clients, in school, agency, organization, or individual settings.
  1) A doctoral degree in a recognized field of human services (e.g., psychology, counseling, social work, medicine, public health, nursing, education, human development, theology/divinity)

including at least one term of field experience in a human services agency supervised by a qualified trainer; **and**
2) certification as a minister, social worker, physician, counselor, nurse, or clinical, counseling, educational, or school psychologist, as recognized by the state wherein employed, or by the recognized state or national professional society in the indicated discipline; **and**
3) at least one year of paid professional experience in a recognized human services agency, supervised by a qualified trainer; **and**
4) advanced study in assertive behavior training/therapy, including at least two of the following:
   a) At least thirty (30) hours of facilitation with clients;
   b) participation in at least two different workshops at professional meetings or professional training institutes;
   c) contribution to the professional literature in the field.

3.3 We recognize that counselors and psychologists are not certified by each state. In states wherein no such certification is provided, unless contrary to local statute, we acknowledge the legitimacy of professionals who: A) are otherwise qualified under the provisions of items 3.1 and 3.2; and B) would be eligible for certification as a counselor or psychologist in another state.

3.4 We do not consider that participation in one or two workshops on assertive behavior, even though conducted by a professional with an advanced degree, is adequate qualification to offer assertive behavior training to others, **unless the additional qualifications** of items 3.1 and 3.2 are also met.

3.5 These qualifications are presented as **standards** for professional facilitators of assertive behavior. No "certification" or "qualifying" agency is hereby proposed. Rather, it is incumbent upon each professional to evaluate himself/herself as a trainer/therapist according to these standards, and to make explicit to clients the adequacy of his/her qualifications as a facilitator.

4. Ethical Behavior of Facilitators

Since the encouragement and facilitation of assertive behavior is essentially a **therapeutic** procedure, the ethical standards most applicable to the practice of assertive behavior training are those of psychologists. We recognize that many persons who practice some form of assertive behavior training are not otherwise engaged in rendering a "psychological" service (i.e., teachers, personnel/training directors). To all we support the statement of "Ethical Standards for

Psychologists" as adopted by the American Psychological Association as the standard of ethical behavior by which assertive behavior training shall be conducted.

We recognize that the methodology employed in assertive behavior training may include a wide range of procedures, some of which are of unproven value. It is the responsibility of facilitators to inform clients of any experimental procedures. Under no circumstances should the facilitator "guarantee" a specific outcome from an intervention.

5. Appropriateness of Assertive Behavior Training Interventions

Assertive behavior training, as any intervention oriented toward helping people change, may be applied under a wide range of conditions, yet its appropriateness must be evaluated in each individual case. The responsible selection of assertive behavior training for a particular intervention must include attention to at least the following dimensions:

A. **Client**: The personal characteristics of the client in question (age, sex, ethnicity, institutionalization, capacity for informed choice, physical and psychological functionality).

B. **Problem/Goals**: The purpose for which professional help has been sought or recommended (job skills, severe inhibition, anxiety reduction, overcome aggression).

C. **Facilitator**: The personal and professional qualifications of the facilitator in question (age, sex, ethnicity, skills, understanding, ethics—see also Principles 3 and 4 above).

D. **Setting**: The characteristics of the setting in which the intervention is conducted (home, school, business, agency, clinic, hospital, prison). Is the client free to choose? Is the facilitator's effectiveness systematically evaluated?

E. **Time/Duration**: The duration of the intervention. Does the time involved represent a brief word of encouragement, a formal training workshop, an intensive and long-term therapeutic effort?

F. **Method**: The nature of the intervention. Is it "packaged" procedure or tailored to client needs? Is training based on sound principles of learning and behavior? Is there clear differentiation of aggressiveness, assertiveness and other concepts? Are definitions, techniques, procedures and purposes clarified? Is care taken to encourage small, successful steps and to minimize punishing consequences? Are any suggested "homework assignments" presented with adequate supervision, responsibility, and sensitivity to the effect upon significant others of the

client's behavior change efforts? Are clients informed that assertiveness "doesn't always work?"
G. **Outcome**: Are there follow-up procedures, either by self-report or other post-test procedures?

6. Social Responsibility

Assertive behavior training shall be conducted within the law. Trainers and clients are encouraged to work assertively to change those laws which they consider need to be changed, and to modify the social system in ways they believe appropriate—in particular to extend the boundaries of human rights. Toward these ends, trainers are encouraged to facilitate responsible change skills via assertive behavior training. All those who practice, teach, or do research on assertive behavior are urged to advocate caution and ethical responsibility in application of the technique, in accordance with these Principles.

REFERENCES

Abrahamson, E. and Pezet, A. *Body, Mind and Sugar.* New York: Pyramid Books, 1971.

Adams, M. The compassion trap. V. Gornick and B. Moran (Eds.) *Woman in Sexist Society: Studies in Power and Powerlessness.* New York: Basic Books, 1971.

Alberti, R. E. Was that *assertive* or *aggressive? ASSERT: The Newsletter of Assertive Behavior*, 1976, *1* (7), 2.

Alberti, R. E. and Emmons, M. L. *Stand Up, Speak Out, Talk Back!* New York: Pocket Books, Inc., 1975.

Alberti, R. E. and Emmons, M. L. *Your Perfect Right: A Guide to Assertive Behavior* San Luis Obispo, California: Impact Publishers, Inc., 1970, 1974.

Altman, S. *Present and Future Supply of Registered Nurses.* Bethesda: National Institute of Health, 1971.

Bandura, A. *Aggression: A Social Learning Analysis.* Englewood Cliffs: Prentice-Hall, 1973.

Bandura, A. Analysis of modeling processes. In A. Bandura (Ed.), *Psychological Modeling: Conflicting Theories.* Chicago: Aldine-Atherton, 1971.

Bandura, A. Behavioral modification through modeling procedures. In L. Krasner and L. P. Ullman (Eds.), *Research in Behavior Modification.* New York: Holt, Rinehart, Winston, 1965, 310-340.

Bandura, A. Influence of models' reinforcement contingencies on the acquisition of imitative responses. *Journal of Personality and Social Psychology*, 1965, *1*, 589-595.

Bandura, A. *Principles of Behavior Modification.* New York: Holt, Rinehart, Winston, 1969.

Bandura, A., Ross, D., and Ross, S. Vicarious reinforcement and imitative learning. *Journal of Abnormal Social Psychology*, 1963, 67, 601-607.

Bandura, A. and Walters, R. H. *Adolescent Aggression.* New York: Ronald Press, 1959.

Bandura, A. and Walters, R. H. *Social Learning and Personality Development.* New York: Holt, Rinehart, and Winston, 1963.

Barber, T. X. and Hahn, K. W. Experimental studies in "hypnotic" behavior: physiological and subjective effects of imagined pain. *Journal of Nervous and Mental Disease*, 1964, *139*, 416-425.

Bart, P. Depression in middle-aged women. In V. Gornick and B. Moran (Eds.), *Women in Sexist Society: Studies in Power and Powerlessness.* New York: Basic Books, 1971.

Bates, H. D. and Zimmerman, S. F. Toward the development of a screening scale for assertive training. *Psychological Reports*, 1971, *28*, 99-107.

Bean, K. L. Desensitization, behavior rehearsal, then reality: a preliminary report on a new procedure. *Behavior Therapy*, 1970, *1*, 542.

deBeauvoir, S. *The Second Sex.* New York: Knopf, 1953.

Bem, D. J. *Beliefs, Attitudes, and Human Affairs.* Belmont: Brooks/Cole, 1970.

Berkowitz, L. The concept of aggressive drive: some additional considerations. In L. Berkowitz (Ed.), *Advances in Experimental Social Psychology*, Vol. 2. New York: Academic Press, 1965.

Berkowitz, L. *Roots of Aggression: A Re-examination of the Frustration-Aggression Hypothesis.* New York: Atherton Press, 1969.

Berne, E. *Games People Play.* New York: Grove Press, 1964.

Bodner, G. E. The role of assessment in assertion training. *The Counseling Psychologist*, 1975, *5* (4), 90-96.

Bongers, L. A developmental study of time perception and time perspective in three cultural groups: Anglo, Indian American, and Mexican American. Doctoral dissertation, University of California, Los Angeles, 1971. Dissertation Abstracts, 32:3774A-3775A, 1972. University Microfilm No. 73-22-656.

Booraem, C. D. and Flowers, J. V. Reduction of anxiety and personal space as a function of assertion training with severely disturbed neuropsychiatric inpatients. *Psychological Reports*, 1972, *30*, 923-929.

Boulette, T. R. Determining needs and appropriate counseling approaches for Mexican American women: a comparison of therapeutic listening and behavioral rehearsal. Unpublished dissertation, University of California, Santa Barbara, June, 1972.

Bronfenbrenner, U. *Two Worlds of Childhood: U.S. and U.S.S.R.* New York: Russel Sage Foundation, 1970.

Broverman, I. K., Vogel, S. R., Broverman, D. M., Clarkson, F. E., and Rosenkrantz, P. S. Sex-role stereotypes: a current appraisal. *Journal of Social Issues*, 1972, *28*, 59.

Buffalo, M. D. and Rodgers, J. W. Behavioral norms, moral norms, and attachment: problems of deviance and conformity. *Social Problems*, 1971, Summer, *19* (1), 101-103.

Buss, A. H. *The Psychology of Aggression*. New York: Wiley, 1961.

Cameron, D. E. The conversion of passivity into normal self-assertion. *American Journal of Psychiatry*, 1951, *108*, 98.

Casavantes, E. Pride and prejudice: a Mexican-American dilemma. In N. Wagner and M. Haug (Eds.), *Social and Psychological Perspectives*. St. Louis: C. V. Mosby, 1971.

Catanzaro, R. J. *Alcoholism: The Total Treatment Approach*. Springfield: Charles C. Thomas, 1968.

Cautela, J. R. A behavior therapy approach to pervasive anxiety. *Behavior Research and Therapy*, 1966, *4*, 99.

Cautela, J. R. Behavior therapy and self-control: techniques and implications. In C. M. Franks (Ed.), *Behavior Therapy: Appraisal and Status*. New York: McGraw-Hill, 1969.

Cautela, J. R. Covert processes and behavior modification. *Journal of Nervous and Mental Disease*, 1973, *157*, 27-36.

Cautela, J. R. Covert reinforcement. *Behavior Therapy*, 1970, *1*, 33-50.

Cautela, J. R. Covert sensitization. *Psychological Reports*, 1967, *20*, 459.

Cheek, D. K. *Assertive Black . . . Puzzled White*. San Luis Obispo, California: Impact Publishers, Inc., 1976.

Chesler, P. *Women and Madness*. Garden City: Doubleday, 1972.

Chittenden, G. E. An experimental study in measuring and modifying assertive behavior in young children. *Monographs of the Society for Research in Child Development*, 1942, 7 (1, Serial #31).

Churchill Films (Producer). *Hopscotch*. California: Churchill Films, 1972.

Clausen, J. A. Family structure, socialization, and personality. In L. W. and M. D. Hoffman (Eds.), *Review of Child Development Research*, Vol. 2, New York: Russell Sage Foundation, 1966.

Cohen, J. Social work and the culture of poverty. In F. Reisman (Ed.), *Mental Health of the Poor*. New York: Free Press, 1964.

Cooley, M. A model for assertive statements. *ASSERT: The Newsletter of Assertive Behavior*, 1976, *1* (6), 2.

Cooper, K. *The New Aerobics*. New York: M. Evans (in association with Philadelphia: Lippincott), 1970.

Coopersmith, S. *The Antecedents of Self-Esteem*. San Francisco: W. H. Freeman and Co., 1967.

Cornell Conference on Therapy. The management of obesity. *New York State Journal of Medicine*, 1958, *58*, 79-87.

Cotler, S. B and Guerra, J. J. *Assertion Training: A Humanistic-Behavioral Guide to Self-Dignity*. Champaign: Research Press, 1976.

Crystal, J. and Bolles, R. N. *Where Do I Go From Here With My Life?* New York: Seabury Press, 1971.

Dalali, I. D. The effect of active-assertion and feeling clarification training on factor analyzed measures of assertion. Doctoral dissertation, University of California, Los Angeles, 1971. *Dissertation Abstracts International*. 1971, *32*, 1B-1291B, University Microfilms No. 71-21, 322.

D'Amico, W. *Revised Rathus Assertiveness Scale for Children, Grades 3-8*. Marblehead, Mass.: Educational Counseling and Consulting Services, 1976.

D'Amico, W. and Gracia, R. *Student Reinforcement Survey Schedule: Grades K-12*. Marblehead, Mass.: Educational Counseling and Consulting Services, 1975.

deBeauvoir, S. (See "Beauvoir"-deBeauvoir.)

Deitche, J. H. The performance of delinquent and non-delinquent boys in the Tennessee Department of Mental Health self-concept scale. Unpublished Doctoral Dissertation, Indiana University, 1959.

Demplewolff, J. *Personal Communication*. Newark: University of Delaware, 1974.

Dengrove, E. Behavior therapy of headache. *Journal of the American Society of Psychosomatic Dentistry and Medicine*, 1968, *15*, 30.

Deutsch, M. and Solomon, L. Reactions to evaluation by others as influenced by self-evaluation. *Sociometry*, 1959, *22*, 92-112.

D'Zurilla, T. J. Reducing heterosexual anxiety. In J. D. Krumboltz and C. E. Thoresen (Eds.), *Behavioral Counseling: Cases and Techniques*. New York: Holt, Rinehart, and Winston, 1969.

Edgerton, R. and Karno, M. Mexican-American bilingualism and the perception of mental illness. *Archives of General Psychiatry*, 1971, *24*, 281-290.

Edwards, N. B. Case conference: assertive training in a case of homosexual pedophilia. *Journal of Behavior Therapy and Experimental Psychology*, 1972, *3*, 55-63.

Eisler, R. M., Hersen, M., and Agras, W. S. Videotape: a method for the controlled observation of nonverbal interpersonal behavior. *Behavior Therapy*, 1973, *4*, 420-425.

Eisler, R. M., Hersen, M., and Miller, P. M. Effects of modeling as components of assertive behavior. *Journal of Behavior Therapy and Experimental Psychiatry*, 1973, *4*, 1-6.

Eisler, R. M., Miller, P. M., Hersen, M., and Alford, H. Effects of assertive training on marital interaction. *Archives of General Psychiatry*, 1974, *30*, 643-649.

Ekman, P., Friessen, W. V., and Taussig, T. VID-R and scan: tools and methods in the analysis of facial expression and body movements. In G. Gerbner, O. Holsti, K. Knippendorff, W. Paisley, and P. Stone (Eds.), *Content Analysis*. New York: Wiley, 1969.

Epstein, D. Aggression toward outgroups as a function of authoritarianism and imitation of aggression models. *Journal of Personality and Social Psychology*, 1966, *3*, 574-579.

Everly, G. S. and Falcione, R. L. Perceived dimensions of job satisfaction for staff registered nurses. *Nursing Research*, 1976, *25*, 346-348.

Fensterheim, H. Personal communication to the editor, January, 1977.

Fensterheim, H. Assertive methods and marital problems. In R. Rubin, H. Fensterheim, J. Henderson, and L. Ullmann (Eds.), *Advances in Behavior Therapy*. New York: Academic Press, 1972.

Fensterheim, H. *Help Without Psychoanalysis*. New York: Stein and Day, 1971.

REFERENCES

Fensterheim, H. and Baer, J. *Don't Say Yes When You Want To Say No*. New York: Dell, 1975.

Feshbach, S. Aggression. In P. H. Mussen (Ed.), *Carmichael's Manual of Child Psychology*, Vol. II. New York: Wiley, 1970.

Feshbach, S. Dynamics of morality of violence and aggression: some psychological considerations. *American Psychologist*, 1971, 26, 281-291.

Flowers, J., Booraem, C., Brown, T., and Harris, D. An investigation of a technique for facilitating patient to patient therapeutic interaction in group therapy. *Journal of Community Psychology*, 1974, 2 (1), 39-42.

Flowers, J. and Guerra, J. The use of client-coaching in assertion training with a large group. *Journal of Community Health*, 1974.

Fodor, I. The phobic syndrome in women. In F. Franks and V. Burtle (Eds.), *Women in Therapy*. New York: Brunner/Mazel, 1974.

Fodor, I. Women's phobias. Presentation given at the Association for the Advancement of Behavior Therapy, Miami, Florida, December, 1973.

Franzini, L. R. Review of *The Assertive Woman*. *Behavior Therapy*, 1976, 7, 418-419.

Fredericks, C. and Goodman, H. *Low Blood Sugar and You*. New York: Constellation International, 1969.

Friedman, A. I. *How Sex Can Keep You Slim*. Englewood Cliffs: Prentice-Hall, 1972.

Friedman, P. H. The effects of modeling and role playing on assertive behavior. In R. Rubin, A. Lazarus, H. Fensterheim, and C. Franks (Eds.), *Advances in Behavior Therapy*. New York: Academic Press, 1971.

Friedman, P. H. The effects of modeling, role playing, and participation on behavior change. In B. A. Maher (Ed.), *Progress in Experimental Personality Research*, Vol. 6. New York: Academic Press, 1972.

Galassi, J. P. *Assertive Training in Groups Using Video Feedback*. Final progress report in National Institute of Mental Health Small Research Grant MH22392-01, 1973.

Galassi, J. P., DeLo, J. S., Galassi, M. D., and Bastien, S. The College self-expression scale: a measure of assertiveness. *Behavior Therapy*, 1974, 5, 165-171.

Galassi, J. P. and Galassi, M. D. Relationship between assertiveness and aggressiveness. *Psychological Reports*, 1975, 36, 352-354.

Galassi, J. P. and Galassi, M. D. Validity of a measure of assertiveness. *Journal of Counseling Psychology*, 1974, 21, 248-250.

Galassi, J. P., Galassi, M. D., and Litz, C. M. Assertive training in groups using video feedback. *Journal of Counseling Psychology*, 1974, 21, 390-394.

Galassi, J. P., Hollandsworth, J. G. Jr., Radecki, J. C., Gay, M. L., Howe, M. R., and Evans, C. L. Behavioral performance in the validation of an assertiveness scale. *Behavior Therapy*, 1976, 7, 447-452.

Galassi, M. D. and Galassi, J. P. A critical review of assertive behavior: definition and assessment. *Psychotherapy: Theory, Research and Practice*, 1976, in press.

Galassi, M. D. and Galassi, J. P. *Assert Yourself! How to Be Your Own Person*. New York: Human Sciences Press, 1977.

Gambrill, E. D. and Richey, C. A. An assertion inventory for use in assessment and research. *Behavior Therapy*, 1975, 6, 550-561.

Gardner, J. E. A blending of behavior therapy techniques in an approach to an asthmatic child. *Psychotherapy: Theory, Research and Practice*, 1968, 5, 46.

Gay, M. L., Hollandsworth, J. G. Jr., and Galassi, J. P. An assertiveness inventory for adults. *Journal of Counseling Psychology*, 1975, 22, 340-344.

Geisinger, D. L. Controlling sexual and interpersonal anxieties. In J. Krumboltz and C. Thoresen (Eds.), *Behavioral Counseling: Cases and Techniques*. New York: Holt, Rinehart, and Winston, 1969.

Ginott. H. *Between Parent and Child*. New York: Avon Books, 1965.

Gittleman, M. Behavior rehearsal as a technique in child treatment. *Journal of Child Psychology and Psychiatry*, 1965, 6, 251.
Gold, M. and Mann, D. Delinquency as a defense. *American Journal of Orthopsychiatry*, 1972, 4223, 463-479.
Goodman, L. S. and Gilman, A. (Eds.). *The Pharmacological Basis of Therapeutics*, 4th ed. London: MacMillan, 1970.
Gordon, E. S. The present concept of obesity: etiological factors and treatment. *Medical Times*, 1969, 97, 142-155.
Gordon, T. *Parent Effectiveness Training.* New York: Wyden, 1970.
Guttentag, M. Group cohesiveness, ethnic organization and poverty. In N. Wagner and M. Haug (Eds.), *Chicanos: Social and Psychological Perspectives*. St. Louis: C. V. Mosby, 1971.
Hall, R. V. *Behavior Management Series: Part I. The Measurement of Behavior.* Lawrence, Kansas: H and H Enterprises, 1971.
Hall, S. M. Behavioral treatment of obesity: a two-year follow-up. *Behavioral Research and Therapy*, 1973, 11, 647-648.
Hammer, S. *Daughters and Mothers.* New York: Quadrangle, 1975.
Havighurst, R. J. *Human Development and Education*. New York: David McKay, 1953.
Hedquist, F. J. and Weinhold, B. K. Behavioral group counseling with socially anxious and unassertive college students. *Journal of Counseling Psychology*, 1970, 17, 237-242.
Henderson, J. M. The effects of assertiveness training on self-actualization in women. Unpublished doctoral dissertation, University of Northern Colorado, 1976.
Herman, S. Nurses' stereotypic views of health professionals. (In Press)
Hersen, M., Eisler, R. M., and Miller, P. M. An experimental analysis of generalization in assertive training. *Behavior Research and Therapy*, 1974, 12, 295-310.
Hersen, M., Eisler, R. M., and Miller, P. M. Development of assertive responses: clinical, measurement and research considerations. *Behavior Research and Therapy*, 1973, 2, 505-521.
Hewes, D. D. On effective assertive behavior: a brief note. *Behavior Therapy*, 1975, 6, 269-271.
Hirsch, S. An experimental investigation of the effectiveness of assertion training with alcoholics. Research Report, Texas Department of Mental Health and Mental Retardation, Austin, Texas, 1975. Contract No. (74-75)-1973, Texas Commission on Alcoholism.
Hokanson, J. E. Psychophysiological evaluation of the catharsis hypothesis. In E. I. Megargee and J. E. Hokanson (Eds.), *The Dynamics of Aggression*. New York: Harper and Row, 1970.
Hollandsworth, J. G. Differentiating assertion and aggression: some behavioral guidelines. *Behavior Therapy*, in press.
Hollandsworth, J. G. Jr., Galassi, J. P., and Gay, M. L. The adult self-expression scale: validation using the multitrait-multimethod procedure. *Journal of Clinical Psychology*, 1976, in press.
Hollingshead and Myers. In Meyers and Bean (Eds.), *A Decade Later: A Follow-up of Social Class and Mental Illness*. New York: John Wiley, 1968.
Homme, L. E. Perspectives in psychology: XXIV. Control of coverants, the operants of the mind. *Psychological Record*, 1965, 15, 501-511.
Homme, L., Csanyi, A., Gonzales, M., and Rechs, J. *How to Use Contingency Contracting in the Classroom*. Champaign: Research Press, 1969.
Huey, L. (Ed.). *First National Conference on Asian-American Mental Health.* Washington, D.C.: Government Printing Office, 1974.

Ivey, A. E., Normington, C. J., Miller, D., and Morrill, W. H. Microcounseling and attending behavior. *Journal of Counseling Psychology*, 1968, *15* (5), 1-12.

Jacobson, E. *Progressive Relaxation*. Chicago: University of Chicago Press, 1938.

Jakubowski, P. A. and Lacks, P. B. Assessment procedures in assertion training. *The Counseling Psychologist*, 1975, *5* (4), 84-90.

Jakubowski-Spector, P. An introduction to assertive training procedures for women. Paper presented to American Personnel and Guidance Association, Washington, D.C., 1973.

Jakubowski-Spector, P. Behavior modification for school personnel. *Focus on Guidance*, 1974, 6, 1.

Jakubowski-Spector, P. Facilitating the growth of women through assertive training. *The Counseling Psychologist*, 1973, 4 (1), 75-86.

Johnson, D. and Sikes, M. Rorschach and TAT responses of Negro, Mexican American and Anglo psychiatric patients. *Journal of Projective Techniques and Personality Assessment*, 1965, *29*, 183-188.

Johnson, R. N. *Aggression in Man and Animals*. Philadelphia: Saunders, 1972.

Johnson, T., Tyler, V., Thompson, R., and Jones, E. Systematic desensitization and assertive training in the treatment of speech anxiety in middle-school students. *Psychology in the Schools*, 1971, 8, 263-267.

Kagan, S. and Madsen, M. Cooperation and competition of Mexican, Mexican-American, and Anglo American children of two ages under four instructional sets. *Developmental Psychology*, 1971, *5*, 32-39.

Kalkhoff, R. and Ferron, C. Metabolic differences between obese overweight and muscular overweight men. *New England Journal of Medicine*, 1971, 284, 1236-1239.

Katz, R. Case conference: rapid development of activity in a case of chronic passivity. *Journal of Behavior Therapy and Experimental Psychiatry*, 1971, 2, 187.

Kaufmann, L. M. and Wagner, B. R. Barb: a systematic treatment technology for temper control disorders. *Behavior Therapy*, 1972, 3, 84.

Kazdin, A. E. Effects of covert modeling and reinforcement on assertive behavior. *Proceedings of the 81st Annual Convention of the American Psychological Association*, 1973, 8, 537-538.

Kovel, J. *A Complete Guide to Therapy*. New York: Pantheon Books, 1976.

Krumboltz, J. D. and Thoresen, C. E. *Behavioral Counseling: Cases and Techniques*. New York: Holt, Rinehart, and Winston, 1969.

Landau, P. L. and Paulson, T. P. Group assertion training for Mexican-American mothers. A paper presented at the seventh Annual Southern California Conference on Behavior Modification. Los Angeles, California, October, 1975. (See Chapter 12.)

Lange, A. J. and Jakubowski, P. *Responsible Assertive Behavior: Cognitive/Behavioral Procedures for Trainers*. Champaign: Research Press, 1976.

Lawrence, P. S. The assessment and modification of assertive behavior. Doctoral dissertation, Arizona State University, 1970. *Dissertation Abstracts International*, 31, 1B-1601B (University Microfilms No. 70-11, 888).

Laws, D. R. and Serber, M. Measurement and evaluation of assertive training. Paper presented at the meeting of the Association for Advancement of Behavior Therapy, Washington, D.C., September, 1971.

Laws, D. R. and Serber, M. Measurement and evaluation of assertive training with sexual offenders. In R. E. Hosford and S. Moss (Eds.), *The Crumbling Walls; Treatment and Counseling of the Youthful Offender*, 1972.

Lazarus, A. A. Behavior rehearsal vs. non-directive therapy vs. advice in effecting behavior change. *Behavior Research and Therapy*, 1966, 4, 209-212.

Lazarus, A. A. *Behavior Therapy and Beyond*. New York: McGraw-Hill, 1971.

Lazarus, A. A. Behavior therapy in groups. In G. M. Gazda (Ed.), *Basic Approaches to Group Psychotherapy and Group Counseling*. Springfield, Illinois: Charles C. Thomas, 1968.
Lazarus, A. A. Behavior therapy, incomplete treatment, and symptom substitution. *The Journal of Nervous and Mental Disease*, 1965, *140*, 180.
Lazarus, A. A. Broad-spectrum behavior therapy and the treatment of agoraphobia. *Behavior Research and Therapy*, 1966, *4*, 95.
Lazarus, A. A. and Fay, A. *I Can If I Want To*. New York: William Morrow and Company, Inc., 1975.
Lazarus, A. A. and Serber, M. Is systematic desensitization being misapplied? *Psychological Reports*, 1968, *23*, 215.
Lear, M. W. "Mother's Day" *New York Times Magazine*. May, 1975.
Lehman-Olson, D. Assertiveness training: theoretical and clinical implications. In D. Olson (Ed.), *Treating Relationships*. Lake Mills, Iowa: Graphics Publishing Co., 1976.
Liberman, R. A behavioral approach to group dynamics. *Behavior Therapy*, 1970, *1*, 141-175.
Logan, D. Need affiliations of Mexican-Americans and Anglo-Americans of South Texas. Doctoral dissertation, Texas Tech University, 1971. *Dissertation Abstracts*, 33:444B, 1972. University Microfilm.
London, P. *The Modes and Morals of Psychotherapy*. New York: Holt, Rinehart and Winston, 1964.
Lyon, H. L. and Iranevich, J. M. An exploratory investigation of organizational climate and job satisfaction in a hospital. *Academy of Management Journal*, 1974, December, 635-648.
Maass, M. Situational role playing: a technique for learning to be more loving. *Marriage and Family Counselors Quarterly*, 1972, 7, 34-39.
MacDonald, M. L. A behavioral assessment methodology applied to the measurement of assertion. Doctoral dissertation, University of Illinois, Urbana, 1974.
MacNeilage, L. A. and Adams, K. A. The method of contrasted role-plays: An insight-oriented model for role playing in assertiveness training groups. Unpublished paper, The University of Texas, 1977.
Mahoney, M. J. *Cognition and Behavior Modification*. Cambridge: Ballinger, 1974.
Maier, H. W. *Three Theories of Child Development*. New York: Harper and Row, 1969.
Manderino, M. A. Effects of a group assertive training procedure on undergraduate women. Unpublished doctoral dissertation, Arizona State University, 1973.
Manis, M. Social interaction and the self-concept. *Journal of Abnormal and Social Psychology*, 1955, *51*, 262-370.
Marks, H. H. Influence of obesity on morbidity and mortality. *Bulletin of the New York Academy of Medicine*, 1960, *36*, 296-312.
Marquez, L. Chicano outlook compared to anglo outlook. Paper presented at the Cultural Awareness Conference, Ghost Ranch, New Mexico, 1972.
Mayer, J. Genetic, traumatic, and environmental factors in the etiology of obesity. *Physiological Review*, 1953, *33*, 472-508.
Mayer, J. *Overweight: Causes, Cost and Control*. Englewood Cliffs, New Jersey, Prentice-Hall, 1968.
Mayer, J. Why exercise pays. *Blue Print for Health*, 1973, *24*, 10-17.
McCarthy, D. and Bellucci, J. The adolescent self-expression scale. Personal communication, 1974.
McClelland, D. C., David, W. N., Kaline, R., and Wanner, E. *The Drinking Man*. New York: The Free Press, 1972.

McCloskey, J. Influence of rewards and incentives on staff nurse turnover rate. *Nursing Research*, 1974, *23*, 239-247.

McFall, R. M. Analogue methods in behavioral assessment: Issues and prospects. In J. Cone and R. Hawkins (Eds.), *Behavioral Assessment: New Directions in Clinical Psychology*. New York: Brunner/Mazel, in press.

McFall, R. M. Assertion training. In B. B. Wolman (Ed.), *International Encyclopedia of Neurology, Psychiatry, Psychoanalysis, and Psychology*. In press.

McFall, R. M. and Lillesand, D. B. Behavior rehearsal with modeling and coaching in assertive training. *Journal of Abnormal Psychology*, 1971, 77(3), 313-323.

McFall, R. M. and Marston, A. R. An experimental investigation of behavior rehearsal in assertiveness training. *Journal of Abnormal Psychology*, 1970, 76, 295-303.

McFall, R. M. and Twentyman, C. T. Four experiments on the relative contributions of rehearsal, modeling, and coaching to assertion training. *Journal of Abnormal Psychology*, 1973, *81*, 199-218.

McLuhan, M. *Understanding Media* New York: Signet Classics, 1964.

McMillan, M. M. Relative efficacy of assertive training and self-control procedures in a weight control program. Unpublished doctoral dissertation, Arizona State University, 1975.

McNamara, J. R. The broad based application of social learning theory to treat aggression in a preschool child. *Journal of Clinical Psychology*, 1970, *81*, 199.

McPherson, E. Selective operant conditioning and deconditioning of assertive models of behavior. *Journal of Behavior Therapy and Experimental Psychology*, 1972, *3* (2).

Megargee, E. I. Undercontrolled and overcontrolled personality types in extreme antisocial aggression. *Psychological Monographs*, 1966, *80* (3) (whole no. 611).

Megargee, E. I. and Mendelsohn, G. A. A cross-validation of twelve MMPI indices of hostility and control. *Journal of Abnormal and Social Psychology*, 1962, 65, 431-438.

Mehrabian, A. and Ferris, S. R. Inference of attitudes from non-verbal communication in two channels. *Journal of Consulting Psychology*, 1967, *31*, 248-252.

Mehrabian, A. Relationship of attitude to seated posture orientation and distance. *Journal of Personality and Social Psychology*, 1968, *10*, 26-30.

Meichenbaum, D. *Cognitive Behavior Modification*. Morristown: General Learning Press, 1974.

Meichenbaum, D. and Cameron, R. Stress-inoculation training: a skills approach to anxiety management. Unpublished manuscript, University of Waterloo, 1973.

Meichenbaum, D. and Turk, D. Stress-inoculation training. In P. O. Davidson (Ed.), *The Behavioral Management of Anxiety, Depression, and Pain*. New York: Brunner/Mazel, 1976.

Metropolitan Life Insurance Company. New weight standards for men and women. Statistical Bulletin #40, 1969, 1-8.

Miller, P. M., Hersen, M., Eisler, R. M., and Hilsman, G. Effects of social stress on operant drinking of alcoholics and social drinkers. *Behavior Research and Therapy*, 1974, *12*, 67-72.

Mischel, W. *Personality and Assessment*. New York: Wiley, 1968.

Montiel, M. The social science myth of the Mexican-American family. *El Grito III*, 1970, (Summer), 56, 63.

Morales, A. The impact of class discrimination and white racism on the mental health of Mexican-American. In N. Wagner and M. Haug (Eds.), *Chicanos: Social and Psychological Perspectives*. St. Louis: C. V. Mosby, 1971.

Morrow, W. R. *Behavior Therapy Bibliography: 1950-1969*. Columbia: University of Missouri Press, 1971.

Murillo, N. The Mexican-American family. In N. Wagner and M. Haug (Eds.), *Chicanos: Social and Psychological Perspectives*. St. Louis: C. V. Mosby, 1971.

Mussen, P. H., Conger, J. J., and Kagan, J. *Child Development and Personality*. New York: Harper and Row, 1963.

Neuman, D. Using assertive training. In J. Krumboltz and C. Thoreson (Eds.), *Behavioral Counseling: Cases and Techniques*. New York: Holt, Rinehart, and Winston, 1969.

Novotny, H. Social competence training. A paper presented at the meeting of the Western Psychological Association, Sacramento, California, May, 1975.

O'Connor, R. D. Modification of social withdrawal through symbolic modeling. *Journal of Applied Behavior Analysis*, 1969, 2, 15-22.

Paulson, T. The differential use of self-administered and group administered token reinforcement in group assertion training for college students. Unpublished doctoral dissertation. Fuller Graduate School of Psychology, 1974.

Peck, E. and Senderowitz, J. *Pronatalism: The Myth of Mom and Apple Pie*. New York: Crowell, 1974.

Pendleton, L., Shelton, J., and Wilson, S. Social interaction training using systematic homework. *The Personnel and Guidance Journal*, 54 (9), 484-487.

Percell, L. P., Berwick, P. T., and Beigel, A. The effects of assertive training on self-concept and anxiety. *Archives of General Psychiatry*, 1974, 502-504.

Perls, F. S. *Gestalt Therapy Verbatim*. Lafayette, California: Real People Press, 1969.

Perls, F., Hefferline, R. F., and Goodman, P. *Gestalt Therapy*. New York: Dell, 1951.

Phelps, S. and Austin, N. *The Assertive Woman*. San Luis Obispo, California: Impact Publishers, Inc., 1975.

Piaget, G. W. and Lazarus, A. A. The use of rehearsal-desensitization. *Psychotherapy: Theory, Research and Practice*, 1969, 6, 264.

Polster, E. and Polster, M. *Gestalt Therapy Integrated*. New York: Brunner/Mazel, 1973.

Prudden, B. *How to Keep Slender and Fit After 30*. New York: Pocket Books, 1970.

Public Health Service Bulletin. Skinfolds, body girths, biacomial diameter, and selected anthropometric indices of adults. Public Health Service Publication No. 1000, Series 11, No. 35. Washington, D.C.: Government Printing Office, 1970.

Ramirez, M. Cognitive styles and cultural democracy in education. *Social Science Quarterly*, 1973, 53, 895-904.

Ramirez, M. Identification with Mexican family values and authoritarianism in Mexican Americans. *Journal of Social Psychology*, 1967, 73, 3-11.

Rathus, S. A. A 30-item schedule for assessing assertive behavior. *Behavior Therapy*, 1973, 4, 398-406.

Rathus, S. A. An experimental investigation of assertive training in a group setting. *Journal of Behavior Therapy and Experimental Psychiatry*, 1972, 3, 81-86.

Reich, W. *Character Analysis*. New York: Orgone Institute Press, 1949.

Reuben, D. R. *The Save Your Life Diet*. New York: Random House: 1975.

Reyes, I. *A Survey of Problems Involved in the Americanization of the Mexican-American*. San Francisco: R & E Research Associates, 1972.

Rich, A. R. and Schroeder, H. E. Research issues in assertiveness training. *Psychological Bulletin*, 1976, 83, 6, 1081-1096.

Rimm, D. C. Thought stopping and covert assertion in the treatment of phobias. *Journal of Consulting and Clinical Psychology*, 1973, 41 (3), 466-467.

Rimm, D. C., Hill, G. A., Brown, N. N., and Stuart, J. E. Group assertive training in the treatment of inappropriate anger expression. *Psychological Reports*, 1974, 34, 791-798.

Rimm, D. C., Keyson, M., and Hunziker, J. Group assertive training in the treatment of antisocial aggression. Unpublished manuscript, Arizona State University, 1971.

Rimm, D. C. and Masters, J. C. *Behavior Therapy: Techniques and Empirical Findings.* New York: Academic Press, 1974.

Rimm, D. C., Snyder, J. J., Depue, R. A., Haanstad, M. J., and Armstrong, D. P. Assertive training versus rehearsal, and the importance of making an assertive response. *Behavior Research and Therapy*, 1976.

Rogers, C. R. *On Becoming a Person.* Boston: Houghton-Mifflin, 1961.

Romanczyk, R. G., Tracey, D. A., Wilson, G. T., and Thorpe, G. L. Behavioral techniques in the treatment of obesity: a comparative analysis. *Behavioral Research and Therapy*, 1973, *11*, 629-640.

Romano, O. The anthropology and sociology of the Mexican-Americans: the distortion of Mexican-American history. *El Grito*, 1968, Fall, 13-26.

Salter, A. *Conditioned Reflex Therapy.* New York: Farrar, Straus, and Giroux, 1949 (Capricorn Books edition, 1961).

Sarason, I. Verbal learning, modeling, and juvenile delinquency. *American Psychologist*, 1968, *23*, 254-266.

Sarason, I. G., and Ganzer, V. J. Modeling and group discussion in the rehabilitation of juvenile delinquents. *Journal of Counseling Psychology*, 1973, *20*, 442.

Schlacter, S. Obesity and eating. *Science*, 1968, *161*, 751-756.

Schwartz, A. Affectivity orientation and academic achievement of Mexican-American youth. Ann Arbor: University Microfilms, 1967.

Seitz, P. F. Dynamically-oriented brief psychotherapy: psychocutaneous exoriation syndrome. *Psychosomatic Medicine*, 1953, *15*, 200.

Seligman, M. E. Fall into helplessness. *Psychology Today*, 1973, June, 43.

Seligman, M. E. For helplessness: can we immunize the weak. *Psychology Today*, 1969, June, 42.

Seligman, M. E. and Maier, S. F. Failure to escape traumatic shock. *Journal of Experimental Psychology*, 1976, 74, 1.

Seligman, M. E., Maier, S. F., and Greer, J. H. Alleviation of learned helplessness in the dog. *Journal of Abnormal Psychology*, 1968, *73*, 256.

Seligman, M. E., Maier, S. F., and Solomon, R. L. Unpredictable and uncontrollable aversive events. In Brush, R. (Ed.), *Aversive Conditioning and Learning.* New York: Academic Press, 1971.

Sheehy, G. Catch-30 and other predictable crises of growing up adult. *New York*, February 18, 1974, 30.

Serber, M. Teaching the nonverbal components of assertive training. *Journal of Behavior Therapy and Experimental Psychiatry*, 1972, *3*, 179-183.

Shelton, J. and Ackerman, M. *Homework in Counseling and Psychotherapy: Examples of Systematic Assignments for Therapeutic Use by Mental Health Professionals.* Springfield, Illinois: Charles C. Thomas, 1974.

Shoemaker, M. E. Group assertiveness training for institutionalized delinquents. Unpublished doctoral dissertation, Fuller Graduate School of Psychology, 1974.

Shoemaker, M. E. and Paulson, T. L. Group assertion training for mothers: a family intervention strategy. In E. J. Mash, L. C. Handy, and L. A. Hamerlynck (Eds.), *Behavior Modification Approaches to Parenting.* New York: Brunner/Mazel, Inc., 1976.

Shure, M. and Spivack, G. Means-end thinking, adjustment, and social class among

elementary school-aged children. *Journal of Consulting and Clinical Psychology*, 1972, *38*, 348-353.
Simon, S. B. *Values Clarification*. New York: Hart Publishing Co., 1972.
Sinning, W. E. Estimating body fat in women. *The Journal of Physical Education*, 1974, July/August, 174-180.
Smaby, M. H. and Tamminen, A. W. Counselors can be assertive. *Personnel and Guidance Journal*, 1976, *54*, 420-424.
Smith, Manuel. *When I Say No, I Feel Guilty*. New York: Dial Press, 1975.
Society of Actuaries. *Statistical Bulletin* (Metropolitan Life Insurance Company), February, 1960, *41*, complete.
Spivack, G. and Shure, M. *Social Adjustment of Young Children*. San Francisco: Josey-Bass, 1974.
Stanislavsky, C. *An Actor Prepares*. New York: Theater Arts, 1936.
Stare, F. J. Overnutrition. *American Journal of Public Health*, 1963, *53*, 1795-1802.
Stevenson, I. and Wolpe, J. Recovery from sexual deviation through overcoming non-sexual neurotic responses. *American Journal of Psychology*, 1960, *116*, 737.
Stuart, R. B. and Davis, B. *Slim Chance in a Fat World: Behavioral Control of Obesity*. Champaign, Illinois: Research Press, 1972.
Stunkard, A. J. New therapies for the eating disorders: behavior modification of obesity and anorexia nervosa. *Archives of General Psychiatry*, 1972, *26*, 391-398.
Sykes, G. M. and Matza, D. Techniques of neutralization: a theory of delinquency. *American Sociological Review*, 1957, *32* (3), 819-823.
Symonds, A. Phobias after marriage: women's declaration of independence. In J. B. Miller (Ed.), *Psychoanalysis and Women*. New York: Penguin, 1973.
Taylor, J. A. A personality scale of manifest anxiety. *Journal of Abnormal and Social Psychology*, 1953, *48*, 285-290.
Thornton, J. W. and Jacobs, P. D. Learned helplessness in human subjects. *Journal of Experimental Psychology*, 1971, *87*, 367.
Ulibarr, S. Differences and similarities between Anglo-American and Hispano-American culture. Paper presented at the Cultural Awareness Conference, Ghost Ranch, New Mexico, 1972.
U. S. Commission on Civil Rights. *Asian Americans and Pacific Peoples: A Case of Mistaken Identity*. Washington, D.C.: Government Printing Office, 1975.
U. S. Department of Public Health. *Obesity and Health*. Publication #1485. Washington, D. C.: Government Printing Office, 1966.
Vaal, J. J. and McCullagh, J. The rathus assertiveness schedule: reliability at the junior high school level. *Behavior Therapy*, 1975, *6*, 566-567.
Varenhorst, B. B. Helping a client speak up in class. In J. E. Krumboltz and C. E. Thoresen (Eds.), *Behavioral Counseling: Cases and Techniques*. New York: Holt, Rinehart, and Winston, 1969.
Videbeck, L. Self-conception and the reaction of others. *Sociometry*, 1960, *23*, 351-359.
Wallace, C. J., Teigen, J. R., Liberman, R. P., and Baker, V. Destructive behavior treated by contingency contracts and assertive training: a case study. *Journal of Behavior Therapy and Experimental Psychiatry*, 1973, *4*, 273.
Walker, W. J., Lawry, E. L., Love, D. E., Mann, G. V., Levine, S. A., and Stare, F. J. Effects of weight reduction and caloric balance on serum lipoprotein and cholesterol levels. *American Medicine*, 1953, *14*, 654-664.
Walters, R. H. and Brown, M. Studies of reinforcement of aggression: III. Transfer of responses to an interpersonal situation. *Child Development*, 1963, *24*, 563-571.
Waters, W. F. and McDonald, D. G. Autonomic response to auditory, visual, and

imagined stimuli in a systematic desensitization context. *Behavior Research and Therapy*, 1973, *11*, 577-585.
White, R. W. The concept of healthy personality: what do we really mean? *The Counseling Psychologist*, 1973, *4*, 3.
Winship, B. J. and Kelley, J. D. A verbal response model of assertiveness. *Journal of Counseling Psychology*, 1976, *23*, 215-220.
Wolfe, J. and Fodor, I. A cognitive behavior approach to assertiveness problems in women. *The Counseling Psychologist*, 1975.
Wolfe, J. and Fodor, I. A cognitive/behavioral approach to modifying assertive behavior in women. *The Counseling Psychologist*, 1975, *5* (4), 45-52.
Wolfe, J. and Fodor, I. Modifying assertive behavior in women: a comparison of three approaches. *Behavior Therapy*, 1976 (in press).
Wolpe, J. Neurotic depression: experimental analog, clinical syndromes and treatment. *American Journal of Psychotherapy*, 1971, *25*, 362.
Wolpe, J. *Psychotherapy by Reciprocal Inhibition*. Stanford: Stanford University Press, 1958.
Wolpe, J. Recpirocal inhibition as the main basis of psychotherapeutic effects. *Archives of Neurology and Psychiatry*, 1954, *72*, 205-226.
Wolpe, J. *The Practice of Behavior Therapy*. New York: Pergamon Press, 1969, 1973.
Wolpe, J. Supervision transcript V: mainly about assertive training. *Journal of Behavior Therapy and Experimental Psychiatry*, 1973, *4*, 141-148.
Wolpe, J. and Lazarus, A. A. *Behavior Therapy Techniques*. New York: Pergamon Press, 1966, (Now out of print).